A SYNOPSIS OF AMERICAN HISTORY

THE BERKELEY SERIES IN AMERICAN HISTORY

A SYNOPSIS
OF
AMERICAN
HISTORY

by

Charles Sellers

UNIVERSITY OF CALIFORNIA AT BERKELEY

and

Henry May

UNIVERSITY OF CALIFORNIA AT BERKELEY

RAND McNALLY & COMPANY · CHICAGO

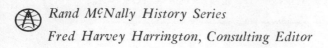 *Rand McNally History Series*
Fred Harvey Harrington, Consulting Editor

PREFACE

A Synopsis of American History is a brief summary, with emphasis on politics, designed for adults who are beginning the study of the subject. Our purpose in offering a much briefer book than the average textbook is not to cut down the *amount* a student reads, but to increase its *diversity*. Use of the *Synopsis*, together with the *Berkeley Readings in American History* and other materials, should help a student to get some idea of the vast diversity of American historical writing and to experience some of the excitement of close, first-hand study of historical sources. At the same time he can acquire some control of the chronological order without which history makes no sense. The very brief chapter bibliographies are restricted to books which are both readily available and readable and provide no more than a bare introduction to the study of each period.

In general, we have said little directly about social and intellectual history, not because we consider these fields unimportant, but because they are best studied in sources and specialized books and do not lend themselves to summary. In our opinion, political history affords the clearest organization of American history. Surprisingly often, American politics reflect with fair accuracy the underlying tendencies in economic, social, and intellectual life.

In reducing this big story to such a small space, we have found it impossible to avoid expressing opinions. While we have tried to keep partisanship to a minimum, we have allowed ourselves to suggest interpretations. Appropriate reading in other books—the whole purpose of the *Synopsis*—should enable students to accept or reject our interpretative statements.

We wish to thank Professor Richard B. Morris, who read the whole manuscript, and Professors Richard Abrams, Harold Hyman, and William E. Leuchtenburg, who read parts of it. Despite much discussion and general agreement, each author is responsible for facts and interpretation in his section of the book—Charles Sellers for chapters 1–15 and Henry May for chapters 16–30.

C.S.
H.M.

TABLE OF CONTENTS

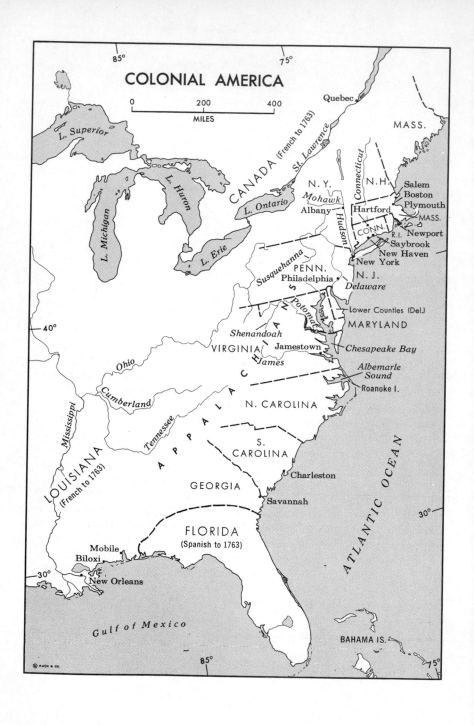

COLONIAL AMERICA

0   200   400
MILES

L. Superior

L. Michigan

L. Huron

CANADA (French to 1763)

St. Lawrence

Quebec

L. Ontario

MASS.

N. Y.

Connecticut

N. H.

Mohawk

Albany

Hartford

Salem
Boston
Plymouth

MASS.

CONN.

R.I. Newport
Saybrook
New Haven

New York

Susquehanna

PENN.

Philadelphia

N. J.

Delaware

40°

Shenandoah

Potomac

Lower Counties (Del.)

MARYLAND

VIRGINIA

Jamestown

Chesapeake Bay

Ohio

James

Albemarle Sound

Roanoke I.

Cumberland

N. CAROLINA

Mississippi

Tennessee

A P P A L A C H I A N S

S. CAROLINA

LOUISIANA
(French to 1763)

GEORGIA

Charleston

Savannah

ATLANTIC OCEAN

30°

FLORIDA
(Spanish to 1763)

Mobile
Biloxi

30°

New Orleans

Gulf of Mexico

BAHAMA IS.

© AHEN & CO.

85°

75°

CHAPTER 1

BEGINNINGS

1607–1700

When Christopher Columbus stepped ashore on the tiny West Indian island of San Salvador, he was opening a new chapter in the history of Europe as well as America. In 1492 the Old World was in the early stages of a four-hundred-year revolution. New intellectual stirrings, growth of trade, and rivalries of emerging nation-states in overseas exploration and commerce were already beginning to move Europe from its feudal past toward the dynamic modern society of the future. The great New World frontier discovered by Columbus suddenly revealed to Europeans vast areas for settlement and resources for exploitation. Quickening the spirit of enterprise and accelerating the pace of economic growth and social change, the very existence of America hastened European man toward the modern world. In addition America's own development was profoundly conditioned by the fact that it took place in the midst of the great transition toward modernity.

The words "modern" and "modernity" are used here not to describe the world of our own time, but rather that social order toward which the Atlantic world was moving in the centuries after the discovery of America, that social order which reached its apogee in the nineteenth century. The central fact of this historical epoch, both as cause and effect, was the increasing importance of autonomous individuals and the growing faith that men could win secular salvation—wealth and "happiness"—by individual enterprise. By the time modern society reached its fullest development in the nineteenth century, this emphasis on the individual had given rise to the social philosophy known as *liberalism*. In its original, historical sense, liberalism was the conviction that the good of everybody would best be served if all were left as free as possible to pursue their individual ends. In the economic sphere, liberal doctrines lent support to *laissez faire* capitalism. In the political sphere liberal doctrines encouraged majoritarian democracy with protection for the rights of minorities. Thus for four centuries following the discovery of America, the Atlantic world was moving toward a modernity characterized by individualism and enterprise, by commercial and industrial capitalism, by liberalism and democracy.

In addition to accelerating the drift toward modernity in the Old World, the New World contained the area—that part of the North American continent which was to become the United States—where the forces of modernity were to find, for good or ill, their freest range and fullest consummation. Curiously enough this area was the last major segment of the New World frontier to be exploited by Europeans. During the sixteenth century the Spanish had expended their enormous colonizing and exploitative energies in bringing most of Central and South America under their control, and the Portuguese had begun developing an empire in Brazil. In the opposite northerly latitudes, French fishermen on the Grand Banks and Jacques Cartier on the St. Lawrence had laid the foundations upon which French Canada would be built after 1600. But the intervening and highly favored domain of temperate and fertile country had lain untouched through most of the sixteenth century while England was slowly made ready for overseas enterprise.

ENGLAND DISCOVERS THE NEW WORLD

English colonization in America differed in its character and consequences from that of other European nations in several crucial respects. First, England itself was closer to a tradition of individual rights and social mobility, and Englishmen exhibited earlier and more fully that spirit of individual enterprise which was to be a major force in the modernization of the European world. The Tudor monarchy of Henry VII and Henry VIII had destroyed the power of the feudal nobility, already weakened by the War of the Roses, and established a strong centralized state. In so doing the Tudor monarchs had encouraged the growth of the business middle classes, the merchants and entrepreneurs who were to be major agents of the modernizing process. Moreover, Henry VIII had welcomed the Protestant Reformation in England, and Protestant theology, with its spiritual individualism and the divine sanction it gave to men's mundane callings, had reinforced the individualistic, enterprising spirit of English middle-class life. All of these tendencies culminated in a burst of national vigor and creativity in the late sixteenth century under the last of the Tudors, Elizabeth I. It was at this point that Englishmen turned their eyes toward the New World.

[4]

A second crucial difference between England and the other major colonizing nations was that England entered upon her colonizing ventures as a small and poor country. Though the Elizabethans dared to challenge the might of Catholic Spain, they were only on the threshold of major-power status, and the Queen's treasury had no funds to support the New World ventures that seemed vital to England's grand strategic design. Private enterprise had to be enlisted for this great national purpose, and Englishmen responded with a mixture of patriotism, Protestant religious zeal, thirst for adventure, and greed for profits.

Sir Humphrey Gilbert died in his effort to found a colony in Newfoundland in 1583. Gilbert's half-brother Sir Walter Raleigh then took up the task. The colonists he planted on Roanoke Island in present North Carolina in 1585 gave up and returned to England after a year, and a second group of settlers sent out in 1587 had disappeared by the time a relief expedition reached Roanoke three years later. These failures demonstrated that a colonizing venture was beyond the financial capacity of any single individual. But English colonization was still to be a private enterprise, and Raleigh had pointed the way by organizing a "joint-stock company" to finance his second colonial venture. The joint-stock device, forerunner of the modern corporation, went back to the time of Henry VIII when English merchants had pooled their capital and spread the risks of trade with Russia by buying shares in the "stock" or capital of the self-governing Muscovy Company. Applied to America, this device not only made English colonization possible, but insured that it would be carried out under the direction of private entrepreneurs seeking private profits as well as national ends.

The private entrepreneurial auspices of English colonization and the individualistic character of English society were to interact with the New World environment to produce important consequences. Everywhere in the New World the absence of established institutions meant that men were free to build a new social order, and rich resources afforded a field for enterprise that might lead Americans toward individualism and modernity.

In contrast, the Spanish quickly found gold and silver in their America, and this ready source of wealth reinforced the authoritarian social structure they had brought with them. The fur trade played a like role in French America. Similarly the English colonizers at first sought gold or a northwest passage that would open to them the Pacific and the riches of the fabled Orient. They, too, attempted to impose on their colonies a rigid form of social organization designed to promote corporate rather than individual ends. But their New World, the temperate zone of North America, yielded no ready riches.

[5]

Instead it proved superbly fitted for the humbler pursuits of farming, fishing, and trade, tasks better adapted to individual than corporate enterprise.

Paradoxically, the English colonies flourished because they failed in their original corporate aims and were thus left as fields of enterprise for individual Englishmen. It was under these circumstances that English America surged into the forefront of the Atlantic world's drift toward modernity. The process can be seen at work, with interesting variations, in the two colonial societies established in the first half of the seventeenth century, one on Chesapeake Bay and the other in New England.

THE CHESAPEAKE COLONIES: VIRGINIA AND MARYLAND

Following Queen Elizabeth's death in 1603, her successor James I made peace with Spain, and English manpower and resources were freed for American ventures. In 1606 King James issued charters to two joint-stock companies to colonize the land that Raleigh had named Virginia in honor of the virgin Queen Elizabeth. The more important of the two Virginia companies, with headquarters at London, promptly sent out an expedition. Reaching Chesapeake Bay in April, 1607, after a voyage of four months, the hundred-odd adventurers proceeded up the great river that they named for King James and founded the first permanent English settlement in the New World at Jamestown.

Hunger, hostile Indians, and disease took a fearful toll in the early years before the settlers learned to cope with the strange environment. At one point the colony was almost abandoned. Much of the trouble arose from the organization and aims of the enterprise. Anxious for quick profits from gold or a northwest passage, the settlers were slow to settle down to the mundane agricultural labor necessary for the colony to sustain itself. Their reluctance arose partly from the fact that all the original settlers went out as employees of the company. All produce went into the company warehouses, and labor was exacted under military discipline by an autocratic governor.

By 1618 officials of the Virginia Company frankly recognized that there would be no quick profits and shifted to a policy of making Virginia so attractive to immigrants that it would grow rapidly and yield eventual profits through the company's control of trade. The famous "headright" system was inaugurated whereby a person received fifty acres for every individual he transported to America.

The "cruell lawes" of former years were replaced by the "free lawes" of England, and the settlers were authorized to send delegates to a representative assembly. When it met in 1619 as the first representative body in the New World, the democratically elected Virginia House of Burgesses organized on the model of the English House of Commons and claimed the right of local self-government.

The shift in company policy was a graceful adaptation to social fact: the fortunes of the colony had begun to pick up only as men found opportunity to pursue their individual ends rather than the corporate ends of the company. John Rolfe is best known as the Virginian who helped gain peace with the Indians by marrying Pocahontas, daughter of the local chieftain. But Rolfe made a greater contribution to Virginia by developing, around 1613, a strain of the Indian weed tobacco that achieved instant popularity in England. When the craze for tobacco in England created a flourishing market and high prices, Virginians poured all their energies into growing tobacco for individual profit, and the company enterprises were left to languish.

The company made one final effort to recruit immigrants to man its corporate enterprises, but the cost of promotion was too great, and the lure of tobacco quickly drew the new workers away. The company fell into factional bickering, and in 1622, after the death of Pocahontas' father, a new and more bellicose chieftain led the Indians in a devastating massacre of the English settlers, extending to the very gates of Jamestown. This disaster so discredited the company that the King revoked its charter in 1624, and Virginia was henceforth a royal colony. The governor and his council were now appointed by the crown, but the Virginians' representative asssembly was left unmolested, and the King interfered in Virginia affairs less than the company had.

The high profits of tobacco culture brought quick recovery from the effects of the Indian massacre and made Virginia a land of opportunity for disadvantaged and discontented Englishmen. A man with no funds at all could go as an indentured servant, agreeing to work three to five years for a Virginian who would pay his ocean passage. Such was the demand for labor and the cheapness of land that at the end of his indenture he could quickly earn enough to buy a farm, plant tobacco, and perhaps within a few years be in a position to acquire indentured servants himself. People who came to Virginia with some funds or the more enterprising among the earlier settlers were able to accumulate both labor and land in substantial amounts by importing indentured servants and acquiring headrights in the process. These more successful planters filled the offices of colony and county government, but during most of the seventeenth century Virginia society remained so fluid that they could not be said to constitute an aristocracy or ruling class.

While Virginia flourished a similar pattern of colonial life was being established under very different auspices farther up the shores of Chesapeake Bay. In 1632 King Charles I, successor of James I, granted to George Calvert, Lord Baltimore, proprietorship of the feudal domain of Maryland lying between the Potomac River and the fortieth parallel. The Calverts were a noble Catholic family who envisioned Maryland as a refuge for their fellow Catholics in Protestant England. The first settlement was established at Saint Mary's in 1634, and soon both Protestants and Catholics were immigrating to Maryland to grow tobacco in emulation of the Virginians.

The proprietor enjoyed absolute political power and ownership of the soil, but in order to attract settlers and make the colony a success it was necessary to share both soil and power with the inhabitants. Large manorial grants were made to some men, mostly Catholics, who presided over numbers of servants and tenants and came to constitute a kind of gentry. Most of the population were yeoman farmers, perhaps employing a few servants and leasing their lands from the proprietor on a basis nearly equivalent to ownership in return for a nominal quit-rent. The Calverts appointed the governor, but eventually allowed the inhabitants to elect an assembly which soon asserted its right to initiate legislation. The most notable piece of legislation was the Act of Toleration of 1649, assuring both Protestants and Catholics of the free exercise of their religion.

NEW ENGLAND: PLYMOUTH AND MASSACHUSETTS BAY

Meanwhile, far to the north of the Chesapeake colonies, a different kind of English colonization was taking place on the less hospitable coast of New England. The New England colonies were a direct outgrowth of a renewal of religious conflict in England. The more thoroughgoing Protestants had never been satisfied with the moderation of the English Reformation as it became institutionalized in the Church of England. Calling themselves Puritans, they demanded a further purification of the English church through the elimination of bishops and the simplification of church services. The essence of Puritanism was a heightened sense of God's sovereignty and man's dependence on divine grace, and the Puritans strove zealously to live strictly in accordance with God's will.

Queen Elizabeth's astuteness had prevented the growing Puritan spirit from causing trouble during her reign, but her successors, the Stuart monarchs James I (1603–1625) and Charles I (1625–1649), invited conflict. James bluntly told the Puritans that they would either conform to the usages of the Church of England or be "harried out of the land." His son Charles married a French Catholic princess and supported Archbishop William Laud's efforts to compel religious conformity.

James had early harried one little band of particularly obnoxious left-wing Puritans out of England to Holland. Not finding Holland to their liking, these Pilgrims had turned their eyes toward America. Getting support from a group of London merchants, they and additional recruits from England set sail in 1620 in the *Mayflower* bound for Virginia. Poor navigation brought them to the American coast at Cape Cod, and rather than brave further winter storms on the Atlantic, they settled at nearby Plymouth. Before landing they subscribed to the Mayflower Compact, an agreement to govern themselves by majority will that was inspired by radical Puritan notions of church government. The Pilgrim settlement at Plymouth developed into a small agricultural colony, important as the first English community in New England but soon overshadowed and eventually swallowed up by a larger Puritan migration.

The main Puritan migration to New England was made possible when a group of well-to-do and influential leaders obtained from King Charles in 1629 a charter for the Massachusetts Bay Company authorizing settlement in the area north of the Plymouth colony. In a bold stroke the leaders resolved to make this charter of a joint-stock company the constitutional basis for a holy commonwealth beyond the King's reach by moving charter and company officers across the Atlantic. All over England Puritans subscribed funds and volunteered themselves, and in the summer of 1630 a fleet of seventeen vessels carried nearly a thousand people to establish a series of towns around Boston harbor. As the prospects for Puritanism worsened in England, these original settlers were followed by thousands more. Within little more than a decade New England had twenty thousand people.

However foreign the Puritans' ideals may seem to later generations, their enterprise for a holy commonwealth was certainly one of the nobler dreams that men have entertained. If one accepts the Puritans' premises that God is sovereign, that man's primary duty is to do God's will, and that the major issue of life is whether one receives God's grace, then it is hard to resist their conclusion that society should be constructed in accordance with the divine plan for men's salvation.

The Puritans' theory of civil government was similar to their "congregationalist" theory of church government, and both were based on the idea of covenant. A true church was a group of the "visible elect" (those who appeared by their lives to be true recipients of God's grace) who had entered into a covenant with God and each other to obey the divine will and establish a church in which the word of God would be truly preached. It was then the business of the church members to choose as minister a man especially qualified by character and education to interpret God's will. This theory contained an element of democracy in that all members participated in the covenant, the choice of a minister, and the admission of new members; an element of aristocracy in that the minister once chosen should be accorded the authority due his special qualifications for interpreting God's will; and an element of monarchy in that God's will was sovereign.

The Puritans similarly believed that their holy commonwealth was founded on an implicit covenant with God and each other and that civil magistrates derived their authority from their special qualifications for interpreting God's will for the society. As a practical matter the Puritan commonwealth took its form from the corporate charter of the Massachusetts Bay Company. The stockholders or "freemen" of a joint-stock company met annually as a "Great and General Court" to decide major company policies and to elect the company's executive officers, a "governor" and a board of "assistants." When the Puritan leaders transferred the charter from England to Massachusetts Bay in 1630, only the governor John Winthrop and a few freemen of the company who were also assistants went along.

At first this handful of magistrates, out of a sincere zeal to protect the religious objectives of the holy experiment, sought to make all rules, judge all cases, and govern alone. But within a year a number of the leading settlers demanded a share in government, and the magistrates decided that henceforth all church members should be considered freemen and allowed to attend the annual General Court to elect the governor and assistants. Within three years the General Court had forced the magistrates to concede it a share in the lawmaking power. As the population increased and the General Court became unwieldy, the practice was adopted of having the freemen in each town elect two deputies to represent them in the General Court. The evolution of the General Court as a representative legislative body was completed in the 1640's when the deputies and magistrates began meeting separately.

The Puritan commonwealth was theocratic in the sense that God's will was supposed to be sovereign, but not in the sense that ministers were given direct political power. The real power of the clergy arose from their authority as interpreters of God's will. Ordinarily this function was performed by the magistrates with respect to civil matters, but when the magistrates disagreed with the deputies, they could usually call the powerful authority of the clergy to their support. Everyone believed that it was the duty of the state to support the church, to require church attendance by members and nonmembers alike, to enforce a strict morality, and to do anything else that would increase the chances of salvation for every member of the community.

The pattern of settlement reflected the religious aims of the holy commonwealth. Individuals could not wander off and buy land wherever they wished. The General Court insisted on compact settlement in contiguous towns. When population increase warranted, the General Court would authorize a group of people to settle a new town adjacent to an already established one. Families were given house lots in a compact village in the center of the town's boundaries from which they went daily to work the outlying agricultural lands they were allotted. The church was located in the village center, and villagers and the town and church officials were encouraged to guard, warn, and reprove each other against moral lapses. Everyone was allowed to participate in the town meeting, which elected town officials and decided town policy.

Deeply believing that a trained intelligence was required to discern God's will, the Puritans were zealous advocates of education. The family was the basic educational unit with every father being required to see that his children and servants mastered reading, writing, and arithmetic and that the boys learned a trade. Fathers were responsible, too, of course, for the religious and moral training and behavior of their families. In 1647 the General Court ordered every town of fifty houses to maintain an elementary school, and some of the larger towns also supported public secondary schools.

Puritan theory required not only a decently educated general population but also a highly-educated magistracy and clergy. Over a hundred graduates of Oxford and Cambridge came to Massachusetts Bay in the first decade to fulfill this need. In 1636 the General Court established at Cambridge a college modelled on the English universities and named after John Harvard, a young English clergyman who bequeathed to it his library and half his estate. Bright boys from ordinary farm families had no trouble attending Harvard, and about half of the graduates became ministers.

RHODE ISLAND, CONNECTICUT, NEW HAMPSHIRE

It was inevitable that the holy commonwealth's efforts to maintain social discipline and a uniform true doctrine would lead to friction in a population filled with gifted, intense, and devout individuals.

The most embarrassing troublemaker in the early days was a brilliant young minister named Roger Williams, who challenged the principle of religious uniformity. Williams was really a radical Puritan who had arrived at the modern principle of separation of church and state on the not so modern ground that enforcement of religious uniformity impeded the soul in its search for religious truth. To tolerate such a view would be to give up the whole enterprise of a holy commonwealth, and Williams' close friend Governor Winthrop warned him of his impending arrest in time for him to escape. Making his way south to Narragansett Bay in 1634, he became the father of the colony of Rhode Island, where he proclaimed the policy of complete religious freedom and inaugurated a democratic system of self-government. Receiving a charter from the English government in 1644, Rhode Island attracted dissenters from Massachusetts and Europe and flourished as a farming and trading community and a thorn in the sides of its orthodox Puritan neighbors.

Another New England colony came into being when the strong-minded Reverend Thomas Hooker and members of his congregation in Cambridge became excited over the fertile Connecticut River Valley a hundred miles inland from the Massachusetts Bay settlements. Rivalry between Hooker and the other leaders probably figured in the situation, and in this case the magistrates departed from their rule of compact settlement and allowed the Cambridge people to go. Travelling overland in 1636, Hooker's followers founded Hartford and organized their own colony of Connecticut on the model of Massachusetts Bay. Other Puritan groups founded settlements at Saybrook and New Haven on the coast and maintained an independent status for a quarter of a century before merging with Hooker's valley settlements as the united colony of Connecticut.

Massachusetts Bay sought to maintain control over the sporadic settlements that grew up to its north. In 1679 the towns beyond the Merrimac River obtained a charter making them the separate royal colony of New Hampshire, but the Maine area beyond continued to be ruled from Boston.

ENGLISH STRIFE AND AMERICAN AUTONOMY

The Stuart monarchy of Charles I had little liking for the stiff-necked independence of Puritan New England, but Charles had his hands too full with Puritanism in old England to undertake any punitive measures across the broad Atlantic. English Puritans had become increasingly important leaders in Parliament's struggle against the arbitrary policies of the Stuarts. The long and bitter conflict culminated in civil war in the 1640's. Oliver Cromwell's Parliamentary army defeated the royalist forces, King Charles was beheaded in 1649, and Cromwell became the dominant figure in a Puritan Commonwealth.

Under these circumstances the English colonies on the Chesapeake Bay and in New England had been left to develop as they pleased. The Virginians cared little who ruled in England so long as they were let alone to grow tobacco and pursue their individual fortunes. In Maryland, however, the Protestant majority took advantage of the English Civil War to overthrow the Calverts and the Catholic ruling class and to repeal the Act of Toleration.

The New Englanders became more independent than ever. The leaders of Massachusetts Bay regarded their holy commonwealth as "a city set upon a hill," a model which England and eventually the whole world would follow. The early success of the Puritan cause in the English Civil War reinforced their faith that they were leading the way to a world organized under the will of God. With redoubled zeal to maintain a pure and undefiled commonwealth, they sought to eliminate religious error wherever it appeared. The Quakers caused them the greatest trouble. These adherents of the Religious Society of Friends represented a kind of radical Puritanism of lower-class origins which enjoined each man to follow the divine promptings coming to him through an "Inner Light" in his own soul. Anti-authoritarian, the early Quakers felt impelled to bear witness to their faith in the most difficult places, and many of them came to Massachusetts Bay for this purpose. When they were banished, they returned at the first opportunity. The authorities tried whipping, then cutting off ears, then the threat of hanging, but still the banished Quakers returned. Finally four were hanged.

Suddenly New England lost its sense of cosmic significance. The Puritan Commonwealth collapsed in England, and the Stuart monarchy returned to power in the Restoration of 1660. The new Stuart king, Charles II, restored Maryland to the Calverts and sought to strengthen his control over the other colonies, but the habit of independence had become so deeply ingrained that he encountered strong resistance. Though the New England magistrates and clergy ceased their persecutions and grudgingly began to tolerate Anglicans and other dissenters, they stubbornly sought in other respects to maintain their autonomy and power in loyalty to the ideal of the holy commonwealth. But by now the ideal was being weakened from within as well as from without.

PURITANISM VERSUS MODERNITY

The Chesapeake colonists had reacted to the New World environment and the lure of profits from tobacco culture by moving easily
and happily toward a society of individual enterprise and liberal institutions. In New England an equally autonomous society had developed, but here institutionalized Puritanism was a brake against the
pull of the New World environment toward modernity.

In emphasizing God's sovereignty and man's dependence, Puritanism (only somewhat more forcibly than Protestantism generally)
was profoundly antagonistic to the modern spirit of optimism and
confident individualism. Yet at the same time Puritanism gave a powerful psychological impetus to individual striving. The Puritans were
"moral athletes" who believed that "right living" was the best evidence that one enjoyed God's grace. Right living included under "the
doctrine of calling" working as hard and being as successful as possible
in whatever worldly calling or business God had placed one. With
these convictions, it was not surprising that Puritans were highly successful in their individual callings, especially under the favoring circumstances offered by the free environment of the New World.

Despite its scarcity of fertile soil, New England had prospered
greatly from the beginning. The cod fisheries had early developed into
a source of profit. Even greater opportunities were opened up by the
establishment of English colonies in the West Indies. These tropical
islands devoted themselves exclusively to the production of tobacco
and sugar for the European market, and New England hastened to
supply them with foodstuffs, lumber, and livestock. In the process the
New Englanders built up a flourishing merchant marine, and this in
turn stimulated a shipbuilding industry.

By the middle of the seventeenth century the Puritan colonies
contained a growing class of successful and wealthy merchants and
entrepreneurs. Such men found it increasingly difficult to put salvation ahead of worldly prosperity and to feel helplessly dependent on
the grace of an omnipotent God. They were not aware of departing
from the orthodox faith, but nevertheless there was a gradual ebbing
of the intense piety that had sustained the ideal of a holy commonwealth. This became apparent when the children of the first generation of church members increasingly failed to give sufficient evidence
of God's grace to be received into full membership themselves. The
churches had to compromise in order to retain their influence, opening their membership under a "half-way covenant" to those baptized

children of church members who led exemplary lives and accepted the orthodox doctrines but who were still unable to testify to a convincing subjective experience of grace.·

At the same time some of the more successful and less pious New Englanders began to argue that religious persecution discouraged immigration and hampered growth and prosperity. Some of these men also chafed at the dominance of the orthodox leadership and disapproved of the continued defiance of royal authority. Thus when the British government finally lost patience with Massachusetts Bay, it found some allies among the Puritans. In 1684 Charles II annulled the Massachusetts charter, and the following year his brother and successor, James II, placed all the New England colonies, along with recently acquired New York and New Jersey, under the Dominion of New England. All legislative bodies were suspended, and the Dominion was arbitrarily ruled by a royally appointed governor, Sir Edmund Andros, and his council. But James's equally arbitrary rule at home was arousing opposition. When the King was overthrown in the "Glorious Revolution" of 1688, a series of popular demonstrations ousted the Dominion authorities in the American colonies.

In 1691 the Massachusetts Bay authorities had to accept from the new English monarchs William and Mary a charter which seriously compromised the ideal of the holy commonwealth. The legislative power of the General Court was restored, but henceforth the governor was to be royally appointed, and property ownership replaced church membership as a qualification for voting. Under the new charter the anticlerical elements gained increasing political influence and finally succeeded even in taking control of Harvard College.

The clergy sought to stem the ebbing of their spiritual and political authority by ever more fervent reminders of God's power and wrath. In the process they unwittingly touched off the Salem witchcraft hysteria of 1691, and twenty innocent people were executed. The revulsion against this outrageous frenzy further undermined the prestige of the orthodox leadership. By the turn of the century the social and political leadership of the Puritan colonies was clearly passing into the hands of the enterprising merchant class that constituted the advance guard of modernity.

FOR FURTHER READING:

Walter Prescott Webb's *The Great Frontier* (1952) presents a bold and stimulating interpretation of the effects of the New World on European development. Wallace Notestein describes *The English*

People on the Eve of Colonization, 1603–1630 (1954)*. The authoritative account of the early colonies is Charles M. Andrews, *The Colonial Period of American History* (4 vols., 1934–1938). The early history of the Chesapeake colonies may be followed in Wesley Frank Craven, *The Southern Colonies in the Seventeenth Century* (1949); and Bradford Smith has written an interesting biography of *Captain John Smith* (1953). A good introduction to Puritanism is Alan Simpson, *Puritanism in Old and New England* (1935)*. The best account of the Plymouth colony is the one written at the time by Governor William Bradford, *Of Plymouth Plantation**. A full and interesting account of the Massachusetts Bay colony is Thomas Jefferson Wertenbaker's *The Puritan Oligarchy* (1947)*; but a better feeling for what the Puritans were trying to do can be derived from Samuel Eliot Morison's *Builders of the Bay Colony* (1930). Morison has also dealt absorbingly with the intellectual life of the American Puritans in *Puritan Pronaos* (1936; reprinted as *The Intellectual Life of Colonial New England*, 1956*); Ola E. Winslow describes the Puritan church in *Meetinghouse Hill* (1952); Bernard Bailyn has analyzed *The New England Merchants in the Seventeenth Century* (1955); Edmund S. Morgan has written a fine brief biography of Governor John Winthrop under the title *The Puritan Dilemma* (1958)*; and the Salem witchcraft hysteria is the subject of Marion Starkey's *The Devil in Massachusetts* (1950)*. The best brief introduction to the spirit behind the founding of Rhode Island is Perry Miller's interpretation of *Roger Williams* (1953)*.

Sigmund Diamond's *The Creation of Society in the New World* (Berkeley Readings in American History, 1963)* brings together a set of documents posing the problem of why the corporate purposes of the early colonies could not be maintained.

---

*Available in paperback edition.

MONARCHS	COLONIES FOUNDED	AUSPICES	COLONIES ROYALIZED
1558 Elizabeth I (Tudor)			
1603 James I (Stuart)			
	1607 Virginia	Virginia Company	1624
	1620 Plymouth	Pilgrims	
1625 Charles I (Stuart)			⎫
	1629 Massachusetts Bay	Massachusetts Bay Co.	⎬ 1691 ⎭
	1632 Maryland	Calvert family	1691–1715
	1634 Rhode Island	Roger Williams and dissidents from Massachusetts Bay	
	1636 Connecticut	Rev. Thomas Hooker and settlers from Massachusetts Bay	
	1630's New Hampshire	Settlers from Massachusetts Bay	1679
1649 Commonwealth			
1660 Charles II (Stuart) *The Restoration*			
	1663 Carolina	Lords Proprietors	S.C. 1719 N.C. 1729
	1664 ⎰ New York ⎱ New Jersey	Duke of York Proprietors	1685 1702
	1681 Pennsylvania and Lower Counties (Delaware)	William Penn	1692–1694
1685 James II (Stuart)			
1689 William and Mary (Orange and Stuart) *The Glorious Revolution*			
1702 Anne (Stuart)			
1714 George I (Hanover)			
1727 George II (Hanover)			
	1732 Georgia	Trustees	1752
1760 George III (Hanover)			

CHAPTER 2

BRITAIN'S NORTH AMERICAN EMPIRE

1660–1763

Before 1660 Englishmen had little or no conception of a colonial empire. The isolated American settlements were rarely thought of, and the British government had been too distracted by political chaos to devise any systematic scheme of beneficial relations between colonies and mother country. The end of civil strife brought a new interest in America. Under the Stuart Restoration, the whole North American seaboard from Maine south to Spanish Florida was organized for settlement and exploitation, and an emerging theory of empire began to be embodied in a set of colonial policies.

THE PROPRIETARY COLONIES

The expansion of the area of English settlement in North America was prompted partly by a desire to gain strategic advantages against other colonizing nations and partly by a desire to reward favored courtiers who had sided with the Stuarts during the Civil War. In 1663 Charles II granted to a group of eight English noblemen the vast domain stretching south from Virginia to the borders of Spanish Florida. This grant of Carolina was modeled on the proprietary grant of Maryland to the Calverts, and the eight Lords Proprietors were given title to the soil as well as political authority over the area. Carolina already contained a small population that had spilled over from Virginia in the area of Albemarle Sound in its northeastern corner. In 1670 an expedition from the British West Indies colony of Barbados established another settlement several hundred miles down the coast at Charleston.

Anxious to encourage immigration and make profits from rising land values, the Proprietors promised religious toleration and adopted

[19]

a liberal land system, including headrights. Settlers in each of the two sections were allowed to elect an assembly and make laws in conjunction with a governor and council appointed by the Proprietors. Coastal sandbars blocked off the northern settlements from good ocean transportation, and this area came to be populated by small landowners whose independent-mindedness made them difficult to govern. The southern settlements around Charleston, on the other hand, quickly developed profitable staple productions for export, at first deerskins and naval stores and then rice and indigo. Great plantations grew up on the tidal estuaries, and the planters came to constitute a tightly knit ruling class with their headquarters in Charleston, where they spent the malarial summer months in breeze-swept town houses along the Battery.

While Carolina was being erected as a buffer against the Spanish to the south, the British were eliminating another competitor farther north: the Netherlands, the European nation most like England in the enterprising qualities of its people. Early in the sixteenth century the Dutch merchant marine had come to dominate the spice trade with the Far East. Though their Far Eastern ventures absorbed so much of their slender resources and manpower that they had little left for the New World, the Dutch had been interested in finding a more direct water passage to the spice islands through North America. It was the search for such a passage that led Henry Hudson in 1609 up the river that bears his name.

The Hudson River proved to be no northwest passage, but it did lead into the heart of the fur-rich Iroquois country, and by 1624 the Dutch had begun to establish trading posts that grew into the colony of New Netherland. New Amsterdam at the tip of Manhattan Island became a cosmopolitan trading center; a scattering of Dutch farmers spread out over Long Island, Staten Island, and across the Hudson from Manhattan; along the Hudson vast manors were granted to wealthy patroons who exercised feudal authority over their tenants. Yet the preoccupation of the Dutch with the Far East, the patroonship system, and the petty tyranny of its governors prevented New Netherland from flourishing like its English neighbors.

The English had always resented this Dutch intrusion in what they regarded as their domain. In 1664 Charles II granted the area between the Delaware and Connecticut rivers to his brother, the Duke of York, who would ascend the throne in 1685 as James II. James promptly organized a fleet and sailed for New Amsterdam, which surrendered without a shot. Renamed New York, the Duke's proprietary domain was larger than he desired, and he transferred the area lying between the Delaware and the Hudson to two of his favorites as the proprietary grant of New Jersey. The New Jersey proprietors later divided the grant into eastern and western sections and sold their rights to other proprietors, with West Jersey eventually coming into the hands of a group of Quakers who included William Penn.

William Penn was responsible for filling the last gap in the continuous band of English settlement along the Atlantic coast of North America. The son of a British admiral who was a close friend of the Duke of York, Penn was converted to Quakerism and spent time in prison for his religious convictions. On missionary tours of continental Europe, he began dreaming of a refuge in America where not just Quakers but the persecuted and poor of all sects and countries could live in peace. The Stuarts had owed Penn's father a large sum of money, and this debt helped persuade Charles II to grant his son in 1681 the province of Pennsylvania, extending west and south from the Delaware River to Maryland.

Penn promptly began advertising his province, offering complete religious freedom, representative government, and the most generous land policy of any of the American colonies. The quick response by English Quakers, Welshmen, and persecuted German sects made Pennsylvania the most rapidly growing and populous area in British America. Penn himself went to Pennsylvania in 1682 to stay several years, laying out the city of Philadelphia between the Delaware and Schuylkill rivers and inaugurating a government that enforced the most humane code of laws in the world. Separate assemblies were provided for Pennsylvania and the "Three Lower Counties" of Delaware below Philadelphia, but both had the same governor who was appointed by the Proprietor. The preponderant Quakers continued for decades to govern the province in the generous spirit of Penn's "Holy Experiment," and Pennsylvania became for European liberals the pre-eminent symbol of a New World society where different sects and nationalities could live together in harmony and prosperity.

Thus by 1682 Great Britain's North American empire had been almost completely rounded out. Georgia, the last remaining colony within the future limits of the United States, was not established until 1732. In that year a group of English philanthropists persuaded the British government to appoint them Trustees of the area south of the Savannah River to be used as a refuge for imprisoned debtors and the unemployed. The leading Trustee and first governor, James Oglethorpe, sailed with a contingent of settlers in 1733 and founded Savannah. The benevolent Trustees tried to insure a moral society of small farmers by limiting each settler to fifty acres of land and prohibiting the importation of rum and slaves. These restrictions had to be relaxed to enable Georgia to compete with its prosperous neighbor South Carolina for settlers, but the colony remained only a small outpost against Spanish Florida.

The failure of the restrictions that the Georgia Trustees sought to impose was merely the final demonstration that corporate purposes, however high minded, could not survive among Englishmen in the New World. This lesson had been forced upon the Virginia Company early, and the holy commonwealth of the Puritans had resisted it only somewhat longer. The proprietory colonies founded after 1660 had all promised religious toleration, representative government, and cheap land—policies designed to attract settlers by guaranteeing individual rights and opportunity. The characteristics of Englishmen and the free environment of the New World led irresistibly toward a society permeated with the spirit of individual enterprise.

THE NAVIGATION ACTS AND THE COLONIAL ECONOMY

While the proprietary colonies were eschewing corporate purposes in the New World, officials in London were developing a series of policies designed to implement the larger corporate purposes suggested by an emerging concept of British empire. These policies were based on the theory of political economy known as *mercantilism* which was generally accepted throughout Europe. Mercantilism presupposed that nations were engaged in a continuous struggle against each other for supremacy. Economic strength was valued for the military and strategic advantages it yielded and was to be measured primarily in terms of the accumulation of gold and silver. Nations lost gold and silver by buying things from other nations, which was taken to mean that the most self-sufficient nations were the strongest and healthiest.

Colonies held an important place in mercantilist thinking. No one questioned that colonies should exist to benefit the mother country. This they could do by furnishing those non-European commodities like sugar, tobacco, rice, molasses, cotton, indigo, naval stores, and furs that the mother country would otherwise have to buy from a rival nation. Colonies could also contribute to the prosperity of the mother country by providing a market for its manufactures. Finally, an extensive trade with colonies would support a large merchant marine, and in a period when merchant ships and seamen were easily converted to naval purposes, this increased the fighting strength of the mother country.

These mercantilist principles were applied to the British colonies in a series of Acts of Trade and Navigation passed by Parliament between 1660 and 1672 and augmented by subsequent legislation. The Navigation Acts contained three major requirements: (1) All trade between England and her colonies must be carried in ships built, owned, and manned by British subjects, including inhabitants of British colonies. (2) All European goods imported into the colonies—with a few special exceptions—must pass through England. This requirement would either allow British manufacturers to undersell their European competitors in British colonial markets or increase the business and profits of the English merchants who handled the European goods in transit, in either case benefiting English businessmen at the expense of their European competitors. Finally, (3) certain "enumerated articles" produced by the colonies could be shipped only to Britain or British colonies even if they were destined for ultimate resale in other European countries. Tobacco was the only important North American product on the "enumerated" list in the seventeenth century, but by the time of the American Revolution the list included nearly every significant export.

The exclusion of Dutch merchantmen from the Chesapeake tobacco trade and the loss of the direct European market for North American tobacco contributed to a period of stringency in Virginia and Maryland in the late seventeenth century, but the effects of the Navigation Acts were by no means uniformly bad for the Americans. The British colonies were given a monopoly of the tobacco market in the mother country, and bounties were paid to colonial producers of indigo and naval stores. The exclusion of foreign built and owned ships from the trade between England and the colonies was a great boon to New England which developed a flourishing shipbuilding industry and merchant marine.

Certainly by the first half of the eighteenth century the colonial economy was in a highly prosperous state. European demand for tobacco, sugar, rice, indigo, and naval stores rose even faster than the rapidly expanding production in the southern and West Indian colonies. As these colonies grew and concentrated ever more exclusively on the profitable staples, they provided an ever greater market for wheat, flour, ground vegetables, salt fish and meat, lumber, and work stock from the middle colonies and New England. Philadelphia and Baltimore became flour milling and exporting centers, and New York was a large exporter of the furs brought into Albany by the far-ranging Iroquois.

New England produced few or no staples for the mother country and at first did not seem to fit the mercantilist prescriptions for usefulness. But the New Englanders quickly made themselves indispensable to the operation of the imperial economic system. It was they who carried provisions from the mainland to the West Indies. Picking up cargoes of sugar, they would proceed to England where they loaded their vessels with manufactured goods for America. In another variation of this "triangular trade," they brought molasses from the West Indies to New England, manufactured it into rum, took the rum to West Africa and traded it for slaves, and then carried the slaves for sale in the West Indies or the southern colonies. Similarly they carried Chesapeake tobacco or Carolina rice to England, bringing back manufactured goods. Prospering greatly from this trade and from its shipbuilding and fisheries, New England eventually contributed to mercantilist aims by becoming the heaviest consumer of British manufactured goods.

As the colonial economy matured, British officials found additional regulations necessary in the interest of mercantilist aims. British West Indian planters resented the fact that the New Englanders got much of the molasses for their rum trade from the West Indian colonies of other countries, and in 1733 Parliament passed the Molasses Act levying a prohibitive duty on foreign molasses or sugar imported into British possessions. But New England evaded the duty by systematic smuggling, and the rum trade continued to flourish.

Some British manufacturers began to fear competition from colonial producers, and in a series of Parliamentary acts passed between 1699 and 1750, the colonists were forbidden to export woolen cloth and beaver hats or to expand their production of finished iron products.

The most serious economic problem of the colonies, money supply, was greatly aggravated by British restrictions growing out of the mercantilist preoccupation with building up the mother country's stock of bullion. Gold and silver coin was the only recognized money at the time, but the export of British coin to the colonies was forbidden, and the colonists were not allowed to mint their own so that they had to rely on Spanish coin acquired in the West Indian trade. Since the colonies, especially the northern ones, were constantly importing from England more than they exported, the coin they acquired was continually being drained away to make up the "adverse balance of trade," and there was never an adequate circulating medium to facilitate exchanges of goods and services within the colonies.

Under these circumstances the colonial governments finally resorted to issuing paper money. These issues were to be redeemed within a certain period and were accompanied by new taxes designed to yield a sufficient fund for their redemption. But if too much paper money were issued or if redemption were delayed, the paper depreciated in value and creditors complained. Moreover this colonial paper money was worthless in England, and it caused trouble to English merchants who tried to collect from American debtors. The British government first sought to remedy the situation by instructing the colonial governors to veto all but the most soundly-backed paper money issues. When this failed to solve the problem, Parliament in 1751 forbade the New England colonies, where the worst abuses had occurred, to issue any further paper that could be used in payment of debts.

ADMINISTERING THE EMPIRE

While British officials were groping their way toward a concept of empire, administrative agencies for colonial planning and control had been evolving in a haphazard fashion in the British government. Soon after the Restoration, the King's principal advisory body, the noble Privy Council, had designated a committee known as the Lords of Trade to consider colonial matters. But not until the Glorious Revolution of 1688 and the accession of William and Mary was much progress made in this direction. A supplementary Navigation Act in 1696 set up a system of admiralty courts in America to enforce the commercial regulations and punish smugglers. This same legislation created in England a Board of Trade and Plantations (a group of bureaucratic experts on colonial matters) to advise the Privy Council through the Lords of Trade. While the Board of Trade had little direct power, it did attain considerable importance as the one agency of the British government which systematically considered all colonial matters. Gradually over many years the Board of Trade was able to implement some consistent policies of colonial control.

One basic aim of the Board was to convert all the corporate and proprietary colonies into royal colonies. This process had begun when the charter of the Virginia Company was revoked in 1624; in 1679, New Hampshire became a royal colony when the British courts overthrew Massachusetts Bay's claim to the area; and New York was perforce converted to royal status when its Proprietor ascended the throne as James II in 1685.

With the accession of William and Mary a process that had hitherto occurred fortuitously became a deliberate aim of policy. Massachusetts Bay, Plymouth, and Maine were organized into the province of Massachusetts under a royal governor in 1691. In the same year the Calverts' Maryland proprietary was royalized, and in

1692, Penn's Pennsylvania and Delaware suffered the same fate. But the new policy was too weak to withstand the political influence of such powerful Proprietors: Penn's domain was restored within two years, and the Calverts finally got theirs back after being converted to Protestantism in 1715. Despite these setbacks the colonial reformers perserved, extracting East and West Jersey from their Proprietors and uniting them as the royal province of New Jersey in 1702. The Carolina Proprietors gave up South Carolina in 1719 and North Carolina ten years later. The Georgia grant to the Trustees was limited in advance to twenty-one years, and in 1752 the province reverted to royal control. Only the strong English respect for property and charter rights enabled Connecticut and Rhode Island to maintain their corporate status, and Penn and the Calverts to regain their domains.

The British government had several means of control over a royal colony. Most important was appointment of the governor who was sent out with a set of detailed instructions drafted by the Board of Trade and who had an absolute veto over the acts of the colonial assembly. Moreover all colonial legislation was sent to the Board of Trade for careful scrutiny, and anything objectionable might be disallowed by the Privy Council. The Privy Council was also a court of appeal from decisions in the colonial courts.

Through these means the Privy Council and the Board of Trade sought to restrain the provincial governments from acts that would damage English merchants or infringe on the royal prerogative. But this regulation was not burdensome. Sir Robert Walpole, who became the king's chief minister in 1721, believed that it was to England's interest to let the colonies flourish without interference; and his policy of "salutary neglect" continued until the 1760's.

Under these circumstances the provinces became virtually self-governing commonwealths. All had a similar form of government. Except in Rhode Island and Connecticut, which continued to elect all their officials, and in Massachusetts, where the assembly elected the council, the governor and his council were appointed by the king or the Proprietor for indefinite terms. The council sitting with an elected lower house formed a bicameral assembly. The assembly could convene only when called by the governor, and he could suspend its sessions or dissolve it at his pleasure. The governor's veto could not be overridden.

While the governor seemed in theory to have a great deal of power, in practice he had a hard time resisting the assembly's will. The assemblies thought of themselves as analogous to the British Parliament and claimed for themselves similar powers. They particularly insisted on the well-established English principle that citizens could not be taxed except by consent of their representatives. The British government let the governors be paid by the colonies, and an assembly's refusal to levy taxes or appropriate funds for the governor's salary could be a powerful political weapon.

Disputes between governors and assemblies over every conceivable matter were the staple of provincial politics. Governors were often incompetent men, and even the better ones found complete success impossible. Caught between the conflicting demands of the London officials and the local assemblies, they could satisfy neither group. The abler governors achieved some success through the astute distribution of appointments and other favors and by horsetrading with leaders of the assembly. At times a governor could fill his council with wealthy and influential provincials who would side with him against the lower house. But except in the few areas of special concern to the Privy Council, the assemblies usually got their way in the end.

As the decades wore on, Americans increasingly assumed that they had an inalienable right to self-government through their assemblies. The recurrent disputes with the governors taught them political sophistication and political skills that would be invaluable if ever this right were challenged.

THE ANGLO-FRENCH WARS

While the English colonies were growing strong and prosperous along the eastern seacoast of North America, the French were developing a different kind of empire to the north and inland. In 1608, one year after the founding of Virginia, Samuel de Champlain began a French settlement at Quebec on the St. Lawrence River. For years Champlain devoted himself to exploring the interior far up the St. Lawrence and into the Great Lakes country and to developing a flourishing fur trade with the Algonquin and Huron Indians of the region. The French fur traders were soon joined by a band of dauntless Jesuit missionaries who ranged far and wide over the wilderness of the north country preaching Christianity to the Indians. By the middle of the seventeenth century there was a narrow zone of agricultural settlement along the St. Lawrence where humble French *habitants* worked peasant-style on the manorial grants of a rather down-at-the-heels class of feudal *seigneurs*.

Despite the numerical weakness of the French in America, their vigor in exploration and their success in maintaining good relations with their Indian allies made them a formidable barrier to English expansion in the direction of the Great Lakes. The powerful Iroquois confederation in upper New York was hostile to the French-oriented Huron and Algonquin tribes, and for many decades shielded Dutch New Netherland and the English colonies from contact with the French. But after the great French king Louis XIV came to the throne in the 1660's, the French pushed their Canadian enterprise more vigorously and assisted their Indian allies in making war on the Iroquois. Meanwhile Louis was seeking to make France the dominant power in Europe as well as to expand her colonial empire in America and other parts of the world. England joined a series of alliances designed to block French ambitions, and the result was a series of four great wars fought mainly in Europe but also between the French and English in America. These wars bore different names in Europe and in the American colonies, as indicated:

COLONIAL NAME	EUROPEAN NAME	DATES
King William's War	*War of the League of Augsburg*	*1689–1697*
Queen Anne's War	*War of the Spanish Succession*	*1702–1713*
King George's War	*War of the Austrian Succession*	*1744–1748*
French and Indian War	*Seven Years' War*	*1754–1763*

In all of the first three, the French and their Indian allies raided the New England and New York frontiers, and Massachusetts expeditions succeeded in capturing important French posts on the coast. Beginning with Queen Anne's War the Spanish were allied with the French, and there was also skirmishing along the southern frontier. But the only American territorial change as a result of the first three wars was the transfer of Nova Scotia, Newfoundland, and the Hudson Bay country in the far north from France to England at the end of Queen Anne's War.

Meanwhile, during the intervals of peace, the French had been moving into the Mississippi Valley behind the English settlements. Around 1700 they set up posts in the Illinois country on the northern Mississippi and established themselves at Biloxi and Mobile on the Gulf Coast near the great river's mouth. New Orleans was founded as the capital of French Louisiana in 1718.

The final phase of the conflict between Britain and France in North America began at the close of King George's War when a group of Virginians sent agents across the Appalachians and into the upper Ohio Valley for the purpose of Indian trade and land speculation. The French responded by building a chain of small forts on the upper Ohio. Young George Washington, sent out in command of a force of Virginia militia in 1754, arrived barely too late to prevent construction of Fort Duquesne at the forks of the Ohio on the site of later Pittsburgh. He was driven off by the French, and the war had begun though it was not to be officially declared for two more years.

All the major European powers were quickly drawn into the fighting, and at first things went badly for the British in America and elsewhere. General James Braddock's army was routed within a few miles of Fort Duquesne, throwing the whole frontier open to several years of pounding by the French and Indians. The British seemed to have no over-all strategy, and the colonies could not be persuaded to contribute very loyally or enthusiastically to the war effort. Delegates from eight of the colonies, meeting at Albany in 1754, had approved Benjamin Franklin's far-sighted, probably visionary, plan for a continental union of all the colonies, but none of the provincial assemblies would touch it.

The situation changed dramatically in 1758 when the vigorous William Pitt took charge of the British government. Making the conquest of Canada his paramount aim, Pitt organized a series of offensives that culminated in the capture of Quebec by General James Wolfe in 1759. By the time the war dragged to a close in Europe, the British were victorious everywhere. In the Peace of Paris (1763), Britain gained both French Canada and Spanish Florida, as well as acquisitions in India and elsewhere. Louisiana was transferred from France to Spain.

No one had more reason to rejoice than the Americans. Suddenly freed from the greatest threat to their security, they now looked west upon an unbounded arena of opportunity lying open to their enterprise. It did not yet occur to them that their new situation of security and confidence might weaken their attachment to the mother country whose emergence as the world's most powerful nation they were now so loyally celebrating.

FOR FURTHER READING:

The final volume of Charles M. Andrews, *The Colonial Period of American History* (1934–1938) traces the development of British imperial policy and administration, while the earlier volumes describe the development of the various colonies. Verner W. Crane has written an interesting account of *The Southern Frontier, 1670–1732* (1929)*. *The Middle Colonies* (1938) are described in a volume by Thomas J.

Wertenbaker. Catherine O. Peare has written a good biography of *William Penn* (1957); and Frederick B. Tolles deals with the changing role of Philadelphia's Quaker merchants in *Meeting House and Counting House* (1948). Francis Parkman's *France and England in America* (8 vols., 1851–1892)* is still the classic account of the development of French Canada and the great struggle for empire in North America. The final phase of that struggle and the period after the French and Indian War are delineated magesterially in Lawrence H. Gipson's *The British Empire before the American Revolution* (10 vols. so far, 1936——).

————————
*Available in paperback edition.

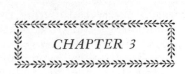

CHAPTER 3

A NEW SOCIETY

Within the loose institutional framework of Britain's North American empire, a distinctly new kind of society had been taking shape. Inside this new society European man was being subtly altered. "What then is the American, this new man?" the French immigrant Crèvecoeur was asking by the 1770's.

THE AMERICANS

Crèvecoeur's American, in the first place, belonged to a numerous and rapidly-multiplying people. The American population grew from about a quarter of a million in 1700 to two and a half million by 1775. A majority of these Americans were of English origin. But English immigration had fallen off in the latter part of the seventeenth century, and the continuing predominance of English stock owed much to the fecundity of Anglo-American mothers.

The spectacular population increase of the eighteenth century was also based on a swelling of non-English immigration. Since the founding of Pennsylvania in the 1680's, Penn's advertising had attracted a steadily mounting flow of impoverished peasants from the war-ravaged states of the German Rhineland. By the 1770's there were around two hundred thousand of these industrious German farm folk in the North American colonies, and in Pennsylvania they constituted a third of the population.

An even larger tide of immigration began flowing in the first decades of the eighteenth century from Ulster in northern Ireland. These people, Protestants of Scottish origin, came to be called Scotch-Irish by their descendants to distinguish them from the indigenous Catholic population of the rest of Ireland. The Scotch-Irish had been transplanted to Ulster in the early seventeenth century as part of the English government's campaign to subdue Ireland. By the beginning of the eighteenth century, they were suffering from English restrictions on Irish trade and industry and by a general raising of farm rents, while simultaneously the English government was enforcing various civil disabilities against them on account of their staunch Presbyterianism. Under these circumstances the Scotch-Irish began crossing the Atlantic in thousands. More than three hundred thousand of them were in the North American colonies by the 1770's, constituting one eighth of the entire population.

Smaller non-English groups from Europe included the Dutch and the French Huguenots. New Netherland had eight thousand Dutch residents at the time of its transfer to English control, and their descendants remained a substantial segment of New York's population. The Huguenots, or French Protestants, began leaving France when the revocation of the Edict of Nantes in 1685 ended religious toleration in that predominantly Catholic country. They did not come to America in large numbers, but their enterprising qualities made them successful and prominent. Probably the largest number came to South Carolina where the Hugers, Legares, Petigrus, and other French families were quickly assimilated to Anglicanism and emerged as a major element of the mercantile-planting aristocracy.

Whether English or non-English, the immigrants of the eighteenth century came mainly from the lower or middling orders of European society. Probably half or more of the settlers in the middle colonies crossed the Atlantic as indentured servants. Many were actually kidnapped and sold to America by unscrupulous dealers in human merchandise. Thousands more—orphans, pauper children, and prisoners— were sent abroad by the public authorities. Under the harsh European penal codes of the day, poor people were often sentenced to long prison terms or execution for minor offenses and welcomed forced transportation to America as an alternative. Some forty thousand English convicts were transported to North America in the six decades before the Revolution, and in Maryland convicts made up the bulk of the servant class.

For the most part, Europeans who embarked on the long ocean voyage to America were the younger and more vigorous people in their home communities. This selective quality of the process of migration enhanced the enterprising quality of American society. Once in America and once having served his indenture, even the lowliest transported convict was free to rise. Colonel John Lamb, a wealthy merchant and prominent political leader in New York in the 1770's, was the son of a man who had been taken from the very gallows in England and transported to America where he established himself as a solid citizen and laid the basis for his son's later success.

But one class of immigrants came most unwillingly and had no chance to rise whatever their vigor or ability. In 1619, the year of the first representative assembly in British North America, a Dutch trading ship dropped anchor at Jamestown with the first cargo of Negro laborers. Initially Negro servants had a status in law similar to that of European servants, and some were actually freed at the end of the customary indenture period. But Negroes were clearly distinguishable by physical characteristics. Unlike European servants, they could not run away and merge into the general population if a master were too exacting or took unfair advantage of them. Gradually masters began holding Negro servants for life and claiming the labor of their offspring, and by the middle of the seventeenth century the law was being modified to define a separate status of permanent and absolute bondage for Negroes. America was to be a land of opportunity for Europeans only.

The slave population did not begin to grow rapidly until the late seventeenth century, and then only in the southern colonies where large amounts of gang labor could be used efficiently in the exhausting but routine tasks required for producing tobacco, rice, and indigo on large plantations. By 1760 Negro slaves outnumbered the white population by more than two-to-one in South Carolina and almost equalled the white population in Virginia.

AMERICAN ENVIRONMENTS: NEW TOWNS AND THE OLD WEST

The acceleration of immigration and economic activity in the eighteenth century created a more diversified society in the American colonies. Towns began to play an increasingly important role in colonial life. The early upsurge of commercial activity in New England was accompanied by a trend toward urbanization as Boston, Newport, and Salem became flourishing trading centers. Philadelphia and New York emerged later as major urban centers but eventually outstripped their predecessors. By the 1770's Philadelphia's population of nearly forty thousand made it the second largest city in the British empire. New York was the second biggest city of British North America followed by Boston, Charleston, and Newport, the last having a population of around seven thousand. The Chesapeake tobacco country, where oceangoing ships could sail directly up to the individual planter's wharf for trade, was the only area that did not develop a major urban center.

Though the colonial towns never contained more than a tenth of the total population, they exercised an influence far out of proportion to their numbers. Here were published the newspapers, pamphlets, and almanacs that were almost the only means of general communication in the colonies. Here flourished the artisan class of shoemakers, weavers, hatters, cabinetmakers, and adepts of countless other trades who produced most of the articles that the colonists used. Here sat the principal courts, and here the lawyers emerged as an influential professional group. The towns in short became the focal points of the economic, intellectual, and political life of the colonies.

While towns were developing along the coast, the pressure of population increase was forcing the line of settlement far inland. Here took shape by the middle of the eighteenth century a new kind of society that has been called the Old West. The distinguishing characteristic of the Old West was that it lay above the "fall line," the point where the rivers descended over rapids into the level coastal plain and became navigable. In the absence of good roads or other transportation facilities, bulky agricultural commodities could be transported to market only by water. Lying too far inland to produce for market, the Old West became an area of pioneer subsistence farming, isolated from the coastal settlements and the Atlantic world. Nevertheless, to those who peopled it, the Old West seemed an agrarian paradise where the ease of acquiring a farm of one's own promised a degree of security, well being, and independence that would have been unthinkable in the land-hungry Europe they had left behind.

New England's Old West was the northern and western hill towns, lying away from the coast and the deep inland extension of coastal society along the navigable Connecticut River. By the late seventeenth century the old Puritan pattern of town planting was breaking down in this area, as the provincial governments began disposing of blocks of new towns to land speculators who in turn sold farms to actual settlers.

South of New England, New York's Hudson River was a magnificent highway north into the interior, while the Mohawk River, flowing east from the Great Lakes country into the Hudson at Albany, afforded the colonies' only easy avenue through the Appalachian mountains to the Ohio and Mississippi valleys. But the fur-trading interests blocked settlement along the Mohawk until the early eighteenth century when the British government sponsored the resettlement of a large number of Germans above Albany.

The main current of German settlement flowed through Philadelphia and on inland to fill the broad and fertile lower valley of the Susquehanna. Beyond the Susquehanna it washed up against the series of Appalachian ridges that run from the northeast through central

Pennsylvania. Diverted down the valleys to the southwest, the Germans settled interior Maryland and crossed the Potomac into Virginia. Here some drifted southeast of the first great Appalachian range, the Blue Ridge, into the rolling Virginia Piedmont, but the main current moved on southwest up the Shenandoah Valley behind the Blue Ridge. By the 1750's, some Germans were pushing southeast from the upper Shenandoah across the Blue Ridge and down into the North Carolina Piedmont.

The German migration was followed and overlapped by the migration of the more aggressive Scotch-Irish. The Scotch-Irish filled in the gaps left by German settlements and then surged beyond them to the west and south. In Pennsylvania these hardy Indian fighters crossed ridge after ridge and filled valley after valley until by the 1770's they were on the waters of the Ohio occupying the area around Pittsburgh. Farther south, in the Carolinas, the Scotch-Irish pushed the Piedmont frontier up against the mountains; while in Virginia they pressed southwest through the mountain valleys toward the headwaters of the Tennessee River.

TENSIONS IN COLONIAL SOCIETY

The people of the Old West—the Yankee farmers of the New England hill towns, the Germans on the Mohawk, and the Germans and Scotch-Irish in their great salient curving southwest against the Appalachians from the Susquehanna to Georgia—soon complained of grievances against the older colonial settlements along the coast. The older areas continued to dominate the provincial governments by refusing to give the new settlements the representation to which their population entitled them. In Pennsylvania the three oldest counties had only a third of the province's population but elected two thirds of the assemblymen. The frontiersmen complained that such unrepresentative assemblies were indifferent to their problems such as the need for an aggressive policy against the Indians. The most extreme case of indifference to frontier needs was in South Carolina where the new settlements were separated from the old planting society along the coast by a wide belt of sandhills. Though the upcountrymen came to be a majority of the free population, the lowcountry not only refused them any representatives whatever in the assembly, but also neglected to provide them with courts or local law-enforcement officers.

The tension between the old and the new settlements was only a phase of a more general tension that accompanied the emergence of sharper class distinctions in the eighteenth century. Paradoxically American society in the seventeenth century had been more democratic in practice than it was in theory; while in the eighteenth century it was becoming more democratic in theory and less democratic in practice.

The Englishmen who came to the New World in the seventeenth century had brought with them the traditional European notion that men should defer to their betters in a society of ranks and orders. But these Old World distinctions rapidly lost their reality in a fluid society of mobile individuals. Class and property qualifications were almost unknown in voting for the early assemblies, not because the society was theoretically democratic but because such distinctions could not be applied where most men were roughly on a par.

Yet the very atmosphere of equal opportunity that eroded the Old World notions of unequal status made for new forms of inequality. In a free, enterprising environment, some men will eventually be more successful than others. In Virginia, for example, the tobacco planters who were harder working or luckier than their fellows or who had started with a bit more capital were in a better position to acquire more headrights and indentured servants. When tobacco prices declined late in the seventeenth century, only the larger and more efficient producers could profit. Also it became apparent that Negro slaves were a more efficient form of labor than indentured servants, but only the better heeled planters could afford the greater capital outlay necessary to acquire them. Thus by the end of the century the larger planters were squeezing out the small tobacco growers. Acquiring political influence along with their wealth, they were able to monopolize the fresh lands necessary to maintain or expand production of the soil-exhausting tobacco. Thus a formerly fluid society of roughly equal yeoman farmers came to be dominated by great planters who increasingly constituted a social and political aristocracy like the English country gentry on whom they modelled themselves. The same process occurred more rapidly in South Carolina where Negro slavery was more promptly adopted as the basic labor system. The successful merchants and professional men similarly emerged as a new elite class in the towns.

The British government actively encouraged the growth and political influence of this colonial elite. After the Glorious Revolution the London authorities replaced the religious qualification for voting with a property qualification in the new Massachusetts charter, and property qualifications became general in the colonies. Usually a voter had to be a "freeholder," the owner of fifty acres or a town lot. Although widespread land ownership softened the effect of property qualifications, they disfranchised over half the men in places like New York where many were tenants.

The royal governors generally sought to secure the support of the elite by bestowing important appointments and other favors on them. The provincial councils became the political strongholds of the wealthiest, while the assemblies were usually controlled by the well-to-do. Thus the eighteenth-century provincial governments were generally dominated by a local ruling class, the wealthiest members of which sometimes sided with the governors in disputes with the assemblies. The unrepresentative character of provincial government was merely made more glaring by the failure to give adequate representation or consideration to the rapidly growing frontier settlements.

This situation led to sporadic tension and occasional outbreaks of violence. As early as 1676 Nathaniel Bacon led an armed rebellion in Virginia against the governor, Sir William Berkeley, who had ruled the province autocratically for twenty-five years in alliance with the wealthiest planters. Similar tensions among New Yorkers figured in Jacob Leisler's rebellion at the time of the Glorious Revolution. The great landlords periodically faced mob violence from their tenants in New York, New Jersey, and elsewhere. There was a bitter struggle between debtor and creditor interests in Massachusetts over an inflationary Land Bank scheme in the 1740's. In 1764 an armed mob of frontiersmen marched on Philadelphia in anger at the pacific Indian policy of the eastern-dominated Pennsylvania assembly. The most spectacular of these outbreaks occurred in North Carolina where the oppressive policies of the local ruling class finally goaded the people of the interior into systematic mobbing of the courts. The governor had to march an army against the insurgents, and in a ragged engagement at Alamance in 1771, the Regulators, as they called themselves, were dispersed.

Most Americans probably acquiesced in rule by gentlemen and in normal times were not unduly disturbed over the unrepresentative character of their provincial governments. But tension was rising in the 1760's and 1770's, and many Americans were becoming ready to follow leadership that moved in the direction of more representative political institutions and a more democratic social order.

THE ENLIGHTENMENT

During the eighteenth century the whole Atlantic world was moving into a climate of thought known as the Enlightenment. The men of this optimistic age believed that a benevolent Creator had designed the world to produce human happiness, that the Creator had prescribed the proper working of all phenomena through "natural laws," and that men could discover these natural laws through observation and reasoning.

This faith of the Enlightenment received a strong impetus from Sir Isaac Newton's description of the physical world (*Principia Mathematica*, 1687) as a harmonious system of bodies regulated by simple natural laws. But it was another English thinker, John Locke, who most persuasively applied the Newtonian kind of analysis to the moral and political spheres. In *An Essay Concerning Human Understanding* (1690), Locke argued that there were natural laws governing human behavior and that man's powers of observation and reasoning enabled him to live in accordance with these laws by understanding what kinds of behavior were conducive to happiness. Thus the Enlightenment exalted "reason" as the human faculty which, predominating over interference from the "passions" or emotions, could lead men toward virtue, happiness, and perfection. Analyzing politics in a similar fashion (*Two Treatises on Government*, 1689), Locke maintained that natural law ordained a government resting on the consent of the governed and respecting the inherent "natural rights" of all.

In its optimism and individualism the Enlightenment expressed the emerging spirit of modernity. Though British North America was too young and too busy to give much attention to metaphysical speculation, the area was in the forefront of the movement into modernity. Americans, therefore, gladly embraced Lockean ideas as explaining what already seemed to them self-evident. Many of the better educated shifted gradually from orthodox Christianity toward the rationalist religion *Deism*, the worship of a wise and kindly Creator who was best served by right living.

The influence of Enlightenment thought can be seen everywhere in eighteenth-century American life. The esthetic principles of rational simplicity, order, and balance were exemplified in the "colonial" or "Georgian" architecture of the period. American writers imitated the simple elegance of the English authors Addison and Steele and sought to persuade their readers by rational argument.

The Enlightenment gave a great impetus to the maturing cultural and intellectual life of the colonies. Beginning with the Boston *News-Letter* (1704), newspapers sprang up everywhere; by 1765 there were twenty-five, and every colony except Delaware and New Jersey had at least one. A hungry market developed for pamphlets on every conceivable topic. Artisans organized clubs for discussion and intellectual self-improvement. Booksellers flourished, many gentlemen developed fine private libraries, and following the example of an enterprise

A NEW SOCIETY

launched by Benjamin Franklin in Philadelphia, subscription libraries
were established in most of the towns.

By placing such a high value on intellect, the Enlightenment reinforced a notable movement in higher education that resulted in the
creation of nine colleges by the 1770's. Harvard (1636) was joined by
Virginia's William and Mary (1693) and Connecticut's Yale (1701);
and the Philadelphia Academy, which was originally founded as a
secondary school by Benjamin Franklin, became in the 1750's the most
modern and secular of the colonial colleges. Five other colleges owed
their founding most immediately to a great religious movement that
seemed at first to oppose the spirit of the Enlightenment and modernity.

THE GREAT AWAKENING

The drift toward modernity had steadily eroded the seventeenth-
century piety which the settlers had brought to all the early colonies
and of which Puritanism was merely the most intense form. Religious
observances were as strictly enforced in early Anglican Virginia as
in New England, but the tobacco prosperity soon converted Anglicanism into a bland and undemanding adornment of Virginia's genial country life. It was this kind of Anglicanism that became the "established"
or official religion, supported by public taxation, in all the southern
colonies and the three lower counties of New York. Anglican religious
zeal was apparent only where the missionaries sent out by England's
Society for the Propagation of the Gospel were at work and in New
England where the Anglicans were an unpopular minority.

Perhaps the most conspicuous example of the erosion of piety in
the New World atmosphere of individualism, optimism, and enterprise
was the quick conversion of the Huguenots, those French counterparts of the Puritans, to the polite Anglicanism of the South Carolina
planter class. Even the Pennsylvania Quakers, growing wealthy as a
result of godly industry, frugality, and honesty, soon arrived at a
point where the counting house seemed to overshadow the meeting
house.

The erosion of piety can be most clearly traced among the theologically sophisticated and articulate Puritan Congregationalists of
New England. By the end of the seventeenth century, the Reverend
Cotton Mather, the last great defender of the orthodox order, was
talking more about the necessity of right living in this world than
about man's dependence on God for salvation in the world to come.
The wealthy Boston merchants who founded the Brattle Street

Church in 1699 did not require an account of conversion for full membership and chose a minister who preached a "free and catholic" version of Christianity emphasizing morality over piety. As the eighteenth century advanced, the most influential ministers in Boston, Charles Chauncy and Jonathan Mayhew, drifted into the "Arminian" heresy which diminished man's dependence on God by regarding him as capable of contributing to his own salvation by right living.

But a people conditioned to piety did not adjust easily to the clear, bland atmosphere of the dawning Enlightenment. The embers of the old intense faith still smoldered beneath the ashes, and in the 1730's and 1740's they were fanned into a bright blaze of religious enthusiasm that burned up and down the length and breadth of the colonies. The American Great Awakening was only part of a general movement in the Protestant world which included such parallel phenomena as an upsurge of Pietism in Germany and the Wesleyan revival in England. In their inception an effort to reassert the earlier extreme piety against the rationalism and optimism of the Enlightenment, these awakenings appealed frankly to the emotions and ended by unconsciously accommodating Christianity to the modern spirit.

The American Great Awakening began in different ways in different places. As early as the 1720's the Reverend Theodore J. Frelinghuysen had touched off emotional revivals of religious feeling among the Germans in New Jersey's Raritan Valley. Nearby a group of ardent Presbyterian ministers had begun trying to stimulate intense religious feeling in place of the cold formalism of Calvinist orthodoxy. And at Northampton, Massachusetts, in 1734, a gifted Congregationalist minister, Jonathan Edwards, stirred up a series of revivals by his powerful appeals to the religious emotions. All of these streams merged into a general revival movement throughout the colonies when England's great Wesleyan evangelist, George Whitefield, made the first of his American tours in 1739–1740.

The Great Awakening was emotional, popular, and anti-intellectual. The revivalists were often poorly educated, and their fervent exhortations sometimes touched off extravagant reactions—barking, the "jerks," and falling down—by their audiences. They maintained that a heart open to the divine spirit was more important than a highly-trained intellect and stirred up much strife by accusing conservative, educated clergymen of spiritual coldness. But people responded to the revivals with enthusiasm, and the more popular Protestant denominations, the Baptists, the revivalistic "New Light" Presbyterians, and later the Methodists, grew by leaps and bounds. In appealing for an emotional response to God's grace, the revival preachers often unconsciously suggested that salvation was available to all, that man played an important part in the process, and the Methodists came to espouse these Arminian (and modern) heresies quite consciously.

Despite its anti-intellectual character, the Great Awakening prompted the establishment of three colonial colleges designed to train ministers for the revivalist wings of the sponsoring denominations: the Presbyterians' College of New Jersey (Princeton, 1746), the Baptists' College of Rhode Island (Brown, 1764), and the Dutch Reformed Rutgers (1766). Two other colonial colleges were founded under nonrevivalist church auspices: Anglican King's College in New York (Columbia, 1754) and Congregationalist Dartmouth (1769), begun as an Indian school in New Hampshire.

It is paradoxical that the often anti-intellectual Awakening should have had as one of its major leaders the most gifted intellectual in colonial America, Jonathan Edwards. This brilliant Congregationalist minister burned with a personal sense of God's majesty and power that would have been exceptional even among the first-generation Puritans. But he also had an understanding of the intellectual implications of Newtonian-Lockean thought that was equalled by few if any men of his generation in either Europe or America. In a series of treatises he impressively utilized the most advanced thought of his day to reconstruct on a new intellectual base the old Puritan vision of God.

Few in Edwards' generation really understood what he was trying to do. His fellow revivalists gladly adopted his advanced principles of human psychology which recognized the importance and legitimacy of emotion. But most Americans had moved too far into modernity to share, even in seasons of religious exaltation, his vision of the beauty and fitness of God's awful sovereignty and sinful man's helpless dependence on the miracle of divine grace.

"THIS NEW MAN"

Crèvecoeur's "new man," then, was a product of New World opportunity, whether the opportunity to acquire a farm of his own in the Old West, to grow rich planting tobacco, to trade with the West Indies, or simply to achieve dignity and independence as an artisan in one of the growing colonial towns. He welcomed the optimistic tendencies of Enlightenment thought as something his New World experience had made self-evident. In politics he stoutly defended the English tradition of individual rights and aspired to control the representative institutions of provincial government in the interest of his group. In religion he tended consciously toward Deism or Arminianism if educated; otherwise he revelled in the emotionalism of the Great Awakening while moving less consciously away from the orthodox piety of his fathers.

"The American, this new man," may be seen in his most fully developed form in the *Autobiography* of Benjamin Franklin. This son of a Boston candlemaker had sat in Cotton Mather's congregation as a boy, had assimilated Enlightenment thought while working on his brother's newspaper and while sowing wild oats in London, and had returned to win wealth and prestige as a Philadelphia printer while still in his forties. Retiring from business, this wise, humane, and practical man spent the rest of his life in scientific experiments that explained the nature of electricity, in developing a host of practical devices and projects for the benefit and improvement of his fellow citizens, and in public service culminating with attendance at the birth of a new nation.

The fascination of Franklin lies largely in the fact that he carried to perfection so many traits that were characteristic of his fellow countrymen. *"He* is an American," wrote Crèvecoeur, "who, leaving behind him all his ancient prejudices and manners, receives new ones from the new mode of life he has embraced, the new government he obeys, and the new rank he holds. . . . Here the rewards of his industry follow with equal steps the progress of his labor. . . . Here religion demands but little of him. . . . The American is a new man, who acts upon new principles; he must therefore entertain new ideas, and form new opinions. From involuntary idleness, servile dependence, penury, and useless labor, he has passed to toils of a different nature, rewarded by ample subsistence. —This is an American."

FOR FURTHER READING:

J. Hector St. John de Crèvecoeur recorded his impressions of the distinctiveness of American life in the eighteenth century in *Letters from an American Farmer* (1782)*. European immigrants to America in the colonial period are described in Marcus Lee Hansen, *The Atlantic Migration, 1607–1860* (1940)*; while Abbott Emerson Smith's *Colonists in Bondage* (1947) deals with indentured servants. Daniel J. Boorstin analyzes the unique institutions and attitudes that emerged in the New World environment in *The Americans: The Colonial Experience* (1958). The colonial towns are described in three works by Carl Bridenbaugh: *Cities in the Wilderness, 1625–1742* (1938), *Cities in Revolt, 1743–1776* (1955), and (with Jessica Bridenbaugh) *Rebels and Gentlemen: Philadelphia in the Age of Franklin* (1942). The best introduction to the Old West, as well as to Frederick Jackson Turner's famous "frontier thesis," is the first three chapters of his volume of collected essays, *The Frontier in American History* (1920)*. The Old West of the southern colonies is described, along with the tidewater societies of Virginia and South Carolina, in Carl Bridenbaugh's *Myths and Realities: Societies of the Colonial South* (1952)*. Thomas J. Wertenbaker analyzes the transition toward an aristocratic society in Virginia in *The Planters of Colonial Virginia* (1922), and Louis B. Wright describes planter life in *The First Gentlemen of Virginia* (1940). Leonard W. Labaree's *Conservatism in Early American History* (1948)* traces the growing influence of the upper classes in colonial politics, while Carl Bridenbaugh deals with the mechanic classes of the towns in *The Colonial Craftsman* (1950)*. The best survey of colonial thought and culture is Max Savelle, *Seeds of Liberty* (1948). William Warren Sweet describes *Religion in Colonial America* (1942) from the point of view of denominations and behavior, while the intellectual and theological transformation of New England Congregationalism may be followed in Conrad Wright, *The Beginnings of Unitarianism in America* (1955). The best single book on the Great Awakening is Edwin S. Gaustad's *The Great Awakening in New England* (1957). Ola E. Winslow has written a good biography of *Jonathan Edwards* (1940)*, and Perry Miller's *Jonathan Edwards* (1949)* is a brilliant interpretation of his thought. Carl Van Doren has written the best biography of *Benjamin Franklin* (1941), but a sense of Franklin's quality is best derived from his own fascinating *Autobiography* (many editions)*.

David Levin's *The Puritan in the Enlightenment: Franklin and Edwards* (Berkeley Readings in American History, 1963)* offers a set of documents comparing and contrasting these two great sons of New England Puritanism in their reactions to the eighteenth-century world.

---

*Available in paperback edition.

EVENTS LEADING TO THE REVOLUTION

BRITISH ACTIONS   AMERICAN ACTIONS

BRITISH ACTIONS		AMERICAN ACTIONS
Revenue (Sugar) Act—laying duties for revenue.	**1764**	
Stamp Act—revenue stamps.	**1765**	Mob action. Nonimportation agreements.
Repeal of Stamp Act. Declaratory Act—asserting right of Parliament to legislate for colonies in all respects.	**1766**	Nonimportation suspended.
Townshend duties—revenue duties on various articles.	**1767**	Mob action. Nonimportation agreements.
Repeal of Townshend duties, except duty on tea.	**1770**	Boston Massacre. Suspension of nonimportation.
	1772	Committees of correspondence organized.
Tea Act—giving East India Co. monopoly of colonial tea trade.	**1773**	Mob action. Boston Tea Party.
Intolerable acts: 1) closing port of Boston. 2) restricting self-government in Massachusetts. 3) allowing royal officers to be tried in England. 4) allowing royal troops to requisition private buildings for quarters. Quebec Act—continuing non-representative government in Quebec, tolerating Roman Catholicism in Quebec, and incorporating Ohio Valley in Quebec.	**1774**	First Continental Congress 1) rejects Galloway's plan of union. 2) adopts Continental Association, establishing committees of safety to enforce commercial nonintercourse with England. 3) encourages Massachusetts to establish revolutionary government and prepare for military defense.
Lexington-Concord — British troops skirmish with Massachusetts militiamen.	**1775**	Committees of safety seize control. Second Continental Congress—appoints Washington to command continental army at Boston.

CHAPTER 4

TOWARD REVOLUTION

1763–1775

At the close of the French and Indian War in 1763, the inhabitants of British North America considered themselves thoroughly patriotic and loyal British subjects. Under British rule the colonies had become flourishing and prosperous societies, affording well-being and oppor- tunities to ordinary individuals to an extent that was unparalleled in Europe and perhaps anywhere in previous human history. The British navigation laws had, by and large, fostered their prosperity; British fleets and armies had defended them against their Spanish, French, and Indian enemies; and a benevolent (or careless) home government had allowed them to develop representative institutions and to regulate their domestic affairs with only minor interference. Nourished on the British Whig tradition stemming from the Glorious Revolution of 1688, the American colonists thought of their political rights and lib- erties as British rights and liberties.

Yet within twelve years these same loyal British subjects were at war with the mother country. The crises of these dozen years grad- ually taught them that they had long since developed a deep attach- ment to the society they were creating in the colonies. Somewhat to their own surprise they learned that they really valued the British con- nection only as far as, and as long as, it was compatible with their desire to preserve and perfect their free and semiautonomous Ameri- can society. In one of history's most notorious instances of bad timing, British officials had chosen to tighten up the lax administration of the Empire at the very moment when the Americans were ripe for the lessons of their experience.

THE NEW IMPERIAL POLICY

When Britain emerged victorious from the great Anglo-French wars, there were a number of conditions making for a new and more vigorous imperial policy. First, King George III, who had come to the throne in 1760, was an ambitious and conscientious monarch who desired to play a larger role in governmental affairs than had his predecessors. Through manipulation of royal patronage and control of Parliamentary elections in the so-called rotten boroughs, he sought to re-establish by political maneuver the royal influence that earlier monarchs had exercised by right. Unfortunately the King and the ministers he picked to run the government proved to be less flexible and astute in dealing with the colonists than their easygoing predecessors had been.

Yet almost any British ministry would have sought to tighten up the imperial system at this time. During the war the colonists had irritated the British by their reluctance to furnish troops, supplies, and money and in too many cases had actually prospered by trading with the enemy. Moreover, the Empire had now been greatly enlarged, and more efficient regulation seemed necessary everywhere if the colonial territories were to serve their purpose of benefitting the mother country.

The most pressing immediate problem was that of revenue to pay off the crushing debt incurred during the war and to support the increased costs of defending and administering the enlarged empire. Compared with English landowners, the American colonists were virtually untaxed, and in London it seemed only fair that they should be made to share some of the heavy burden laid on English taxpayers for the defense of American territory.

The new imperial policy that grew out of these conditions was inaugurated by the ministry of George Grenville in the years 1763–1765. A permanent military force was established in the American colonies, the control over Indian relations was transferred from the colonial governments to imperial officials, the advance of settlement on the western frontier was restricted and placed under imperial regulation, and the colonial assemblies were forbidden to issue paper money. Particularly important was the Revenue Act of 1764 (often called the Sugar Act) which for the first time levied import duties avowedly for revenue rather than regulation of trade and provided machinery insuring that the duties would really be collected.

Most disturbing was the duty on molasses from the French West Indies. For years New England merchants had been evading an earlier duty levied under the Molasses Act of 1733 in order to import molasses for manufacture of rum. The molasses duty was now lowered to half its former rate but now it was rigorously enforced, and the effect was to cripple the flourishing commerce of New England. Shocked by the sudden vigor of imperial control after decades of "salutary neg-

[46]

lect," the colonists quickly took the position that they could not rightfully be taxed except by their own representatives.

Underestimating the strength of colonial opposition or not caring how strong it was, Grenville proceeded the following year, 1765, to push through Parliament the even more provocative Stamp Act. This measure required the colonists to purchase revenue stamps and affix them to all kinds of legal and commercial documents, newspapers, almanacs, playing cards, dice, and liquor licenses. This was taxation (without representation) in a highly visible and odious form. Moreover, it offended most those who were most influential in shaping colonial opinion—merchants, lawyers, printers, and tavern keepers. The explosion of protest indicated not only how averse the colonists were to taxation of any kind, but also how attached they were to the representative tradition of British Whiggery and to the home rule they had enjoyed with so little interference.

Colonial mobs blocked the sale of stamps and intimidated the stamp agents into resigning. More effective in the long run was a non-importation agreement sponsored by the colonial merchants that led to a boycott of British goods. This had such an effect on British manufacturers and exporting merchants that Parliament was persuaded in 1766 to repeal the Stamp Act. But Parliament did not surrender its claim to tax the colonists, for repeal was accompanied by a Declaratory Act asserting Parliament's right to legislate for the colonies in any and all respects.

That this was no idle claim was shown the very next year, 1767, when Charles Townshend, Chancellor of the Exchequer, pushed through Parliament the so-called Townshend Acts levying duties for revenue on a new class of previously untaxed articles. The new taxes were rendered more unpalatable by provisions for further strengthening the enforcement and collection machinery and by the stipulation that revenues from the act would be used to pay the salaries of royal officials in the colonies, thus robbing the colonial assemblies of their most potent weapon, the power to withhold salaries from uncooperative royal officers. Again the Americans resorted to mob action and the proven weapon of nonimportation, and again, in 1770, Parliament backed down, repealing all the duties except the one on tea.

Most of the colonists were willing to accept this action as settling the controversy, and the next few years were a period of prosperity and relative peace between colonies and mother country. Yet the British ministers were badly deceived if they supposed that imperial relations were as cordial as they had been before 1763. The Americans had moved far toward a consciousness of having a separate and quasi-national interest during the seven years of controversy. They had been able to defy the home government successfully for the sake of this separate interest, and they were now more committed than perhaps they themselves realized to the principles of local home rule and no taxation without representation.

THE RADICALS

Especially dangerous for continued harmony was the fact that the controversies of the 1760's had developed a small but well-organized and ably led group of American "radicals" who opposed the slightest British effort to tax the colonies or to regulate their internal affairs. Usually these radicals were the men who had led the more violent phases of the agitation against the Stamp Act and the Townshend duties, and their hostility toward the British was often combined with a democratic resentment toward their more aristocratic fellow Americans. In Virginia, for example, Patrick Henry's radical opposition to the Stamp Act was simultaneously a challenge to the control of the House of Burgesses by the most conservative wing of the planter oligarchy. In Boston the radical leader Samuel Adams, though strongly backéd by the wealthy merchant John Hancock, drew most of his support from mechanics and shopkeepers who welcomed an opportunity to strike at those aristocratic Bostonians who held royal offices or had close ties with the royal officials. In Charleston mechanics and other "middling" types constituted most of the radical group, but their leader was the young aristocrat Christopher Gadsden. Americans of every social level had joined in the protests against the Stamp Act and Townshend duties, but the wealthier and more conservative of them had been dismayed by the excesses of mob action. These more conservative American Whigs were satisfied when Parliament repealed all the offensive duties except the one on tea, while the radicals insisted on continuing the agitation against the tea duty. The most dangerous of the radical leaders was that superb organizer, agitator, and propagandist Samuel Adams. Through his control of the Boston town meeting, Adams kept Boston in an uproar while quiet was returning to other areas. By precipitating incidents like the "Boston Massacre" of 1770 (an unruly crowd goaded a small party of British soldiers into firing and killing three persons) Adams gained material for distorted propaganda designed to keep the colonists alarmed over an encroaching British tyranny.

Simultaneously Adams and his allies were creating a radical organization. Operating from his base in the Boston town meeting, Adams induced other Massachusetts towns to establish "committees of correspondence." The idea spread, and shortly the planter radicals in Virginia urged the establishment of a provincial committee of correspondence in every colony. Naturally these committees came to be dominated by men with relatively radical attitudes. While the radicals were unable to dispel the complacency that prevailed in the prosperous years 1770–1773, they had created an organization that could seize the initiative whenever an opportunity arose.

THE SECOND CRISIS

Opportunity came when the British ministry of Lord North, in all innocence, undertook to aid the British East India Company by pushing through Parliament the Tea Act of 1773. The company was given the exclusive privilege of selling its tea directly to American consumers without paying the English export tax, thus increasing the company's profits, lowering the price of tea to Americans, eliminating widespread smuggling and evasion of the American tea duty, and depriving American importing merchants of any share in the tea trade.

The resentment of the conservative American merchants drove them again into alliance with the radicals, and the radicals made the most of this opportunity to renew violent agitation. Claiming that the British were using lower tea prices to seduce Americans into surrendering their liberties, the radicals again resorted to mob action which was climaxed by the famous Tea Party in Boston. Boarding the vessels that had arrived with East India tea, Sam Adams' followers dumped Boston's entire consignment overboard.

This open defiance of authority and destruction of property shocked many Americans, while it convinced the British government that punitive measures must be adopted to bring the rebellious colonists to heel. Promptly, Parliament passed a series of four "Intolerable Acts," closing the port of Boston until the Bostonians paid for the tea they had destroyed, drastically reducing the representative and self-governing features of the Massachusetts provincial government, allowing royal officials to be tried in England when accused of crimes in the colonies, and permitting the British army to requisition American buildings as quarters. About the same time Parliament also passed the Quebec Act, adding to the province of Quebec much western territory claimed by several of the colonies, providing the kind of unrepresentative government in Quebec that had prevailed under the French, and affording complete religious toleration to the overwhelmingly Catholic Quebec population.

These measures threw the radical propaganda machine and committee organization into high gear. "The cause of Boston is the cause of all British America" was the message trumpeted everywhere during the spring and summer of 1774. Food, fuel, and money were collected for the relief of the beleaguered Bostonians, local nonimportation agreements sprang up on all sides, and a proposal for a continental congress to coordinate resistance won quick endorsement from the assemblies or from extralegal meetings of the assemblymen in most of the colonies.

THE FIRST CONTINENTAL CONGRESS

In September, 1774, an extralegal Congress of delegates from every colony except Georgia assembled in Philadelphia. Because the delegates had been chosen at the height of the anti-British excitement following the Intolerable Acts, the already organized radicals gained a majority in the Congress over the confused and unorganized conservatives. Nevertheless, the conservatives were ably led and made a strong fight for moderate measures. The most promising conservative proposal was Joseph Galloway's plan for a colonial union under a royally appointed president-general and a council representing the colonial assemblies, with the latter having power to legislate for the colonies and to veto Parliamentary legislation affecting the colonies. When the Congress narrowly refused to endorse this plan, the radicals were given a green light to proceed with more aggressive measures.

After a hard fight they finally persuaded the Congress to adopt the Continental Association. This was a detailed plan for nonimportation, nonconsumption, and nonexportation of goods between the colonies and Great Britain, combined with a plan of enforcement that laid the basis for an extralegal governmental system. Committees of safety were to be elected in every county or town. These committees were to circulate the Association among all citizens for endorsement and then to single out violators for boycott and for denunciation as "enemies to the rights of British America." Goods imported in violation of the Association could be seized, and the work of the local committees was to be coordinated in each colony by a provincial Congress and a provincial committee of safety.

During the winter and spring of 1774–1775 the radicals began vigorously putting this revolutionary scheme to work in every colony. A drastic decline in British imports quickly demonstrated the Association's effectiveness as an instrument of economic warfare; but it was probably even more important as an instrument of political persuasion and coercion.

While nearly all Americans favored efforts to secure concessions from the British government, it is probable that only a minority supported the aggressive tactics of the radicals. Many were decidedly hostile to any action that threatened to break the British connection, and many more were simply confused or indifferent. The Association and its committee system gave the organized and purposeful radicals a highly efficient means of committing the passive and often hostile majority to their program.

Though the committees were supposed to be elected, they were frequently in fact self-constituted bodies of the local radical leaders and in some cases were merely the old committees of correspondence continued under a new name. Where public denunciation failed to secure compliance with the Association, they did not hesitate to employ threats and even physical violence. More and more as the revolutionary crisis deepened the committees assumed the powers of government, fixing prices, levying fines, and taking charge of local militia units.

Yet radical control was far from complete by the spring of 1775. The mercantile and officeholding aristocracy was putting up strong opposition in the northeastern port towns; upcountry Carolina farmers were disposed to side with the royal governors against the provincial politicians who had oppressed them in the past and who were now leading the radical movement; and everywhere there were wide areas still so unexcited over British oppression that the radicals had made little headway. An additional impulse was needed, and once again Sam Adams' Massachusetts radicals supplied it.

WAR

British despotism was anything but a remote and idle threat to the Massachusetts radicals during the winter and spring of 1774–1775. As part of the British plan to crush the spirit of insubordination in Massachusetts, additional troops had been sent to Boston, and their commander, General Thomas Gage, was designated military governor of the province. With the endorsement of the Continental Congress, the radicals took the momentous step of establishing a revolutionary provincial government under the suspended charter and began training troops and collecting military supplies.

The inevitable clash came on the morning of April 19, 1775, when General Gage sent a detachment of British soldiers from Boston to seize the powder and arms that had been collected at nearby Concord and to arrest Samuel Adams and John Hancock. Warned by Paul Revere and William Dawes, the farmer "minutemen" of Lexington and Concord boldly challenged the British regulars, and by the time the harassed soldiers had run the gauntlet of farmers' muskets on the road back to Boston, they had lost 273 dead, wounded, and missing. Instantly the radicals sent special riders flying through the colonies with exaggerated accounts of the massacre of innocent Massachusetts farmers by bloodthirsty British soldiers. Everywhere there was a burst of patriotic indignation, enabling the radical-dominated committees of safety to gain complete control. Royal governors were driven from their posts, troops were drilled, and royal forts and powder magazines were seized.

On May 10, a Second Continental Congress was hastily assembled in Philadelphia. As a gesture to the timid, this radical-dominated body made a final appeal to the King for a peaceful settlement, but most of its energies were devoted to preparations for war. The thousands of armed New Englanders who had rushed to besiege Gage's redcoats from the hills overlooking Boston were taken under the aegis of the Congress, and Virginia's George Washington was named to command this emerging continental army.

FOR FURTHER READING:

Charles M. Andrews has written an excellent brief account of *The Colonial Background of the American Revolution* (1924)*. John C. Miller's *Origins of the American Revolution* (1943) is the best general account of the developing conflict between the colonies and the mother country. Somewhat differing interpretations of British politics as they affected the imperial crisis are given in Sir Lewis Namier, *England in the Age of the American Revolution* (1930) and in Herbert Butterfield, *George III and the Historians* (1959). The internal workings of the developing American protest movement are described in Arthur M. Schlesinger, *The Colonial Merchants and the American Revolution* (1917), while Philip G. Davidson illuminates the methods of the protest movement in his study, *Propaganda and the American Revolution* (1941). John C. Miller has written a good biography of *Sam Adams, Pioneer in Propaganda* (1936), and Catherine Drinker Bowen's *John Adams and the American Revolution* (1949)*, though cast in semifictional form, is historically sound and makes absorbing reading.

A good understanding of the conflict of loyalties that the Revolutionary crisis caused for many Americans may be derived from the contrasting reactions presented in Jackson T. Main, *Rebel versus Tory: The Crises of the Revolution, 1773–1776* (Berkeley Readings in American History, 1963)*.

*Available in paperback edition.

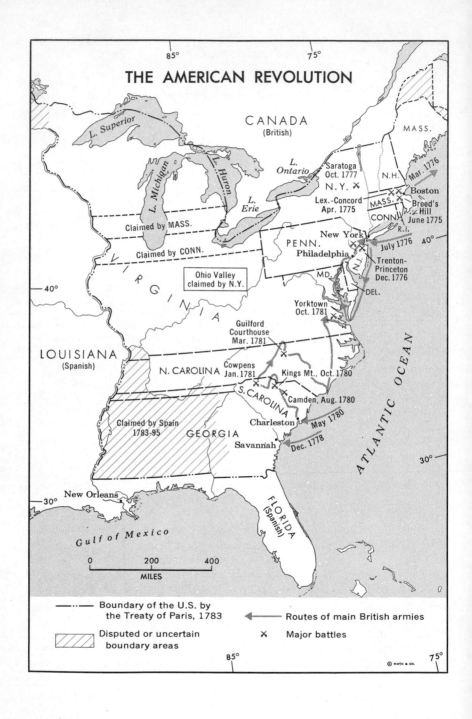

THE AMERICAN REVOLUTION

85°   75°

CANADA
(British)

MASS.

L. Superior

L. Michigan

L. Huron

L. Ontario   Saratoga
Oct. 1777   N.H.   Mar. 1776

N.Y. ✗   Boston

L. Erie   Lex.-Concord   MASS.   Breed's
              Apr. 1775   CONN.   Hill
                                       June 1775

Claimed by MASS.   R.I.

New York   July 1776   40°

Claimed by CONN.   PENN.
                    Philadelphia

Ohio Valley   Trenton-
claimed by N.Y.   MD.   Princeton
                           Dec. 1776

40°   DEL.

VIRGINIA

Yorktown
Oct. 1781

Guilford
Courthouse
Mar. 1781

LOUISIANA
(Spanish)   Cowpens
              N. CAROLINA   Jan. 1781   Kings Mt., Oct. 1780

S. CAROLINA

Camden, Aug. 1780

Claimed by Spain   Charleston   May 1780
1783-95   GEORGIA

Savannah   Dec. 1778

ATLANTIC OCEAN

30°

New Orleans

30°   FLORIDA
                        (Spanish)

Gulf of Mexico

0   200   400
├────────┼──────────┤
        MILES

—··—··— Boundary of the U.S. by
         the Treaty of Paris, 1783   ◄────── Routes of main British armies

▨▨▨ Disputed or uncertain   ✗   Major battles
      boundary areas

85°   75°

© RMSN & CO.

CHAPTER 5

INDEPENDENCE ACHIEVED

1775–1783

THE FIRST YEAR OF WAR

The military struggle began slowly, and during the first year no really decisive engagements occurred. In June, 1775, shortly before Washington arrived to take command of the poorly organized American forces on the hills surrounding Boston, General Gage managed to drive his besiegers from one of their strongest positions, Breed's Hill. But the misnamed Battle of Bunker Hill cost the British some 40 per cent of their force, and these frightful losses demonstrated that the Americans could not easily be dislodged. During the months that followed Washington methodically converted his untrained militiamen into a disciplined army and tightened the ring around the British.

With Gage's army encircled in Boston, the ebullient Americans undertook, during the winter of 1775–1776, a two-pronged offensive against Canada. The valiant forces led by Richard Montgomery and Benedict Arnold surmounted great hardships and won some early successes; but in the end the reluctance of the Canadian population to join the rebellion forced a retreat.

Perhaps the most important struggle going on during the first year of the war was within the colonies to consolidate support for the Revolution. It had quickly become clear that neither the British nor the American leaders were prepared to recede from their positions and that the issue would be decided only by full-scale war. So strongly rooted were the British loyalties of the colonists that many of them could not bring themselves to support open war against the mother country, despite all the coercion the Revolutionary leaders exerted. Nearly one hundred thousand of these Loyalists were forced into exile, while those who remained suffered ostracism, disfranchisement, confiscation of property, and other penalties for their loyalty to the King. Still, the American Revolution produced none of the wholesale imprisonments or executions of dissidents that have marked other revolutions, and the penalties imposed on the Loyalists do not seem disproportionate to the threat they represented to the success of the Revolutionary cause.

In March, 1776, General Gage finally abandoned the increasingly difficult task of holding Boston and sailed away with his army and hundreds of Loyalists to the British stronghold at Halifax, Nova Scotia. His departure did not mark a decisive American victory, but instead the approaching end of a year of stalemate in which each side had consolidated its position and prepared for the real struggle yet to come. During that fortunate year of respite a new American nation animated by fresh and exciting ideals had been coming to birth.

"CONCEIVED IN LIBERTY"

For months after the Revolutionary War began, almost no Americans were willing to admit that they sought independence from England. Yet the pressure of events increasingly forced them to act as though they were in fact independent and steadily prepared them for an open break.

The question of independence was connected in an indirect but important way with the acceleration of democratic tendencies that exhibited itself in the Revolutionary movement. While "home rule" was the primary issue in the Revolution, the political upsurge of the "lower orders" during the agitation had raised the important secondary issue of "who should rule at home." The Liberty Boys who rioted against the Stamp Act or the Townshend duties were making a bid for political status. Perhaps more important was the fact that the Revolutionary agitation opened an avenue by which ambitious men of the "middling sort"—Sam Adams, Patrick Henry, and their counterparts in other colonies—could rise to power and influence. The Revolutionary movement offered such "new men" an opportunity to gain power by espousing radical measures and appealing indirectly to the inchoate democratic aspirations of those who had heretofore had little influence in government.

The success of these "new men" was due in considerable measure to a favorable climate of ideas. The Revolutionary era was one of those periods in history when ideas have had great consequences. All Americans, including the most conservative and aristocratic, believed that the Glorious Revolution of 1688 and its great Bill of Rights had guaranteed to every British citizen certain rights—especially rights of "liberty" and "property"—upon which no monarch or government could rightfully infringe. The colonists pegged their opposition to the New Imperial Policy on the claim that it was an arbitrary violation of these rights. "Liberty and Property" became the slogan of the Revolutionary movement.

But the Whig slogans carried some democratic implications that could be applied to government within the colonies. When the colonial leaders argued for the Whig principle of "no taxation without representation" in imperial relations, it required no great imagination for inadequately represented Americans to apply the same argument to domestic affairs or even to expand it into the more general principle that government should be representative of the governed, meaning all the governed.

These democratic implications of the British Whig tradition were powerfully reinforced by the larger thought stream of the Enlightenment. Confident that the Creator desired human happiness, the men of the eighteenth century were drifting toward the notion that all men were equal in their "natural rights" and that the only just end of government was to maintain a state of society in which every man could enjoy his rights to the fullest possible extent. Since liberty was the most precious of these rights, government should be restricted to the smallest possible compass that would enable it to keep individuals from invading each others' liberty, and since all men were potentially rational, government should rest on the consent of the governed.

During the later stages of the Revolutionary crisis, the colonial leaders had broadened the basis for their claim to autonomy from their rights as British citizens, according to the Whig tradition, to their rights as men, according to the natural-rights tradition. The second of John Locke's *Two Treatises on Government* (1689) was the most trenchant justification of revolution on the basis of the natural-rights argument. Directly or indirectly, Americans were thinking in Lockean terms as they decided for revolution, drafted their Declaration of Independence, and established a new governmental system.

This is not to say that the Americans rebelled against England because they deliberately sought to extend democracy at home. Rather, large segments of the population rallied to the movement for colonial autonomy more enthusiastically than they might otherwise have done because they were aroused by the democratic implications of Revolutionary rhetoric. Moreover, in the process of creating broad support for their movement, the Revolutionary leaders were compelled to seek the participation of groups that had previously played little part in public life. Consequently the new provincial congresses that were

organized in the early months of the war had a far broader membership than the colonial assemblies and councils that they succeeded.

This rise of the lower orders affected the ways in which members
of the old colonial ruling group reacted to the Revolutionary crisis.
Many of them were so alarmed that they became Loyalists. A larger
number (conservative Whigs) continued to furnish leadership to the
Revolutionary movement but resisted independence. They hoped to
win colonial autonomy while restoring the British connection as a
means of preserving the predominance of gentlemen within the colonies. A third segment of the gentry (radical Whigs) were so deeply
infected with the Revolutionary ideology that they worked closely
with the "new men" who spoke for the lower orders, espousing independence and paving the way for a new distribution of political power.

It was this last group of men, especially Richard Henry Lee of
Virginia and Samuel and John Adams of Massachusetts, who controlled
the Continental Congress in the early years of the war. On the question of independence, they were aided by the drift of events. The
British government showed little disposition to conciliate the Americans and every disposition to wage vigorous war against them. The
importance of aid from Britain's ancient enemy France became increasingly apparent, and independence might pave the way for a French
alliance. Finally, Americans of all classes were gradually beginning to
sense the exciting possibility of building a new and independent society
on the natural-rights and implicitly democratic principles of Revolutionary rhetoric. How rapidly this feeling had spread was demonstrated by the tremendous public response to Thomas Paine's pamphlet
Common Sense, published in January, 1776. Advocating both independence and democracy, Paine's slashing pamphlet sold several hundred thousand copies.

Paine did not create the sentiment for independence, but merely
crystallized a feeling that had been growing by leaps and bounds while
remaining largely unspoken. Once catapulted into the arena of open
debate, the idea of independence rapidly overcame conservative opposition. On July 2, the Continental Congress resolved that "these United
States are, and of right ought to be, free and independent states"; two
days later the Declaration of Independence was adopted.

Drafted by Thomas Jefferson, with the help of Benjamin Franklin
and John Adams, this memorable document was for the most part a
long and exaggerated catalogue of British violations of American
rights. What made the Declaration a momentous factor in history,
however, was its opening section distilling in a few sentences of noble
and enduring prose the essence of the Lockean, natural-rights theory
of government: "We hold these truths to be self-evident, that all men

are created equal, that they are endowed by their Creator with certain inalienable Rights, that among these are Life, Liberty, and the pursuit of Happiness. That to secure these rights, Governments are instituted among Men, deriving their just powers from the consent of the governed. That whenever any Form of Government becomes destructive of these ends, it is the Right of the People to alter or abolish it." Much of subsequent American history would be a working out of the implications of the principles here so ringingly enunciated.

THE NEW STATE CONSTITUTIONS

By the time the Declaration of Independence was adopted, four of the colonies had already translated its liberal principles into political institutions by drafting new state constitutions. Shortly all the other states followed suit, except Rhode Island and Connecticut which simply continued to operate under their unusually liberal colonial charters. The very drafting of written constitutions was unprecedented and significant. With British authority destroyed, the Americans were left free to perform in literal fact the act which, according to Lockean theory, lay at the root of all legitimate government: they entered into a "social contract." The new state constitutions were conceived of as voluntary compacts among all the people whereby governments of limited and explicitly defined powers were created. Several of the states exemplified this theory of constitution-making by having the people elect a special convention to draft the fundamental compact, and in several others the constitution was submitted for popular ratification; but in a majority of cases the existing provincial congress drafted and promulgated the new constitution itself.

However adopted, the new constitutions uniformly reflected the distrust of governmental power, and especially executive power, that arose from the Enlightenment's liberalism and from the colonists' experience with British authority. Most states followed the distinguished example of Virginia by including a Bill of Rights specifying in detail those rights of the citizen—freedom of speech, freedom of the press, trial by jury, and the like—which no government could rightly abridge. All the constitutions sought to minimize the danger of arbitrary power by building "checks and balances" and a "separation of powers" into the very structure of government. The executive, legislative, and judicial functions were to be exercised by separate bodies, and except in Pennsylvania and Georgia the legislature was divided into two houses that were expected to act as a check on each other.

The "checks and balances" principle was greatly weakened, however, by memories of the long struggles between the colonial assemblies and the royal governors. Actually, the new constitutions made the legislatures dominant, and the governors—in most cases elected annually by the legislatures and denied the veto or appointive powers —were relatively impotent.

Along with their restrictions on the power of government, the new constitutions also manifested a marked tendency toward greater political democracy. Both of these impulses were reflected in the common provision that the voters should exercise close supervision over the legislators through annual elections. Also the new constitutions extended the privilege of voting, either by reducing the freehold (landowning) requirement that had prevailed in colonial days or by opening the polls to all taxpayers. It seems likely that the great majority of white adult males were given the vote in most of the states. As a result of these changes and of the Revolutionary circumstances that produced them, there emerged into political leadership a whole class of "new men" who would have had little chance for political prominence in colonial days.

THE ARTICLES OF CONFEDERATION

The Continental Congress was still a body with no regular constitutional authority. At the same time it decided for independence, the Congress began working on a plan for a confederation with sufficient powers to conduct the war and to unite the states once victory was achieved. After protracted debate, the Articles of Confederation were finally approved by Congress in 1777, but a dispute over the western lands claimed by some of the states delayed final ratification by all the states until 1781.

The Articles of Confederation did not establish a government, but a confederation of sovereign states. The Revolution was being fought to abolish central control, and liberty was deemed safe only when government was sharply restricted and kept close to home where the governed could watch it. The Confederation was given just the powers to: (1) conduct foreign affairs by negotiating treaties and making war and peace, (2) control Indian affairs, (3) set standards of coinage, weights, and measures, (4) settle disputes among the states, and (5) conduct a postal service. It could not raise money or troops except by requisitions on the states. It had no power to make laws binding on individual citizens and no means of enforcing its will either on citizens or on the states. Each state was to have a single vote in the Confederation Congress, the votes of nine states were required to approve all important measures, and the Articles could be amended only with the approval of Congress and the legislature of every state. The Articles did not even provide an executive agency to carry out whatever policies Congress might succeed in adopting.

THE CAMPAIGNS OF 1776–1777

The Declaration of Independence had just been adopted and the constitution-making process was well under way in the states and the Congress when the British launched the American war in earnest. In July, 1776, the greatest military force Britain had ever sent abroad sailed into New York harbor—hundreds of ships carrying 32,000 soldiers under the command of Sir William Howe. Anticipating the British strategy, Washington had moved his army to the vicinity, but his greatly outnumbered forces were easily pushed off Long Island, then out of Manhattan, then steadily through New Jersey and across the Delaware River into Pennsylvania.

Washington was probably no great military genius, but it was his courage and tenacity under these disheartening circumstances that kept his army intact and the American cause alive. Wisely avoiding decisive engagements, he waited until the British ceased offensive operations for the winter, and then, on Christmas night, 1776, he daringly ferried his troops back across the Delaware and fell upon unsuspecting British forces at Trenton and nearby Princeton, New Jersey. With these small but brilliant victories to keep American hopes alive, he then went into winter quarters at Morristown.

The following summer of 1777 was the time of greatest military peril for the infant American nation. From Canada, General John Burgoyne launched a British offensive by way of Lake Champlain toward Albany and the lower Hudson Valley. Sir William Howe might have moved up the Hudson from New York City and effected a junction with Burgoyne, thus cutting the colonies in two. Instead the indecisive Howe succumbed to the temptation of occupying the rebel capital at Philadelphia, which he managed to do after brushing aside what resistance Washington's outmanned army was able to offer at the Battle of Brandywine.

Thus freed from the threat of Howe in their rear, the American commanders in the Hudson Valley, Horatio Gates and Benedict Arnold, were able to put up a stubborn resistance against Burgoyne's advance from the north. Far from his base of supply and harassed on every side by farmer militiamen, the British commander was finally hemmed in at Saratoga in October, 1777, and forced to surrender his entire army. The importance of this victory and the narrowness of the American escape from a crushing military catastrophe would be hard to exaggerate. Thanks to a combination of British lethargy and American valor, it now appeared for the first time that the rash bid for independence might succeed.

THE FRENCH ALLIANCE AND THE
SOUTHERN CAMPAIGNS

Yet even the victory at Saratoga could not cure the feebleness of the American war effort. Driven from Philadelphia to York, Pennsylvania, Congress struggled ineffectually during the winter of 1777–1778 with the problems of supply and funds as the paper money with which it was trying to finance the war plunged toward worthlessness. Meanwhile, cold and hunger in the winter camp at Valley Forge decimated Washington's ill-fed, ill-clothed, ill-paid army.

Across the Atlantic, however, the Saratoga victory was bearing fruit. From the beginning of conflict, the Americans had hoped that France would seek to avenge her recent defeat at the hands of Britain by giving them aid, and as soon as independence was declared, the Congress had sent Franklin to Paris to seek an alliance. The French government proved willing to furnish supplies and funds secretly, but it wanted assurance that the Americans had a real chance of winning before siding with them openly. Saratoga furnished this assurance, and in February, 1778, the treaty of alliance was signed. As a result France's ally Spain was pulled into the war with Britain, and soon afterwards the Netherlands were also drawn into the conflict because of their insistence on continuing to trade with the French and the Americans. Spain and the Netherlands furnished much-needed loans for the American war effort, but France became the main source of both the money and the munitions that enabled the Americans to keep fighting. In addition the French sent over an army and a powerful naval force without which victory would not have been possible.

Military activity was at a stalemate for a year following Saratoga as the British prepared for another offensive, this time aimed at the southern colonies. Landing at Savannah, Georgia, in December, 1778, the British army under the aggressive Lord Cornwallis easily took Charleston and occupied most of South Carolina. When the Americans finally marched against him in August, 1780, they were soundly defeated at Camden; and Cornwallis was able to push his invasion northward. By this time the American forces in the South had come under the able command of Nathanael Greene. At King's Mountain and at

[62]

Cowpens severe defeats were inflicted on contingents of Cornwallis' army, and in March, 1781, the British army sustained heavy losses in a hard-fought but inconclusive battle at Guilford Court House, North Carolina. The seriously weakened Cornwallis, finally despairing of subduing the vast and hostile southern interior, withdrew his army to Yorktown on the peninsula between the York and James rivers in tidewater Virginia where he could be evacuated by the British fleet.

It was not the British fleet that appeared. By a miracle of good fortune and good timing, Washington and the French commanders were able to march the combined Franco-American army down from the north just as the French fleet appeared off the Virginia coast. Thus caught between a hostile army and a hostile navy, Cornwallis had no alternative but to surrender on October 17, 1781.

THE TREATY OF PEACE

Cornwallis' surrender finally convinced the British that the effort to subdue the Americans was too difficult and too expensive to continue. Although the British armies had usually been able to advance at will and to defeat American armies when they could catch them, such success brought them little closer to their goal. The country was too vast, the population was too deeply committed to resistance, and the cost of supporting a large army three thousand miles away was becoming an intolerable burden on an already debt-ridden treasury. The debacle at Yorktown forced Lord North to resign, and a new ministry came to power prepared to treat with the Americans.

Already John Adams, Benjamin Franklin, and John Jay were in Europe as a commission to negotiate a peace treaty, but a settlement was delayed for some time by the crosscurrents of international politics. The Franco-American alliance committed each party to continue fighting as long as the other was fighting, while the Franco-Spanish alliance committed France to staying in the war until Spain won Gibraltar from England. This seemed to mean that the Americans could not make peace with England until Spain regained Gibraltar. But when the American commissioners uncovered evidence that the French were proposing a settlement by which the Spanish and British would control the northern and southern portions of the section lying between the Allegheny mountains and the Mississippi, they felt absolved of their obligation to negotiate in concert with the French.

Seeing an opportunity to detach the Americans from French influence, the British accepted the American proposal for separate Anglo-American negotiations. By thus playing off one power against the

1783
Treaty:

other, the American commissioners won an exceedingly favorable
treaty. Besides recognizing the independence of the United States, the
2. British also acquiesced in a generous extent of territory for the new
nation, stretching from the Atlantic to the Mississippi and from the
Canadian border on the north to the Florida border on the south. These
terms were agreed upon by late 1782, but peace did not come officially
until Spain and France ended hostilities in early 1783. In this general
settlement, Florida was transferred from Britain to Spain to compensate
for Spain's failure to win Gibraltar.

FOR FURTHER READING:

John C. Miller's *Triumph of Freedom* (1948) is an excellent general account of the American Revolution. There are also two excellent
briefer accounts of the military history of the war: Howard Peckham,
The War for Independence (1958)*; and Willard M. Wallace, *Appeal
to Arms* (1951). Also excellent for military and naval history are two
biographies: Douglas S. Freeman, *George Washington* (7 vols., 1948–
1957); and Samuel Eliot Morison, *John Paul Jones: A Sailor's Biography*
(1959). C. H. Van Tyne has written the best account of *The Loyalists
in the American Revolution* (1902). For the political thought that
influenced the development of new political institutions during the
Revolutionary years, see Clinton Rossiter, *Seedtime of the Republic*
(1953; a section of which has been republished under the title, *The
First American Revolution*, 1956*); and Carl L. Becker, *The Declaration of Independence* (1922)*. Elisha P. Douglass, *Rebels and Democrats* (1955), describes the conflict between the democratic-minded
and the elite-minded in the formation of the new state governments,
and Merrill Jensen has written a controversial analysis of a similar
conflict over the drafting of *The Articles of Confederation* (1940)*.
Charles S. Sydnor delineates the political leadership of the Virginia
gentry in *Gentleman Freeholders* (1952; republished as *American
Revolutionaries in the Making*).

---

*Available in paperback edition.

CHAPTER 6

A NATION EMERGES

1780–1788

The new nation brought into being by the Revolution covered a vast expanse of territory six times the area of England and Wales combined but thinly populated. Ninety-five per cent of its three million people lived in the countryside. Most of them were near the seacoast, but even here they were so dispersed that there were only six cities with over eight thousand inhabitants. Philadelphia, with some forty thousand, was largest, followed by New York, Boston, Charleston, Baltimore, and Salem. Transportation facilities from one part of this far-flung republican empire to another were rudimentary, and communication was so infrequent that the letters carried by the postal service amounted to only one per capita per year.

Nevertheless, the shared experience of the Revolution had given Americans a sense of national pride and optimism about the future of their experiment in liberty. But not all Americans agreed what that future should be. As a result the 1780's were a decade of conflict.

THE AGRARIAN-MINDED AND THE COMMERCIAL-MINDED

One fundamental division was between what might be called the *agrarian-minded* and the *commercial-minded* portions of the population. The great majority of the people were small farmers. Measured against the Europe which they or their peasant forebears had left behind—the Europe of arbitrary government, heavy taxes, military conscription, state churches, and rigid social distinctions—America seemed a virtual paradise. Above all, in America the dream of land ownership, the key to security, independence, and dignity, could be realized by the great majority.

[65]

To these small landowners, secure on their acres, far from cities, often illiterate or semiliterate, the American utopia was already at hand. Provincial and typically adhering to the more orthodox brands of Protestantism, they regarded the farmer's way of life as morally superior to all others. They were deeply suspicious of cities, of change, and of those ambitious and probably evil men in cities who grew rich by commercial manipulations. The agrarian mystique was also shared in good part by many southern planters and by many of the great landlord families in New York's Hudson Valley.

Less numerous but equally influential were the men who saw America's future in terms of economic growth and national strength. Commercial-mindedness was centered in the cities, especially among the merchant and professional classes, the best-educated and most cosmopolitan parts of the population. Included also were a good many farmers and planters who lived close enough to transportation and cities to produce commercial crops for the foreign and domestic markets.

The division between the commercial-minded and the agrarian-minded merged into the other major division in the politics of the 1780's: that over the increasingly democratic character of American society and government. There was a tendency for the agrarian-minded to be democratic-minded and for the commercial-minded to resist democratic tendencies, but the two alignments did not coincide completely. Thomas Paine, for example, was among the most effective advocates of both democracy and commercial expansion, while much of the leadership for the agrarian forces was provided by high-toned gentlemen from the great landholding families.

With some important exceptions, then, the political struggles of the 1780's involved two rough groupings. On one side were those who favored leadership by gentlemen, vigorous and more centralized government, and policies designed to foster national strength and economic growth through encouragement to enterprising businessmen. On the other side were men resentful of any pretensions to superiority, deeply suspicious of all government, and mistrustful of even their own elected representatives and who consequently wanted government kept as decentralized as possible, as inactive and inexpensive as possible, and subject to the check of frequent and democratic elections.

CONFLICT IN THE STATES

The state governments were the principal arenas of conflict between the two groups. The agitation was in part a straight struggle for control, as in Pennsylvania, where the displaced conservatives warred unrelentingly against the ultrademocratic constitution of 1776 and the power it gave to western farmers and the lower orders of Philadelphia.

Religion was frequently a divisive issue. In New England (outside Rhode Island where religious freedom had always prevailed) the Congregationalists surrendered only part of the exclusive privileges they had enjoyed by law before the Revolution; but in New York and the southern states the formerly established Anglican church was reduced to an equal footing with other denominations. In Virginia, the Anglicans of the wealthy and conservative tidewater area managed to stave off this movement until 1786 when James Madison's coalition of liberal gentry with backcountry Baptists, Methodists, and Presbyterians finally pushed through the legislature Jefferson's Statute for Religious Freedom.

The greatest cause of alarm to conservatives was the apparent disregard of democratic legislatures for property rights. In some states property-minded men fought against wholesale confiscations of the property of Loyalists; but they were even more alarmed by the movement for debtor laws and state-issued paper money.

Paper money had been used during the colonial period with both good and bad results, but the collapse of the Continental currency during the Revolution had utterly discredited the whole idea with merchants and creditors. Yet the return to a specie (gold and silver) currency at the end of the Revolution, the collapse of the brief boom that followed, and the ensuing depression of 1785–1786 had produced a severe deflation. People who had borrowed money during inflationary times found that they had to repay their debts in money that was worth much more than the money originally borrowed, and at a time when money of any kind was hard to obtain.

Under the pressure of desperate debtors, seven state legislatures authorized issues of paper money, while in several other states creditors and merchants had a hard time fighting off such demands. These paper issues were relatively beneficial where taxes were levied to retire them, but in other instances the old story of rapid depreciation was repeated. Some states tried to compel creditors to accept the paper money in payment of debts, and in Rhode Island the situation got so bad that creditors were said to be fleeing the state to avoid being forced to accept payment in depreciated paper.

The conflict became most violent in Massachusetts, where debtors and small farmers of the interior simply could not find enough of the scarce specie to pay their debts and heavy state taxes. As the courts began imprisoning large numbers of defaulting debtors or foreclosing

on their farms, armed mobs started breaking up sessions of the courts. By the winter of 1786–1787 the interior was swarming with a virtual insurrectionary militia whose principal leader was a Revolutionary veteran named Daniel Shays. Finally a state army of four thousand men marched into the area and quelled the disorders after a series of minor skirmishes. Meanwhile exaggerated accounts of "Shays' Rebellion" had further alarmed property-minded conservatives in all the states.

PROBLEMS OF THE CONFEDERATION

Already, in the early 1780's, conservative men had sought to erect a bulwark against the localism and democratic irresponsibility of the states by strengthening the Confederation government. Under the leadership of Robert Morris, a Philadelphia merchant who had grown wealthy from war contracts, they had persuaded Congress to appoint full-time executives to superintend departments of finance, war, foreign affairs, and marine. Morris himself became superintendent of finance, but exercised great influence in all areas. Continental paper money was abandoned, and Morris sought to finance the government by borrowing, partly from American citizens. In the process he encouraged the creation of a powerful class of public creditors who had a vested interest in seeing the government strong enough to pay its debts.

Yet the Confederation government could neither pay its debts nor carry on its ordinary operations effectively as long as it had to depend for income on voluntary contributions by the recalcitrant states. Morris' whole program hinged on getting the states to approve the "Impost of 1781." This proposed amendment to the Articles of Confederation would give Congress the power to levy limited import duties which were to be used to pay the Confederation debt. But Rhode Island refused to ratify, and all further efforts to give Congress a limited taxing power failed to get the required unanimous approval of the states. Meanwhile the coming of peace had dissipated the atmosphere of emergency, and the drive to add vigor to the Confederation government stalled.

Through the mid 1780's national-minded men could only grumble helplessly at the impotence of the Confederation in many areas. Lacking any means of enforcing its policies either on the states or directly on their citizens, the Confederation was unable to deal effectively with unseemly quarrels among various states over boundaries, western lands, and state-levied tariffs and trade restrictions.

The Confederation's weakness was most evident in foreign relations. Partly because the United States could not enforce uniform commercial regulations in its own territory or threaten uniform retaliatory regulations against other countries, it was unable to secure favorable commercial treaties with the leading European powers. More serious, Spain and Great Britain threatened the very territorial integrity of the new nation in the Southwest and Northwest respectively.

Spain had lost Florida to Great Britain at the end of the Seven Years' War in 1763, but in place of it had gained formerly French Louisiana (the entire western watershed of the Mississippi and the "island" of New Orleans east of the river). Then, in 1783, she regained Florida, making her the dominant power on the southwestern borders of the United States. Moreover Spain was not bound by the 31° northern boundary of Florida specified by the Anglo-American treaty, but actually occupied territory north of that line and claimed the greater part of the Southwest. These claims she actively buttressed in the 1780's by gaining control over the southwestern Indians and restricting the Mississippi River trade through New Orleans. When the Confederation proved powerless to protect the new settlements in the Tennessee-Kentucky area against the Indians or to secure them a right to trade down the Mississippi, many of their leaders sought the protection of Spain, and for a time there was a serious danger that the western settlers would cooperate in making the entire Southwest Spanish territory.

Great Britain understandably treated her former subjects with even greater contempt, closing her West Indian possessions to American trade, restricting American trade with England, refusing to enter negotiations for a commercial treaty, and not even sending a minister to the new nation. Most threatening of all, she continued to occupy military posts along the northern frontier within territory she had ceded to the United States, and from these posts she retained dominion over the Indians of the northern Ohio Valley and encouraged them to resist the advance of American settlement.

It must be added that the British found justification for these actions in the failure of the American states to live up to their obligations under the Treaty of Paris. Congress technically complied with the treaty by urging the states to restore confiscated property to Loyalists, but it could not force the states to do so. Nor could it prevent the states from violating the treaty by impeding the collection of debts that Americans owed to British merchants. The Confederation authorities could counter British complaints on these points only by demanding payment for several thousand slaves which the British armies had carried away from the southern states.

[69]

THE CONFEDERATION AND THE WEST

For all its weaknesses, the Confederation had one magnificent achievement to its credit: the creation of a great national domain west of the Appalachian mountains and the formulation of a system for land sales and territorial government by which this West and later Wests would become a spectacularly expanding "empire for liberty."

Even before the Revolution pioneers had crossed the mountains to form pockets of settlement in a few areas. New Englanders had moved up and across the Connecticut River to populate the green hills of Vermont. Resisting the claims of New York and New Hampshire to the area during the Revolution, Ethan Allen and his "Green Mountain Boys" had created an independent republic which was not admitted as one of the United States until 1790.

Farther south other pioneers had established themselves on the upper waters of the Ohio River in the Wheeling-Pittsburgh area, and still others had pushed southwestward through the valleys of the Virginia mountains to found the Watauga settlement on the headwaters of the Tennessee River in what was to become the northeastern corner of Tennessee. During and immediately after the Revolution, these outposts became staging areas for further advances of settlement into the country north of the Ohio, through Cumberland Gap into the Bluegrass region of what would later be central Kentucky, and over the Cumberland Plateau into the Nashville basin of what would later be central Tennessee.

Seven states laid claim to various parts of the trans-Appalachian empire. Virginia, making the most of the vague boundaries specified by its colonial charter, claimed Kentucky and all the territory north of the Ohio River. New York had a shadowy claim resting on Indian treaties, while Massachusetts and Connecticut argued that their boundaries extended indefinitely westward, cutting across the Virginia claim. Farther south the two Carolinas and Georgia asserted without challenge that their boundaries extended all the way to the Mississippi.

Even before the war was over, under heavy pressure from the landless states, Congress had urged that these western claims be ceded to the Confederation to create a great common domain. Virginia led the way in 1781 by offering its lands north of the Ohio, and by the end of the 1780's all except one of the landed states had followed suit. Georgia finally ceded its western lands in 1802, while in 1792 Virginia had passed the sovereignty over its remaining western territory directly to the new state of Kentucky that was created from it.

Congress lost no time in providing for land sales and a governmental system in the new public domain. The Ordinance of 1785 established the "rectangular" system of survey. North-south and east-west lines were to be run through the public domain at intervals of one mile. "Townships" six miles square were to be laid off, each of which would contain thirty-six one-mile-square (640 acres) "sections." As the line of settlement advanced, these sections were to be auctioned off to the highest bidders, with a minimum price of two dollars an acre.

A year earlier, in the Ordinance of 1784 (drafted by Thomas Jefferson), Congress had declared that territorial governments in the public domain should evolve as quickly as possible into new states fully equal to the original states. The process by which this would happen was altered by the so-called Northwest Ordinance of 1787. Congress adopted the ordinance to meet the wishes of the Ohio Company, a group of New England land speculators who were promoting a settlement in the Muskingum Valley of what was to become southeastern Ohio.

The Ordinance of 1787 established a Northwest Territory in the area north of the Ohio and east of the Mississippi rivers, which was to be administered at first by a governor appointed by Congress. When the population of the territory reached five thousand, the people were to elect a representative assembly and a nonvoting delegate to Congress. Eventually the Old Northwest was to be divided into not less than three and not more than five states, and when the population of any of these proposed states reached sixty thousand, it could be admitted to the union on an equal footing with the original states. During the territorial stage, civil liberties and religious freedom were guaranteed, a system of free public education was called for, and, in the Northwest Territory, slavery was excluded. Thus Congress laid down the pattern of territorial evolution by which the United States was to become a continental nation of equal states.

THE MOVEMENT FOR A STRONGER GOVERNMENT

However satisfied many Americans may have been with the limited successes and modest potency of the Confederation, others grew steadily more disgusted with its weakness and more desperately determined to secure a strong national government in its place. The unpaid public creditors constituted a standing lobby for change. Merchants wanted a uniform commercial policy that could force concessions from the great trading nations. The artisan class and infant manufacturers wanted a uniform tariff policy that would protect them from the competition of British manufactures. The elite dreaded the vulnerability of many of the states to popular control. Creditors and men of wealth cried out for protection against debtor legislation, paper money, and the assaults of the unpropertied on the sanctity of property. Frontiersmen demanded more vigorous defense against the Indians and their British and Spanish abettors. And the more cosmopolitan and national-minded patriots wanted their country to assume a position of greater strength and dignity among the nations of the world.

As the 1780's wore on, events pushed some of these national-minded elements into an almost revolutionary mood. Robert Morris' drive to strengthen the Confederation from within had stalled when the urgency of war was removed in 1783; and all further attempts to remedy the inadequacy of the Articles by amendment failed. More important, the brief economic boom that followed peace collapsed into a commercial and financial depression in the mid-1780's, and inevitably merchants, financiers, and artisans began to think that their distress was related to the Confederation's weakness. As a result of the depression, the panic of conservative men over paper money and debtor legislation reached its peak, and in the autumn of 1786 the conservatives' worst fears of the lower orders and anarchy seemed confirmed by exaggerated accounts of Shays' Rebellion.

By this time a concerted movement was already under way to by-pass the prescribed method for amending the Articles and to create a stronger government by constitutionally questionable means. The movement had been initiated by a small group of national-minded men, particularly George Washington and James Madison in Virginia and Alexander Hamilton in New York. Washington shared the exaggerated fears of anarchy held by other men of the upper classes, but his nationalism was more than a class prejudice. His views reflected his position as the pre-eminent personal symbol of American nationality, and he cared deeply about the strength, dignity, and perpetuity of the nation he had done so much to bring to birth.

Hamilton and Madison were younger men. After serving as Washington's aide-de-camp during the Revolution, Hamilton had become a highly successful lawyer in New York, where he had married into one of the leading families and had proved himself a staunch defender of property rights. But Hamilton was not primarily a servant of propertied interests. Instead he was obsessed with the need for vigor and strength in government and sought to ally wealth with government in the interest of strong government rather than wealth.

Madison was a nationalist on more theoretical grounds. A close friend of Jefferson and, like him, a member of the liberal wing of Virginia's planting gentry, Madison had combined study of ancient and modern governments with a quiet but increasingly influential role in Virginia politics. His nationalism was a matter of intellectual conviction, stimulated by his association with Washington and buttressed by his wide reading and disinterested reflection on political problems.

In 1785, on Madison's initiative, a conference of commissioners from Virginia and Maryland met at Mount Vernon and Alexandria to consider improving navigation of the Potomac. Madison and Washington persuaded the commissioners that other states should be brought into the consultation, and the Virginia legislature invited all the states to send delegates to a convention at Annapolis in 1786 to deliberate on "a uniform system in their commercial regulations." When delegates from only five states appeared at Annapolis, Hamilton, a delegate from New York, persuaded the convention to send out a call for another convention in Philadelphia in May, 1787, to "devise such further provisions as shall appear . . . necessary as to render the constitution of the federal government adequate to the exigencies of the union."

The call for the Philadelphia convention was grudgingly endorsed by the Confederation Congress with the explicit stipulation that any amendments it proposed must be endorsed by all the states as the Articles required. During the spring, delegates were selected by the legislatures of every state save debtor-dominated Rhode Island. With only a few exceptions, those who were satisfied with the Articles as they stood refused to serve as delegates, thus permitting men who were inclined to a stronger government to represent even those states where they were in a minority. The legislature of Hamilton's New York was dominated by his opponents; they permitted him to be a delegate but only as a member of a three-man delegation controlled by two staunch opponents of change.

THE CONSTITUTIONAL CONVENTION

Except for the two New Yorkers, then, and a few scattered delegates from other states, the convention was composed of men from the national-minded side of the political spectrum. Predominantly lawyers, merchants, and planters, the delegates were drawn heavily from urban and seaboard areas and from the upper classes. Collectively they presented an impressive showing of youth, education, ability, and disinterested patriotism. Yet from the circumstances of their selection the crucial political decision that faced the convention—whether the government should continue to be a weak "confederated" government with some additional powers to raise revenue and regulate commerce or whether it should become a "national" government acting directly on the citizens of the states—was settled before the delegates ever met. Had this not been the case, Madison could never have scored such a resounding victory for a national plan at the very outset of the convention. The Virginia delegation had arrived in Philadelphia some days before the convention opened, and Madison had had his fellow Virginians hard at work on a "Virginia Plan" which became the basis for the convention's early deliberations. By accepting the Virginia Plan as its basis for deliberation, the convention made the momentous decision that it would propose not simply amendments to the Articles but an entire new frame of government. It also indicated a disposition in favor of a government radically different from the Confederation.

The two principal features of the Virginia Plan were the sweeping
1. powers it conferred on the central government and the fact that
2. representation in the national legislative body was to be in proportion to population. It was the second feature that raised the only fundamental disagreement in the convention's proceedings, for delegates from the small states rightly feared that basing representation on population would allow the large states to control the new government. Consequently the small-state delegates presented a "New Jersey Plan" which called for amending the Articles rather than drawing up an entirely new constitution. The heart of the New Jersey Plan was the continuance of a one-house Congress in which each state would have one vote. By adhering to the form of the Articles, the small-state men were also proposing a confederated government of limited powers, though their plan did give Congress the power to levy import duties, regulate commerce, and admit new states. Yet it was the matter of representation rather than the question of confederation versus nationalism that was at the bottom of the disagreement. On this point a compromise was finally effected whereby there was to be a two-house Congress with representation in the lower house apportioned by population and with the influence of the small states safeguarded in an upper house composed of two senators from each state. Once the small states won this concession, their delegates showed less zeal in defending a confederated structure. From this point on, the convention was able to work out the detailed powers and structure of the new government without serious disagreement.

Though the delegates were predominantly national-minded and though many of them feared the influence of popular majorities, they were also political realists who recognized that whatever they proposed would have to be accepted by a society that was considerably more confederationist and democratic-minded than the convention itself. Consequently, and to Hamilton's discomfort, the document that resulted from their deliberations was a compromise between the two poles of political thought. Its basic feature was the creation of a "federal" system in which powers and responsibilities were distributed between the state and national governments. On the one hand, the powers given Congress were specified in detail with the implication that only these powers could be exercised; but on the other hand, the specified powers were quite ample. The new government was to have virtually unlimited authority to levy taxes, borrow money, regulate domestic and foreign commerce, conduct foreign relations, and maintain an army and navy. Moreover the states were specifically forbidden to engage in diplomatic negotiations, maintain armies, or— closing the door on debtor legislation and paper money—"emit Bills of Credit, make any Thing but gold and silver Coin a Tender in Payment of Debts; pass any . . . Law impairing the Obligation of Contracts. . . ." Finally, and most important, the new national government was to operate directly upon the citizens rather than upon the states, and the proposed national constitution and laws and treaties made in pursuance of it were declared to be "the supreme Law of the Land."

Following the eighteenth-century doctrine of separation of powers and fearful of a concentration of power anywhere in government, the convention was at pains to create, in addition to Congress, a strong and independent executive and judiciary so that the three branches would be organized as "checks and balances" on each other. The vesting of the executive function in a single president with ample authority was a particularly important departure from existing practices in the states and the Confederation. The president was given a veto over congressional legislation (unless repassed by two thirds of both houses), he was to appoint judges and other officers (with consent of the Senate), he was given primary responsibility for foreign relations and the making of treaties (with the advice and consent of two thirds of the Senate), and he was to be commander in chief of the armed forces.

The convention spent much of its time working out the method for choosing the personnel of the legislative, executive, and judicial branches. Nearly all the delegates recognized that popular majorities must have a voice somewhere in the governmental structure they were planning, but they were equally anxious to erect ample safeguards against the workings of popular passions and temporary enthusiasms. Popular majorities were allowed direct sway in the House of Representatives, whose members were to be elected every two years by those who were qualified to vote for the popular branches of the legislatures in the respective states. But laws passed by the House of Representatives also had to be approved by the Senate, and the Senators were to be chosen for six-year terms by the state legislatures. Even after passage by both houses of Congress, laws still needed the approval of the president, and the convention worked long and hard before devising a method of selecting the president that would leave him independent of state legislatures, Congress, and popular majorities. The result was that famous invention, the electoral college. Each state was to appoint, as its legislature directed, as many electors as it had members of Congress, and the electors were then to elect a president who was to serve for four years. Finally, the members of the judiciary were to be appointed by the president for life.

The system as a whole seemed admirably contrived to frustrate direct popular control of all branches of the government at any one time and to ensure that the various branches would pull in such different directions as to hobble effective government. The convention did not foresee that the rise of political parties would quickly subvert its intentions in both respects, and indeed the government under the Constitution would probably have proved unworkable if it had operated exactly as its architects intended that it should.

RATIFICATION

It was September, 1787, before the convention lifted the veil of secrecy with which it had covered its debates and presented its handiwork to the country. Only then did men outside the convention discover that the delegates had exceeded their authority by not only drafting an entirely new Constitution, but also by providing that it should go into effect when approved by special ratifying conventions in only nine of the thirteen states.

The supporters of the Constitution, calling themselves Federalists, won quick and decisive ratifications in the small states of Delaware, New Jersey, and Connecticut, whose powerful neighboring states had taken advantage of them under the Confederation, and in the small and exposed frontier state of Georgia. Two states, Rhode Island and North Carolina, were so well satisfied with the virtually independent course they had been pursuing that they refused even to consider ratification until after the new government was in full operation.

The crucial struggles occurred in the great states of Pennsylvania, Massachusetts, Virginia, and New York which had been able to take care of themselves under the confederated system. Anti-Federalist delegates were probably in a majority when the ratifying conventions of several of these states opened—certainly overwhelmingly so in New

York—but ratification finally carried in all of them. Federalist superiority in initiative, organization, and debate counted heavily in these close contests as did the strategy of agreeing to recommend whatever amendments the anti-Federalist delegates wished to propose. Thus it would seem not only that the Constitution was adopted by extra-constitutional means, but that the Federalists' tactical advantages may well have given them victory over a potentially opposed but ineffectively organized majority of the country.

When due allowance is made for the multitude of particular interests affecting men's attitudes toward the Constitution, there still seems to be a more general pattern of division. The urban and seaboard areas were almost solidly in favor of the document, not just because particular interests were stronger here, but because in these wealthier, more commercial, more cosmopolitan areas, general commercial-mindedness and elite-mindedness were more prevalent. Conversely the Constitution tended to be strongly opposed in the more provincial backcountry areas of small farms because of the great prevalence of agrarian- and democratic-mindedness. The numerically predominant small farmers were well satisfied with things as they stood and saw little need for stronger government.

While the agrarian-minded majority might have defeated the Constitution if it had been effectively mobilized, the very fact that it was not should warn us against assuming that the opposition was terribly intense. Politics beyond the local and state level was still a matter of indifference to most farmers. Only a small proportion of the eligible voters bothered to vote at all for delegates to the ratifying conventions, and when the Constitution went into effect, it was readily accepted by all elements of the population. Within little more than a decade, under a Constitution whose operations had been transformed by political parties that the farmers did not envisage, the hitherto apathetic agrarian- and democratic-minded majority would come into its own.

FOR FURTHER READING:

The standard account of the Confederation period is Merrill Jensen, *The New Nation* (1950). Marion L. Starkey, *A Little Rebellion* (1955), deals with Shays' Rebellion. The long conflict of historical interpretations about the adoption of the Constitution was opened when Charles A. Beard published *An Economic Interpretation of the Constitution* (1913)*. The extent to which Beard's interpretation must be modified is shown in Forrest McDonald, *We the People: The Economic Origins of the Constitution* (1958), while Jackson T.

Main's *The Antifederalists* (1961) explains the strong opposition to the Constitution. The classic interpretation of the Constitution by its sponsors is found, of course, in the series of essays written by Alexander Hamilton, James Madison, and John Jay, under the title *The Federalist* (many editions)*. The second and third volumes of Irving Brant's biography of *James Madison* (6 vols., 1941–1961) give an excellent detailed view of both the Confederation period and the Constitutional Convention.

---

*Available in paperback edition.

PRESIDENTIAL ELECTIONS AND MAJOR EVENTS, 1789–1800

1789   **George Washington** elected without opposition.

1790–1791   Hamiltonian program enacted.

Funding the national debt.

Assumption of state debts. Bargain involving location of the national capital.

First Bank of the United States.

Excise taxes. Whiskey Rebellion, 1794.

1792   **George Washington** re-elected without opposition.

1793   Wars of the French Revolution begin. Neutrality Proclamation.

1795   Jay's Treaty with Great Britain.

1796   Pinckney's Treaty with Spain.

John Adams (Federalist) elected over Thomas Jefferson (Republican).

1797–1798   American commissioners to France insulted.

1798   Undeclared naval war with France begins.

Alien and Sedition Acts.

1798–1799   Virginia and Kentucky Resolutions.

1800   Convention of 1800 resolves differences with France.

Thomas Jefferson (Republican) elected over John Adams (Federalist).

CHAPTER 7

FEDERALISTS AND REPUBLICANS

1789–1800

The new Constitution as written and ratified was merely a grand outline. An actual government was created only as the Constitution was put into practice, through adaptation and conflict, in the 1790's. During this stormy decade there were three major developments that lastingly affected the nature of the federal government. First, precedents were set with regard to the detailed composition and functioning of the various branches of government. Second, the real and potential scope and authority of the new government were enormously broadened by Alexander Hamilton's vigorous program of exercising to the limit every power granted or even implied by the Constitution. Finally and most important, Hamilton's policies provoked a growing opposition around which a political party formed; and by the end of the decade a two-party system was well established, with the most profound influence on the way the new government operated.

LAUNCHING THE NEW GOVERNMENT

It was only natural that friends of the Constitution should be chosen to put it into effect. To no one's surprise, the first electoral college agreed unanimously on Virginia's George Washington for president. To provide geographical balance while avoiding the suspect Samuel Adams and John Hancock, the electors turned for vice president to that sturdy patriot and nationalist, Massachusetts' John Adams. And when the first Congress tardily assembled in New York's City Hall in April, 1789, both houses were dominated by Federalists.

While the Senators squabbled behind closed doors about titles and ceremonial procedures, James Madison was pushing through the House of Representatives a series of laws that would put the new govern-

[81]

ment into practical operation. Income was provided by a tariff act levying import duties at a moderate rate designed for revenue purposes only. An organization for the executive branch was provided by the creation of departments of state, treasury, and war. The Judiciary Act of 1789 specified that the Supreme Court should consist of six justices, that there should be a district court for each state, and that two Supreme Court justices sitting with a district judge should constitute an intermediate court of appeals. The Act also provided for an Attorney General and explicitly specified that any decision in the state courts that questioned federal as opposed to state powers could be appealed to the Supreme Court, thus authorizing the Supreme Court to pass on the constitutionality of state laws.

Finally, this first Congress took cognizance of the seventy-eight amendments to the Constitution that had been proposed by the state ratifying conventions. Somewhat reluctantly the House approved seventeen of these, the Senate approved twelve of the seventeen, and by 1791 sufficient states had ratified ten of the twelve. These first ten amendments, to be known as the Bill of Rights, guaranteed citizens that the federal government would not invade such rights as trial by jury and freedom of religion, speech, and the press. All the proposed amendments that substantially modified the powers of the federal government had been carefully omitted from the approved list, and the disgruntled anti-Federalists could take only small comfort from the Tenth Amendment which "reserved to the States respectively, or to the people" all powers not mentioned by the Constitution.

Meanwhile President Washington was enhancing the dignity of the new government by formal and ceremonial behavior which some critics thought too high toned for a republic. Also, during the first years of his administration, he contributed to the popularity of the new regime by exhausting tours through all parts of the country. But the President influenced the course of events most by his appointments, especially Alexander Hamilton as Secretary of the Treasury and Thomas Jefferson as Secretary of State. He consulted with them regularly, along with his Secretary of War and Attorney General, and soon the Cabinet, nowhere mentioned in the Constitution, emerged as a major governmental institution.

THE HAMILTONIAN PROGRAM

Alexander Hamilton had no sooner taken office than he became the master spirit of the administration; indeed he thought of himself as Washington's prime minister. This remarkable man burned with

a vision of national greatness. Aiming at a powerful, unified nation,
he detested the localistic tendencies of the states. Convinced that
vigorous leadership by the able few, especially in the executive branch
of the government, was the only way to build a powerful nation,
he feared the turbulence and irresponsibility of the democratic masses.
Astutely aware of the relationship between political power and economic power, he was determined to promote the rapid economic
growth of the country and to forge firm ties, political and economic,
between the government and the wealthy.

Hamilton was far from satisfied with the Constitution as an instrument for realizing his vision of national power and economic growth.
Yet he recognized that it was the best that could be secured, and he
came into office resolved to strengthen it by stretching its provisions
and by vigorous administration. Seizing from Congress the initiative
for public policy, he outlined in a series of four masterly reports a
set of proposals that added up to a brilliant, tightly integrated program for achieving all his objectives.

Hamilton's first proposal was that the long unpaid Continental
debt, to a face value of over $50 million, be funded at par—that is,
that the old and greatly depreciated securities be called in and exchanged for new federal bonds on which interest would be regularly
paid and which would be redeemed at full value when they matured.
This would not only restore American public credit with dramatic
suddenness, but would at the same time bolster the private credit of
American entrepreneurs, making it easier for them to obtain the European capital the economy needed if it were to grow rapidly. Funding
would also place in the hands of American holders of Continental
securities a large amount of gilt-edged federal bonds which could
themselves form the basis for investment capital. Moreover, the whole
class of wealthy investors (or speculators) in Continental securities
would be greatly enriched, for many of them had obtained their
securities from the original holders for as little as twenty or twenty-
five cents on the dollar. On all these grounds, funding would have
the political effect of attaching the wealthy to the idea of a strong
federal government.

Hamilton next proposed that the federal government assume, in
similar fashion, over $20 million in unpaid debts that the various states
had incurred in fighting the Revolution. This would have all the
advantages of funding the national debt, plus the additional benefit of
attaching the large class of state creditors to the federal government
rather than to the states, strengthening the prestige of the former at
the expense of the latter.

Funding and assumption required additional revenue, and Hamil-

3. ton recommended that this be raised by increasing tariff duties and by a direct excise tax on spirituous liquors. He advocated the latter *a.* tax frankly on the ground that it would increase the power of the government to collect a tax from individuals, and he was especially anxious to have the whiskey-making farmers of the localist and democratic interior feel the power of the federal government directly.

4. The capstone of Hamilton's financial system was his proposal for a national bank. The bank was to be chartered for twenty years as a mixed public-private corporation controlled by private investors who were to purchase four fifths of the $10 million worth of capital stock. Investors could pay three fourths of their stock subscriptions in the form of federal bonds and one fourth in gold or silver coin (specie). On the basis of this capital the bank was to issue specie-redeemable bank notes for loan to borrowers. The fact that these notes were to be receivable for all dues to the government would *a.* tend to keep up their value. Such an institution, Hamilton argued, would provide an ample and uniform circulating medium, a source *b+e.* of credit for businessmen, and a profitable investment for capitalists. *d.* More particularly it would convert into fluid and expandable capital the funded Continental and state securities. In all these ways it would be another instrument for binding the wealthy to the federal government. A final advantage of the bank, from Hamilton's point of view, *e.* was that it was nowhere authorized in the Constitution; it could be chartered only under a "broad construction" of that instrument and would help to establish a doctrine of "implied powers."

One major element in Hamilton's economic vision remains to be mentioned. As a pioneer student of what today would be called the economic growth of underdeveloped countries, he was far ahead of his time in recognizing the importance of promoting manufacturing, *5.* and a major factor in his financial proposals was the desire to provide capital for industrial development. The last of his four great reports was devoted wholly to this subject, calling for tariff rates that would give "infant industries" a competitive advantage in the domestic market until they could become well established.

Hamilton did not rely on the persuasiveness of his reports to carry his proposals through Congress, but fought for them with every political weapon at his command. The more agrarian-minded section of the country had taken immediate alarm, and the first battle *1.* came over funding the Confederation debt. Critics objected particularly to the windfall profits of speculators who had acquired Continental securities at greatly depreciated rates, and the opposition was so strong in Virginia that Madison parted with Hamilton, proposing that current holders be paid at only the depreciated rate with the remainder going to the original holders. However, the cumbersomeness of this

[84]

method and the strength of commercial-minded Federalists in the first Congress enabled the measure to pass as originally proposed.

Assumption of state debts aroused even stronger opposition, especially from states like Virginia that had already paid off many of their own debts, and again Madison was in opposition. This time the measure was stalled, until Hamilton adroitly connected it with the simultaneous controversy among New York, Pennsylvania, and the southern states over the permanent location of the national capital. At a dinner with Madison and Jefferson it was agreed that the two Virginians would draw off some of the opposition to assumption and that in return the national capital would be moved for ten years to Philadelphia and then permanently to a ten-mile-square tract to be selected by Washington on the Potomac River between Virginia and Maryland.

Hamilton's revenue proposals met their strongest opposition not in Congress but among backcountry farmers who violently resisted the tax on whiskey, their only easily transported and salable product. By 1794 this resistance had culminated, in Pennsylvania, in a Whiskey Rebellion, and only when Washington sent an army of some thousands into the disaffected area were the armed mobs dispersed and order restored.

The serious constitutional objections to the national bank gave even Washington pause, and before signing the bill he requested written opinions from members of his Cabinet. Hamilton pointed out that the Constitution authorized Congress to "make all laws which shall be necessary and proper for carrying into Execution" the specifically enumerated powers. "Necessary" should be construed, he thought, as meaning *"needful, requisite, incidental, useful,* or *conducive to,"* and he argued that powers "ought to be construed liberally in advancement of the public good." Jefferson, on the other hand, contended that all powers not expressly granted (restricting "necessary" to the narrowest sense) were reserved by the Tenth Amendment to the states or the people, and hence he felt the bank was unconstitutional. Washington finally followed the opinion of Hamilton and signed the bank bill.

Hamilton's proposals for encouraging manufacturing were the only part of his program that got nowhere in Congress. Manufacturing was still in an infant state in the country, most of it carried on by independent artisans and in people's homes, and there was no strong interest group to back Hamilton's plans. Indeed, the wealthy mercantile capitalists who were his strongest supporters on other measures were opposed to tariff barriers that would impede the flow of international trade.

On the whole Hamilton had been brilliantly successful, and his

[85]

policies gave to the new government a vigor and direction that profoundly affected its future development. At the same time, however, the forceful financier had provoked a rising opposition from agrarian-minded men. By 1791 there was a recognizable group in Congress opposed to the Hamiltonian policies, and Madison and Jefferson were beginning to work together to organize resistance to the New Yorker's influence. Already men were beginning to speak of a Republican or Antifederalist "interest" as opposed to the Federalist "interest" of Hamilton and his followers. At the time of Washington's re-election in 1792 this nascent Republican party was strong enough to garner fifty electoral votes for New York's George Clinton for vice president, against John Adams' seventy-seven.

THE WARS OF THE FRENCH REVOLUTION

The outbreak of the French Revolution in 1789 was greeted with enthusiasm by most Americans for it confirmed their faith that their own Revolution had lighted a road to liberty that would eventually be taken by all mankind. But conservative Americans, the people who tended toward Federalism in domestic politics, were soon shocked by the execution of Louis XVI, and the advent of the Terror in France drove many into hysterical fears of mob rule, atheism, and Jacobinism at home. On the other hand, more democratic-minded Americans, those who tended toward Republicanism in domestic politics, became more enthusiastic in their championing of liberty, equality, and fraternity and more convinced that their domestic opponents were really monarchist reactionaries.

The French Revolution also precipitated a great European war, lasting with brief interruptions from 1793 until 1815 and pitting France against a series of European coalitions headed by Great Britain. American leaders of all persuasions agreed that their infant nation should avoid becoming directly involved on either side, but there were sharp differences in sympathies. The Hamiltonians favored the British, partly out of a preference for British conservatism as opposed to French radicalism and partly because the large trade with Great Britain enriched the merchant class and provided 90 per cent of the tariff revenues that were essential for maintaining the Hamiltonian financial policies. Jefferson and his friends, more sympathetic to French aims, pointed out that the country owed its independence to the Franco-American alliance of 1778, which was still in force, and argued for a neutrality that would be benevolent toward France.

Actually France did not want to invoke the alliance to bring the

United States into the war as a belligerent. The powerful British navy was sweeping French merchant ships from the seas, and the French hoped that if the United States remained neutral, American merchantmen could supply her with foodstuffs and raw materials. Britain, too, as she devoted more of her resources to war, relied increasingly on American shipping. As a result, commercial interests and producers of exports in the United States entered upon a period of unparalleled prosperity.

Thus Washington's proclamation of American neutrality in 1793 made considerable sense economically, but it did not begin to solve all the problems created by the European war. Existing American grievances against Great Britain over the northwest posts, incitement of the northwestern Indians, and discrimination against American trade were compounded in 1794 when Great Britain moved to cripple the newly flourishing American commerce on the high seas. Determined to starve France into submission, the British navy suddenly seized some three hundred American ships under newly promulgated rules that forbade neutrals to carry grain or flour to France, to carry any French-owned goods whatever, or to engage in trade with the French West Indies, which had been closed to such trade before the war. Adding insult to injury, British naval commanders began stopping American merchantmen and forcibly taking off seamen thought to have deserted from the British navy, including some who were American citizens.

Despite a storm of indignation, Hamilton was determined to avoid a break with Great Britain at all costs. Jefferson had already resigned in disgust at Hamilton's domination of the administration and interference in the affairs of the State Department, leaving no one in the Cabinet strong enough to oppose the iron-willed Treasury Secretary. The only diplomatic weapon the United States had was the threat to join the Armed Neutrality of smaller European trading nations that was forming to resist British restrictions on international trade. But when Chief Justice John Jay was sent to London to negotiate, Hamilton undercut his mission by assuring the British minister that the United States would not join the Armed Neutrality.

As a result Jay had to accept whatever terms the British offered. The British did agree to pay indemnities for seized American shipping and to withdraw by 1796 from their posts within the northwestern boundary of the United States. But in return Jay had to agree that the United States should pay the old claims of British merchants against American citizens and tacitly accept the restrictive British definitions of the rights of neutrals in international trade. Not a word was said about British impressment of American seamen, British inter-

Jay Treaty

ference with the northwestern Indians, or indemnity for the slaves carried away by British armies.

Hamilton's outraged opponents charged that these terms were a humiliating surrender to British power; and it was in the violent debate over Jay's treaty during 1795 that the emerging line of division between Federalists and Republicans finally crystallized. Yet the only alternative to accepting the treaty was war with England. Ratification by the Senate guaranteed a return of commercial prosperity and gave the young nation a further period of freedom from European embroilments during which it could further strengthen its independence and institutions.

In another area of diplomacy, the Washington administration was able to capitalize on Spain's involvement in the European wars to achieve a brilliant diplomatic triumph. When Spain shifted in 1795 from the British to the French side and when the Jay Treaty appeared to align the United States with Great Britain, the Spanish authorities recognized that their possessions on the southwestern border of the United States had become exceedingly vulnerable. Consequently, the American minister, Thomas Pinckney, had little difficulty negotiating a treaty, ratified in 1796, that granted all the American demands: fixing of the Florida boundary at the thirty-first parallel, free navigation of the Mississippi and a right of "deposit" (the right to bring goods down the Mississippi and land them while awaiting oceangoing ships) at New Orleans for American citizens, and a Spanish promise to restrain the Indians along the frontier.

Thus by the end of Washington's second term, the Jay and Pinckney treaties had settled America's difficulties with two of the three European powers with which the United States was dangerously involved. Washington's policy of preserving American neutrality so as to strengthen American independence while taking advantage of opportunities afforded by the involvements of European nations was firmly established. Whether this policy could be adhered to in the face of difficulties with a third European power, France, was the major problem that faced Washington's successor, John Adams.

THE TRIALS OF JOHN ADAMS

Washington's determination to retire at the end of two terms cost the Federalist party its greatest political asset at the very moment it was under heavy attack because of the Jay Treaty. Consequently the election of 1796 was the first hard fought and closely contested presidential election. Hamilton had made too many bitter enemies to be a successful candidate, and moreover his ultracommercial and elitist views were too extreme even for many Federalist voters. Vice President John Adams, to whom the party leaders therefore turned as their candidate, represented a more moderate federalism, nationalist and interested in commercial prosperity, but also tinctured with agrarian-mindedness and suspicious of wealthy speculators and manipulations of money and credit. The Republican opposition almost without discussion accepted Jefferson as their candidate. After a vituperative campaign, Adams barely edged Jefferson, seventy-one electoral votes to sixty-eight, with Jefferson becoming vice president.

At the time of Adams' election the French were enraged by the Jay Treaty. Truculently they ordered seizure of American ships carrying British goods, and this time it was the Hamiltonians who beat the drums for war. Resisting Hamiltonian pressure, however, Adams sent a special three-man commission to France to try to settle the difficulties. When the French treated the commissioners insultingly and made impossible demands, including bribes, the war spirit again flamed high in the United States. By the spring of 1798 the President and Congress were making preparations for war, and an undeclared naval war broke out between French and American vessels on the high seas. Yet Adams was never quite swept away by the war fever, and in early 1799, against bitter Hamiltonian opposition, he resolved to make one last effort for peace. Another three-man commission was sent to France and succeeded in concluding an agreement which recognized American principles of neutral rights and which abrogated amicably the Franco-American alliance of 1778.

While John Adams must be credited with great courage and disinterestedness for single-handedly resisting the war hysteria at the cost of his own popularity and the political success of his party, there was one respect in which he went along with the Hamiltonian extremists. As in other periods of national crisis, the popular mood was highly suspicious of dissenters and foreigners while the Federalists were all too ready to regard the Republicans, and especially vitriolic Republican editors, as traitorous sympathizers with the nation's enemies. Indeed the ideas of free speech, a free press, and the legitimacy of partisan opposition were not yet firmly established. Under these circumstances the Federalists, including President Adams, took advantage of the war hysteria to push through Congress in 1798 four measures known as the Alien and Sedition Acts. Three of these laws lengthened the minimum residence requirements for new American citizens from five to fourteen years and authorized the president to deport any alien he thought dangerous and imprison or deport dangerous aliens during war. The fourth, the Sedition Act, prescribed fines up to

$5,000 and imprisonment up to five years for persons who conspired to oppose measures of the government, who promoted riots or unlawful assemblies, or who published "any false, scandalous, and malicious writing" against the government or its officials.

No aliens were deported under the new laws, although many left the country in fear of prosecution. But partisan Federalist district attorneys and judges used the Sedition Act to secure indictments against fifteen Republican editors and convictions of ten, one of them a congressman from Vermont.

No man in the United States was more alarmed by the Alien and Sedition Acts than Thomas Jefferson. Seeking some means of arousing protest, he drafted a set of resolutions and sent them by a friend to Kentucky where the legislature adopted them. Meanwhile Madison had secured adoption of similar resolutions by the Virginia legislature. These Kentucky and Virginia resolutions of 1798 took the position that the Alien and Sedition Acts, being contrary to the Constitution, were null and void. Rather than invoking the state power to obstruct enforcement of the obnoxious laws, however, as the later nullifiers of South Carolina were to do, these resolutions simply called on the other states to join in asking Congress to repeal them.

THE REVOLUTION OF 1800

The Kentucky and Virginia resolutions opened the campaign for the return match between Adams and Jefferson in the presidential election of 1800. Again there was a close, hard-fought contest. The Republicans had been greatly weakened by the charge of Francophilism during the war hysteria, but with the passing of the threat of war, the reaction against the Alien and Sedition Acts gave hope of a Republican comeback. Moreover the Federalists were weakened by mounting friction between the Adams and Hamilton wings of the party and by unpopular taxes levied to support the preparedness program. This time Jefferson edged ahead of Adams, seventy-three electoral votes to sixty-five.

This "revolution of 1800" inaugurated no revolutionary change in public policy nor even, as yet, a revolutionary shift in the balance of strength between the parties. What had happened was that the working of the constitutional system had been transformed beyond the intention of the framers by the growth within it of a system of two opposing political parties, representing divergent constituencies, holding divergent ideologies, and proposing divergent policies. The potentially overwhelming majority of the electorate that was represented by one of the parties was not yet very fully mobilized for political action in pursuance of its democratic- and agrarian-minded objectives. But already that party had overcome the great initial advantages of its competitor and won a majority. Thus the revolutionary principle of peaceful competition and transfer of power between parties was established. Meanwhile, the Federalists, though often out of tune with the slowly awaking majority, had given the new government a vigorous start, steered it safely through the shoals of international war, and presented it thriving and intact to the party of Thomas Jefferson.

FOR FURTHER READING:

A good general account of the politics and leaders of the 1790's is Nathan Schachner, *The Founding Fathers* (1954)*. The most influential interpretation of the difference between Federalists and Republicans is Charles A. Beard, *The Economic Origins of Jeffersonian Democracy* (1915). Joseph C. Charles has presented a series of stimulating essays on the divergence in *The Origins of the American Party System* (1956)*. For the Federalists, Marcus Cunliffe's *George Washington: Man and Monument* (1958)* is a brilliant brief interpretation. Manning J. Dauer has distinguished between two wings of the Federalist party in *The Adams Federalists* (1953), Nathan Schachner has written a good biography of *Alexander Hamilton* (1946)*, Gilbert Chinard a good one of *Honest John Adams* (1933), and Stephen G. Kurtz has described in detail *The Presidency of John Adams* (1958)*. On the Republican side, Eugene P. Link has described those forerunners of the Republican party, the *Democratic-Republican Societies* (1942), Leland D. Baldwin has written a good book about *The Whiskey Rebels* (1939), and Noble E. Cunningham has analyzed the development of the Republican party organization in *The Jeffersonian Republicans* (1957). There is a single-volume biography of *Thomas Jefferson, The Apostle of Americanism* (rev. ed., 1939)* by Gilbert Chinard, but the best biography is still being written, Dumas Malone, *Jefferson and His Time* (3 vols. so far, 1948–   ). Adrienne Koch interprets the thought of the Republican leaders and the formulation of the Virginia and Kentucky resolutions in *Jefferson and Madison: The Great Collaboration* (1950). James M. Smith, *Freedom's Fetters* (1956), is a fine study of the Alien and Sedition Acts.

A fascinating relationship between two great men may be traced, in their own words, in Adrienne Koch, *Adams and Jefferson: "Posterity Must Judge"* (Berkeley Readings in American History, 1963)*.

---

*Available in paperback edition.

1800 **Thomas Jefferson** (Republican) elected over John Adams (Federalist).

1803 Marbury *vs.* Madison. John Marshall's Supreme Court declares a law of Congress unconstitutional.

Louisiana Purchase.

1804 **Thomas Jefferson** (Republican) re-elected over Charles C. Pinckney (Federalist).

1804–1806 Lewis and Clark expedition.

1805–1807 Mounting seizures of American shipping under British Orders in Council and Napoleon's Decrees.

1807 Chesapeake-Leopard affair.

Embargo Act.

1808 **James Madison** (Republican) elected over Charles C. Pinckney (Federalist).

1809 Nonintercourse Act replaces Embargo Act.

1810 Macon's Bill No. 2 replaces Nonintercourse Act.

1811 Recharter of First Bank of the United States defeated.

Power of northwestern Indians broken at Tippecanoe.

1812 **James Madison** (Caucus Republican) re-elected over DeWitt Clinton (Independent Republican).

1812–1815 War of 1812.

1814–1815 Treaty of Ghent.

1816 **James Monroe** (Republican) elected over Rufus King (Federalist).

1817 Rush-Bagot Agreement with Great Britain demilitarizes the Great Lakes.

Andrew Jackson invades Spanish Florida.

1818 Convention of 1818 settles outstanding differences with Great Britain.

1819–1821 Transcontinental Treaty with Spain acquires Florida.

1820 **James Monroe** (Republican) re-elected without opposition.

1823 Monroe Doctrine enunciated.

CHAPTER 8

THE JEFFERSONIAN REPUBLIC
IN A THREATENING WORLD
1800–1823

Thomas Jefferson wisely recognized the political foolhardiness, if not the practical impossibility, of trying to erase completely the legacy of Hamiltonian measures that he had inherited. The national bank was allowed to run its course undisturbed until its twenty-year charter expired in 1811, and the funded federal debt continued to be honored. Yet there was a significant shift in the tone and direction of public policy. The government had just moved to the new Washington City. In sharp reaction to the formality and ceremony which his more aristocratic predecessors had cultivated, Jefferson invested the muddy little capital on the Potomac with an almost ostentatious unostentation. This lack of pretension symbolized his deliberately negative policy: to eschew ambitious measures, to keep the federal establishment as plain and simple as possible, to practice the most rigorous economy, and, thus, to pay off as rapidly as possible the federal debt that Hamilton had designed as semipermanent.

In taking this line, Jefferson was not only following his own agrarian and democratic preconceptions, but also proving himself a shrewd reader of the mood of the country. The Hamiltonian system, for all its brilliant success, had been premature, resting on the transitory and fortuitous ascendancy of a commercial-minded minority that was out of tune with the bulk of the population. Even in the Federalist stronghold of New England, religious and sectional considerations had contributed more to that party's strength than commercial-mindedness, and the Adams brand of Federalism was more popular than the Hamilton brand. Despite a flourishing overseas commerce that was gradually pulling more farmers and planters into producing staples for market, the country as a whole remained wedded to the vision of a simple, unprogressive, democratic utopia, dominated by self-sufficing and therefore independent and virtuous farmers. Once Jefferson's reasonable behavior in office discredited the caricature drawn by his enemies, the eloquence of his statements and policies in behalf of the agrarian, democratic ideal won him overwhelming political strength, even in New England.

During these Jeffersonian years Americans appeared to believe that their utopian republican order might endure without change forever. They failed to realize that history will not leave societies, much less utopias, alone. The only problems that most of them saw were those arising out of the continuing international conflict. These were indeed to be severe problems for Jefferson and his successor Madison and would lead ultimately to war. Yet it was not war that was to undermine the republican utopia, but the unsuspected forces of westward expansion and economic change that were already gaining momentum.

VESTIGES OF FEDERALISM

Jefferson's disciplined majorities in Congress had moved promptly, of course, to repeal the whiskey tax, the unpopular preparedness taxes, and the parts of the Alien and Sedition Acts that had not already expired. The only serious battle over remnants of Federalism arose in connection with the judiciary.

The federal courts were staffed entirely by Federalists serving for life, and some of the judges had conducted themselves with egregious partisanship. In the last days of the Adams administration the Federalists had sought to strengthen their judicial bastion by an act establishing a series of new courts, and President Adams had spent his last hours in office signing commissions for the "midnight judges" and other officials who were to staff the new courts. Adams had made his most important contribution to perpetuating Federalist principles a month earlier by appointing as Chief Justice of the Supreme Court John Marshall, a Virginian of the Washington rather than the Jefferson-Madison stamp, whose nationalistic ideas were to dominate the Court from 1801 until 1835.

The Republicans had no sooner assumed power than they repealed the act establishing the new courts, and Jefferson ordered his Secretary of State, James Madison, to withhold the commissions of the Federalists who had been appointed to staff them. The stage was set for a showdown when one of these appointees applied to the Supreme Court for a writ of mandamus ordering Madison to deliver his commission. Chief Justice Marshall's famous decision in the case of Marbury vs. Madison was handed down in 1803. Marshall knew that he had no means of forcing Madison to deliver the commission so he skillfully sidestepped a direct confrontation with the administration

[94]

while he gained an advantage in another quarter. Declaring that the petitioner was entitled to his commission, he contended nevertheless that the Supreme Court was not empowered to act in this kind of case. It had been given such jurisdiction by the Judiciary Act of 1789, but Marshall argued that the Judiciary Act had contravened in this respect the definition of the Court's jurisdiction found in the Constitution. Therefore, said Marshall, this section of the Judiciary Act was unconstitutional and consequently void. The Court for the first time asserted the power, nowhere explicitly given it, to invalidate an act of Congress on constitutional grounds.

Even before Marshall's decision the Republicans had begun a campaign to neutralize the Federalism of the judiciary. Incensed by the prosecutions under the Sedition Act and fearful of keeping any branch of the government from popular control, Jefferson favored making the judiciary amenable to political influence. This he thought might be accomplished by congressional impeachment of the more notorious judges. The Republicans had little difficulty getting one drunken and incompetent district judge removed from office. In the key case, however, they failed to get enough votes to convict Supreme Court Justice Samuel Chase. This failure preserved the principle of an independent judiciary and left Chief Justice Marshall free to develop the Supreme Court in later years into a fortress of nationalistic and anti-Jeffersonian influence.

AN EMPIRE FOR LIBERTY

Early in Jefferson's administration the exigencies of international war again, as in the case of the Pinckney Treaty, presented the United States with a splendid diplomatic opportunity. Napoleon had just forced Spain to return Louisiana, which had been in Spanish hands since 1763, to France, hoping to use it as the granary for a growing French empire in the western hemisphere. Louisiana in weak Spanish hands was no great threat to the United States, but the prospect of having Napoleonic France astride the Mississippi with an economic stranglehold on the whole interior of the country was another matter. Promptly Jefferson sent James Monroe to aid the American minister in Paris, Robert R. Livingston, in securing American interests at the mouth of the Mississippi, if possible by purchasing the isle of New Orleans, that small portion of Louisiana that lay east of the lower Mississippi.

By the time the negotiations opened, in 1803, the collapse of the French expeditionary force in the West Indies and the resumption of the European war after a brief truce had caused Napoleon to abandon

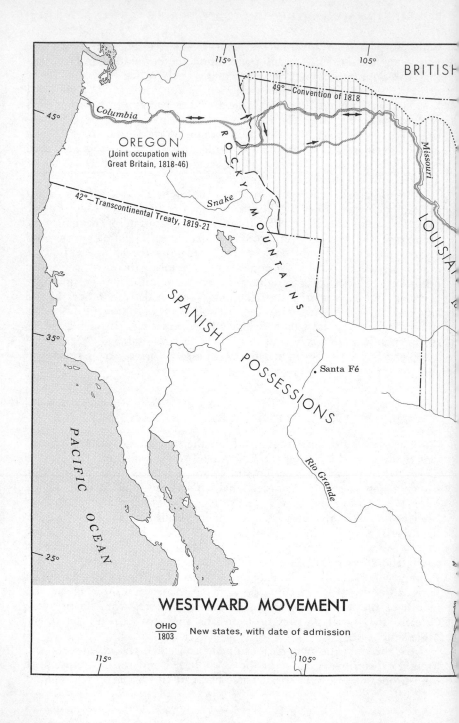

115° 105° BRITISH

49°—Convention of 1818

Columbia

45°

OREGON
(Joint occupation with
Great Britain, 1818-46)

R O C K Y

Snake

42°—Transcontinental Treaty, 1819-21

M O U N T A I N S

Missouri

LOUISIANA

35°

S P A N I S H

P O S S E S S I O N S

. Santa Fé

Rio Grande

PACIFIC

OCEAN

25°

WESTWARD MOVEMENT

OHIO
––––   New states, with date of admission
1803

115° 105°

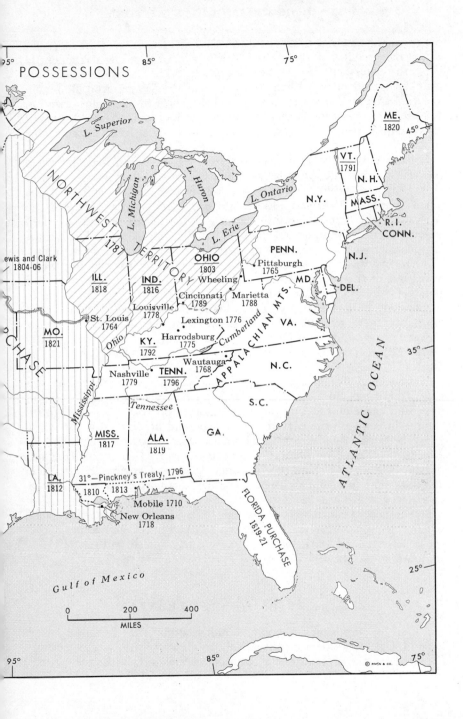

POSSESSIONS

95°　85°　75°

L. Superior

L. Michigan

L. Huron

L. Ontario

L. Erie

NORTHWEST TERRITORY 1787

ewis and Clark
1804-06

ILL.
1818

IND.
1816

OHIO
1803

Pittsburgh
1765

PENN.

N.Y.

VT.
1791

N.H.

MASS.

R.I.

CONN.

ME.
1820

45°

N.J.

MD.

DEL.

Wheeling

Cincinnati
1789

Marietta
1788

St. Louis
1764

Louisville
1778

Lexington 1776

Ohio

MO.
1821

KY.
1792

Harrodsburg
1775

Wautauga
1768

Cumberland

APPALACHIAN MTS.

VA.

N.C.

35°

PCHASE

CHASE

Nashville
1779

TENN.
1796

Tennessee

Mississippi

S.C.

MISS.
1817

ALA.
1819

GA.

LA.
1812

31°—Pinckney's Treaty, 1796

1810　1813

Mobile 1710

New Orleans
1718

FLORIDA PURCHASE
1819-21

ATLANTIC OCEAN

25°

Gulf of Mexico

0　200　400

MILES

© RMCN & CO.

95°　85°　75°

his plans for Louisiana. To the astonishment of the American negotiators, the French offered to sell the whole of Louisiana, the entire western watershed of the Mississippi. A price of $15 million was quickly agreed upon. When the news reached Washington, Jefferson worried briefly about the lack of specific constitutional authorization for such purchases of territory, but his doubts were easily dissipated in his enthusiasm for so vast an extension of his agrarian "empire for liberty."

Even before the Louisiana Purchase was consummated, Jefferson had evinced his interest in the western country by beginning preparations for the exploration led by Meriwether Lewis and William Clark. Between 1804 and 1806 Lewis and Clark's party ascended the Missouri River to its sources, crossed the Rocky Mountains, and descended the Columbia River to the Pacific, returning with a wealth of information about the vast domain the United States had acquired.

During these years a strong tide of migration was running westward out of the original states, but the line of regular settlement had not yet reached the Mississippi River. The first of the new states (Vermont, 1791, Kentucky, 1792, Tennessee, 1796, and Ohio, 1803) were becoming populous commonwealths, while the French-Spanish settlements around New Orleans were attracting sufficient immigrants from the older states to enter the union as the state of Louisiana in 1812.

Thomas Jefferson and his party showed a special solicitude for the agrarian, democratic West. One demonstration of this was the provision made at the time of Ohio's admission that a percentage of the public land proceeds from the state would be used to construct a great National Road from Cumberland, Maryland, on the Potomac River above Washington across the mountains to Wheeling, Virginia, on the Ohio. From there the National Road was eventually extended about on the line of the fortieth parallel through Ohio and Indiana and surveyed as far as St. Louis.

The new western states returned Jefferson's solicitude with overwhelming support for the Republican party. But so, increasingly, did the other states. In 1804, Jefferson was elected to a second term by the resounding margin of 162 electoral votes to 14.

THE PERILS OF NEUTRALITY

During Jefferson's second administration the European war entered a more desperate phase. Napoleon's authority was extending over the whole of continental Europe, while conversely the British were achieving unchallenged supremacy on the high seas. As the great land power and the great naval power moved into their final mortal struggle, each increasingly sought to cripple the other by economic warfare, and Americans, the leading neutral traders, were caught in the middle.

Out of self-interest and principle the United States had asserted the most advanced doctrine of neutral rights, claiming the right to trade unmolested with all belligerents. This doctrine had been tenable in connection with the limited warfare characteristic of the sixteenth and seventeenth centuries, and it was supported by the code of international law that had emerged to win considerable acceptance during that period. But the wars of the French Revolution had brought a new kind of general warfare, precursor of the total war of the twentieth century, ranging whole populations against populations and waged by mass armies with sweeping ideological and nationalistic objectives in place of small professional armies seeking limited national goals.

Under these circumstances it was not realistic to expect belligerents to respect the doctrines of neutral rights that the United States sought to maintain. The Federalists had recognized the realities of the world power situation in accepting Jay's Treaty as an alternative to war. Now faced with these same realities, Jefferson was just as anxious as the Federalists had been to avoid American involvement in the war, but more reluctant to compromise American principles of neutral rights. Believing, as he had in the 1790's, that the belligerents needed American trade too much to risk war with the United States, he embarked on the difficult task of using American commerce as a weapon to coerce the belligerents into respecting neutral rights.

During Jefferson's first administration, American shippers had been able to pile up such tremendous profits as to more than offset their losses from seizures under the temporarily relaxed British and French restrictions. But in 1805, in the *Essex* case, the British admiralty courts outlawed the most lucrative part of this trade, involving goods shipped from the French West Indies to France by way of the United States. This was but the first in a series of admiralty decisions and Orders in Council blockading the Continent so as to shut off the flow of commodities useful to the French war effort, and as a result seizures of American shipping mounted alarmingly. Even more intolerable to American pride was an increase in British impressments of seamen from American ships.

Congress responded in 1805 by barring certain British goods from American ports, and the Jefferson administration sought to use this Nonimportation Act as a counter in negotiations in London. The

British were willing to relax their restrictions on the French West Indian trade, but since they refused to renounce altogether the right of impressment, Jefferson would not submit the resulting treaty to the Senate for ratification. British indignities culminated in 1807 when the British naval vessel *Leopard* opened fire on the unsuspecting American naval vessel *Chesapeake*, stopped her, and impressed at cannon's mouth four seamen.

Now, like Adams before him, Jefferson had to resist the clamor for war, meanwhile pushing through Congress the Embargo Act of 1807. This extreme measure of economic coercion forbade American ships to sail for Europe. Jefferson hoped, of course, to force the British to terms by denying them desperately needed American goods and shipping. Unfortunately the effects of the Embargo were felt more severely by American commercial and exporting interests than they were by the British. New England, its economy prostrate and its people bitter, moved back into the Federalist orbit. Finally even Jefferson concluded, just before he left office in the spring of 1809, that the Embargo could no longer be sustained. Congress repealed the Act, and it was left to Jefferson's successor James Madison to seek some better solution to the prickly problem of neutral rights.

MADISON TRIES HIS HAND

By the time of Madison's accession, French depredations on American commerce were becoming as serious as those by the British. Napoleon had responded to the British blockade of the Continent with a series of decrees declaring the British Isles blockaded, and though he did not have the naval power to enforce a blockade, he could and did order the seizure of American ships reaching French ports after having submitted to British regulations. Such seizures reached wholesale proportions early in the Madison administration.

Shifting from one expedient of economic coercion to another, Madison and his congressional followers tried first supplanting the Embargo with a Nonintercourse Act (1809), freeing American shippers to trade with all nations except France and England and promising to resume trade with whichever of these nations would first remove its restrictions. Profits were so high, however, that American shippers preferred to take their chances on the British and French trade even under the restrictions, and in 1810 Congress supplanted the Nonintercourse Act with a measure known as Macon's Bill No. 2. This over-ingenious measure reopened the whole world to American trade, but declared that whenever either of the major belligerents rescinded its restrictions on neutral shipping, nonintercourse would be reinvoked against the other.

American embarrassment was compounded by the pathetic eagerness of the Madison administration to seize upon any indication that its policy of economic coercion was having effect. First, under the Nonintercourse Act, the President used favorable negotiation with a too pliable British minister as a pretext for announcing resumption of trade with Great Britain, only to have to eat his words when the British minister's work was disavowed in London. Napoleon exploited Macon's Bill No. 2 with even greater cynicism. A carefully ambiguous French promise to rescind the obnoxious decrees against neutral shipping hoodwinked Madison into reinvoking nonintercourse against Great Britain, whereupon the French resumed seizing American ships.

Thus by 1811 the pacific, agrarian-minded diplomacy of economic coercion had been tried in every way that could be imagined, all to no avail. The nation had never seemed so powerless to avert indignities, and the only alternatives seemed to be humiliating submission or war.

THE WAR OF 1812

Submission was utterly unacceptable to a remarkable group of vigorous young men who were elected to the Congress that convened in December, 1811, and who came to be known as the War Hawks. Led by the captivating Henry Clay of Kentucky and the intellectually impressive John C. Calhoun of South Carolina, the War Hawks represented a new generation of Republican politicians who were eager to wrest leadership from the tired hands of Madison and his dispirited companions of the Revolutionary generation.

These new Republicans were nationalistic, not only in their patriotic love of country but also in their freedom from the agrarian-minded localism that animated the companions of Jefferson. This was especially true of Clay, whose Kentucky Bluegrass constituency had been drawn into flourishing hemp production for the international market by way of New Orleans, and Calhoun, whose South Carolina upcountry was undergoing a heady transformation into a land of cotton plantations. Such areas of recent economic boom, based on the production of agricultural staples for national and international markets, shared the cosmopolitanism, progressivism, and nationalism of the older commercial-minded areas and might be characterized as agrarian-commercial in spirit. From such areas was beginning to emanate a new-style Republican nationalism whose spokesmen par excellence were Clay and Calhoun.

It was no accident that the spokesmen for the agrarian-commercial areas were War Hawks in 1811 and 1812. In the older, strictly commercial areas of the Northeast, merchants and shipowners could run the risk of British and French seizures and still make great profits; they opposed both the Republican measures of economic coercion and the talk of war. But in the agrarian-commercial enclaves of the South and West, exhilarating booms had been stalled by the disorganization of international trade. As loyal Republicans, men in these areas had been willing to give the policies of economic coercion a trial, but now their patience had run out. Only war could save the national honor and enable the march of progress and prosperity to resume.

Embarrassingly enough, Great Britain and France had been equally obnoxious, and the United States could hardly take on both. But there were special reasons for hostility to Great Britain. The British officials in Canada were thought to have encouraged Indian unrest in the Old Northwest and the organization of an ominous Indian confederacy, headed by Tecumseh and his brother the Prophet, to oppose the advance of American settlement. Though a frontier army destroyed Tecumseh's power at Tippecanoe in 1811, the bumptious Republicans of the Ohio Valley were clamoring for the conquest of Canada.

Similarly the Southwest was calling for the conquest of Spanish Florida, and Spain was again allied with Great Britain in the European war. Through Spanish Florida ran the rivers on which the men of the Georgia, Alabama, and Mississippi country depended for trade, the Spanish authorities were suspected of encouraging Indian hostility, and their territory was a haven for the runaway slaves of the Americans. The United States asserted a doubtful claim under the Louisiana Purchase to West Florida, roughly the territory between Mobile Bay and New Orleans, and already in 1810 the Madison administration had taken advantage of a "revolution" by immigrants from the United States to annex part of this area. War with Great Britain would provide an opportunity to complete the conquest of Florida.

Thus the stalling of economic booms in several agrarian-commercial areas, resentment of British and Spanish tampering with the Indians, and a desire for Canada and Florida made the war fever especially intense in a great arc running along the frontier from northern New England out through Kentucky and Tennessee to South Carolina and Georgia. Yet more important than any of these specific grounds for war was the widespread desire, especially among younger Republicans of the War Hawk stripe, to avenge the national honor and dignity. The callous impressments of American seamen made Great Britain the inevitable enemy.

By the spring of 1812 the Madison administration, not knowing what else to do, was ready to go along with the agitation for war, and in June, on the President's recommendation, a declaration of war was pushed through a seriously divided Congress. Two days before the declaration, the British government decided in London to repeal all its restrictions on neutral trade. The Republican diplomacy of economic coercion had finally accomplished its purpose, barely too late to save the country from a disgraceful war.

The War of 1812 was a military debacle. But for British preoccupation with Napoleon, it would have been an utter disaster. Feeble administration in Washington and feebler generalship in the field brought defeat after defeat. Grandiose western boasts about the easy conquest of Canada eventuated in the disgraceful surrender of the American army at Detroit. In 1814 the defeat of Napoleon enabled the British to pay serious attention to the American war. One invading army easily captured Washington and burned the public buildings. Another, marching down from Canada to cut the country in two along the line of the Hudson, would have succeeded if its timid general had not been unduly discouraged by the success of a small American flotilla in maintaining naval control of Lake Champlain along his line of march. A final formidable force, fresh from victories over Napoleon, was sent to seize New Orleans with the aim of wresting much of the West from the United States. It was this seasoned army that was annihilated by Andrew Jackson and his western militiamen in the only significant American triumph of the war. Americans could also take pride in the naval victories of individual ships, but these could not prevent the mighty British navy from establishing unquestioned control of the seas along the American coasts.

Much of the American weakness arose from internal dissension. Southerners had little enthusiasm for the conquest of Canada, and Northerners had little for the conquest of Florida. The whole war was bitterly opposed in commercial areas, especially New England. New England banks and capitalists would not loan money to rescue the bankrupt federal treasury, the New England governors refused to supply troops, and in December, 1814, a convention of the New England states met at Hartford to seek redress against the tyranny of the federal government. Some participants advocated the secession of New England, but the more moderate majority contented itself with proposing constitutional amendments that would protect the interests of their section.

The unfortunate war had hardly started when the Madison administration began efforts to end it, but it was 1814 before a group of British and American commissioners got down to negotiating in earnest at Ghent in Belgium. The treaty they finally agreed on in December simply restored the state of things existing at the beginning of the war without mention of neutral rights, impressment, or any of the other questions that had been in dispute between the two countries. Actually the United States escaped without loss of territory only because the British were too war weary at the end of their long struggle with Napoleon to go on fighting. Indeed, had the British defeated Jackson, as expected, at New Orleans in January, 1815, two weeks after the peace terms were agreed upon at Ghent, they would probably have insisted on territorial concessions before ratifying the treaty.

THE CENTURY OF SECURITY

However ignominious the War of 1812 seemed at the time, the independence of the United States was not really secure until it had been fought and, by great good luck, survived. It also began a century such as no other western nation has ever had the good fortune to enjoy, a century in which to develop free from any external threat.

This marvelous security was guaranteed primarily by British domination of the seas. By the end of the War of 1812 Great Britain was ready to accept the permanence of the United States and to look for advantage in flourishing trade between the two countries. Seeing great commercial opportunities throughout the Americas, British ministries observed with satisfaction the crumbling of the Spanish Empire, the last great colonial empire in the New World, and resisted any efforts by other European powers to extend their influence across the Atlantic.

This happy turn in British-American relations was signalled when the outstanding questions between the two countries were amicably settled shortly after the War of 1812. The Rush-Bagot Agreement of 1817 provided for demilitarization of the Great Lakes, and in the Convention of 1818 American fishing rights in Canadian waters were specified, the northern boundary of the United States was set at the forty-ninth parallel from the head of the Mississippi to the Rocky Mountains, and the two countries agreed to joint occupation of the Oregon country beyond the Rockies for a period of ten years. In 1827 the joint occupation agreement was extended indefinitely until such time as either nation should give a year's notice for terminating the arrangement.

The Anglo-American rapprochement facilitated another diplomatic achievement of this period: the liquidation of American difficulties with Spain through the acquisition of Florida. After acquiring West Florida as far east as the Pearl River (the area now a part of the state of Louisiana) through "revolution" in 1810, the Madison administration had taken advantage of the war to annex, in 1813, another chunk extending beyond Mobile Bay east to the Perdido River (the coastal areas of the present states of Mississippi and Alabama). Following the war Spain was wracked by political turmoil at home and revolution in her South American colonies. Forays on American territory by Florida Indians intensified southwestern demands for annexation and furnished the pretext that Spain was not living up to her obligations under Pinckney's Treaty. When Andrew Jackson was sent to pacify the Indians along the Florida border in 1817, he moved on into Florida and seized the whole northern Gulf Coast area.

The administration in Washington could not sanction this rash and unauthorized occupation, but Secretary of State John Quincy Adams finally persuaded his Cabinet colleagues that Jackson should not be censured. Instead Adams told the Spaniards that the incident revealed their inability to maintain their treaty obligations along the Florida boundary, indicating the propriety of ceding Florida to the United States. Under this implied threat of forcible seizure, Spain yielded. By a treaty signed in 1819 but not ratified until 1821, Florida was ceded to the United States in exchange for the sum of $5 million. What is sometimes called the Transcontinental Treaty also defined the boundary between the United States and the Spanish possessions to the southwest as running from the Gulf of Mexico up the Sabine River (the western boundary of the state of Louisiana), then west and north to the Rocky Mountains, then west along the forty-second parallel to the Pacific.

The Florida treaty was consummated by the administration of James Monroe, who had succeeded Madison in 1817 and who was to provide the classic definition of America's diplomatic position in the Century of Security. The Monroe Doctrine was enunciated in the President's annual message to Congress in December, 1823, and contained two principal parts. The first was the assertion that the American continents were no longer open to colonization by European powers. The second was a warning against any interference by European powers with the revolutionary new nations of Latin America or any extension of the political systems of Europe to the Americas.

The noncolonization declaration was prompted by an expansion of the sphere of Russian activity down the northwest American coast from Alaska, and in 1824 the Russians agreed to limit their interests to the area north of 54°40′, leaving the United States and Great Britain as the only claimants of the Oregon country between that line and the Spanish-Mexican boundary at 42°.

The other part of the Monroe Doctrine was prompted by the fear that the major continental powers might join in an effort to subdue Spain's rebellious American colonies. The British foreign secretary had suggested that the United States join his country in opposing any such action, but Secretary of State Adams and President Monroe decided that it would be better for the United States to make a unilateral statement, knowing that British seapower would back up the policy. The European powers had no enthusiasm anyhow for the reconquest of Spanish America against British opposition so the Doctrine had little effect on the immediate situation. But it did clarify, for Americans and for others, the idea of the proper relation between the Old World and the New that was to be the basis for American diplomacy during the Century of Security.

FOR FURTHER READING:

Henry Adams' *History of the United States during the Administrations of Jefferson and Madison* (9 vols., 1889–1891) is one of the great classics of American historical writing. Irving Brant's *James Madison* (6 vols., 1941–1961) utilizes much material on the Jefferson and Madison administrations that has come to light since Adams wrote. For the Lewis and Clark expedition and western development during the Jeffersonian era, see Bernard De Voto's *Course of Empire* (1952)*, and his edition of *The Journals of Lewis and Clark* (1953). On the coming of the War of 1812, there are differing interpretations in Julius W. Pratt, *Expansionists of 1812* (1925) and A. L. Burt, *The United States, Great Britain, and British North America* (1940). Much can be learned from Bernard Mayo's account of the earlier career of one of the leading War Hawks in *Henry Clay, Spokesman of the New West* (1949). F. F. Beirne has written the best book on *The War of 1812* (1949). The Treaty of Ghent and postwar diplomacy are splendidly delineated in Samuel Flagg Bemis, *John Quincy Adams and the Foundations of American Foreign Policy* (1949); while Dexter Perkins, *Hands Off: A History of the Monroe Doctrine* (1941), is the standard account of that subject.

*Available in paperback edition.

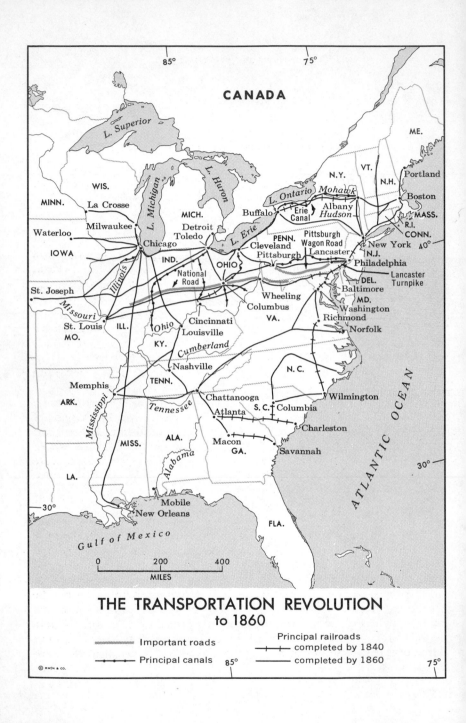

CANADA

L. Superior

WIS.
MINN.
La Crosse
Waterloo
IOWA
Milwaukee
Chicago
St. Joseph
Missouri
St. Louis
MO.
ILL.
Memphis
ARK.
LA.
New Orleans
Mobile

L. Michigan
L. Huron
MICH.
Detroit
Toledo
IND.
National Road
Illinois
Ohio
Cincinnati
Louisville
KY.
Cumberland
Nashville
TENN.
Chattanooga
Atlanta
Tennessee
MISS.
ALA.
Macon
GA.
Alabama
Mississippi

L. Ontario
Mohawk
Buffalo
Erie Canal
Albany
Hudson
L. Erie
Cleveland
Pittsburgh
Pittsburgh Wagon Road
Lancaster
OHIO
Wheeling
Columbus
VA.
Richmond
Norfolk
N. C.
S. C.
Columbia
Charleston
Savannah
Wilmington

ME.
N.Y.
VT.
N.H.
Portland
Boston
MASS.
R.I.
CONN.
New York 40°
N.J.
Philadelphia
DEL.
Lancaster Turnpike
Baltimore
MD.
Washington

ATLANTIC OCEAN

30°

FLA.

Gulf of Mexico

85°
75°

| 0 | 200 | 400 |
MILES

THE TRANSPORTATION REVOLUTION
to 1860

Important roads   Principal railroads
completed by 1840
Principal canals   completed by 1860

85°   75°

© RAND & CO.

CHAPTER 9

THE MARKET VERSUS
THE AGRARIAN REPUBLIC

It is one of the ironies of history that the Century of Security into which the Republican statesmen finally ushered the country was also supremely the Century of Enterprise. Freedom from all entanglements with the Old World, except a free and peaceful trade, had been deemed essential to the simple and therefore virtuous republic that Jefferson and his colleagues sought to perfect. Yet this freedom and security helped to foster a spirit of enterprise and rapid change that undermined the agrarian ideal.

The spirit and direction of American life became so strikingly different after the War of 1812 that the period around 1815 must be regarded as one of the major turning points in American history. The change was not quite so abrupt as it may appear—war has a way of temporarily damming up certain latent tendencies in a society and accelerating others so that they all seem to burst forth at the end of the conflict and as a result of it. In this case economic changes were primary.

THE MARKET REVOLUTION

The American economy has developed through three main stages. The economy of the colonial period was a *staple-exporting economy*, in which people either concentrated on producing tobacco, grain, and other staples for overseas markets or on the carrying trade or were largely self-sufficing in their economic activities. About the middle of the eighteenth century, as population flowed heavily into the interior where poor transportation prevented staple production, the self-sufficing sector of the economy began to grow relative to the staple-exporting and therefore commercial sector. It was this develop-

ment that set the stage for the struggle between commercial-mindedness and agrarian-mindedness in the last quarter of the century.
From the point of view of economic development, however, the important thing about the staple-exporting economy was its static quality, its lack of any tendency to self-acceleration or change. In fact the overseas markets for American staples were seriously disturbed by the Revolution, and with the steady growth of the self-sufficing sector toward the end of the century, the economy was becoming, if anything, more set in its ways. It was this unprogressive staple-exporting economy, with its sizeable self-sufficing sector, that undergirded the stable agrarian utopia of Thomas Jefferson.

How, then, did this economy become a dynamic *industrial economy?* The "industrial revolution" that brought factories, large-scale enterprises, and rapid technological change did not really gain full momentum in the United States until after the Civil War. But the critical shift in the pace, direction, and spirit of the economy had occurred decades before, as a result of the "market revolution" that brought most American economic activity into the orbit of an intricately intermeshed national market system. Between the *staple-exporting economy* of the eighteenth century and the *industrial economy* of the late nineteenth century there intervened a *national market economy* which did not until the 1850's begin to become significantly industrial.

The essence of the market revolution was a vast extension of the division of labor or, in other words, specialization of economic activities. Areas and individuals that formerly had been self-sufficing or that had engaged in mixed enterprises began to concentrate on the one product or service they could produce most efficiently, selling it for money and then buying with that money the other goods and services they needed. Areas and individuals that had formerly engaged in only barter or limited local trade were inexorably drawn into a national and international market system linked together by the mysterious mechanisms of money and credit. It was the resulting gains in efficiency and productivity that overnight jolted the formerly static economy into rapid growth. And it was in this atmosphere of rapid growth and ready profits that an economically conservative population became deeply infected with the spirit of enterprise, progress, and economic individualism.

The market revolution seemed to spring full blown from the War of 1812. With a staple-starved Europe paying high prices for American products, the long dammed-up flood of European imports pouring into American harbors, and settlers swarming over the newly opened lands of the West, the country was swept into an unprecedented four-year boom (1815–1818). Lured by high profits and easy credit into venturing their all on enterprises ranging from farms to steamboats, countless Americans were drawn for the first time into the money-market nexus. Yet this spectacular boom ended in the even more spectacular bust of 1819 and the depression of the 1820's to be followed by another boom-bust cycle in the 1830's.

The short-term boom-bust cycle of 1815–1819 arose immediately from the abnormalities of war and peace, but it had deeper roots in the market revolution and in the greater interdependence of the economy that the market revolution produced. The roots of the market revolution itself were in certain long-term developments that began before and continued long after the War of 1812. One of these was the accumulation of investment capital from the high profits of the American carrying trade during the Napoleonic Wars. Others will be discussed in the following sections.

THE ADVANCE TO THE MISSISSIPPI

A major stimulus to the growth of the American economy after 1815 was the rapid settlement and economic development of the West up to and across the Mississippi River. Much of this area was not open to settlement until William Henry Harrison destroyed the Indian power in the Northwest and Andrew Jackson crushed the Creeks and Cherokees of the Southwest during the War of 1812. Following the war the broken tribes yielded to repeated demands for additional cessions of territory. Finally in the 1820's, John C. Calhoun, Monroe's Secretary of War, inaugurated a policy of resettling the remaining Indians beyond the Missouri River, and by the middle 1830's this objective had been substantially accomplished.

With the return of peace in 1815 a flood of settlers poured west to take up rich lands under the liberal Harrison Land Act of 1800. A tract of as little as 160 acres could be bought for a minimum down payment of fifty cents an acre with four years to make the remaining payments of $1.50. Overnight great plantations appeared on the fertile river lands of Alabama and Mississippi as planters from the worn soils of eastern Virginia, the Carolinas, and Georgia moved west with slaves, stock, and plantation gear. Along the line of the Mohawk Valley and the Great Lakes came a torrent of refugees from the stony hill farms of northern and western New England, blanketing the productive plains of northern Ohio, Indiana, and Illinois with townships, churches, and school houses on the New England pattern. The older western states of Kentucky and Tennessee became thickly settled, and from them and from farther south and east a stream of immigrants moved into southern Ohio, Indiana, and Illinois, establishing a pattern of life that differed from the New England-based style in the northern sections of those states.

During the boom years this great migration attained staggering proportions. Federal land sales, which had risen from 67,800 acres in 1800, to over 500,000 acres in 1813, abruptly shot to 1,306,400 acres in 1815, and reached a peak of 3,491,000 acres in 1818. Even during the depressed twenties the tide continued to run strongly. The population of the country beyond the Appalachians doubled between 1810 and 1820 and again between 1820 and 1830. In quick succession the late wilderness produced five new states: Indiana (1816), Mississippi (1817), Illinois (1818), Alabama (1819), and Missouri (1821).

The typical western migrant was no solitude-loving Daniel Boone, but a man of enterprise, bent on bettering himself through shrewd investment, hard work, and a ride on a rising market. The market revolution in its early stages fostered the western boom that stimulated migration, and the great migration in turn accelerated the market revolution. The great migration cannot be understood, therefore, apart from other major factors in the market revolution.

COMMERCIAL AGRICULTURE

The most important feature of the market revolution was the spectacular expansion of commercial agricultural production with cotton leading the way. The development in England during the latter part of the eighteenth century of machinery which could manufacture cotton cloth cheaply had created a heavy demand for cotton. Cotton production was restricted for a time by the difficulty of separating the fibers from the seeds, but after Eli Whitney in 1793 perfected a gin that performed this task, cotton plantations mushroomed across the interior of Georgia and South Carolina. Checked for a time by the Embargo and the War of 1812, the cotton boom roared ahead with the return of peace and the opening of the rich southwestern lands to cultivation. Production rose from 146,000 bales in 1814 to 209,000 bales in 1815 and 349,000 bales in 1819. Within a few years after 1815, a wide belt extending from North Carolina around to Louisiana had been converted into the world's largest cotton-producing area, and cotton was the country's leading export.

Unlike the staple-exporting sector of the colonial economy, the new cotton sector was intimately tied to the national as well as the international market system. While the bulk of the cotton shipped from New Orleans, Mobile, and Charleston went to Europe, much of it went by way of northeastern ports, especially New York. The proceeds of the crop paid for imports from Europe that found their way back to all parts of the United States through northeastern mercantile houses. Importations from Europe were financed to a great extent in the Northeast by the services of merchants in shipping and selling the South's cotton crop and by the South's purchases of northeastern manufactures; and in the Northwest by foodstuffs and livestock the farmers shipped to southern cotton planters. For some decades after 1815 the ever-mounting cotton exports were the most important factor in the growth of the economy.

Cotton production was merely the biggest segment of an expanding commercial agriculture. Tobacco cultivation never recovered from its post-Revolutionary slump in the old tidewater area of Virginia and Maryland, but new tobacco belts developed along the North Carolina-Virginia border and in sections of Kentucky, Tennessee, and Missouri. Not until the 1840's, however, did tobacco production flourish and become highly profitable. Rice culture benefited from improved seed selection and methods of cultivation, but could not expand beyond its long-established locale in the coastal region of South Carolina and Georgia. The development of an improved variety of ribbon cane fostered a booming sugar plantation economy in Louisiana following the War of 1812, and hemp, used especially for baling cotton, similarly afforded a profitable commercial crop for areas in Kentucky and Missouri.

While the great export staples were concentrated in the South, other sections were not lacking in an extensive commercial agriculture producing mainly at first for the national market. Areas of commercial wheat production expanded steadily west from Pennsylvania's Susquehanna Valley to New York's Mohawk and Genesee valleys to Ohio, Indiana, and Illinois. In the decade after 1815 a mounting stream of wheat, flour, corn, pork, beef, and livestock began pouring from the Old Northwest into the East and South. Cincinnati became the country's leading center of flour milling and meat packing, and by the 1840's the flood of cheap wheat and flour from the fertile Northwest was becoming a major item in American exports to Europe.

Farmers on the less productive soils of the Northeast, forced out of cereal and meat production by the cheap western products, turned to producing perishables—fruits, vegetables, poultry, and dairy products—for the growing eastern cities. Improved breeds of wool-bearing sheep and increased demand from an expanding woollens industry made wool production a profitable enterprise in many parts of the Northeast as well as the Northwest.

Thus within a brief space of time, mainly following the War of 1812, countless self-sufficing or general farmers had responded to the lure of cash returns held out by a mushrooming national and international market system and were concentrating on those staples that they could produce most efficiently. Yet little of this would have occurred had it not become possible to transport bulky products cheaply from one part of the country to another.

THE CONQUEST OF DISTANCE

So important were the dramatic improvements in transportation facilities in the early nineteenth century that some historians have called the market revolution a transportation revolution. Like the great westward migration, the transportation revolution was part cause and part effect of the broader market revolution.

During the colonial period production for market had been confined to areas along navigable waterways, and at the beginning of the nineteenth century almost the only transportation elsewhere was by wagon or pack team over primitive dirt roads. As late as 1816 a ton of goods could be shipped three thousand miles from England for what it cost to transport the same goods thirty miles overland in America. The cost of moving a bushel of wheat from Buffalo to New York City in 1817 was three times the market value, for corn it was six times the market value, and for oats twelve times the market value. Cheaper transportation was an obvious prerequisite to a national market economy.

The first attempts to solve the problem were through improved roads. In 1794 a company chartered by the Pennsylvania legislature opened between Lancaster and Philadelphia the first major turnpike, or graded and paved road on which tolls were charged. So dramatically did it lower wagoning rates and stimulate commercial development in the country it traversed and so profitable did it prove, that a wave of turnpike construction followed. By the War of 1812 most of the major cities in the Northeast were connected by turnpikes, but not until after the war did the turnpike craze reach its peak while spreading into the West. One of the major turnpikes led west from Baltimore to Cumberland, Maryland, and it was here that the federal government had begun constructing the National Road. By 1818 this great highway had reached Wheeling, Virginia, on the Ohio River, and by 1833 it had been extended to Columbus, Ohio. The National Road quickly became a major artery of east-west trade, while elsewhere the turnpikes reduced transportation costs and brought previously isolated areas into the market.

More important than better roads, especially in the West, was the introduction of the steamboat. Flatboating down the Ohio and Mississippi rivers to New Orleans had permitted some production for market from the early days of settlement, but this mode of transportation was extremely slow even downriver while upriver shipping by oar-driven keelboat was so slow, backbreaking, and expensive as to inhibit any extensive commerce. A new era was predicted when Robert Fulton operated the first commercially successful steamboat, the *Clermont*, on the Hudson River in 1807. By 1812 a few forerunners of the classic shallow-draft sternwheeler had appeared on the Mississippi. The development of western steamboating came with a rush at the end of the war, and by 1820 there were sixty steamboats on the Mississippi-Ohio system (by 1860 there would be more than a thousand) and others on the river systems of Alabama and Mississippi. Steamboat freight rates were only 5 to 10 per cent of what keelboats had charged to haul goods upriver and only 25 to 30 per cent of what it had cost to flatboat goods down the river, and there were proportionate gains in speed of shipment. Able to operate far up the network of tributaries that laced the West, the shallow-draft sternwheeler made possible the production of cotton, wheat, and other bulky commercial commodities in widespread areas that could not otherwise have entered the national market.

While the steamboat was accelerating the market's conquest of the West, another transportation development was providing a direct water link between East and West. In 1817 the New York legislature, prodded by Governor DeWitt Clinton, authorized the construction of a canal from Albany on the Hudson River west along the Mohawk Valley to Buffalo on Lake Erie, and by 1825 the 364-mile Erie Canal was completed. Traffic on the new canal was so heavy that tolls equalled the cost of construction within nine years. Given cheap water communication with New York City and Europe, a flood of commodities from the whole Great Lakes region soon flowed eastward along the canal, meeting a returning flow of eastern and European manufactured and other goods destined for the entire West.

The success of the Erie Canal prompted Pennsylvania to build a competing system linking Philadelphia with Pittsburgh on the Ohio, and in the 1830's and 1840's the states of the Old Northwest completed a series of canals connecting the Great Lakes with the Ohio and the Mississippi.

The development of a railroad network in the 1840's and 1850's gave added efficiency to a transportation system that had already succeeded in bringing most parts of the country within the orbit of the irresistible market. Baltimore began constructing its railroad west toward the Ohio in 1828, and in the next decade several thousand miles of short lines were built. Not until the 1850's, however, did the railroad boom reach its height. It was in this decade that the great trunk lines connecting East and West were completed, and by 1860 the country had more than thirty thousand miles of railroad.

In 1815 the shipment of goods from Cincinnati to New York by keelboat and wagon had required over fifty days. In 1850 they could be sent by steamboat to New Orleans and thence by packet to New York in twenty-eight days, by the Ohio and Erie canals and the Hudson River in eighteen days, and by railroad in six to eight days. In 1815 overland freight rates by wagon had ranged from thirty to seventy cents per ton per mile. By the 1850's the railroads were charging two to nine cents per ton-mile and the canals around one cent per ton-mile. Behind these simple figures lay a revolutionary transformation of American life.

ENTERPRISE AND PUBLIC POLICY

The transportation revolution and the market revolution would have come much more slowly if the men of the early republic had followed the *laissez-faire* notions of political economy that are often mistakenly ascribed to them. Instead, as the market advanced and the spirit of enterprise quickened, Americans demanded that their governments ally themselves with private enterprise to speed the march of progress.

The most notable alliance of public and private enterprise at the state and local level was in the field of transportation, where progress demanded undertakings too vast for individuals or even groups of individuals. The early turnpike companies raised much of their capital from stock subscriptions by states and towns through which they ran. The great canals were built directly by states, while other states spent large sums on improving navigable rivers. Governmental aid to transportation reached its peak in the construction of railroads. No one has yet calculated how many millions of dollars towns, cities, and states expended for all these purposes, but it is certain that the revolutionizing transportation network could not have gotten far without this governmental aid.

The turnpike, steamboat, and railroad companies were the forerunners of the modern corporation. These early corporations were born out of the theory of "mixed enterprise," the idea that government should ally itself with private enterprise to accomplish ends beneficial to the public. In the simple days of the staple-exporting economy all enterprise had been carried on by individuals or partnerships. Economic combinations of many individuals or their capital in large enterprises were thought to be dangerous to the public interest and were frowned upon by the law. Only where some great public purpose was to be accomplished were they thought justified, and then only when chartered by special act of the legislature.

Such corporate charters usually facilitated the raising of capital by granting the privilege of "limited liability," making stockholders in the corporation (unlike members of partnerships) liable for debts of the corporation only to the extent of the stock they held. Charters also usually granted, either explicitly or implicitly, monopolies or semi-monopolies, as when a company was given the exclusive right to develop a certain transportation route. Thus the early corporate charter was thought of as a privilege conferred by government in order to enlist private enterprise for the accomplishment of a public purpose.

The corporate device found much of its early use not only in transportation but also in banking, and the rapid growth of banking was another of the major factors in the acceleration of economic development. The banking system before the War of 1812 had consisted of the Hamiltonian national bank, chartered by Congress, and a small number of private banks which were called state banks because they were chartered by state legislatures. In theory at least, stockholders bought stock in these banks by paying in gold and silver. On the basis of this "specie" capital the banks made loans, with the interest they collected from their borrowers providing profits that could be paid back to the stockholders as dividends. What made the banks extremely profitable was the fact that they could safely loan out more than their capital. Instead of loaning specie, a bank gave borrowers bank notes, or pieces of paper resembling modern paper money, each bearing a promise that the issuing bank would redeem the note on demand with a specified sum of specie. These bank notes then circulated as money in the vicinity of the bank and, as long as people had confidence in the bank, were not returned for redemption in specie. Thus the bank could safely print, loan, and collect interest on considerably more bank notes than it had specie to cover.

Though conservatively managed and restrained by the national bank at first, the state banks were potentially capable of expanding the supply of credit and investment "capital" almost infinitely and thus of stimulating feverish economic activity. This began to happen when the national bank's demise in 1811 and the economic stimulus of the war prompted enterprising politicians and businessmen to secure legislative charters for a large number of new state banks designed to operate on more generous and lucrative principles than their predecessors. The bank mania reached its peak after the war, and the rapid multiplication of banks and bank credit contributed greatly to the boom-and-bust cycle of 1815–1819. Yet bust was again followed by boom, and the expansion of bank credit reached even greater heights than before in the 1830's. In spite of the violent short-term fluctuations which the banks fostered, they also contributed greatly to the spectacular long-term prosperity of the economy due to their active stimulation of its growth.

REPUBLICAN NATIONALISM

The spirit of enterprise was strong in the new generation of Republican leaders who had pushed Madison into war in 1812 and who dominated a transformed Republicanism after the war. Federalism, despite a momentary comeback in Embargo days, was so weakened by the steady swelling of the Republican electorate and so discredited by the Hartford Convention that in 1816 only three states voted for the Federalist presidential candidate. To succeed Madison the Republicans picked James Monroe, the last prominent Virginian of the Revolutionary generation, and in 1820 Monroe was re-elected without opposition.

Monroe himself retained some of Jefferson's agrarian-minded and strict constructionist scruples and rejoiced that the death of federalism had ushered in an "Era of Good Feelings" when parties would no longer be necessary. In truth the younger men surrounding the President had moved, in the enterprising atmosphere of the boom years, so far toward the nationalist and commercial-minded views of the Federalists that Federalism had become superfluous. Monroe's State Department was headed by that ardent nationalist John Quincy Adams, who had deserted the party of his father, President John Adams, over the Embargo issue. Monroe's Secretary of the Treasury, William H. Crawford of Georgia, had been working for a new national bank. Presiding over the War Department was John C. Calhoun, vigorous champion of a strong army, protective tariffs, and federal road and canal construction. And in Congress the dominant figure was Speaker of the House Henry Clay, who for a generation would symbolize a broad program of federal action—the "American System" he would call it—to aid enterprise and speed progress.

These men were preaching Hamiltonianism shorn of its elitist overtones. The onrushing market revolution was democratizing business, and the rapid spread of the spirit of enterprise through all levels of society made the new Republican nationalism more dynamic than the old Federalist nationalism of conservative merchants and financiers.

The war was no sooner over than several problems growing out of wartime developments were attacked in the spirit of Republican nationalism. The overexpansion of state banks had led to a financial *l.* crisis early in the war. Outside New England the overextended banks had had to "suspend specie payments" (stop redeeming their bank notes in gold or silver coin on demand), their notes had depreciated, and the resulting financial chaos had contributed greatly to the government's difficulties in carrying on the war. To get the federal government out of its financial troubles and to furnish a sound paper currency and credit system as a basis for orderly business growth, the younger Republicans pushed through Congress in 1816 a charter for a Second Bank of the United States.

This institution, with headquarters in Philadelphia and branches elsewhere, was to have a capital of $35 million as compared with the *a.* $10 million of Hamilton's national bank. It was to be the depository *b.* for all federal funds, and its bank notes were declared receivable for all sums due the government. It was to serve public purposes by making loans to the government and also by regulating the state *c.* banks, aiding them to resume specie payments at the earliest possible moment, and thereafter keeping them on a sound basis by sustaining them in periods of financial stringency and restraining them in periods of boom. Its power to do this resulted from its large capital and from the fact that it was constantly receiving large quantities of state bank notes in its role as federal depository. By promptly presenting these notes to the state banks for redemption it could force them to curtail their issues, while by expanding its own loans and note issues it could ease any pressure on the state banks. Yet this was to be essentially a private, profit-making institution with the government subscribing only one fifth of its capital and designating only one fifth of its directors.

Going into operation in 1817, the Second Bank did help secure a general resumption of specie payments, but then succumbed to the boom spirit itself. Inefficient and often dishonest officers so overextended the Bank's own loans and note issues that it lost all power to restrain the expanding state banks. The inevitable reaction, the Panic of 1819, was much more severe than it might otherwise have been because the national Bank suddenly reversed its policy and saved itself by ruthless pressure against its debtors and the state banks. Not until Nicholas Biddle became the Bank's president in 1823 did it begin to realize its great potential as a balance wheel and regulator for the economy as a whole.

A second problem growing out of the war was the desperate *d.*

situation of American manufacturers. Most American manufacturing before the War of 1812 had been of the "domestic" variety—spinning, weaving, shoemaking, hatmaking, and countless other enterprises carried on in homes or shops of independent artisans. Large-scale industrial production would develop only in response to the market revolution and the vast national market it created. Yet even before 1812, small cotton textile factories had begun to spring up in New England, iron works were attaining some size in Pennsylvania, and other enterprises in cities like New York and Philadelphia were outgrowing their independent-artisan origins and beginning to employ substantial numbers of journeyman artisans on a wage basis. By cutting off imported European manufactures, the war stimulated a rapid growth in this manufacturing activity. But when the war ended, British manufacturers dumped on the American market their stored-up surplus of products at cut-rate prices, threatening the promising American manufacturing establishment with sudden death.

In the mood of generous nationalism that followed the war, Republican congressmen from all sections of the country responded to the plight of the beleaguered northeastern manufacturers by passing the first tariff act designed primarily to protect American producers from foreign competition. The Tariff of 1816 required foreign imports that competed with such leading American manufactures as cotton and woollen cloth and iron to pay import duties ranging around 20 to 25 per cent of their value. Additional protection was granted to iron and textiles in 1818 and 1819.

One of the greatest ambitions of the national-minded Republicans was frustrated by the lingering constitutional doubts of presidents Madison and Monroe. In the closing days of his administration Madison vetoed as unconstitutional Calhoun's Bonus bill of 1817, a measure reserving the $1.5 million bonus which the new national Bank paid the government for its charter to be used for beginning a great national system of roads and canals. On assuming office, President Monroe similarly declared that the Constitution did not authorize federal expenditures for internal improvements.

JUDICIAL NATIONALISM

In the congenial atmosphere of Republican nationalism following the War of 1812, the Federalist nationalism of Chief Justice John Marshall and the Supreme Court he dominated came to full fruition. Having asserted the Court's authority on constitutional questions in Marbury *vs.* Madison back in 1803, Marshall now used this authority in a series of remarkable decisions to establish his Federalist and nationalist views on questions of property rights, constitutional interpretation, and federal and state powers.

In Dartmouth College vs. Woodward (1819), the Court overruled an attempt by the New Hampshire legislature to change the college's colonial charter. Marshall's Court had already made itself the defender of property rights against state legislatures in an earlier case, and now Marshall declared that charter rights, too, were sacred. This decision was to become increasingly significant with the growing importance of chartered corporations in American economic life.

The biggest corporation of Marshall's day, the Second Bank of the United States, was involved in his most far-reaching decision, McCulloch vs. Maryland (1819). This case arose from Maryland's attempt to tax out of existence the Bank's branch at Baltimore. The power to tax was the power to destroy, he argued, and no state could be allowed to destroy an instrumentality of the federal government. Perhaps the most important part of this decision was Marshall's argument, based on the doctrine of implied powers, that Congress had acted constitutionally in chartering the Bank. Here he echoed Hamilton's argument to President Washington at the time the first national Bank was chartered, maintaining that if the end Congress sought to attain were sanctioned by the Constitution, then "all means which are appropriate, which are plainly adapted to that end" are constitutional.

Of various other decisions affirming federal over state powers, one may be singled out as particularly important. In Gibbons vs. Ogden (1824), the Court invalidated a monopoly that New York had granted over steamboat service between New York and New Jersey. In giving Congress the power to regulate interstate commerce, Marshall declared, the Constitution meant that *only* Congress should have such power. Furthermore he defined "interstate commerce" so broadly as to include the carrying of passengers or any other variety of commerce between states. Marshall's sweeping extension of the commerce clause not only invalidated the New York monopoly as an invasion of Congress' exclusive power to regulate, but also laid the basis for the vast future extensions of federal regulatory powers.

Thus in the first flush of the market revolution, the spirit of enterprise and nationalism seemed pervasive everywhere in American life—in the entrepreneurial undertakings of countless citizens, in the efforts of the states to hasten progress through transportation projects and corporate charters, in the tariff and banking legislation of Congress, in the diplomacy of President Monroe's Doctrine, and in the decisions of the Supreme Court. The only marring note seemed to be the doubts of old-fashioned Virginia presidents about federal appropriations for roads and canals, and even this slight barrier to progress would be removed when one of the younger, national-minded Republicans entered the White House in 1825. Yet an unprogressive, agrarian society had not—could not have—changed so totally and quickly as this one momentarily appeared to have done. Two decades of crisis and conflict were to elapse before Americans would be at ease in the new world of enterprise.

FOR FURTHER READING:

The indispensable starting point for the economic history of this period is Douglass C. North's somewhat technical but rewarding analysis of *The Economic Growth of the United States, 1790–1860* (1961). This should be supplemented with the detailed accounts of the factors of economic growth in George R. Taylor, *The Transportation Revolution, 1815–1860* (1951) and Paul W. Gates, *The Farmer's Age: Agriculture, 1815–1860* (1960). Special aspects are well treated in Louis C. Hunter, *Steamboats on the Western Rivers* (1949); Carter Goodrich and others, *Canals and American Economic Development* (1961); Samuel Eliot Morison, *The Maritime History of Massachusetts, 1783–1860* (1921)*; R. G. Albion, *The Rise of New York Port, 1815–1860* (1939); and Bray Hammond, *Banks and Politics in America from the Revolution to the Civil War* (1957). For western development, Frederick Jackson Turner's famous essay on "The Significance of the Frontier in American History" is reprinted, along with many of the arguments from other historians that it evoked, in George R. Taylor, ed., *The Turner Thesis Concerning the Role of the Frontier in American History* (rev. ed., 1956, Amherst Problems in American Civilization)*. Ray A. Billington has written the best general account of *Westward Expansion* (1949); Richard C. Wade describes early western cities in *The Urban Frontier* (1959); and an absorbing contemporary account of the boom years in the Southwest is Joseph G. Baldwin, *The Flush Times of Alabama and Mississippi* (1853)*. A general account of the political history of the era of Republican nationalism is George Dangerfield, *The Era of Good Feelings* (1952); and the first volume of Charles M. Wiltse, *John C. Calhoun* (3 vols., 1944–1951) deals superbly with one of the leading Republican nationalists.

The decisions of the Marshall Court are analyzed in Charles Warren, *The Supreme Court in United States History* (rev. ed., 2 vols., 1926); and Albert J. Beveridge has written a good *Life of John Marshall* (4 vols., 1916–1919).

———————
*Available in paperback edition.

PRESIDENTIAL ELECTIONS AND MAJOR EVENTS, 1816–1828

1816   **James Monroe** (Republican) elected over Rufus King (Federalist).

Tariff of 1816, the first deliberately protectionist tariff act.

1817   Second Bank of the United States chartered.

Madison vetoes Calhoun's Bonus bill for internal improvements.

1817–1826   Erie Canal constructed.

1818   National Road reaches the Ohio River.

1819   Dartmouth College *vs.* Woodward. John Marshall's Supreme Court defends charter rights against state legislation.

McCulloch *vs.* Maryland. John Marshall's Supreme Court upholds the constitutionality of the national Bank.

Panic of 1819 forces a general suspension of specie payments and inaugurates a long and severe economic depression.

1820   Land Act of 1820. Lower land prices and abolition of credit system.

Missouri Compromise.

James Monroe (Republican) re-elected without opposition.

1824   Tariff of 1824. Higher protection.

Gibbons *vs.* Ogden. John Marshall's Supreme Court extends the federal power to regulate interstate commerce.

John Quincy Adams (Republican) elected over Andrew Jackson, William H. Crawford, and Henry Clay (all Republicans).

1826   Anti-Masonic movement begins.

1828   Tariff of Abominations. Extremely high protective duties.

Andrew Jackson (Democratic Republican) elected over John Quincy Adams (National Republican).

CHAPTER 10

DEPRESSION DECADE:
SECTIONALISM AND DEMOCRACY
1819–1828

The Panic of 1819 was the first severe economic crisis ever seriously to affect the American people as a whole. Part of an international economic dislocation following a long period of war, it was especially intense in the United States because of the reckless expansion of banks, credit, and entrepreneurial investment that preceded it. When the prices of cotton and other commodities suddenly plummeted on the world markets, countless Americans faced the loss of their homes, farms, workshops, and other property because they could not meet the debts they had incurred to finance their entrepreneurial ventures. The banks suspended specie payments, and bank notes, the only circulating medium, skidded toward worthlessness in the hands of their holders. Merchants went bankrupt, city workers lost their jobs, and the economy ground to a standstill. The paralysis maintained its grip through the early 1820's, and not until the end of the decade did prosperity return.

Yet the economic effects of the Panic were no more momentous than its psychological and political effects. In rapid succession the American people had been drawn from the settled ways of the old agrarian order into a national market economy of dizzying prosperity, unlimited optimism, and headlong change, and then suddenly plunged into privation and despair. The shock of this experience made the 1820's a decade of soul searching and tension. The postwar mood of generous nationalism evaporated as sections and interest groups became narrowly concerned with their own welfare and jealous of rival sections and interest groups. There was a striking revival of Jeffersonian orthodoxy as prodigal agrarians eschewed the fleshpots of the market and resolved to return to the old ways of frugality and honest toil. Class antagonisms sharpened as impoverished farmers and urban workers blamed political and business leaders—above all, the banking fra-

[125]

3. ternity—for the disaster. And finally there was a growing interest in politics, a dissatisfaction with the political leadership that had allowed hard times to come, and a demand for new leaders who would be more responsive to the popular will in using government to relieve the distress.

POLITICAL SECTIONALISM

The resurgence of sectional rivalries was dramatically demonstrated by the heated congressional controversy in 1820 over admitting Missouri as a slave state. Slavery had been a source of conflict in the constitutional convention and on several occasions since, but it had not yet become a major issue. The Quakers had been bearing testimony against human servitude for some time, and by 1804 every state north of Delaware had provided for the ultimate emancipation of slaves within its borders. But there was as yet no strong general movement against slavery as a moral and political evil, for most men of good will, both north and south, continued to indulge Jefferson's hope that it would eventually disappear everywhere through the gradual operation of economic and moral forces.

Thus when northern congressmen sought to amend the Missouri admission bill to require the gradual emancipation of Missouri slaves, they were acting less from moral repugnance to the institution than from a revival of the traditional northeastern resentment at southern political domination. Much of the South's political power was derived from the constitutional provision that three fifths of its slaves be counted in apportioning congressional representation and electoral votes. Northeasterners seized upon the Missouri question as a means of blocking the extension of this political injustice throughout the Louisiana Purchase. Southern congressmen, on the other hand, reacted violently to this attack on their vulnerable system of labor. Admission of Missouri as a free state would upset the even balance between slave and free states and destroy the protection that this gave the South in the Senate against any future antislavery measures.

A Missouri Compromise was finally reached because of the simultaneous movement to make the geographically separated eastern appendage of Massachusetts (now Maine) a separate state. Maine was admitted as a free state, Missouri was admitted as a slave state, and it was provided that no further slave states were to be created from that part of the Louisiana Purchase lying north of latitude 36°30′ (the latitude of the southern boundary of Missouri).

What many northern congressmen had in mind when they opposed the admission of any more slave states was illustrated at this same session of 1820 by the fate of a bill to extend further tariff protection to the hard-pressed manufacturers. Representatives from slave-holding states voted almost five to one against this measure in the House and provided most of the votes that killed it in the Senate. By 1824, when the manufacturers tried again for higher duties, the South was opposed fifty-seven to one in the House. This time the Northeast was heavily in favor, the only opposition there coming from representatives of international merchants and shippers who resisted any diminution of international trade. But now western farmers had been convinced that the growth of manufacturing might create a flourishing home market for their unprofitable products, and western representatives provided the margin by which the tariff bill squeaked through Congress. The Tariff of 1824 raised duties on textiles to 33⅓ per cent, sharply increased the rate on iron, and won rural support by duties on raw wool and hemp.

RELIEF AND DEMOCRACY

Manufacturers were not the only ones who had learned from the doctrines of Republican nationalism to look to government for aid. Thousands of western settlers were now unable to complete their payments for public lands under the credit system inaugurated by the Land Act of 1800. In response to their outcries, Congress forgave interest charges, extended payment periods, and allowed delinquent purchasers to retain an amount of land proportionate to the payments they had made. At the same time, in the Land Act of 1820, it abolished the credit system while lowering the minimum price of public lands from $2 to $1.25 an acre. The minimum tract that could be purchased had recently been reduced to eighty acres, and all these changes enabled a settler to buy a farm for as little as $100 cash.

But it was to the state governments that the people looked for relief from the most desperate problem created by the Panic, the disappearance of money and the collapse of the pyramid of debt that had been built up during the boom. Men could neither collect the debts owed them nor pay the debts they owed, property could not be sold, and a sweeping liquidation through foreclosures and bankruptcies threatened the whole community.

Legislatures, especially in the hard-hit South and West, responded to the demands of their aroused constituents by various schemes to circumvent the constitutional prohibition against issuing paper money or making anything except gold and silver legal tender. Some states established "banks" or "loan offices" to print state-backed paper money for loan to desperate debtors. Usually these measures were coupled with "stay laws" requiring creditors who refused to accept the state-backed paper money to delay executions on their debtors' property. Relief was also provided through "property laws" whereby a "disinterested" jury composed of the debtor's neighbors set a minimum value below which his property could not be forcibly sold to satisfy his debts.

The violent political struggles over debtor relief laws and the closely related banking question accelerated the drift toward a more democratic political system in many of the states. A few socially complex states like New York and Pennsylvania were already far along the road toward a well-developed two-party or bifactional system in which evenly matched candidates campaigned against each other with the aid of party newspapers and stable party organizations expert in the techniques of garnering votes. Under such circumstances voter interest and participation were high, and public policy was responsive to majority wishes.

In most of the country, however, widespread interest in politics had appeared only sporadically before the 1820's. Having little sense that government—at least the remote state and national governments—affected them much anyhow, most people were willing to leave politics to those well-to-do and socially superior men in their communities who had something to gain from political power, whether land grants or bank charters or simply office. This resulted in a *personal-factional* political system in which a group of leaders allied through personal or family ties normally maintained unchallenged predominance in a county or other district. In the legislatures, representatives from the various local oligarchies formed shifting alliances, again based on personal or family ties.

This system was sanctioned by Jeffersonian political theory. Jefferson had never maintained that the people as a whole should decide public policy, but only that the people were wise enough and virtuous enough to select the wisest and most virtuous among them as political leaders. Candidates pretended that they did not seek office, certainly did not electioneer, but only reluctantly consented to serve when called upon by their fellow citizens. The voters did not tell their chosen representatives what to do once elected, and certainly the representatives did not seek votes by promising to do thus and so. Instead, according to Jeffersonian theory, these unusually wise and virtuous men should be left free to reach wise and virtuous decisions through rational debate and compromise with each other in legislatures and Congress.

The personal-factional system was best adapted to homogeneous communities where conflicts of interest were not very important. It mustered enough genuine wisdom and disinterestedness to function satisfactorily until the market revolution began multiplying the number of specialized economic roles and competing interest groups in the community, while at the same time making men more conscious of the connection between enterprise and public policy. This caused no difficulty during the boom years when there seemed to be enough for everybody. But the Panic made people suddenly aware of their separate and competing interests at the very moment they began looking to government for mutually contradictory kinds of aid. With debtors clamoring for stay laws and loan offices while creditors denounced them, the Jeffersonian notion of a harmony of interests served by wise and virtuous leaders could no longer be sustained. Voters wanted to know where candidates stood on questions of vital concern to them, and the more alert politicians began telling the voters what they thought a majority wanted to hear.

As elections began to be transformed into popular referenda on public policy, a current of discontent with the established political leadership manifested itself. The main target of popular resentment was the banking system, which was blamed for causing the collapse by its reckless overexpansion of credit. While the banks were refusing to pay their own debts by not redeeming their notes in specie and while the depreciation of bank notes was the most conspicuous source of loss to the whole community, the banks were foreclosing on the property of their debtors, continuing to pay dividends, and extending special accommodations to their favored borrowers. The state banks managed to shift some of the resulting resentment to the national bank against which they had similar complaints. But in the eyes of many newly aroused voters, the banking system as a whole was to blame and along with it the politicians and businessmen who had fostered it and profited from it. Moreover these same politicians and businessmen were often leading the opposition to debtor relief.

As voters came to the polls in increasing numbers to repudiate the established leaders, a new-style democratic politics began to supplant the personal-factional system. The new-style democratic politician not only promised the voters what they wanted, but also portrayed himself as fighting the battle of the plain people against a group of unscrupulous "aristocrats." The old loose and shifting factional groupings in state politics began to stabilize as "democratic" and "aristocratic" alignments. In Kentucky, and to a lesser extent in some other southern and western states, something very like a two-party system developed out of the violent conflict over debtor relief.

In the East, where debtor relief was not such a pressing problem, other issues led to similar results. In New York, DeWitt Clinton capitalized on some high-handed maneuvers by Martin Van Buren's long entrenched Albany Regency to make a smashing political come-back as gubernatorial candidate of the "People's Party." In the same state in 1826, the disappearance and presumed murder of a man who had revealed the secrets of the Masonic order caused an astonishing anti-Masonic outburst, which within a few years became a political movement and eventually a short-lived political party. Since Masonic lodges were usually composed of the most prominent men in their communities and since many of the dominant politicians were Masons, the Antimasons attacked the order as a secret, oath-bound, aristocratic conspiracy against the rest of the community.

The urban counterpart of Antimasonry was the labor movement that began to flourish late in the 1820's. By fostering larger and more specialized units of production, the market revolution was making it more difficult for artisans and mechanics to complete the traditional progression from apprenticeship through the wage-earning journey-man status to independent proprietorship. The depression and unem-ployment highlighted the insecurity of the permanent wage-earning status in which more and more workingmen were finding themselves. Journeymen organized labor unions and called strikes for the ten-hour day. On the political front they joined with small entrepreneurs whose middle-class status was likewise threatened, to form workingmen's parties in Philadelphia and New York City. Under the banner of "Equal Rights" these parties advocated free public education, opposed imprisonment for debt, and agitated against banks and other "monop-olies" through which a favored few could exploit the many.

Amid the frustrations and conflicts of the 1820's the long drift toward actual popular sovereignty in the United States was reaching its culmination. From the beginning of settlement the cheapness of land and the demand for labor had created an atmosphere of universal opportunity and rough social equality that was quickly reflected in the quasi-democratic political institutions of the colonies. The Revolu-tion, consigning the destiny of Americans to their own hands, had cut off elitist tendencies and firmly established the ideal of equal political rights. In the following decades state after state had alleviated restrictive suffrage requirements and other denials—often more sym-bolic than real—of the Revolutionary ideal. Meanwhile the egalitarian tendency of American life had been reinforced by the process of west-ern settlement, and the new western states had been free to adopt con-stitutions reflecting the increasingly democratic tone of the country.

Yet it remained for the market revolution to democratize enter-prise, to give a final push to the egalitarian tendency, and to arouse a hitherto apathetic electorate to the importance of public policy and politics. The boom-bust cycle simply made this popular political awakening more abrupt than it might otherwise have been. Appearing first in a variety of contexts at the local and state levels, the new-style democratic politics began to manifest itself at the national level in the presidential election of 1824.

THE ELECTION OF 1824

The institutional symbol of the personal-factional system at the level of presidential politics was the caucus. Every four years the Republican Senators and Representatives had met in caucus at Washington to designate their party's presidential candidate, and since 1800 the caucus designation had been tantamount to election. As the election of 1824 approached, the foreordained choice of the caucus was William H. Crawford of Georgia, Monroe's Secretary of the Treasury and the favorite of the large congressional delegations representing Virginia and New York. Crawford's strongest support came from areas that had been relatively immune to the postwar boom and the Republican nationalism that accompanied it (landlocked North Carolina, the wornout plantation country of eastern Virginia, and the conservative Dutch farming counties along the Hudson River), and he ran as the candidate of a resurgent Jeffersonianism.

This time, however, the caucus system itself was challenged by the sectional and personal rivalries that had rendered Monroe's second term anything but an "Era of Good Feelings." Secretary of State John Quincy Adams came forward as the presidential choice of New England and Speaker Henry Clay as the choice of the West. In addition, Secretary of War John C. Calhoun proposed to take his state of South Carolina away from Crawford in the South and counted on his record of support for tariffs, internal improvements, and the national Bank, to give him Pennsylvania's electoral vote and additional nationwide backing. All of these anti-Crawford candidates, in fact, were unrepentent champions of Republican nationalism. Calhoun led them in attacking the caucus as undemocratic, and the refusal of their supporters to attend it resulted in Crawford's being nominated by only a minority of the Republican Congressmen.

The ultimate beneficiary of all these currents was none of these candidates, but Andrew Jackson, hero of the Battle of New Orleans. In order to gain an advantage in a local factional struggle, some Tennessee politicians had pushed through their legislature a resolution nominating Jackson for president, never expecting him to be a serious candidate. But there was a surprising response to the nomination from quarters that politicians had not heretofore taken seriously. No one knew where the Tennessee general stood on public issues. To people disenchanted with the old leaders, it was enough that he was a popular hero, the people's man against the established leadership. The strength of this sentiment became apparent when a grass-roots movement swept the Pennsylvania Republican convention out of the control of the leaders who had intended to endorse Calhoun and forced them to pledge Pennsylvania for Jackson. Calhoun promptly withdrew from the presidential race, running unopposed for vice president and carrying South Carolina into the Jackson camp.

When the election took place, Jackson led the four-man field in both popular and electoral votes, but no one had a majority. The Constitution directed that the House of Representatives, voting by states, should choose among the three highest candidates. This eliminated Clay, low man in electoral votes, and Crawford was also removed from serious contention by a physical collapse. This left Clay to wield his great influence in the House on behalf of either Jackson or Adams. Clay chose Adams, and Adams was elected by the narrowest of margins.

THE TRIBULATIONS OF THE SECOND ADAMS

John Quincy Adams was among the ablest and most patriotic presidents, but also one of the least successful. Partly through circumstances and partly through insensitivity to public sentiment, he defied and was overwhelmed by the most powerful political currents of the 1820's.

The Jackson men would have regarded Adams' election, in any case, as a flouting of the people's will. But when he appointed Henry Clay to the Secretaryship of State, traditional stepping stone to the presidency, their fury knew no bounds. The cry of "Bargain and Corruption" rang throughout the land, touching off a four-year campaign to vindicate popular sovereignty by placing Jackson in the White House.

Adams compounded his difficulties by underestimating the depression-bred reaction against Republican nationalism. Adams and Clay sought to build a National Republican party, based on a coalition of the Northeast and the Ohio Valley and dedicated to Clay's "American System" of protective tariff, national bank, and internal improvements. In addition, the President's first annual message called for a national university and federally sponsored scientific research and exploration, while cautioning Congressmen against being "palsied by the will of our constituents."

The Adams-Clay program outraged the neo-Jeffersonian Crawford men, now led by New York's Martin Van Buren, and drove them into alliance with the Jackson and Calhoun factions. Calling itself the Democratic Republican party, this Jacksonian coalition for four years blocked the President's program in Congress and harassed him in every way possible. The only significant legislative product of these four years was a tariff act passed in 1828. With both parties trying to win presidential votes by juggling the complicated tariff schedules, this "Tariff of Abominations" pushed duties on both manufactured and agricultural products to absurdly high levels and satisfied almost no one.

The presidential election of 1828 was marked by the return of the two-party system to national politics and by a scurrility on both sides that was unmatched since the last closely contested two-party election in 1800. Questions of public policy were hardly discussed, the real issue being whether the people's man Jackson should prevail over the seasoned statesman and old-style political leader Adams. This was enough to produce a substantial increase in the number of voters and a substantial majority for Jackson.

FOR FURTHER READING:

The best general account of the 1820's is Frederick Jackson Turner, *The Rise of the New West, 1819–1829* (1906)*. Even more suggestive, though it deals only with the southern states, is Charles S. Sydnor, *The Development of Southern Sectionalism, 1819–1848* (1948). Some idea of the political transformations going on in the states in the 1820's may be gained from Dixon Ryan Fox, *The Decline of Aristocracy in the Politics of New York* (1919), and from Charles G. Sellers, Jr., *James K. Polk, Jacksonian: 1795–1843* (1957). The presidency and subsequent political career of John Quincy Adams are splendidly narrated in Samuel Flagg Bemis, *John Quincy Adams and the Union* (1936).

---

*Available in paperback edition.

1828   **Andrew Jackson** (Democratic Republican) elected over John Quincy Adams (National Republican).

1830   Jackson vetoes the Maysville Road bill.

1832   Tariff of 1832. Remedies the worst abuses of the Tariff of Abominations, but fails to satisfy the South Carolina Nullifiers.

Jackson vetoes the bill to recharter the Second Bank of the United States.

Andrew Jackson (Democratic Republican) re-elected over Henry Clay (National Republican).

South Carolina nullifies the tariff laws.

1833   Compromise Tariff. Gradual reduction of all tariff duties to 20 per cent.

Force Act. Authorizes president to use military to enforce the laws.

Jackson transfers the federal deposits from the national bank to selected state-chartered deposit banks.

1836   Jackson issues Specie Circular requiring specie for purchase of federal lands.

Distribution Act distributing the federal surplus among the states.

Martin Van Buren (Democrat) elected over William Henry Harrison, Daniel Webster, and Hugh Lawson White (all Whigs).

1837   Panic of 1837 forces a general suspension of specie payments and initiates a severe and prolonged economic depression.

Van Buren proposes the independent treasury system.

1838   New York Free Banking Act, a forerunner of general incorporation laws. One of the many efforts by the states to reform and regulate banking.

1840   Independent treasury system finally approved by Congress after three years of debate.

William Henry Harrison (Whig) elected over Martin Van Buren (Democrat).

CHAPTER 11

THE JACKSONIAN ERA

1828–1840

With Andrew Jackson's inauguration, the forces of egalitarianism swept over the federal government. Though Jackson had risen to become master of a large plantation and one of the leading men of his state, he had never abandoned the egalitarian habits of his earlier surroundings in small-farmer North Carolina and frontier Tennessee. On Inauguration Day he opened the White House reception to an unruly mob of the high and the low, shocking the older official society but unmistakably announcing the new regime's conviction that one man was as good as another.

The same point was made with more substantial effect by Jackson's extension of the "spoils system" and his frank advocacy of "rotation in office." The new President was accompanied to Washington by a host of new-style democratic politicians demanding office as a reward for their support. Jackson took the position that any honest citizen could discharge the duties of a government office as well as any other. Furthermore public offices should not be the property of their holders for life. They should be passed around, with a preference shown for friends of the administration that the people had elected. The numerous removals and appointments that Jackson made on these principles somewhat impaired the efficiency of government service, but also made it more representative of and responsive to the country as a whole. Moreover the spoils system helped make possible the new-style political parties through which the popular will could be translated into public policy.

Jackson was the first president to operate on the principle that the people themselves should decide public policy. Arguing that the president was the only federal official elected by the people as a whole, he was supremely certain that his policies represented the popular will. And so great was the popular confidence he inspired that the people, or a majority of them, usually agreed.

By assuming this role of democratic tribune, Jackson greatly increased the power of the presidency relative to Congress. All of his predecessors combined had vetoed only nine congressional measures, usually on the ground that they were unconstitutional. Old Hickory used the veto twelve times, against legislation he thought inexpedient as well as legislation he thought unconstitutional. And by taking his differences with Congress to the voters, he was highly successful in making recalcitrant legislators compliant or in getting them replaced.

JACKSONIAN POLICIES

Though the people's candidate had been elected, it was by no means clear what policies a people's administration would follow. Jackson himself had little political experience, and it was supposed that much would depend on whether Calhoun or Van Buren controlled his administration and became his heir for the presidential succession. Calhoun wanted to base the Jacksonian Democratic-Republican party (which gradually came to be called simply the Democratic party) on an alliance between the South and the West, which would reduce tariffs for the South and liberalize federal land policy for the West. The issue which was most embarrassing for Calhoun's plans was that of internal improvements which the West favored and the South increasingly opposed.

Van Buren, on the other hand, wanted to resurrect the old Jeffersonian coalition between southern planters and the "plain Republicans" of the Northeast. Such a coalition could unite on neo-Jeffersonian grounds to oppose internal improvements (New York wanted no federally financed competition for its Erie Canal) and the national bank (New Yorkers resented the bank as a Philadelphia institution that gave New York City's rival an undeserved financial dominance). The one issue that was dangerous to Van Buren's plans was the tariff, over which Northerners and Southerners were disagreeing with mounting vehemence.

The Calhoun men had seemed to have the upper hand in the party until Jackson's inauguration produced a sudden reversal. Calhoun's friends were almost frozen out of the Cabinet, while Van Buren himself was given the Secretaryship of State. Relations between Jackson and Calhoun steadily deteriorated until the South Carolinian was finally driven from the party. This result was produced in good part by Van Buren's astute use of the information that Calhoun, while a member of Monroe's Cabinet, had advocated punishing Jackson for his rash invasion of Spanish Florida. The New Yorker was aided, too, by the "Eaton imbroglio," when the socially prominent $\mathcal{2}$. women of Washington tried to ostracize the somewhat disreputable wife of Jackson's old friend and Secretary of War John Eaton. Mrs. Calhoun was among the ladies who angered the President by snubbing Peggy Eaton, while the widower Van Buren was free to treat her with conspicuous gallantry.

But more fundamental than any of these considerations was the $\mathcal{3}$. fact that the old general found Van Buren more congenial than Calhoun, both personally and in political outlook. Jackson came to Washington without a very well thought-out position on the major issues. But he did have some deeply rooted political instincts which he trusted implicitly, and it was these that determined the policies of his administration. His instinctive egalitarianism has already been noted. Joined to this was an instinctive neo-Jeffersonian agrarian-mindedness.

Jackson himself had once long before engaged in extravagant land and commercial speculations based on credit. The bankruptcy that ended these operations and the long struggle to pay off his debts and regain solvency through farming were the experiences that were most decisive for his political outlook. A thoroughly chastened advocate of the virtues of agriculture, hard work, and economy, abhorring debt and fearing the get-rich-quick atmosphere fostered by easy credit, he interpreted the boom-bust cycle of 1815–1819 as reproducing on a national scale his own personal experiences. Consequently when he assumed the presidency, his one clearly-defined objective was to administer a simple, economical government so as to pay off the national debt as rapidly as possible.

Jackson's mood was, of course, more congenial with Van Buren's neo-Jeffersonianism than with the Republican nationalism that had heretofore been Calhoun's trademark. The influence that this gave Van Buren became most apparent when the advocates of a nationwide federal road system managed to push through Congress in 1830 the Maysville Road bill. Though this bill only provided that the federal government should buy stock in a company building a turnpike from Maysville to Lexington in Kentucky, it was regarded as the test measure for the whole internal improvements program. Expenditures for internal improvements would delay Jackson's cherished project for paying off the national debt, and Van Buren had little difficulty persuading him that the measure should be vetoed. The veto message not only condemned the Maysville project as local rather than national, but by its sweeping reservations about the constitutionality and expediency of federal expenditures for internal improvements killed for several decades the dream of a great nationally financed transportation network.

THE TARIFF AND NULLIFICATION

Yet Jackson and Van Buren were not ready to assault all the works of Republican nationalism. To undertake a thoroughgoing downward revision of the Tariff of Abominations would be to delay payment of the public debt and to disrupt the North-South alliance that Van Buren sought to perfect. Consequently the President urged his first Congress to handle the question with "utmost caution," and the resulting tariff revisions of 1830 hardly touched the more abominable features of the system.

At this point South Carolina exploded. No state had enjoyed a more uninterrupted prosperity from colonial days to 1819 than South Carolina. First rice, indigo, and sea island cotton had created a wealthy ruling class in the lowcountry, and then the upland cotton boom had spread comparable riches through the rest of the state. No state was harder hit or more permanently damaged by the depression of the 1820's. The disruption of business coincided with the rise of more efficient cotton-producing areas in the Gulf States, and South Carolina never really recovered. South Carolina's reaction to its prostration was the more violent because of the long period of heady prosperity that had preceded it and because no state had developed a prouder or touchier group of political leaders.

Until the depression the Republican nationalism of Calhoun and his friends had been ascendant in South Carolina. The hard times enabled a rival "State Rights" faction to blame Calhoun's favorite policies for all the state's woes. By the mid-twenties the state-rights men had stirred up a storm of resentment against the protective tariff and were close to winning political control of the state. Calhoun and his friends were forced to retreat from Republican nationalism as rapidly and unobtrusively as possible. When Congress passed the Tariff of Abominations in 1828, the Calhoun men confounded their state-rights rivals by outdoing them in violent agitation against protection and by adopting an even more radical version of the state-rights doctrine.

The famous doctrine of nullification was announced in the South Carolina Exposition and Protest of 1828, secretly written by Calhoun and issued as a report of a legislative committee. The Nullifiers maintained that the Constitution was a compact among states which retained their essential sovereignty and which had delegated only limited and clearly specified powers to the federal government. The states themselves were the only proper judges of whether their common agent, the federal government, had exceeded the powers delegated to it by the constitutional compact. If a state judged that some federal law was

[138]

a violation of the compact, it could declare it null and void whereupon the federal government must desist unless and until three fourths of the states, through the amending process, explicitly granted it the nullified power.

The South Carolinians counted on the Jackson administration to push tariff reform, and only after its failure to do so in 1829–1830 did Calhoun's friends begin a campaign in the state for actual nullification. The Jacksonian Congress responded by eliminating some of the worst excesses of the Tariff of Abominations in 1832, but the rates were still decidedly protectionist. Meanwhile Calhoun had openly broken with Jackson and put himself at the head of the Nullifiers; the Nullifiers won the two-thirds majority in the state legislature necessary to call a state convention, and in November, 1832, the state convention declared the tariff laws null and void and forbade their enforcement in South Carolina.

When Congress met in December, Jackson called for thoroughgoing tariff reform but at the same time announced his determination to enforce all federal laws throughout the land, by military means if necessary. It was this situation that produced the Compromise Tariff of 1833. Snatching from the Jackson party the credit for tariff reform, Clay and Calhoun united to push through a measure by which all tariff rates were to be reduced by gradual steps over a ten-year period to a uniform rate of 20 per cent. Congress also complied with Jackson's demand that it simultaneously pass a Force Act, authorizing him to use the armed forces to uphold the laws. The South Carolina convention then reassembled and rescinded its nullification of the tariff laws, but got in the last word by nullifying the Force Act.

The seemingly inconclusive outcome should not obscure the important long-range effects of this dangerous crisis. The fact that the Nullifiers could claim victory—the tariff had been reformed—heightened their intransigence against the federal government and gave them complete dominance over South Carolina. From this time on, the state and its magnetic leader, Calhoun, sought to unite the South in radical resistance to federal tyranny, and the incessant agitation from this source was a major factor in producing the eventual secession of the southern states.

Yet in the shorter run nullification and disunion were discredited. Every other southern legislature denounced the South Carolina doctrine, the aged Madison denied that it derived from the Kentucky and Virginia resolutions of 1798, and the country as a whole responded enthusiastically to the nationalistic sentiments that Jackson expressed in opposing the Nullifiers. In fact Jackson's zeal for preserving the Union led him to embrace a nationalistic interpretation of the Constitution that greatly embarrassed Van Buren and other state-rights Jacksonians. Heretofore the state-rights idea had been associated with democratic-mindedness in American politics, but now that the people's candidate was in the White House proclaiming federal pre-eminence over the states, federal power seemed less threatening. Perhaps the most significant result of the nullification crisis was the decline of state-rights sentiment in the face of a rising democratic nationalism.

THE BANK WAR

Simultaneously with the nullification controversy another great conflict had begun to take shape, this one between Andrew Jackson and the Second Bank of the United States. Jackson's experience with debt and depression had made him distrustful of all banks. On the bank question his democratic-mindedness merged with his agrarian-mindedness to produce the conviction that banks fostered an unhealthy atmosphere of speculation, created boom-and-bust cycles, and transferred wealth from the many to the few. The national Bank was open to special objection because it concentrated so much power in private hands and because it violated the Jeffersonian principles of strict construction and limited government. Jackson's views in all these respects reflected the resurgent agrarian-mindedness and neo-Jeffersonianism produced by the depression, as well as the antibank animus of the emerging workingmen's movement.

Actually, since Nicholas Biddle had become president of the Bank in 1823, it had acted to restrain the numerous state-chartered banks from the tendencies Jackson feared, and most businessmen and politicians had become convinced that the Bank was indispensable to a soundly growing economy. Yet the opponents of banking in general saw the national Bank as the head of the whole odious system, and the only part of the system that the federal government could readily reach. And as a new boom gathered strength in the early 1830's, they were joined by some incongruous allies against the Bank, the forces of entrepreneurial democracy.

Once again, as in the boom years following the War of 1812, the glittering promise of profits held out by a rapidly expanding market economy was creating a host of new entrepreneurs. For these men of enterprise easy credit was the key to success, and the more reckless of the state-chartered banks became the citadels of the entrepreneurial spirit. By restraining the state banks from overexpansion, the national Bank curtailed the profits and dimmed the prospects of the state banks and their borrowers. Consequently the new entrepreneurs, the more speculative elements of the economy, regarded the Bank as an aristocratic and repressive institution, representing established wealth and using its privileged position to hobble newcomers who attempted to join the race for success.

Both the new entrepreneurs and the agrarian-minded had been heavily attracted to Jackson's Democratic party. Both groups opposed the Bank on somewhat egalitarian grounds, but their common hostility to Mr. Biddle's institution could not indefinitely conceal the fact that their ultimate objectives were diametrically opposed.

When Jackson became president, Biddle was already thinking about getting a bill passed to renew the Bank's charter, which was due to expire in 1836. Thus Jackson dismayed the Bank's supporters when he questioned its constitutionality and expediency in his first message to Congress. Their dismay turned to alarm when it became clear that Jackson would be a candidate for re-election in 1832. The old Adams-Clay alignment, calling itself the National Republican party, was planning to run Clay against Jackson, and Clay was urging Biddle to press for recharter before the election. Clay argued that this would force Jackson to approve a recharter bill, for a veto would be a damaging issue against him in the election. Biddle finally agreed, and in July, 1832, a recharter bill passed Congress by substantial majorities.

Jackson promptly returned the measure to Congress with a veto message declaring the Bank unconstitutional and demagogically denouncing the foreign ownership of much of the Bank's stock. But the heart of the message was an eloquent paragraph expounding the Jacksonian social philosophy. The President granted that natural inequalities existed in every society. "But," he said, "when the laws undertake to add to these natural and just advantages artificial distinctions, to grant titles, gratuities, and exclusive privileges, to make the rich richer and the potent more powerful, the humble members of society—the farmers, mechanics, and laborers—who have neither the time nor the means of securing like favors to themselves, have a right to complain of the injustice of their government."

The Bank men did not have the votes in Congress to override the veto, but they confidently expected that both the veto and its author would be repudiated in the ensuing presidential election. When the returns were in, Jackson had 219 electoral votes to 40 for Clay.

Yet the Bank was far from dead. Jackson rightly feared that Biddle was determined to use the Bank's great economic and political power to push a recharter bill through Congress over his veto. Equally determined to cripple the Bank, the President resolved to remove the government's mounting deposits from its vaults. Federal receipts were booming along with the economy, the national debt had been paid off, and a federal surplus of millions of dollars was beginning to accumulate. These surplus federal deposits greatly extended the Bank's lending ability, profits, and power, but it took the administration a year to find a way of removing them from the Bank. After discharging one and then another uncooperative Secretary of the Treasury and after protracted negotiations with nervous state bankers, Jackson announced in September, 1833, that henceforth the Treasury would deposit the federal funds in selected state banks, the so-called deposit banks or pet banks.

Enraged by the removal of deposits, Biddle recklessly threw the full economic power of the Bank against the government. Removal and Jackson's hostility made some contraction of the Bank's loans necessary, but Biddle resolved to force such a severe contraction and to create such widespread distress that Congress would be compelled to restore the deposits and eventually recharter the Bank. As a result the "Panic Session" of Congress was under intense pressure during the winter of 1833–1834 to relieve the country from mounting bankruptcies, unemployment, and distress by restoring the deposits. But Jackson's anti-Bank majority held firm, Biddle was finally forced to relax the pressure, and the Bank's doom was sealed.

BOOM AND BUST AGAIN

Yet the destruction of the Bank was only a Pyrrhic victory in the Jacksonians' larger campaign to reform banking in general. Jackson and many of his principal followers were "hard-money" men who wanted all bank notes driven from circulation, leaving only gold and silver coin as a circulating medium. Their attack on the national bank was only the first step in their deflationary, agrarian-minded program, and they hoped to use the state-bank deposit system to reform the state banks. The deposit banks would be required, as a condition for receiving the deposits, to cease issuing notes in denominations under $5 or accepting such notes in their transactions with other banks. Gradually the prohibition would be extended to notes under $10 and then $20. Driving small notes from circulation would create a steady demand for specie for small transactions, and all banks would have to reduce their loans and note issues in order to have enough specie on hand to meet the demand.

But this scheme did not have time to get under way before it was overwhelmed by a massive inflation. The Jacksonians had destroyed the national Bank's stabilizing influence on the economy just at the moment when powerful inflationary forces were pushing the country into a boom even more wildly speculative than the one that followed the War of 1812. With the national Bank's restraining influence removed, the state banks expanded their loans, note issues, and profits; new state banks were chartered by the hundreds; the deposit banks themselves got out of control, and the wave of inflation and speculation rolled ominously higher toward its inevitable cresting and crash.

The hard-money men could only shout futile warnings. Their Jeffersonian constitutional scruples prevented them from attempting direct federal regulation of the state banks. Regulation at the state level was equally impossible because the uneasy alliance between hard-money (or agrarian-minded) Democrats and enterprise-minded Democrats began breaking down as soon as their common enemy, the national Bank, was finally defeated.

Nevertheless, in 1836, Jackson attempted a drastic remedy with his Specie Circular. The flood of bank notes had stimulated an especially frantic speculation in public lands, and the Circular directed that thenceforth lands must be paid for in specie or specie-redeemable bank notes. Coming too late, the Specie Circular succeeded only in putting a strain on the vastly overextended structure of credit. The strain was increased by the Distribution Act that Jackson had reluctantly signed a few weeks before. Congress had decided to distribute the bulging federal surplus, approaching $40 million, among the states; and the federal deposit banks were suddenly called upon to transfer vast sums to the state treasuries. Finally, in the spring of 1837, only weeks after Jackson left office, a financial crisis in England set off a wave of bankruptcies in the United States, the banks suspended specie payments, and the Panic of 1837 brought the whole towering pyramid of credit crashing down.

Jackson's hand-picked successor Van Buren was left to cope with a severe and prolonged depression. Aligning himself with the hard-money wing of the Democratic party, Van Buren proposed that the government sever its connections with all banks and keep its funds in its own "independent treasury" offices. He further proposed that the government accept and pay out only gold and silver coin, which would have some deflationary effect by creating a constant demand for specie; but in the main the proposal meant that the federal government would wash its hands of responsibility for the economy. As a result of the split between hard-money and soft-money Democrats, Congress wrangled throughout Van Buren's term over the independent treasury. The bill was finally passed in 1840.

Meanwhile the depression had forced most state legislatures to attempt some kind of banking reform. A few states prohibited banks entirely, others gave a monopoly of the banking business to a state-owned or mixed public-private bank, and most states adopted stricter regulations to prevent an overextension of credit by private banks. New York's widely imitated Free Banking Act of 1838 sought to provide state regulation and at the same time to divest banks of the monopolistic special privileges they enjoyed through their legislative charters. Foreshadowing general incorporation laws for all kinds of enterprises, it provided that anyone could engage in the banking business if he complied with certain regulations. Thus by the early 1840's the country had reached a modus vivendi on the banking question: banks would continue to stimulate economic growth, but they would be restrained through free competition and state regulation rather than through a national bank.

The long and hotly contested struggle over banking was important in two respects. On the most obvious level it reflected the efforts of an economy newly swept forward by the market revolution to develop a credit and currency system that would sustain growth and broaden opportunity without causing disastrous boom-and-bust cycles. But at a deeper level it reflected the psychological ambivalence of a conservative, agrarian society toward the whole new world of rapid change and growth into which it had been suddenly thrust. During the first great boom, 1815–1819, the country as a whole succumbed with uncritical enthusiasm to the new spirit of enterprise. The depression of the 1820's produced an equally decided reaction in the other direction—against banks, easy credit, paper money, and entrepreneurial ambition. Thus the return of prosperity and the second great boom, 1834–1837, evoked more ambivalent reactions. Some again saw unlimited opportunity and clamored for unlimited credit; others, the neo-agrarians who remembered the 1820's, championed hard money; still others, perhaps the majority, oscillated between the two extremes. By the time of the second great depression following 1837, the ever-advancing market had sufficiently undermined agrarian-mindedness, and the boom-bust cycle had sufficiently chastened the enterprise-minded to make a rough consensus possible. The American people had finally made their adjustment to the new world of enterprise created by the market revolution.

THE NEW POLITICS

Just as the Jacksonian era saw the evolution of financial institutions and practices to serve the emerging spirit of enterprise, so also did it see the evolution of political institutions and practices to serve the emerging spirit of egalitarian democracy. The basic feature of the new politics was the two-party system, which had flourished briefly and imperfectly around 1800 but which re-emerged to reach its full development only in the 1830's.

By carrying to the national level the new-style democratic politics that had emerged in the states during the 1820's, the Jacksonians created a strong political party and forced their opponents to imitate their organization and techniques for wooing a mass electorate. The anti-Jacksonians were at first an ill-organized coalition of Clay-Adams National Republicans, Nullifiers, and—out of hostility to the Van Buren organization in New York—the democratic-minded Antimasons. These elements were unable to unite to stem the Jacksonian tide in the presidential election of 1832, but they were already beginning to learn the lessons of Jacksonian politics. In fact the Antimasons had anticipated the Democrats in calling a national party convention, representing the grass-roots elements of the party, to replace the discredited caucus method of nominating candidates.

A powerful, unified opposition party developed only in 1833–1834 when Jackson's removal of the deposits caused the defection of many business-minded Democrats and enabled his opponents to unite on the platform of resistance to executive tyranny. Taking the name "Whigs," to identify themselves with earlier defenders of liberty, they stood for sound business enterprise and a program of Republican nationalism. Though the Whigs drew increasing support from all sections and classes, they appealed especially to the wealthier and more established members of the business community, to the manufacturing interests, and to the larger southern planters whose staple crops involved them extensively in the commercial network. Calhoun's Nullifiers cooperated with the Whigs for a few years, but after 1837 returned to the Democratic party.

In 1836 the new Whig party sought to capitalize on political sectionalism by running three presidential candidates, hoping to throw the election into the House of Representatives. But the magic of Jackson's popularity was sufficient to win his candidate Van Buren a slim majority over all three Whigs. The Whigs' day finally came in 1840 when the Democrats were discredited by the depression and when the Whigs outdid the Democrats at the game of democratic politics. Running the popular old Indian fighter William Henry Harrison as the people's candidate against the "aristocratic" Van Buren, the Whigs whipped up enthusiasm with monster rallies, torchlight parades, songs, and log-cabin symbolism to win a sweeping majority.

The presidential election of 1840 also produced by far the largest outpouring of voters yet seen. Only 27 per cent of the estimated eligible voters had voted for president in 1824, the Jackson-Adams contest of 1828 had raised the figure to 56 per cent, but the contest of 1840 brought out 78 per cent of the eligible electorate, a proportion that may never have been equalled since. This dramatic rise in political interest was a result of the full development of the two-party system. By 1840 the two parties were almost equally strong not only at the national level but also in every section, in most of the states, and in a majority of counties. This meant closely contested elections for all offices from sheriff to president with no efforts being spared to woo hesitant voters. Each party maintained an elaborate network of stridently partisan newspapers in Washington, the state capitals, and countless villages and towns. Rival orators stumped every neighborhood for months before every election. Competing systems of party committees at county, state, and national levels issued a constant stream of broadsides and pamphlets, organized parades and rallies, and made sure that no voter stayed away from the polls on election day. This incessant political activity not only brought voters to the polls in droves, but also made politics a leading form of American recreation, while providing the population with a massive political education.

But the parties were as much affected by the voters as they affected the voters. The new-style democratic politicans of both parties developed an acute sensitivity to shifts in public opinion and became expert in building coalitions that would yield a majority or near-majority. The Whigs continued to appeal more strongly to businessmen, the well-to-do, manufacturing interests, and large planters, while the Democrats attracted smaller farmers, workingmen, and frontier areas. But both parties needed additional support to achieve a majority, and both quickly learned the techniques for constantly adjusting their positions to changing public moods. As a result the parties tended not to differ sharply in normal times and to maintain a nearly even balance of strength. From Jackson's day to our own, with only brief interruptions, this two-party system has remained a marvelously sensitive instrument for translating majority opinion into public policy while moderating the sharpness of conflict among the diverse groups that compose American society.

FOR FURTHER READING:

Historians have disagreed widely over the proper interpretation of Jacksonian politics. The differing points of view are presented in the following stimulating books: Arthur M. Schlesinger, Jr., *The Age of Jackson* (1945)*; Bray Hammond, *Banks and Politics in America from the Revolution to the Civil War* (1957); Marvin Meyers, *The*

Jacksonian Persuasion (1957)*; and Lee Benson, *The Concept of Jacksonian Democracy: New York As a Test Case* (1961). Moisei Ostrogorski unhappily traces the emergence of the new-style political parties in *Democracy and the Organization of Political Parties* (2 vols., 1902); John W. Ward explores the American attitudes that were reflected in current popular conceptions of *Andrew Jackson: Symbol for an Age* (1955)*; and Walter Hugins focusses on New York City in discussing *Jacksonian Democracy and the Working Class* (1960). There are many good biographies of leading figures: Marquis James, *Andrew Jackson* (2 vols., 1933–1937)*; Glyndon G. Van Deusen, *The Life of Henry Clay* (1937); Glyndon G. Van Deusen, *Thurlow Weed, Wizard of the Lobby* (1947); William N. Chambers, *Old Bullion Benton: Senator from the New West* (1956); E. B. Smith, *Magnificent Missourian: The Life of Thomas Hart Benton* (1958); Thomas P. Govan, *Nicholas Biddle: Nationalist and Public Banker* (1959); and Margaret L. Coit, *John C. Calhoun: American Portrait* (1950)*. A firsthand impression of Martin Van Buren may be gained from his *Autobiography* (1918). For the nullification controversy, see David F. Houston, *A Critical Study of Nullification in South Carolina* (1896); Chauncey S. Boucher, *The Nullification Controversy in South Carolina* (1916); and the second volume of Charles M. Wiltse, *John C. Calhoun* (3 vols., 1944–1951). The analyses of Jacksonian America by European observers are extremely illuminating. Here the classic is Alexis de Tocqueville, *Democracy in America* (2 vols., 1835–1840)*, but also fascinating are Michael Chevalier, *Society, Manners, and Politics in the United States* (1839)*; Francis J. Grund, *Aristocracy in America* (1839)*; Harriet Martineau, *Society in America* (1837)*; and Frances Trollope, *Domestic Manners of the Americans* (1832)*.

The nullification controversy and its consequences may be analyzed through the documents presented in Charles Sellers, *Andrew Jackson, Nullification, and the State-Rights Tradition* (Berkeley Readings in American History, 1963)*.

*Available in paperback edition.

CHAPTER 12

ROMANTICISM, REFORM, SLAVERY

*The country had no sooner developed a two-party system, superb-
ly fitted for reflecting the majority will while moderating conflict,
than it ran head-on into the one conflict that could be neither resolved
by majority will nor moderated: the conflict over Negro slavery.* The
age of enterprise and egalitarianism that produced the two-party system had also brought Americans to their highest pitch of confidence
about the possibilities of individual men and of optimism about the
future of their society. It was a reforming age, abounding in schemes
for wiping out the remaining blemishes that marred the full perfection of man. It was a utopian age, spattered with perfectionist communities and looking forward to the early perfection of the whole
society. Such an age was bound to find intolerable the most glaring
affront to the liberal principles of the Declaration of Independence.
Yet Negro slavery was so deeply rooted as a social and economic institution that the slaveholders, though themselves heirs of the American
liberal tradition, could not surrender it.

ROMANTICISM

Underlying the reformist spirit of the age was a new configura-
tion of ideas and attitudes called *Romanticism.* A vast and complicated
movement in the intellectual and literary history of the Western
world, Romanticism took different forms and led toward different
conclusions in different countries, periods, and individuals. As used
here the term denotes the central tendencies of thought in the United
States in the first half of the nineteenth century.

Romanticism grew out of the thought of the eighteenth-century
Enlightenment and was akin to it. Both assumed that the world was

designed for man's happiness and both emphasized man's ability. In America, at least, both led in the direction of optimism, individualism, and liberal political principles. But Romanticism was a reaction against the Enlightenment's mechanical view of the natural world and its emphasis on intellect. Where the Enlightenment ascribed man's competence to his ability through reason to understand the natural laws by which a watchmaker Creater regulated both the physical and moral universes, Romanticism distrusted intellect and valued man's emotional and intuitive qualities. Regarding the natural world as the embodiment of a divine spirit, Romanticism held that the natural and the spontaneous were the good and that the highest truth was derived through the instantaneous spiritual intuition of the individual.

American Romanticism reached its most sophisticated and self-conscious form in the Transcendentalism of Ralph Waldo Emerson and the group of New England intellectuals he inspired. While most of Emerson's contemporaries were probably unaware of Transcendentalism or Romanticism as an explicit body of doctrine, the pervasiveness of Romantic assumptions was apparent in every aspect of American life. The overwhelming theme of popular literature and the popular stage was the primacy of feeling over intellect. In more serious writing, James Fenimore Cooper celebrated the moral perfection and superior wisdom of the "natural" but untutored woodsman Leatherstocking and the "noble savage" Chingachgook, while Nathaniel Hawthorne and Herman Melville explored, from a Romantic standpoint, some of the darker implications of Romantic doctrine. The landscape painters of the Hudson River School sought to capture on their canvases the emotion of the "sublime" evoked by natural scenes. Architects turned from the intellectually satisfying simplicity, harmony, and proportion of the eighteenth century's "colonial" or "Georgian" style to exotic and more titillating models—Gothic, Moorish, and Egyptian. Even in laying out gardens and parks, Americans abandoned formal patterns and tried to reproduce artificially the wildness and irregularity of nature as in Frederick Law Olmsted's design for Central Park in New York City.

Yet the influence of Romanticism extended far beyond intellectuals, writers, and artists. Jacksonian egalitarianism was reinforced by some widely-accepted Romantic assumptions. The Enlightenment's emphasis on reason and education, its insistence that reason was more highly developed in some men than in others, had prevented even the more liberal men of the eighteenth century from endorsing full egalitarianism and popular sovereignty. Thus Jefferson had relied on a "natural aristocracy" to rule, trusting the people to elect the "natural aristocrats" to office, yet not trusting them to dictate public policy.

But if intuition rather than reason is seen as the source of truth, the situation changes. The Romantic doctrine of democracy was expounded most baldly by the Jacksonian politician and distinguished historian George Bancroft: "if the sentiment of truth, justice, love, and beauty exists in every one then it follows, as a necessary consequence, that the common judgment in taste, politics, and religion is the highest authority on earth." Indeed, by Jackson's time, the semiliterate farmer who lived simply and close to nature was often regarded as being superior in virtue and real wisdom to a city dweller whose "natural" impulses had been stifled by the artificialities of education and culture.

Jackson's enormous popularity may be attributed in considerable measure to the prevalence of such attitudes. The contest between Jackson and John Quincy Adams in 1828 was widely interpreted as pitting a "natural" man of virtue, a product of the American frontier, against the Harvard-educated, highly-cultured, and therefore suspect Adams, who had the additional disadvantage of having spent much of his early life in the artificial surroundings of an overcivilized and decadent Europe. The Whigs turned the tables in the presidential election of 1840 by using a log-cabin symbolism that appealed to the same attitudes and generated the same kind of enthusiasm in giving William Henry Harrison his smashing victory over the Jacksonian city slicker Van Buren. The voters who responded to these appeals had never heard of Romanticism as a body of doctrine, but their behavior demonstrated their unconscious conversion to some key Romantic assumptions.

ROMANTIC CHRISTIANITY

Apart from political behavior, it was in religious behavior that the extensive popular acceptance of Romantic assumptions was most evident. Well into the nineteenth century, the story of religion in the United States was a story of the gradual erosion of the originally dominant Puritan-Calvinist strain of Protestant Christianity. In an increasingly self-reliant, optimistic, and individualistic society, it continually became more difficult to sustain a view of life that emphasized the awful sovereignty of God, the sinfulness and helplessness of man, and the necessity for salvation by God's miraculous and arbitrary grace.

Under the impact of the eighteenth-century Enlightenment, a large segment of the more sophisticated classes had abandoned the inscrutable, omnipresent God of the Calvinists for Deism's remote and kindly Creator. Others had moved in the same direction more gradually, retaining the outward forms and language of orthodox Christianity, but coming to believe that a reasonable God was favorably disposed toward all men, that men were sufficiently endowed with reason to be capable of goodness, and that the objective of a religious life ought to be goodness in this world rather than God's arbitrary salvation in a world to come. Such opinions spread rapidly even among the direct descendants of seventeenth-century Puritanism, the New England Congregationalists, and violent controversy broke out between the liberal and orthodox factions. By the end of the century the liberal Congregationalists, who tended to be the wealthier and better educated, were breaking off to form separate churches and taking the name Unitarians.

While Unitarianism was a minority movement in the churches, Christian orthodoxy unquestionably was at a low ebb in the last quarter of the eighteenth century. The mighty orthodox counteroffensive, the Great Awakening of the 1730's and 1740's, had spent its force, the Revolution had brought with it the spiritual and moral laxity usual in wartime, Deism was growing popular and militant, and the orthodox themselves had become listless and begun to acquiesce in compromises with the spirit of the age.

It was under these circumstances that the orthodox clergy resorted to the emotional techniques of the Great Awakening to launch another vigorous counteroffensive known as the Great Revival. Really a series of revival movements beginning around the turn of the century, the Great Revival kept the country in religious ferment for twenty-five years, obliterating the last traces of Deism and for the first time bringing a majority of Americans into the Protestant churches. But America did not return to Calvinism. For in the process of capturing America, Protestant Christianity was itself captured and transformed by the Romantic optimism and individualism of American culture.

One phase of the Great Revival began with a series of spectacular "camp meetings" in Kentucky. These week-long extravaganzas of religious enthusiasm spread rapidly over the West, spawning a host of poorly educated but highly effective revival preachers. Travelling up and down the West, these emotional revivalists left in their wake a host of new churches, mainly of the less sophisticated popular denominations, Baptists and Methodists.

Meanwhile President Theodore Dwight of Yale and his protégé Lyman Beecher were showing the conservative clergy in the East how to use a more restrained revivalism as a technique for combating Unitarianism and maintaining the hegemony of orthodox Congregationalism. At the same time the Congregationalists were cooperating with the Presbyterians in a joint campaign to evangelize the frontier areas of western New York and the Old Northwest. The revival movement and the western missionary effort both culminated in the 1820's in the spectacularly successful evangelism of Charles Grandison Finney. This former lawyer combined emotional intensity with some shrewdly devised new techniques—cottage prayer meetings preceding his revival meetings, the full participation of women, the "holy band" of zealous young helpers to pray individually with the religiously smitten —to produce an explosion of emotional piety that entrenched a revivalistic "Presbygationalism" in the western regions.

Nearly all the revivalists started from positions they would have regarded as theologically orthodox, but they were more interested in the effectiveness, the preachability, of what they were saying than in its theological correctness. They quickly found that it was easiest to evoke the desired emotional response by preaching that God was anxious to save sinners, that sinners need only accept God's love. Many Presbyterians and the more conservative Protestants of all denominations in the South resisted this tendency, but the main body of American Protestantism moved gradually and unconsciously toward a Romantic theology. Love was viewed as the essence of the Christian life. God was love, freely offering his love to all who would accept it. Conversion was the emotional experience of acceptance and loving response. In some versions, as with many Methodists and in the theology that Finney himself finally taught, conversion was viewed as carrying with it a kind of spiritual perfection. The tone of this Romantic Protestantism was clearest perhaps in hymns like "O Love That Will Not Let Me Go" and its juvenile counterpart "Jesus Loves Me."

UTOPIANISM AND HUMANITARIANISM

Wherever the Great Revival burned—and especially in the frequently ravaged "burnt over district" of western New York—it left behind a bed of glowing embers ready to be fanned into all kinds of extravagant perfectionist and utopian movements. Most of these movements were millennialist, expecting Christ's early return to establish the Kingdom of God on earth. There was an excited outburst of expectation when the Reverend William Miller calculated from Biblical prophecies the time of Christ's return, but believers were disillusioned when the event did not occur, either in the originally predicted spring of 1844 or, after Miller had corrected his calculations, on October 21 of that year.

Various groups that looked forward to an early millennium sought in the meantime to gather together those who had been "perfected" through conversion into communities that would be without sin or blemish. Because they emphasized the primacy of love in all relationships and the freedom from sin that comes with salvation, these perfectionist utopians had particular difficulty with conventional notions about the proper relations between the sexes. One group, led by John Humphrey Noyes, established a flourishing community at Oneida, New York, that rejected private property for common ownership and exclusive marriage for a carefully regulated system of "complex marriage." An even more successful group, the Shakers, solved the problem of exclusive love by practicing celibacy in their many communities. The most durable of all these movements was Mormonism, which derived from Joseph Smith's claim that he had discovered in upstate New York some golden plates containing new revelations from God and which for a time sanctioned the practice of polygamy.

In addition to the religiously-oriented utopian movements, the Romantic age produced many secular utopian communities. Perhaps the best known was Brook Farm at Roxbury, Massachusetts, which was supported by many people on the fringes of the Transcendentalist movement. A more ambitious community at New Harmony, Indiana, was founded by Robert Dale Owen, son of the English textile manufacturer and social reformer Robert Owen. The most extensive movement in secular communitarianism was inspired by Charles Fourier, a French social philosopher who had calculated rationally the optimum size and organization for the ideal socialistic community which he called a "phalanx." Attracting the support of the prominent New York editor Horace Greeley, the Fourierists established some forty or fifty phalanxes in the United States. In general, the secular utopias did not fare as well as those that had a religious motivation to keep their members loyal to the communitarian ideal. Many of the latter survived late into the nineteenth century, dwindling away only as the ebbing of religious revivalism dried up their source of recruits.

The perfectionist impulse that produced the utopian communities also inspired a broader series of movements aimed at wiping out every individual and social evil that the age could identify. Much of this reformist activity was devoted to previously neglected classes of unfortunates. Dorothea Dix led the crusade that persuaded state legislatures to establish institutions for the care of the mentally ill. A related movement induced a number of states to undertake extensive programs of penal reform, emphasizing rehabilitation rather than merely punishment of criminals. For the first time facilities were developed for educating the deaf, dumb, and blind. Indeed, the great movement for publicly supported common schools for all children got its real start in this perfectionist age with Horace Mann's ambitious program in Massachusetts leading the way. Women assumed prominent roles in the whole spectrum of reform activity and along with their other involvements agitated for an equal status for members of their sex.

The reform movements that had the greatest impact were those most closely associated with the Great Revival. In the early stages of his revivalist campaign in Connecticut, Lyman Beecher had devised the technique of organizing through local churches voluntary societies of laymen to promote various moral and evangelical objectives. By the late 1820's these local societies had developed into a group of regional and national federations with paid agents to organize new local societies, raise funds, and carry out the various objectives of the federations. The American Home Missionary Society, which hired evangelists to carry the Great Revival into the West, was one of the first of the national federations. It was soon joined by other national societies that devoted themselves to such religious objectives as foreign missions, distributing Bibles and religious tracts, promoting Sunday schools, and saving sailors. Leadership and financing for all these societies came from the same group of revivalistic "Presbygational" ministers and philanthropists led by Beecher and Finney.

The developing Romantic theology of the Great Revival soon inspired a reform impulse that went beyond the evangelical objectives of the earliest societies. Finney in particular was preaching that conversion caused a disposition of "disinterested benevolence" in the converted, and his revivals left behind numbers of converts anxious to find some object on which to lavish their disinterested benevolence. The first object to be discovered was the drunkard.

The fantastic consumption of alcoholic beverages in the early republic unquestionably constituted a serious social problem. Lyman Beecher had early been shocked by the extent of drunkenness at ministerial ordinations, and as the revival spirit spread he helped inspire the organization of local temperance societies, which aimed at moderation rather than complete abstinence in the consumption of alcohol. When this proved ineffective, Beecher began campaigning for total abstinence, and in 1826 the American Society for the Promotion of Temperance was organized with total abstinence as its goal. Sending evangelists through the country to persuade people to sign a pledge of total abstinence, the Society claimed five thousand local branches with a million members by 1834.

Turning to politics, the temperance forces secured a local option law in Massachusetts in 1838 and the first statewide prohibition law in Maine in 1846. Soon most of the northern states had legislated against alcohol. By contrast with twentieth-century prohibitionism, the nineteenth-century movement was much weaker in the South, where only the border states of Delaware and Tennessee resorted to legislative prohibition.

The temperance movement was merely the first of the reform movements inspired by the Great Revival. By the 1830's the head-quarters for the benevolent societies had shifted from Boston to New York City where Finney had been established as pastor of a great "free" church (charging no pew rents) for the poor and where re-sided the two leading financial angels of the general benevolence move-ment, the merchant brothers Arthur and Lewis Tappan. Into New York every May poured an army of the benevolent-minded from every part of the country to attend a series of annual conventions of all the societies. New societies were continually being organized for every conceivable purpose: to promote peace, to stop the carrying of mails on Sunday, to stop the wearing of corsets. Amid this welter of do-goodism, the unfocussed impulses of disinterested benevolence created by the Great Revival finally found their great and absorbing object: the institution of Negro slavery.

ABOLITIONISM

Before 1830 the organized antislavery movement had been small and ineffectual, drawing its support mainly from those persons, notably Quakers, having strong religious scruples against human bondage. A scattering of manumission societies, principally in the upper South, sought to encourage owners to free their slaves, and Benjamin Lundy had maintained for some years an effective antislavery journal. In addition the American Colonization Society had been seeking without much success to promote the migration of free Negroes to Africa, a conservative approach to the problem that aroused the suspicion of both the defenders and critics of slavery.

Only when the British Parliament's widely-publicized debates over emancipation caught the attention of the leaders of the American benevolence movement did antislavery begin to become a major force on this side of the Atlantic. In 1830 the Tappan brothers helped organize an antislavery society in New York. The following year young William Lloyd Garrison left Benjamin Lundy's employment to set up his own militant antislavery newspaper *The Liberator* in Boston. Over the years to come Garrison and the small group of zealous anti-slavery men he inspired in New England were to furnish an uncom-promising ideology for the growing antislavery movement, while the Finney-Tappan benevolence movement was to commit its mass base of support, stretching west from New York, almost wholly to the cause.

At first antislavery was only one among the many causes espoused by the Tappans and their associates. The turning point came when one of Finney's ablest young converts and apprentice evangelists Theodore Dwight Weld became wholly committed to the antislavery cause. In 1833 Weld enrolled at Lane Seminary in Cincinnati, a school that had just been established under Lyman Beecher's presidency to train Finney's converts for the ministry. Proselytizing among his fellow students, Weld provoked the famous Lane Debate, a revivalistic discussion of slavery that lasted for eighteen days and nights and ended with the conversion of virtually the entire student body to the abolitionist cause. Meanwhile the Tappan and the Garrison groups had come together in uneasy alliance to form the American Anti-Slavery Society, which now employed Weld and his fellow Lane converts as agents. During the mid-thirties these men and others conducted a whirlwind evangelistic campaign through New England, New York, Pennsylvania, and the Old Northwest, which resulted in the conversion of some whole communities to antislavery and the organization of over a thousand local antislavery societies with more than one hundred thousand members.

The abolitionism preached by Weld and his associates emphasized the moral evil of slavery and the religious duty of good men to align themselves against it. At times the abolitionists seemed more interested in demonstrating their own moral purity by taking a stand against slavery than in pressing for any practical steps to eradicate it. At first they naively hoped to persuade slaveholders to abandon the institution by sending into the South tons of pamphlets portraying the sin of holding human beings in bondage.

Despite the rapid growth of the movement, abolitionism remained highly unpopular in much of the North. Many Northerners who had no great fondness for slavery feared that antislavery agitation endangered the Union. Still others were deeply infected with the same race prejudice that bolstered slavery in the South. Prominent abolitionists had to face hostile mobs, and one editor, Elijah Lovejoy, was actually killed for his antislavery views.

Yet the abolitionists gained support far beyond their own ranks when they moved into politics in the mid-thirties with a petition campaign asking Congress to abolish slavery and the odious slave trade in the District of Columbia. Many Northerners who shied away from the constitutionally difficult question of abolition in the slave states were glad to support the abolitionist petitions with reference to the national capital over which Congress had unquestioned jurisdiction. Northern opinion generally was indignant when Congress responded to southern pressure in 1836 by adopting a "gag rule" refusing to consider petitions relating in any way to slavery. At this point ex-President John Quincy Adams, serving out the remainder of his life in the House of Representatives, took up the cause. Originally not an abolitionist, "Old Man Eloquent" was infuriated by this denial of the constitutionally guaranteed right of petition. Supported by a growing body of northern opinion, he carried on a dogged fight against the gag rule until it was eventually repealed in 1844. Though the North was still far from abolitionized, the steady agitation of the question was gradually conditioning increasing thousands of voters to view the slaveholding section of American society with hostility.

THE SOUTH AND SLAVERY

Meanwhile white Southerners were being forced to re-examine their attitudes toward their "peculiar institution." Christianity and the liberal principles of the Declaration of Independence affected Southerners just as much as Northerners. During the latter part of the eighteenth century many of the South's outstanding leaders had emancipated their slaves, denouncing slavery as incompatible with the ideals of the Revolution. Thomas Jefferson and other liberal Southerners had counted on the gradual operation of economic forces to eliminate slavery in the South as was already being done in the North. As late as the Missouri debate in 1820, southern Congressmen refused to defend slavery in the abstract, arguing instead that the unfortunate institution had been inherited and was difficult to eradicate.

Yet southern opinion had already begun to shift in a direction that would ultimately lead to civil war. The fundamental cause for change was the market revolution. Until the end of the eighteenth century, the stronghold of slavery had been in the Chesapeake tobacco region of Virginia and Maryland. The economic depression in this region following the Revolution had encouraged the spread of anti-slavery sentiment and afforded some grounds for Jefferson's hope that the institution might wither away. But farther south, along the coast of South Carolina and Georgia, the slave plantation system had continued to flourish, and with the invention of the cotton gin in 1793, the high profits of cotton culture stimulated the rapid spread of plantation slavery into the upcountry of these two states. These two were the only states that permitted a resumption of the barbarous foreign slave trade until its prohibition by Congress in 1808.

The most spectacular expansion of plantation slavery came during the boom years following the War of 1812 when it flooded over the newly opened lands of Alabama, Mississippi, and Louisiana. Taking deep root as a flourishing economic system, the chief source of wealth and spur to enterprise, slavery became increasingly impossible for white Southerners to surrender. The cotton boom in the lower South dampened antislavery tendencies in the upper South by creating a heavy demand at high prices for the surplus slaves of the declining tobacco kingdom. Nonslaveholders, too, came to feel that they had a stake in the institution. Only about a fourth of the white families in the South ever owned slaves, and even among the slaveholding minority only 12 per cent owned as many as twenty slaves. But the South was as deeply infected as any other part of the country with the spirit of enterprise that the market revolution generated, and in the South the acquisition of slaves was becoming the primary and almost the exclusive means of raising one's economic and social status.

At the same time another factor was reinforcing the white South's growing economic attachment to slavery. Thomas Jefferson had assumed that deep antipathies between white men and Negroes would make emancipation unthinkable without some plan for removing the emancipated slaves from the United States. This conviction that the two races could not live side by side in freedom received a powerful impetus in the 1790's when the slaves on the nearby French West Indian island of Santo Domingo rose in rebellion, murdering or forcing into exile thousands of their former masters. From this time on, the more the white South became attached to slavery as an economic institution, the more it feared its slaves, and consequently the more it insisted on slavery as an institution for controlling this dangerous population. Alarms over threatened slave insurrections became more frequent, some with a basis in fact and others arising more from imaginations made excitable by fear and guilt.

A real insurrection finally came in August, 1831, when a slave named Nat Turner led an uprising in Southampton County, Virginia. Over sixty whites were killed before the rebels were crushed. A wave of hysteria washed over the whole domain of slavery, and the Virginia legislature was frightened into the Old South's only full and free debate over the peculiar institution. Not a voice was raised to justify slavery in the abstract, and proposals for gradual emancipation were barely defeated.

The entire South sensed that a fateful choice had been made. The fears of slave insurrection had culminated just at the time when slavery was becoming too entrenched as an economic institution to be surrendered and at the very moment when the American antislavery movement was launching a massive propaganda barrage against slavery appealing to Christian and liberal values that white Southerners shared. Slowly and reluctantly Southerners faced the fact that, if slavery were to be retained, they could no longer ease their consciences with hopes for its eventual disappearance or tolerate the expression of such hopes in their midst. Southern minds must be nerved for a severe struggle in defense of the institution to which they now saw themselves committed. So southern leaders of the Calhoun school began trying to convince themselves and others that slavery was a "positive good," while southern legislatures abridged freedom of speech and the press, made manumission difficult or impossible, and imposed tighter restrictions on both slaves and free Negroes.

Yet the proslavery arguments never succeeded in relieving the majority of white Southerners from varying degrees of moral uneasiness or feelings of guilt. Like all men unsure of their ground but unable to change it, Southerners responded to attacks on slavery with mounting vehemence. Even in the 1830's, when both Southerners and Northerners were still preoccupied with the Jacksonian political issues, the abolitionists' petitions provoked such violent congressional debates that the gag rule had to be imposed. Within another decade the explosively emotional quarrel over slavery would move to the center of the political stage, there to remain until blood was shed.

FOR FURTHER READING:

In the absence of an adequate general account of Romanticism in American thought, the starting point must be the series of essays by George Boas and others, *Romanticism in America* (1940). Van Wyck Brooks presents a rich mosaic of cultural and intellectual life in *The Flowering of New England, 1815–1856* (1936)*. The older work by Octavius B. Frothingham is still the fullest account of *Transcendentalism in New England* (1876), and Henry Steele Commager's *Theodore Parker: Yankee Crusader* (1936)* describes a major figure on the fringes of the Transcendentalist movement. Institutional aspects of religion in the Romantic era are treated in William Warren Sweet, *Religion in the Development of American Culture, 1765–1840* (1952). For the Great Revival in the West, see Charles A. Johnson, *The Frontier Camp Meeting* (1955); and the *Autobiography* (1856)* of a famous western revivalist, Peter Cartwright. For the Great Revival in the East and revivalism's connection with perfectionism and reformism, see Whitney R. Cross, *The Burned-over District* (1950); and Timothy L. Smith, *Revivalism and Social Reform in Mid-Nineteenth Century America* (1957). A general account of religion, utopianism, and reform in this period is Alice Felt Tyler, *Freedom's Ferment: Phases of American Social History to 1860* (1944)*. In *No Man Knows My History: The Life of Joseph Smith* (1945), Fawn M. Brodie traces the beginnings of Mormonism, one of the more fascinating outgrowths of the period's religious ferment.

Louis Filler has written a fine account of *The Crusade against Slavery* (1960). Gilbert H. Barnes, *The Anti-slavery Impulse, 1833–1844* (1933) is the classic study of the origins of the abolition movement in the Great Revival. The most important of the revivalist-abolitionists is treated in Benjamin P. Thomas, *Theodore Weld: Crusader for Freedom* (1950); the New England abolitionists, slighted by Barnes, are given their due in Russel B. Nye, *William Lloyd Garrison and the Humanitarian Reformers* (1960); and a prominent Negro abolitionist is best revealed through his autobiography, *The Life and Times of Frederick Douglass* (1881)*. On the Old South, the early chapters of W. J. Cash, *The Mind of the South* (1941)* are a brilliant interpretation; and Clement Eaton, *A History of the Old South* (1949) is a comprehensive account. Special aspects of the Old South are ably treated in Frank L. Owsley, *Plain Folk of the Old South* (1949); and Clement Eaton, *Freedom of Thought in the Old South* (1940). The best account of slavery is Kenneth M. Stampp, *The Peculiar Institution* (1956); while Stanley Elkins, *Slavery* (1959), is a series of suggestive essays. William S. Jenkins has surveyed *Pro-Slavery Thought in the Old South* (1935); a leading pro-slavery theorist is described in Harvey Wish, *George Fitzhugh: Propagandist of the Old South* (1943); and Wish has reprinted Fitzhugh's most important works, *Sociology for the South* (1854) and *Cannibals All!* (1857), in a modern edition under the title *Ante-Bellum* (1960)*.

Conflicting attitudes toward the antislavery movement can be compared in the documents presented in Bernard Weisberger, *Abolitionism: Disrupter of the Democratic System or Agent of Progress?* (Berkeley Readings in American History, 1963)*.

*Available in paperback edition.

1840   **William Henry Harrison** (Whig) elected over Martin Van Buren (Democrat).

1841   Vice President **John Tyler** becomes president on death of Harrison.

Whig Congress repeals the independent treasury system.

Land Act of 1841. Pre-emption principle allows settlers to buy public lands they occupy at minimum price.

Tyler vetoes successive bills chartering a national bank and is disowned by the Whig party.

1842   Tariff of 1842. Whig measure extending substantial protection to American manufactures.

Webster-Ashburton Treaty with Great Britain, settling the Maine boundary and other disputed matters.

1844   Tyler's treaty for the annexation of Texas defeated in the Senate.

James K. Polk (Democrat) elected over Henry Clay (Whig).

1845   Texas annexed by joint resolution of Congress.

1846   Democratic Congress reinstitutes the independent treasury system.

Tariff of 1846. Substantial reduction of rates.

Polk's veto of Rivers and Harbors bill checks policy of internal improvements.

Oregon controversy with Great Britain compromised.

Polk precipitates Mexican War by insisting on extreme Texas boundary claim.

Wilmot Proviso proposed to bar slavery from any territories acquired from Mexico.

1848   Treaty of Guadelupe Hidalgo. Ends Mexican War, with the United States paying Mexico for a vast cession in the Southwest.

Zachary Taylor (Whig) elected over Lewis Cass (Democrat) and Martin Van Buren (Free Soiler).

1849   Gold Rush to California.

1850   Vice President **Millard Fillmore** becomes president on death of Taylor.

Compromise of 1850: (1) California admitted as free state; (2) Utah and New Mexico territories organized on principle of squatter sovereignty; (3) Texas surrenders claims to area in New Mexico, and United States assumes Texas debt; (4) slave trade abolished in the District of Columbia; (5) a more stringent Fugitive Slave Law enacted.

1852   **Franklin Pierce** (Democrat) elected over Winfield Scott (Whig).

CHAPTER 13

MANIFEST DESTINY AND
SECTIONAL CONFLICT
1840–1852

Though the Whig and Democratic leaders continued to battle each other in the early 1840's over tariff, national bank, and internal improvements, these old issues no longer excited Americans as they had in Jackson's day. The market revolution had completed its psychological conquest of the country, and with hard times receding an enterprising generation was engrossed in the pursuit of wealth and status.

For countless thousands the pursuit led west toward the perennial American goal of cheap land and a fresh start. But now, for the first time in the American experience, there seemed a limit to the supply of cheap, fertile land. In the South the tide of settlement rolled up to the boundary of the Mexican province of Texas. Farther north it was nearing the treeless Great Plains which were thought unfit for cultivation.

Yet neither political nor geographical boundaries were to halt the two-hundred-year advance of the American frontier. Since the 1820's American settlers had been pouring into Texas, where in 1836 they had rebelled against Mexican authority, defeated a Mexican army, and set themselves up as an independent republic looking toward union with the United States. During the same period wagon trains from the Missouri frontier had been crossing the Plains along the northern borders of Texas and pushing on to trade with the ancient Spanish-Mexican settlement of Santa Fe on the upper Rio Grande. Still farther north fur traders had followed in the track of Lewis and Clark, exploring the Rocky Mountains and bringing back tales of new promised lands beyond in the Oregon country and Mexican California. Meanwhile, the enterprising merchants of Boston and Salem and New York, sending their ships around the Horn to pick up hides on the California coast, were becoming excited about the possibility of dominating trade

[163]

with the Orient from the magnificent Pacific harbors at San Diego, San Francisco, and Puget Sound.

While Americans were discovering the farther West, romantic assumptions were intensifying their faith in the superiority and glorious destiny of their free institutions. Rapidly the idea grew that it was the "manifest destiny" of these free institutions to spread over all the vast, thinly inhabited, and lightly held territories between the Mississippi Valley and the Pacific Ocean.

The growing enthusiasm for territorial expansion further confused an already tangled political situation while raising an ominous question. The decade of the 1840's opened with the Whigs and Democrats still battling inconclusively over old issues that no longer stirred the voters, and both parties were for different reasons somewhat demoralized. Under these circumstances the issue of expansion was a godsend to ambitious politicians with various axes to grind. But it was a dangerous issue. The controversy over slavery was making the country edgy. The mounting hostility between North and South was becoming too apparent to be wished out of consciousness. A great crusade to fulfill the manifest territorial destiny of the United States might reunite Americans in enthusiastic patriotism. But it could also incite a disastrous sectional conflict over the territorial spoils.

TIPPECANOE—AND TYLER TOO

Such possibilities were still far from most men's minds as the Whigs took over the national government following their great victory in the presidential election of 1840. Under the guidance of Senator Henry Clay, President Harrison called a special session of Congress to pass the traditional Whig program—repeal of the independent treasury system, a new national bank, a higher protective tariff, and a scheme for distributing the federal land revenues among the states. Yet the Whigs were the unluckiest of the major political parties. Within a month after his inauguration, "Old Tippecanoe" died, leaving the Whig program at the mercy of the vain, stubborn Vice President, John Tyler of Virginia.

Tyler had left the Democratic party when Jackson threatened to coerce the South Carolina Nullifiers in 1832, and he retained much of the old-fashioned Virginian attachment to state rights. He went along with Clay in repealing the independent treasury system, but after indicating a willingness to approve the right kind of national fiscal agency, he vetoed two successive bills chartering a new national bank. By other vetoes, Tyler made it clear that Clay could have either

[164]

a higher protective tariff or distribution, but not both together. Clay chose increased protection for manufacturers, and the Tariff of 1842 raised duties generally to the levels that had existed before the Compromise Tariff of 1833. Meanwhile, in a futile effort to secure distribution also, the Whig Congress had included in the Land Act of 1841 the principle of *pre-emption*. Pre-emption enabled any head of a family to settle on 160 acres of the public domain before they were offered for sale at the customary auction and then to bid them in at the minimum price of $1.25 an acre.

Thus the stubborn Virginia President had frustrated every part of the Whig program except the higher tariff and had caused Clay to accept a pre-emption system for which he had no great enthusiasm. The overwhelming majority of the Whig Congressmen, both northern and southern, turned on Tyler in fury and read him out of the Whig party. Every member of his Cabinet resigned, only Secretary of State Daniel Webster tarrying a little longer than the others. Webster's delay was partly to enable him to complete the negotiations with England that led up to the Webster-Ashburton Treaty of 1842, compromising a dispute over the boundary between Maine and Canada. Bereft of party support, Tyler took up the issue of expansion, hoping that it might enable him to run for president in 1844. Secretly his administration began negotiating with the Texas authorities for a treaty of annexation.

The Texas question had long been regarded as a threat to the delicate sectional balances that held the two parties together as national organizations. From the moment of the Texas Revolution in 1836, antislavery men had been denouncing it as a plot by southern filibusterers to extend the area of slavery, and even Jackson, despite his warm friendship for the Texas leader Sam Houston, had delayed recognition of the new republic until after Van Buren was safely elected. Van Buren had similarly avoided the question of annexation during his administration as being too dangerous to the harmony of the Democratic party.

Thus, by pushing the Texas question to the fore, Tyler might greatly embarrass the old party leaders and either run for president as the candidate of a pro-Texas third party or displace Van Buren as the Democratic nominee. The potential for sectional conflict over the Texas issue was increased when Tyler brought in Calhoun as his Secretary of State to complete the secret negotiations for an annexation treaty. The treaty was signed and sent to the Senate in April, 1844. Along with it Calhoun sent a copy of a dispatch he had written to the British minister, Richard Pakenham, denouncing British interference in Texas, defending slavery as a positive good, and justifying annexation mainly as a measure in defense of slavery. Calhoun's Pakenham letter, irritating even moderate antislavery men, doomed the treaty to defeat in the Senate and produced violent political turmoil on the eve of the presidential nominating conventions.

THE PRESIDENTIAL ELECTION OF 1844

Clay and Van Buren had both seemed assured of nomination by their respective parties, and both wished to keep the Texas issue out of the campaign. At the end of April, hard on the heels of Calhoun's Pakenham letter, they published simultaneous letters opposing immediate annexation. Shortly thereafter Clay was nominated by the Whig convention, but Van Buren's Texas letter aroused a storm of opposition against him at the Democratic convention.

Although a majority of the delegates to the Democratic convention had originally been instructed for Van Buren, the late-developing Texas excitement had produced, especially in the southern and western states, a decided popular reaction in favor of a pro-Texas candidate. Van Buren's Texas letter was the signal for Texas men and anti-Van Buren men to join forces in a last-ditch fight to block his nomination. Their strategy was to insist on a two-thirds majority for nomination. Many delegates who felt bound by their instructions to vote for Van Buren on the early ballots were nevertheless able to vote for the two-thirds rule that made his nomination impossible.

But if Van Buren could not muster a two-thirds majority, neither could his leading rival Lewis Cass of Michigan. The deadlock might have destroyed the Democratic party if the convention had not finally hit upon a compromise candidate. James K. Polk had recently suffered two successive defeats in campaigns for governor of Tennessee, but he was almost the only Democrat of any prominence who could command the confidence of all the feuding factions. The hard money Van Buren wing of the party respected him as a protégé of Jackson and able leader of the Democratic forces in the House of Representatives during the Bank War, while as a slaveholding Southerner and outspoken advocate of immediate annexation, he was acceptable to the expansionist, anti-Van Buren wing.

Having nominated Polk by acclamation, the convention adopted a platform calling for "the reoccupation of Oregon and the reannexation of Texas, at the earliest practicable moment." The Oregon question had recently generated considerable enthusiasm in the Northwest, but even there it had been overshadowed by the Texas question. The Oregon plank seems to have been included primarily to remove the sectional sting from the inescapable Texas issue.

The ensuing election reflected the nearly equal division of popular strength that the matured two-party system had by this time produced. In the closest presidential result to this time, Polk received 49.6 per cent of the popular votes to 48.1 per cent for Clay. His margin in the electoral college was provided by New York, where the diversion of a small number of normally Whig votes to an antislavery third-party candidate swung the balance in favor of the Democrats.

The Texas men interpreted this narrow victory as a mandate for annexation. Just before Polk's inauguration in early 1845 Congress approved, by joint resolution rather than treaty, the admission of Texas as one of the United States.

THE POLK ADMINISTRATION

Polk was one of the hardest working and most effective men ever to occupy the White House. Unimaginative, undramatic, and without much prestige when he entered office, he was nevertheless spectacularly successful in getting what he wanted from a deeply divided Democratic party and Congress and from other countries. He wanted a great deal.

Polk was first of all an old-fashioned, doctrinaire, Jacksonian Democrat. He wanted an independent treasury system reinstituted, and from his first Congress in 1846 he got it. He wanted a drastic downward revision of the tariff, and the same Congress gave him a tariff act incorporating the antiprotectionist principle of moderate rates designed chiefly for revenue and expressed in uniform percentages with only moderate discrimination in favor of the most important American manufactures. He wanted an even further reduction in the already circumscribed federal expenditures for internal improvements, and his vetoes of long-sanctioned appropriations for river and harbor improvements were sustained. Thus under Polk the traditional Democratic policies were finally established, to remain substantially unchanged until the Civil War.

While cleaning up this unfinished Democratic business, Polk was simultaneously moving aggressively along the new line of expansionism. With the Texas issue settled, he wasted not a moment in turning his attention to the Oregon country. This vast expanse of territory, stretching from the Rockies to the Pacific and from the border of Mexican California at 42° on the south to Russian Alaska at 54°40′ on the north, had been jointly occupied by the United States and Great Britain with the proviso that either nation could terminate the joint occupation by giving one year's notice. In the early 1840's, American settlers began finding their way to Oregon in substantial numbers and disputing possession of the land with the well-established British posts of the Hudson's Bay Company. This migration had created considerable interest in Oregon in the states of the upper Mississippi Valley, northwestern Democrats had begun agitating for a more vigorous assertion of American claims to the country, and the Democratic platform had declared that "Our title to the whole of the Territory of Oregon is clear and unquestionable."

Polk's inaugural address echoed the Oregon plank in the Democratic platform, but he felt bound to renew once more his predecessors' offer of a compromise boundary along the forty-ninth parallel, an offer the British had rejected several times. When the British minister rudely rebuffed this proposal without even referring it to his government, Polk took a more bellicose line. Calling on Congress to give notice of the termination of joint occupancy, he asserted the American claim to the whole of the territory.

For a time war threatened, but both sides were ready for any face-saving solution along the forty-ninth parallel. Polk allowed intimations to reach the British that if they made a proper proposal he would submit it to the Senate for advice. Such a proposal came in June, 1846, and the Senate advised its acceptance. The 49° boundary already established east of the Rockies was extended west to the Pacific with a short detour down the Straits of Fuca to leave Britain the whole of Vancouver Island.

THE MEXICAN WAR

Polk's bold Oregon game with the British was rendered more dangerous by his bellicose diplomacy in another quarter. For a time he seemed to be courting simultaneous wars with Great Britain and with Mexico. The principal prize in the latter case would be Mexican California with its splendid Pacific harbors. There can be little doubt that Polk was determined to secure the vast domain between the southwestern borders of the United States and the Pacific and that he deliberately provoked war when the Mexicans refused to sell it.

Having won its independence from Spain in 1821, Mexico was a proud young republic with a political system so unstable that any government compromising the national honor was sure to be driven from office. The Texas Revolution had been a severe blow to Mexican pride. Stubbornly refusing to recognize Texan independence, the Mexicans regarded the annexation of Texas by the United States as an act of aggression and had broken off diplomatic relations.

It was at this point that Polk entered the White House. One of his first acts was to order an American army to the western frontier of Texas to ward off any attack by Mexico while the formalities of annexation were being completed. He was less justified in authorizing the army to advance beyond the traditional Texan boundary at the Nueces River and in announcing his determination to enforce the highly questionable Texas claim that its territory extended to the Rio Grande River. Then he sent a minister to Mexico with an offer that the United States would assume the unpaid claims of American citizens against Mexico for property losses during the Mexican Revolution in return for Mexican acceptance of the Rio Grande boundary. In addition the envoy was to try to purchase New Mexico and California.

Since the Mexicans had not indicated any willingness to reopen regular diplomatic negotiations, it should not have been surprising that they refused to receive Polk's minister. Nevertheless Polk chose to regard this rebuff as a cause for war. He had already ordered the American army to advance to the Rio Grande, and now he prepared to ask Congress for a declaration of war. The Mexicans saved him the trouble of precipitating hostilities. A Mexican force encountered an American patrol just east of the Rio Grande, and in the ensuing skirmish sixteen Americans were killed or wounded. Polk got the news just in time to modify his war message. Mexico, he told Congress, "has invaded our territory, and shed American blood upon the American soil." War was declared on May 13, 1846.

The Mexican War was morally the least justifiable of American wars but militarily the most successful. General Zachary Taylor led the army on the Rio Grande into north central Mexico and at Buena Vista in February, 1847, won a brilliant victory over a superior Mexican force commanded by General Santa Anna. Shortly thereafter another American army under General Winfield Scott landed at Vera Cruz on the Gulf Coast and by September had occupied the enemy capital, Mexico City. Meanwhile Colonel Stephen Kearney had led another American army across the plains from Missouri, seizing Santa Fe on the upper Rio Grande, and then moving on west across the mountains and deserts to establish American authority in California.

When General Scott captured Vera Cruz, President Polk had sent Nicholas P. Trist, chief clerk of the State Department, to accompany Scott's army and seize upon any opportunity for negotiating a peace that would give the United States the territory it wanted. The fall of Mexico City reduced the country to political chaos, and by the time Trist found a government stable enough to negotiate, he had infuriated President Polk by insubordinate behavior. Defying an order to return home, Trist went ahead and negotiated the Treaty of Guadalupe Hidalgo, signed in February, 1848. By this treaty, Mexico recog-

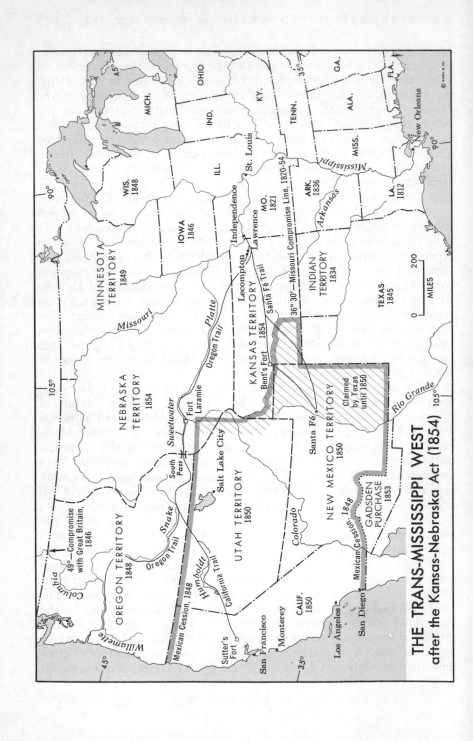

THE TRANS-MISSISSIPPI WEST
after the Kansas-Nebraska Act (1854)

nized the Rio Grande boundary and ceded New Mexico and California, while in return the United States was to assume the claims of its citizens against Mexico and pay Mexico $15 million. Since these were the terms Polk had instructed the repudiated diplomat to secure, he signed Trist's treaty, and the Senate ratified it.

TOWARD THE FIRST SECESSION CRISIS

Despite the brilliance of its military victories and the vastness of its territorial acquisitions, the United States emerged from the Mexican War more deeply divided and distracted than ever. The enthusiastic expansionism of men like President Polk had been partly an effort to find a cause that would unite all Americans in a new burst of patriotic nationalism and furnish a vaccine against the insidiously spreading infection of sectional enmity. But the infection had already taken too firm a hold, and the remedy served to intensify rather than alleviate the disease.

The enthusiasm for expansion was most widespread in the Northwest and the Southwest and among Democrats, whereas in the East and among Whigs the transparently aggressive character of the Mexican War had made it unpopular with many from the beginning. The Whigs carried on a constant criticism of the administration's war policy, and in the North they began to denounce the war as a southern project for expanding the area of slavery. Northern voters were told, too, that a slavery-dominated Democratic party had demonstrated its indifference to the interests of the free states by reducing the tariff, cutting off appropriations for rivers and harbors, and surrendering the American claim to the whole of Oregon. Thus the war helped to crystallize in thousands of northern minds the conviction that the area of slavery and the political power of slavery must not be allowed to expand.

In the summer of 1846, while Congress was debating a bill appropriating money for negotiations with Mexico, a Pennsylvania Democrat named David Wilmot offered an amendment declaring that slavery should be forever barred from any Mexican territories to be acquired. The Wilmot Proviso, though defeated when first introduced, infuriated southern Congressmen and provoked a struggle of such mounting violence that within three years it would bring the country to the brink of secession and civil war.

The end of the Mexican War made it indispensable to enact some legislation for government in the new territories, but no legislation could be passed without settling the status of slavery there. Northerners dominated the House of Representatives and insisted on the Wilmot Proviso while Southerners, relying on a Senate still evenly balanced between slave and free states, asserted their right to migrate with their property, including slaves, into the territory they had helped to win. President Polk urged that the Missouri Compromise line of 36°30′ be extended to the Pacific as the boundary between slave and free territory, telling Northerners that slavery could never get a foothold in the arid Southwest no matter what Congress provided. But Polk had made the serious blunder of announcing that he would under no circumstances accept a second term. Having expended his patronage in getting his ambitious program through his first Congress, he was less and less able to control Democratic Congressmen as his term neared its end, and the extremists, both North and South, defeated his and all other efforts to reach a compromise solution.

It was in this atmosphere that the presidential election of 1848 occurred. The free-soil issue had split both parties deeply along sectional lines. The rift was potentially deeper among the Whigs because antislavery sentiment was stronger in the northern wing of their party, but they successfully obscured their differences by again adopting the strategy of nominating a military hero. This time he was General Zachary Taylor, the hero of Buena Vista, a plain, honest old soldier who owned a plantation and slaves in Louisiana. Democratic differences were more conspicuous because Polk's no-second-term position had prompted a prolonged intraparty struggle over the nomination. At the cost of great bitterness the Democratic convention finally nominated Senator Lewis Cass of Michigan, hated by the Van Burenites for his role in blocking their chieftain's nomination four years previously.

The major-party nominations provoked the formation of a formidable antislavery third party. Deeply suspicious of the slaveholding Taylor, the more fervently antislavery Whigs organized a Free Soil party with the Wilmot Proviso as their platform. They were quickly joined by the "Barnburners," or Van Buren Democrats, who were just as anxious for revenge against Cass and the rival "Hunker" faction of the New York Democratic party as they were to stop the spread of slavery. The new party nominated Van Buren for president and Charles Francis Adams, Whig son of John Quincy Adams, for vice president.

Taylor's personal popularity, his nonpartisan posture, the special appeal that his slaveholding status gave him in the South, and the Barnburner secession from Cass in the North made the outcome a foregone conclusion. "Old Rough and Ready" did not have to say where he stood on the territorial question, while Cass advanced a compromise solution of great future significance but little immediate appeal to the more zealous defenders of the southern and northern positions. This was the doctrine of popular sovereignty by which the settlers in the territories would be left to settle the status of slavery for themselves. Taylor won handily while the Free Soilers garnered a substantial popular vote and elected nine congressmen.

THE COMPROMISE OF 1850

By the time Taylor took office in March, 1849, the discovery of gold in California had attracted a horde of unruly immigrants and created a desperate need for legislation providing government in the new territories. Meanwhile Southerners had been further infuriated by proposals in Congress to abolish slavery and the slave trade in the District of Columbia. Calhoun was passionately exhorting Southerners to abandon the old parties and unite in a new sectional party to defend the South's rights and safety. The more radical Southerners were demanding that the South secede if the Wilmot Proviso were applied in any form to any territory, and a number of southern governors and legislatures took measures looking toward secession in such an eventuality. In this crisis the new President, to the shock of those Southerners who had supported him because he was a slaveholder, encouraged the Californians to bypass the territorial stage, to draw up a state constitution without congressional authorization, and to apply directly for admission as a free state. Thus Taylor's first Congress met in December, 1849, to find a free California waiting on its doorstep and passions running so high that members carried Bowie knives and revolvers and the House of Representatives took three weeks and sixty-three ballots to elect a Speaker.

The aged Henry Clay now stepped forward to rally the forces of moderation and compromise, presenting a series of proposals as an "omnibus" settlement of all the disputed questions arising from the slavery issue. (1) California was to be admitted as a free state. (2) The remainder of the Mexican cession was to be organized into two territories, Utah on the north and New Mexico on the south, leaving the status of slavery for their inhabitants to settle. The Utah territory was to provide a government for the large body of Mormons who had migrated to the shores of the Great Salt Lake in 1846 after being driven out of their settlements in Missouri and Illinois. The New Mexico territory involved an additional complication because Texas claimed that its territory extended to the upper Rio Grande, embracing Santa Fe and half of the old Spanish-Mexican province of New Mexico. Clay therefore further proposed that (3) Texas should give up its claims to the New Mexican area in return for which the United States would assume the Texas public debt; (4) the slave trade but not slavery should be abolished in the District of Columbia; (5) the old federal fugitive slave law of 1790, the enforcement of which had been increasingly defied and impeded in the North, should be strengthened.

Southerners complained that Clay's compromise would cost the South its equal strength in the Senate while making only the single concession to the South of a stronger fugitive slave law. Equally formidable opposition came from President Taylor and the bulk of the northern Whigs who were determined that the advance of slavery should be decisively halted. Even after Taylor died in July, 1850, and was succeeded by the procompromise Vice President Millard Fillmore, Clay was unable to gain a majority for his omnibus proposal. Only when the Illinois Democrat, Stephen A. Douglas, took command and broke Clay's omnibus bill into separate proposals did the various compromise measures pass.

The success of the Compromise depended on the willingness of the aroused lower South to accept it. In Georgia, Mississippi, and other states, party lines broke down as Whigs and moderate Democrats joined forces to defeat the advocates of secession. The country breathed sighs of relief, and the majority of politicans everywhere committed themselves to the Compromise measures as a "final solution" of the slavery controversy.

In the presidential election of 1852 the Democratic nominee, Franklin Pierce of New Hampshire, won because of his allegiance to the Compromise. Again the Whigs had turned to a military hero, nominating General Winfield Scott. But Whigs could no longer sustain themselves in the South as copartisans of the increasingly antislavery northern Whigs. With southern Whigs being forced into the Democratic party, the Whig party was already moribund as a national entity, and Scott was its last presidential candidate.

FOR FURTHER READING:

Ray A. Billington has written the best general account of *The Far Western Frontier, 1830–1860* (1956); and Henry Nash Smith, *Virgin Land* (1950)*, is a brilliant interpretation of the meaning of the West for the American imagination. The trade between Missouri and Santa Fe is described by a participant in Josiah Gregg, *Commerce of the Prairies* (1844)*; the fur trade is vividly and soundly reconstructed in Robert G. Cleland, *This Reckless Breed: Trappers of the Southwest* (1950) and Bernard De Voto, *Across the Wide Missouri* (1947); and Francis Parkman's account of his experiences along *The*

Oregon Trail (1849)* is a classic. Bernard De Voto has written a distinguished book about the momentous developments on the western and expansionist fronts during *The Year of Decision, 1846* (1943)*; while Norman A. Graebner's *Empire on the Pacific* (1955) emphasizes the commercial ambitions that sharpened American appetites for the Pacific coast. Marquis James's *The Raven* (1929)* is a vivid biography of the Texas leader Sam Houston; the near disintegration of the Democratic party over the Texas question is described in James C. N. Paul, *Rift in the Democracy* (1951)*; and the third volume of Charles M. Wiltse's *John C. Calhoun* (3 vols., 1944–1951) is invaluable for the political history of the 1840's. Alfred H. Bill, *Rehearsal for Conflict* (1947) is a good account of the Mexican War; and Holman Hamilton's *Zachary Taylor* (2 vols., 1941–1951) is excellent on both the war and the Taylor administration. Allan Nevins' biography of *Fremont, Pathmarker of the West* (1955) throws light on many aspects of western exploration and the Mexican War; and Nevins' *Ordeal of the Union* (2 vols., 1947) is the best analysis of the sectional controversy leading to the Compromise of 1850.

*Available in paperback edition.

PRESIDENTIAL ELECTIONS AND MAJOR EVENTS, 1852–1860

1852   **Franklin Pierce** (Democrat) elected over Winfield Scott (Whig).
Harriet Beecher Stowe publishes *Uncle Tom's Cabin.*

1854   Kansas-Nebraska Act. Repeals Missouri Compromise and organizes Kansas and Nebraska territories on principle of squatter sovereignty.

1856   **James Buchanan** (Democrat) elected over John C. Fremont (Republican) and Millard Fillmore (American).

1857   Dred Scott *vs.* Sandford. Roger B. Taney's Supreme Court declares that Congress cannot bar slavery from the territories.

Buchanan fails to force the admission of Kansas to statehood under the proslavery Lecompton Constitution.

Hinton Rowan Helper publishes *The Impending Crisis of the South.*

1858   Lincoln-Douglas Debates. In his contest with Abraham Lincoln for Senator from Illinois, Stephen A. Douglas argues, in his "Freeport Doctrine," that slavery cannot survive in a territory without positive supporting legislation.

1859   John Brown's Raid.

1860   Radical Southerners break up the Democratic party by withdrawing when the Charleston convention refuses to endorse their demand for a congressional slave code.

Abraham Lincoln (Republican) elected over Stephen A. Douglas (Northern Democrat), John C. Breckinridge (Southern Democrat), and John Bell (Constitutional Unionist).

1860–1861   Seven states of the lower South secede and organize the Confederate States of America.

CHAPTER 14

A HOUSE DIVIDING

1843–1860

Hoping that the Compromise of 1850 had finally settled the slavery controversy, the American people again turned their energies to the march of enterprise. The fifties were a decade of unprecedented economic growth and prosperity, the climax of the market revolution and the beginning of the industrial revolution. Yet the very process of economic growth and physical expansion provoked a renewal of sectional conflict that could be resolved only by civil war.

CULMINATION OF THE MARKET REVOLUTION

The exuberance of the forces generating the market revolution had also generated boom-and-bust cycles that had periodically inhibited the country's full potential for economic growth. Not until the years between 1843 and 1857 did the developed market economy have a chance to show what it could do in an extended period without a major depression.

The results were spectacular. Between 1844 and 1854 the total value of all commodities produced rose by 69 per cent, the highest gain for any decade until the 1880's. Accompanying this rise in gross production was an equivalent gain in the efficiency of production with output per worker increasing by 10 per cent in the 1840's and 23 per cent in the 1850's, the latter increase again to be unequalled until the 1880's. This rapid economic growth was in part simply a further acceleration of the market revolution in its various aspects after a slackening of pace during the depression of 1837–1843.

Commercial agriculture resumed its growth at a faster rate than ever. By 1846 the formerly protectionist Northwest was exporting so much wheat to foreign markets that it turned toward free trade and provided the votes by which the tariff reductions of that year were passed. By 1850 the Northwest exceeded the Northeast in wheat production, and this was only a prelude. The advance of the agricultural frontier north into Wisconsin and west across Iowa into eastern Kansas and Nebraska, coupled with the widespread use of Cyrus McCormick's mechanical reaper, pushed northwestern wheat production from some thirty million bushels in 1850 to almost one hundred million bushels in 1860. Meat packing and the production of corn and hogs expanded almost as spectacularly.

Similarly in the South the cotton crop increased by 60 per cent in the 1840's and 100 per cent in the 1850's. Sugar production in Louisiana rose fourfold between the mid-1830's and 1859. The increasing productivity and profitability of southern agriculture were reflected in the rising price of slaves. In the 1790's a prime field hand could have been bought for $300. By 1840 the price had risen to $1,000, and by 1860 it ran up to $1,500.

The impressive growth of a regionally specialized commercial agriculture was closely related to the perfection of a national system of transportation and communication, providing facilities for swift, cheap, and efficient interregional and international exchanges of goods and services. Turnpikes, canals, and steamboats had been efficacious enough for the earlier stages of the market revolution, but not until the 1850's was the transportation system brought to full efficiency by the creation of a great railroad network.

Although railroad construction had received a start in the 1830's, only local lines had been completed before the depression of 1837–1843 stalled further progress. As late as 1848 the country had only six thousand miles of track. Mileage doubled in the next four years and reached thirty thousand by 1860. By 1857 the country had invested a billion dollars in railroads, two thirds of it during the preceding seven years.

Particularly important was the completion in the early 1850's of five great trunk lines connecting the Atlantic ports of Boston, New York, Philadelphia, Baltimore, and Charleston with the Ohio and Mississippi valleys by way of Albany and Buffalo, Pittsburgh, Wheeling, and Atlanta and Chattanooga. From these terminals the eastern trunk lines rapidly developed connections by new western railroads to the emerging transportation and commercial centers of Chicago, St. Louis, and Memphis. By 1855 a passenger could travel in two days from one of the Atlantic cities to Chicago or St. Louis for a fare of $20. Radiating out from the terminals and junctions of the trunk lines were a series of feeder lines bringing cheap transportation and commercial production to virtually every part of the country.

The flood of products harvested by an expanded agriculture and brought to tidewater by a perfected transportation system helped push American exports from $144 million worth of commodities in 1850 to $334 million in 1860. Imports climbed to an even higher level, the trade deficit being bridged by exports of California gold which rose from $5 million in 1850 to $58 million by the end of the decade. This swelling of foreign commerce brought with it a vigorous revival of the American carrying trade.

Another element in the economic expansion was the upsurge of immigration from abroad, especially from Ireland and Germany after the potato famine created widespread destitution in 1846. Immigrants to the United States had not numbered more than ten thousand a year before 1825, but exceeded one hundred thousand in the mid-1840's and reached an annual level of around four hundred thousand in the early 1850's. Between 1844 and 1854 nearly three million new Americans arrived from abroad. Many of these people supplied the labor for the factories that were springing up in the East, others did the hard, dirty work in railroad and canal construction. The Germans established strong colonies in such northwestern cities as Cincinnati, St. Louis, and Milwaukee, while still other immigrants swelled the tide of agricultural migration into Wisconsin, Iowa, and beyond.

THE RISE OF INDUSTRY

The impressive economic gains of the late 1840's and the 1850's were more than a matter of growth along established lines. The rounding out of the vast and lucrative national market set the stage for the industrial revolution in the United States. A new sector of the economy was moving into the dynamic role. Earlier the profits of the American carrying trade during the Napoleonic Wars had provided the initial impetus that jarred the economy out of its static staple-exporting phase. Then the swelling flood of commercial crops, cotton above all others, had fueled the transportation revolution and the creation of a national market economy. Now, from the 1850's on, industry was to be the primary stimulant for a sustained and massive expansion of production that would create the most abundant economy that history had yet known.

Large-scale factory production had been developing gradually since the War of 1812, but not until the 1840's did the expansion of the industrial sector spurt ahead. The value of manufactured products in 1850 for the first time exceeded the value of agricultural products, and between 1850 and 1860 it nearly doubled: from just over $1 billion to just under $2 billion. Probably the best measure of industrial growth is increase in value added by manufacture, which is the difference in value between the raw materials used and the final manufactured products. Between 1839 and 1849 the value added by American manufacturing is estimated to have risen by 157 per cent, and between 1844 and 1854 by 134 per cent. These ten-year increases were not to be equalled in any subsequent decade of the nineteenth century.

Cotton textile manufacturing had been the pioneer industry in the United States. In 1791 the successful Rhode Island merchant Moses Brown had employed Samuel Slater, who understood the recently developed English textile machinery, to set up a small spinning plant. Soon there were a number of such small enterprises putting out the yarn they spun to be woven into cloth on hand looms in homes. When imports of English cloth were cut off during the War of 1812, the infant American textile industry spurted ahead to meet the demand.

Besides giving American manufacturers a temporary monopoly of the domestic market, the war also caused large amounts of capital to be diverted from the disrupted shipping business to manufacturing. Beginning in 1813 a group of wealthy Boston merchants led by Francis Cabot Lowell poured the unprecedented capital of $600,000 into the Boston Manufacturing Company at Waltham, Massachusetts. This was the first really large-scale and completely integrated manufacturing enterprise in the United States. The Waltham operation included every step in the manufacturing process from raw cotton to the final printed cloth with the most advanced machinery used at every stage. The healthy profits at Waltham encouraged the promoters to erect similar plants at Lowell and other places in New England where water power was available.

The example of the Waltham system hastened the development of large plants using power-driven machinery in other industries: woolens, flour, shoes, carpets, stockings, and paper. The assembly-line or continuous-process system was even adopted for nonmachine operations, as in the great pork butchering and packing establishments that grew up at Cincinnati and later Chicago. The small, scattered iron works of the colonial period expanded, with the adoption of the rolling mill and the substitution of coal for charcoal fuel, into larger-scale enterprises. The demand for iron created by the railroad boom helped quadruple the output of pig iron between 1842 and 1860.

By the 1840's stationary steam engines had been developed to the point where they could substitute for water power in industrial production. This strengthened the tendency for industry to locate in cities, and industrial growth contributed greatly to a marked trend toward urbanization. In 1820 only 6 per cent of the American people had lived in places of 2,500 or more population. By 1860 the figure had risen to nearly 20 per cent, and New York had become the first city to pass the 1,000,000 mark. The greater part of this urban growth had occurred during the 1840's and 1850's. Much of it was produced by the increased volume of international and interregional trade that funnelled through the cities, but industrial development was becoming almost as important. Five of the fifteen largest cities in 1860 had more than 10 per cent of their population engaged in manufacturing, while some of the newer and smaller cities like Newark, Lowell, and Lynn were almost wholly industrial.

The steady trend toward concentrating production in larger and larger industrial units had undermined the independence of the old artisan class and created a growing new working class of permanent wage earners. This shift in the status and prospects of workingmen had given rise in the 1820's and 1830's to a number of labor unions of skilled artisans in such crafts as printing, shoemaking, and the building trades. The craft unions had organized city federations in New York and Philadelphia, workingmen's parties had entered local politics, there had been strikes for the ten-hour day, and in 1834 a National Trades Union had been formed.

This early labor movement was swept under by the Panic of 1837, but as prosperity returned in the 1840's so did the craft unions. Strikes became numerous and successful enough so that the ten-hour day was general by the middle 1850's. Again a National Trades Union was organized, and again, in 1857, a depression wiped out labor's organizational gains. This time, though, several nationally organized craft unions survived the debacle.

The union movement largely bypassed the growing body of unskilled or semiskilled workers who manned the new mechanized factories. For several decades after the establishment of the Waltham plant, the New England cotton mills had recruited their labor force mainly from young, unmarried New England girls who lived in paternalistically managed company boarding houses and worked in the mills until they married. This system broke down after the Panic of 1837, and from this time on the labor force for all kinds of factories was recruited increasingly from unskilled immigrants. Factory hours were long, and factory wages provided only a mean living. Not for many decades would the industrial worker begin to share in the vastly expanded wealth created by the industrial revolution.

CONFLICT AGAIN

With North and South riding the greatest tide of prosperity either section had ever known, it may seem strange that the decade of the 1850's ended in civil war. Indeed direct conflicts of economic interest between the sections over national legislation seemed at the lowest ebb since the Panic of 1819. Southerners were no longer frustrating the Northwest's demands for federal aid to internal improvements: between 1850 and 1860 the federal government granted eighteen million acres of the public lands to aid construction of forty-five railroads in ten states. The tariff issue no longer engaged men's passions as northern industry continued to flourish under the low rates of 1846.

Yet the very lushness of prosperity and growth was fostering imperial visions in the two sections: in the South visions of an expanding cotton-slavery empire and in the North visions of an expanding free-soil empire. As these competing expansionist impulses headed toward a collision, they were inevitably intensified by the moral dimensions of the slavery question.

The South's growing insecurity over the institution of slavery was particularly dangerous. By the 1850's the North was rapidly outstripping the South in population and potential political power, while Northerners were demonstrating their deepening disapproval of slavery by blocking enforcement of the stringent new Fugitive Slave Law, one of the few concessions to the South in the Compromise of 1850. These circumstances help explain the mounting stridency with which southern spokesmen proclaimed the merits of slavery—and more specifically the South's hysterical reaction to two famous books published during the 1850's. The first, Harriet Beecher Stowe's novel *Uncle Tom's Cabin* (1852) was a sentimental portrayal of slavery's brutal impact on some appealingly drawn slave characters. The second, Hinton Rowan Helper's *Impending Crisis of the South* (1857) was an all too effective argument by a nonslaveholding North Carolinian that slavery was disastrous to the nonslaveholding white majority in the South. Both books were not only denounced but violently suppressed in the South, while in the North they won wide audiences and helped harden antislavery sentiment.

Paradoxically, not since Jeffersonian days had the South had as much power in the federal government as it had in the 1850's. The campaign of 1852 had demonstrated that the northern and southern wings of the Whig party were too far apart on the slavery question to hold together any longer, leaving the Democrats as the one great national party. Northern Democratic politicians competed against each other for promotion in the party and in the federal government by going as far as they could toward satisfying southern demands and thereby winning southern support. Therefore the South came to have the dominant voice in the Democratic presidential administrations of

Franklin Pierce and James Buchanan. As long as the Democrats remained a national party and the South's northern Democratic allies could win elections in a good part of the North, the South could in effect control the country and counteract the northern advantage in population and representation. Eventually the South, out of its insecurity, demanded more from its northern Democratic allies than they could grant without losing elections in the North.

What the South was demanding in the 1850's was the right for slavery to expand, but this insistence grew out of complicated motives. It was in part simply the cotton-slavery imperialism of a prosperous and expansive social and economic system. It was also an effort to bolster the South's slipping proportion of representation in the federal government through the creation of additional slave states so as to defend slavery better from political attack. It was finally a demand that Northerners recognize the moral legitimacy of slavery by acknowledging its right to grow and thus relieve the white South from the intolerable burden of justifying and defending an unjustifiable and indefensible social system.

THE TERRITORIAL QUESTION

It seemed clear by the 1850's that there was no further room for new slave states within the territorial limits of the United States under the political arrangements that prevailed. The Missouri Compromise barred slaves from the remaining unorganized parts of the Louisiana Purchase, the Oregon territory had been organized on free-soil principles, and geography seemed to prohibit slavery's spread over the arid wastes of the New Mexico and Utah territories.

Under these circumstances, expansionist Southerners turned their attention to the Caribbean area, and the Pierce administration attempted to purchase Cuba from Spain. This effort had the advantage of appealing on nonsectional grounds to a nationalistic "Young America" group who wanted to continue the expansionism of the 1840's. But when a trio of southern-oriented diplomats issued the Ostend Manifesto proposing that Cuba be seized if it could not be purchased, there was such a reaction in the North and in Spain that the Cuba project had to be dropped. Despite this setback, many Southerners continued to agitate throughout the 1850's for expansion into the Caribbean area and to support illegal filibustering expeditions that sought to overturn weak Central American governments and pave the way for American annexations.

With the outlook for foreign expansionism dim, a small group of southern politicians began a fateful effort to push slavery into that part of the Louisiana Purchase hitherto reserved as free soil. Democratic Senator Stephen A. Douglas of Illinois was anxious to pass a bill providing territorial government for the Kansas and Nebraska country, partly to facilitate the start of a transcontinental railroad that might terminate in his home town of Chicago. Senator David R. Atchison of Missouri, representing a slaveholding constituency across the Missouri River from the area in question, had staked his political life on a promise that his constituents would be able to take their slaves into the new territory. Atchison joined with a group of powerful southern Senators to insist that no territorial bill would pass unless it contained a clause repealing the Missouri Compromise prohibition of slavery. Douglas gave in to their demand, a weak President Pierce was persuaded to use all the power of the national administration to secure enough northern Democratic votes to pass the bill, and the Kansas-Nebraska Act of 1854 was the result.

Douglas argued that the Act was simply an extension of the democratic "popular sovereignty" principle already applied to the New Mexico and Utah territories by the Compromise of 1850. But indignation blazed up in the North at this cynical abrogation of a sacred compromise and at the servile northern Democrats who obeyed an "aggressive slavocracy." While only a small minority of Northerners were disposed to interfere with slavery where it already existed, far more were ready to stop its further spread. With the Kansas-Nebraska Act, cotton-slavery imperialism provocatively challenged free-soil imperialism. The immediate response was the organization of a new sectional party in the North calling itself "Republican" and vowing its opposition to the least extension of the area of slavery.

Meanwhile Kansas, the more southerly of the two new territories, was filled with violence and bloodshed as proslavery and antislavery factions contended for control of the territorial government. New England abolitionists contributed guns and funds for free-soil immigrants, while "border ruffians" from Missouri crossed the river to furnish illegal ballots and armed support to the proslavery faction. When President Pierce again yielded to southern pressure and recognized a proslavery legislature elected largely by illegal voters from Missouri, the enraged free-soilers elected their own legislature and governor. A proslavery force raided the free-soil capital, and in retaliation a fanatical free-soiler named John Brown invaded an isolated proslavery settlement and butchered five inoffensive residents. In the sporadic violence that followed more than two hundred people were killed.

In retrospect the demand for repeal of the Missouri Compromise appears to have been a suicidal strategy from the standpoint of southern interests. Southern opinion generally was not strongly in favor of such a demand, and even many of the more radical Southerners admitted that slavery would probably never be established in any of the disputed territories. What the South was really demanding was an acknowledgment of its technical right to take slaves into all territories, an acknowledgment of the legitimacy of slavery. But for the sake of this technical right, southern leaders put their northern Democratic allies in an untenable position in their home constituencies and called into existence a formidable antislavery party that would soon destroy their control of the federal government.

BUCHANAN RIDES THE STORM

The new Republican party, drawing heavily from former Whigs and outraged Democrats, grew by leaps and bounds in the North. As the presidential election of 1856 approached, the Democrats were also threatened by another new party, the Americans or Know-Nothings, who appealed to anti-immigrant, anti-Catholic sentiment. To meet this double challenge, the Democratic national convention dropped the discredited Pierce and nominated the cautious, conservative, and pro-southern James Buchanan of Pennsylvania. The new American party nominated ex-President Fillmore and drew a substantial vote, especially from former Whigs in the South, but carried only one state. The major feature of the election was the strong showing of the new Republican party which carried all but five of the free states for its candidate John C. Fremont. Only by the lavish use of money in Pennsylvania and Indiana and by the support of an almost solid South, did the Democrats squeak through with a bare electoral majority.

Meanwhile the attempt to apply the popular sovereignty principle was deepening the chaos in Kansas and Washington. Southerners were insisting that popular sovereignty did not allow the people of a territory to bar slavery until they came to draft a constitution preparatory to admission as a state. Shortly after Buchanan's inauguration in March, 1857, a southern majority on the Supreme Court upheld the southern contention in the celebrated case of Dred Scott. Chief Justice Roger B. Taney's opinion denied the slave Scott's contention that he had been made free by residence in the free territory of Iowa, saying that Congress could not bar slavery from the territories—and it was a logical inference that territorial legislatures could not either.

While northern opinion reacted to this further evidence of slave power aggression, President Buchanan was trying to remove the issue from politics by pushing Kansas into statehood. Failing in his efforts to get a fair referendum on slavery in Kansas, the President unwisely succumbed to southern pressure and endorsed a proslavery state constitution drafted by a notoriously unrepresentative convention at Lecompton. At this point Senator Douglas and a number of other northern Democrats, fighting for political survival at home, revolted against the President and blocked the admission of Kansas under the Lecompton Constitution.

At the height of the Kansas crisis in 1857, the country's nerves were further strained by a severe financial crisis. The Republicans capitalized on the hard times to broaden their appeal. The southern-dominated Democratic Congress had just passed the Tariff of 1857, reducing protection to the lowest level since 1812. It was easy to blame the depression on the new tariff and to win support from hard-hit manufacturers and industrial workers by promises of higher rates. At the same time the Republicans made themselves more appealing to northwestern farmers by agitating for a homestead act giving free homesteads of 160 acres to actual settlers on the public lands. A wave of religious revivals followed the financial crash, further exciting the public mind and intensifying the North's moral sensitivity on the slavery question.

THE ELECTION OF 1860

It was under these unsettling circumstances that the slavery debate began to be dominated by the approaching presidential election of 1860. Stephen A. Douglas of Illinois was the leading aspirant for the Democratic nomination and perhaps the only one who could win enough support in the North to be elected. But Douglas was in an exceedingly difficult dilemma, one reflecting the dilemma of the Democratic party. In order to be nominated he had to allay southern suspicions arising from his opposition to the Lecompton Constitution, but it was questionable whether he could allay these suspicions and win the nomination without taking a position so prosouthern that he would lose the subsequent election. And in the meantime he had to win re-election to the Senate against the leading Illinois Republican, a shrewd Springfield lawyer named Abraham Lincoln.

In his famous series of debates with Lincoln across Illinois in 1858, Douglas sought to escape his predicament by taking an ambiguous position. On the one hand he maintained his doctrine of popular sovereignty which would technically permit Southerners to take their slaves into the territories and deny territorial legislatures the right to bar slavery before statehood. But at the same time he assured the Illinois voters, in what came to be called the Freeport Doctrine, that slaves could never be successfully held in a territory unless the territorial legislature had passed a slave code or positive legislation for protecting and policing slave property. Douglas won the senatorial election by a narrow margin, but his Freeport Doctrine made him even less acceptable to Southerners as a presidential nominee.

By now southern demands were reaching an extreme of presumption and folly. The more radical Southerners had already begun to suspect that slavery, as Douglas claimed in the Freeport Doctrine, could not be sustained in the territories without a slave code. Now they moved beyond the claim that neither Congress nor territorial legislatures could bar slavery from the territories and began demanding that the federal government positively protect and guarantee slavery in the territories through enactment of a congressional slave code. Most Southerners were not insistent on this radical demand, and certainly very few Southerners had any real thought of taking slaves into any of the territories in any case. But as tension increased and excitement mounted, southern politicians feared to be outdone in defending their constituents' supposed interests, and the most extreme positions came to the fore. Southern insecurity had generated demands for more and more guarantees and assurances, these apparently aggressive movements of the slaveholding section had frightened the North into more determined resistance and spawned the Republican party, and this hardening resistance in the North had intensified southern insecurity and generated even greater demands.

Southern insecurity reached a peak of near hysteria in October, 1859, when the violent abolitionist John Brown, of Kansas fame, led a raid on the federal arsenal at Harper's Ferry, Virginia, seizing guns and ammunition with which he planned to arm a wholesale slave rebellion. Though Brown and his followers were quickly subdued, a paroxysm of terror ran through the South, and terror quickly turned to rage when it was learned that respectable antislavery men in the North had backed the plot.

Against this background the Democratic national convention assembled at Charleston, South Carolina, in April, 1860. Radical Southerners insisted that the convention endorse their demand for a congressional slave code. When the pro-Douglas majority refused, after violent debate, the delegates from eight states of the lower South withdrew, and the convention had to adjourn. Two separate Democratic conventions then met in Baltimore, the northern-dominated one nominating Douglas and the southern-dominated one nominating John C. Breckinridge of Kentucky. Meanwhile the Republicans had met in

Chicago to nominate Abraham Lincoln, and union-minded old-line Whigs from the border states, calling themselves the Constitutional Union party, had put John Bell of Tennessee into the running as a fourth candidate.

Lincoln had no support outside the free states, but there he made an almost clean sweep which was by itself enough for a majority in the electoral college. For the rest, Breckinridge carried most of the South handily; Bell won three border slaves states; and Douglas, though running second to Lincoln in popular votes, won the electoral votes of only Missouri and half of New Jersey.

SECESSION

For years the small but steadily growing body of radical southern fire-eaters had been looking forward to this day, and they lost no time in making the most of their opportunity. South Carolina had been in a secessionist mood since the days of nullification, impatiently waiting for her stolid sister-states to awaken to their danger. At last enough of the southern population was sufficiently aroused by the election of a "Black Republican," and South Carolina could lead the way. Hastily calling a state convention, the Palmetto State formally repealed its ratification of the federal constitution on December 20, 1860. Within six weeks she had been followed by the six Gulf States where the fire-eaters were strongest: Mississippi, Florida, Georgia, Alabama, Louisiana, and Texas.

As the border states hesitated, the waning Buchanan administration fretted in helpless impotence. The politicans at Washington scurried about seeking a formula for compromise, but the victorious Republicans would not listen to a proposal that countenanced the slightest extension of slavery, while the Southerners demanded at least a token concession on the territorial question. Meanwhile the seceded states had sent delegates to Montgomery, Alabama, organized themselves as the Confederate States of America, and chosen Jefferson Davis of Mississippi as their president.

FOR FURTHER READING:

For economic development in the 1840's and 1850's, the references listed in Chapter 9 will continue to be useful. Marcus Lee Hansen, *The Atlantic Migration, 1607–1860* (1940)*, has a good account of the upsurge of immigration during these years. John R. Commons and others have written the standard *History of Labour in the United*

States (4 vols., 1918–1935); and Hannah Josephson's *The Golden Threads* (1949), is a good account of the girl workers in the New England textile mills. William O. Scroggs describes Caribbean adventures of various Americans in *Filibusters and Financiers* (1916). The drift toward Civil War is traced with distinction in Avery O. Craven, *The Growth of Southern Nationalism, 1848–1861* (1953); Roy F. Nichols, *The Disruption of American Democracy* (1948)*; and Allan Nevins, *Ordeal of the Union* (2 vols., 1947) and *The Emergence of Lincoln* (2 vols., 1950). The more important biographies include: Laura A. White, *Robert Barnwell Rhett* (1931); David Donald, *Charles Sumner and the Coming of the Civil War* (1960); and George Fort Milton, *The Eve of Conflict: Stephen A. Douglas and the Needless War* (1934). Indispensable to an understanding of secession is Ollinger Crenshaw, *The Slave States in the Presidential Election of 1860* (1945). Modern readers will also gain much insight from those two famous books of the 1850's, Harriet Beecher Stowe, *Uncle Tom's Cabin* (1852)*, and Hinton Rowan Helper, *The Impending Crisis of the South: How to Meet It* (1857)*.

Every reader may analyze the secession crisis for himself through the documents presented in Philip Staudenraus, *The Secession Crisis, 1860–1861* (Berkeley Readings in American History, 1963)*.

*Available in paperback edition.

1860   **Abraham Lincoln** (Republican) elected over Stephen A. Douglas (Northern Democrat), John C. Breckinridge (Southern Democrat), and John Bell (Constitutional Unionist).

1860–1861   Seven states of the lower South secede and organize the Confederate States of America.

1861   Confederates bombard Fort Sumter, beginning the Civil War.

Virginia, North Carolina, Tennessee, and Arkansas secede and join the Confederacy.

Morrill Tariff. Substantial upward revision of duties, beginning a long period of high protection.

Trent affair. Union naval officer seizes two Confederate diplomats from a British vessel.

1862   Homestead Act. Free farms of 160 acres to actual settlers.

Morrill Land Grant Act. Land grants to the states for agricultural and mechanical colleges.

Pacific Railroad Act. Federal subsidies for a railroad from Omaha to California.

Slavery abolished in the territories and the District of Columbia.

Second Confiscation Act. Freeing escaped or captured slaves of Confederates.

1863   Lincoln's Emancipation Proclamation. Declaring free all slaves in Confederate areas.

National Bank Act. With a supplementary act of 1864 establishes a system of banks issuing a uniform paper currency based on holdings of federal bonds.

Turning point of the war in July, when Union forces capture Vicksburg on the Mississippi and stop Lee's invasion at Gettysburg.

Lincoln announces his "ten per cent plan" for the easy restoration of the seceded states to the Union.

1864   Lincoln vetoes the Wade-Davis bill, containing a harsher congressional plan for restoration of the seceded states to the Union.

Abraham Lincoln (Republican) re-elected over George B. McClellan (Democrat).

1865   Lee surrenders to Grant at Appomattox Courthouse.

Lincoln assassinated.

The Thirteenth Amendment abolishes slavery throughout the United States.

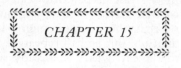

CHAPTER 15

THE CIVIL WAR

1861–1865

When Abraham Lincoln arose to deliver his inaugural address on March 4, 1861, few people had any very clear idea of how the secession problem should be handled. Some voices in the North counselled letting the "erring sisters depart in peace." The abolitionist minority called for a holy war to free the slaves. Majority opinion in the North was increasingly convinced that the Union must somehow be preserved, but there was no clear mandate for military coercion of the seceded states. The war that finally came, like most wars, came not because anyone deliberately willed it, but out of a fortuitous chain of circumstances whose outcome reflected only imperfectly the conscious collective will of North or South. Insofar as a guiding will affected the outcome, it was the will of Abraham Lincoln.

LINCOLN AND THE SECESSION CRISIS

The new President was known to the country only as a lanky and apparently uncultivated lawyer-politician from the prairies of Illinois. He had won brief notice years earlier when his opposition to the Mexican War caused Illinois voters to repudiate him after a single term in Congress. Not until his debates with Douglas in the senatorial campaign of 1858 had he attracted national attention. Elected president by a minority of the voters, he had given little public indication of his policy in the months between the election and the inauguration. Actually he had blocked all efforts at compromise by privately opposing any arrangement that left the slightest room for the expansion of slavery. But this position could be put down to political expediency—compromise on the territorial question would have left the infant Republican party little reason for existence—and gave no clue as to what he would do when he assumed office.

Certainly Lincoln was not prepared to lead a crusade to free the slaves. He had insisted that slavery was wrong and that its expansion should be stopped so that the country might look forward to its eventual peaceful extinction. But he had repeatedly denied any disposition to interfere with slavery where it already existed. He had also denied in his debates with Douglas that he was "in favor of bringing about in any way the social and political equality of the white and black races." A "physical difference" would prevent the two races from ever living together on equal terms, he had said, and, therefore, "I, as much as any other man, am in favor of having the superior position assigned to the white race." He wanted slavery excluded from the territories so that "white men may find a home—may find some spot where they can . . . settle upon new soil and better their condition in life . . . as an outlet for *free white people everywhere*."

The inaugural address revealed both a leader of unsuspected stature and a position around which northern opinion could rally. With an eloquence that no president since Jefferson had attained, Lincoln pleaded for preservation of the Union. "The mystic chords of memory," he said, "stretching from every battlefield and every patriot grave to every living heart and hearthstone all over this broad land, will yet swell the chorus of the Union, when again touched, as surely they will be, by the better angels of our nature." In trying to touch these chords, he reassured the South in the most positive terms that he would countenance no act against slavery in the states where it already existed.

But the address also had a vein of iron. The Union, said Lincoln, was perpetual, any violent acts against the authority of the United States were "insurrectionary or revolutionary," and these statements were to be taken "as the declared purpose of the Union that it *will* constitutionally defend and maintain itself." Though the federal government would not initiate hostilities, the President told the South, it would "hold, occupy, and possess" the federal forts and other property in the seceded states and collect the import duties there.

It is clear in retrospect that Lincoln thus committed himself to a course that led directly to one of the bloodiest wars in history. But war was not his purpose. Eight of the fifteen slave states were still in the Union. By refusing to recognize secession while at the same time declining to proceed forcibly against the secessionists, Lincoln was seeking to reinforce the manifest Unionist sentiment in the upper South. Apparently he wanted to keep the upper South from seceding, hoping that latent Unionism would eventually overcome secessionism in the seven seceded states of the lower South.

There were several difficulties with this Union-saving strategy. One was that Lincoln exaggerated the strength of Unionist sentiment in the lower South. Another was the likelihood that the effort to hold the federal forts in the seceded states would lead to armed conflict. Armed conflict was the more likely because many of the secessionists were quite ready to provoke a crisis that would force the upper South to choose sides. The issue of peace or war came to a focus in the harbor of Charleston, South Carolina.

Practically all the federal forts and other property in the lower South had been taken over by the seceding states before Lincoln's inauguration. Of the few posts remaining in federal hands, the unfinished and lightly garrisoned Fort Sumter, located in the entrance to Charleston's harbor, had become the symbolic focus of the whole controversy over federal property. Sumter had sufficient supplies to hold out only six weeks, and a decision about its future could not be postponed. Lincoln finally informed the Confederate authorities that he was sending a naval expedition to reprovision Sumter. They in turn ordered their general at Charleston to demand the fort's immediate evacuation and in case of refusal to bombard it. The demand was made and refused, and on April 12, 1861, the Confederate shore batteries opened fire.

Lincoln responded by calling on the states for seventy-five thousand troops. Rather than make war on their fellow Southerners, four states of the upper South—Virginia, North Carolina, Tennessee, and Arkansas—now reluctantly followed the lower South out of the Union. The four slave states of Delaware, Maryland, Kentucky, and Missouri remained with the Union, though the last two had strong secessionist movements and furnished many soldiers to the Confederacy. The tables were turned on the secessionists when the strongly Unionist western section of Virginia seceded from Virginia and laid the basis for the new state of West Virginia under the aegis of the Union. Meanwhile the Confederacy had acted to consolidate the adhesion of the upper southern states by moving its capital from Montgomery to Richmond.

THE WAR BEGINS

A spirit of martial ardor swept over both sections in the spring of 1861. Northerners expected a short and easy war, while Southerners seemed oblivious of the overwhelming superiority in human and material resources against which they would have to contend. The five and a half million free people of the eleven Confederate states faced a population of twenty-two million in the twenty-three Union states. The North had a four-to-one advantage in free males of fighting age and would muster twice as many soldiers. Even if one southern soldier was worth two Yankees (as Southerners loudly proclaimed), how were southern armies to be supplied and transported? The North had 80 per cent of the country's factories and most of the coal and iron. Twenty-two thousand miles of railroad traversed the North as compared with nine thousand in the South, and the North's rail network included a series of vital trunk lines between East and West while the sprawling southern regions were but circuitously and inefficiently bound together.

Under the circumstances the South made a remarkable military showing. This was due in part to the advantage of fighting a defensive war. The North was compelled not only to invade but occupy the South, and southern commanders had the additional advantage of shorter interior lines of communication for shifting troops from one front to another. Moreover Jefferson Davis could utilize from the beginning a galaxy of outstanding generals, Albert Sidney Johnston, Joseph E. Johnston, Thomas J. ("Stonewall") Jackson, and, pre-eminently, Robert E. Lee; while Lincoln spent several years trying a succession of variously unsatisfactory commanders before he found a really able one.

The Appalachian highlands, thrusting deep into the South, divided the theater of war into two zones. Throughout the conflict the greatest public attention was focussed on the East, where the rival armies menaced each other's capitals only a hundred miles apart. Here the Confederate armies, magnificently led by Joseph E. Johnston and then by Robert E. Lee, repeatedly repelled Union invasions aimed at Richmond. General Irvin McDowell's army was turned back at Bull Run in northern Virginia in July, 1861. Lincoln's next general, George B. McClellan, tried another tack, ferrying an enormous invasion force down Chesapeake Bay and up the York River to the eastern outskirts of Richmond only to be beaten off in the series of hard-fought battles that constituted the Peninsula Campaign of May–June, 1862. Later that summer Lee trounced another Union army led by John Pope in the second battle at Bull Run and followed up this victory with an audacious advance across the Potomac River into Maryland. McClellan caught up with him at Antietam Creek, some fifty miles northwest of Washington, in September, 1862, and in a closely contested battle inflicted so much damage that the Confederates had to withdraw to Virginia.

Back on his home ground Lee was again invincible, trouncing Ambrose E. Burnside at Fredericksburg in December and Joseph E. Hooker at nearby Chancellorsville the following May. Once again the great Confederate general sought to capitalize on his success by invading the North, gambling on the hope of a decisive victory that would cut the east-west trunk railroads in Maryland and Pennsylvania, imperil Washington, and persuade the North to make peace before its superiority in manpower and material became irresistible. On July 1, 1863, Lee's seventy thousand men and the ninety thousand Union soldiers of George G. Meade faced each other from opposing ridges outside the little town of Gettysburg in southern Pennsylvania. For three days wave after wave of Confederates swept up against the strong Unionist position barely failing to flood over it. Lee was again forced to retreat to Virginia, and the South's last hope of victory was gone.

While Lee's brilliant gamble was failing in the East, the Confederacy's military doom was being more plainly spelled out in the West. Here the Mississippi, Tennessee, and Cumberland rivers afforded natural invasion routes for the combined operations of Union gunboats and armies, and here an obscure Union commander Ulysses S. Grant had been steadily and inexorably crunching deeper and deeper into the South. Forts Henry and Donelson, guarding the Tennessee and Cumberland rivers, had fallen in February, 1862. Pressing on south up the Tennessee River, Grant had inflicted a severe blow on the main Confederate army in the west at Shiloh in April and moved on into northern Mississippi. Meanwhile Union gunboats had steamed up the Mississippi from the Gulf to take New Orleans and down the Mississippi from the north to take Memphis. The last Confederate stronghold on the Mississippi, Vicksburg, fell to Grant in July, 1863, while Meade was turning back Lee at Gettysburg, and the Confederacy was cut in two.

THE CONFEDERACY AT WAR

The burden of directing the Confederate war effort fell almost wholly on the shoulders of Jefferson Davis. Lacking able subordinates in his cabinet and in the Confederate Congress, Davis perhaps took on too much of the burden of detailed administration and sometimes exercised poor judgment in decisions about military strategy and commanding officers. But only an able and conscientious executive could have kept the Confederacy operating and its armies in the field under the staggering difficulties that he faced for as long as he was able to.

At the beginning of the war Davis had high hopes of aid from Europe. France's Napoleon III was openly sympathetic as were the ruling upper classes in Great Britain, and both of these countries went so far as to recognize the Confederacy's belligerent status. But Davis was counting on the economic power of the South's cotton to produce more substantial aid—full diplomatic recognition, financial assistance, and perhaps even military intervention. The South might have built up large credits for the purchase of supplies in Europe by shipping its cotton abroad. Instead the Confederate authorities placed an embargo on cotton exports, expecting that this would force British cotton mills to close and thus bring pressure on the British government to intervene more openly on behalf of the Confederacy. Unfortunately the British mills had a year's surplus of raw cotton on hand, some alternative sources of supply were available, and although some of the cotton mills eventually shut down, their unemployed workers remained sympathetic to the more democratic North and exerted their influence against any aid to the South.

The South's best chance to drive a wedge between Great Britain and the North came in November, 1861, when a United States naval vessel stopped the British ship *Trent* on the high seas and took off the Confederate diplomats James M. Mason and John Slidell. But the United States promptly released Mason and Slidell, and Lincoln's skillful minister in London, Charles Francis Adams, was increasingly successful in preventing the British from aiding the Confederacy either directly or indirectly. And France refused to act without British support.

Meanwhile Lincoln had ordered the Union navy to blockade southern ports; and by the time the Confederacy decided to ship cotton to Europe in exchange for supplies, this was no longer possible. Cut off from all outside goods (except a trickle brought in by swift blockade runners), the Confederacy was increasingly hard put to supply its armies with munitions or its people with the ordinary necessities of life.

As the war wore on and as the Confederacy's prospects dimmed, the early enthusiasm was replaced by growing discouragement, apathy, and disaffection. The Confederate conscription law, which exempted overseers and owners of twenty slaves, was especially resented by poorer Southerners who began to say that this was "a rich man's war and a poor man's fight." Desertions became an increasingly serious problem. The South's state-rights tradition was also a source of weakness as fractious governors like Joseph E. Brown of Georgia and Zebulon B. Vance of North Carolina defied the policies of the Richmond government. It seems fair to conclude that the South's commitment to the war had been less than wholehearted in the beginning and that a growing disenchantment with it was a major factor in the Confederacy's eventual collapse.

LINCOLN AND THE WAR

Lincoln was having his problems too. The North had a large contingent of "Peace Democrats" who as the war dragged unsuccessfully on demanded a negotiated settlement. The draft law of 1863, from which the wealthy could escape by paying $300 or hiring a substitute, provoked a bloody two-day riot in New York City. At the other end of the political spectrum, Lincoln was ceaselessly hounded by a group of "Radical" Republicans who wanted to make the war an antislavery crusade and who advocated a punitive policy toward the South. Under the leadership of men like Senator Charles Sumner of Massachusetts and Representative Thaddeus Stevens of Pennsylvania, the Radicals gained great power in Congress where they set up a Joint Committee on the Conduct of the War, which constantly criticized and interfered with the President's conduct of military operations.

The split between Radical Republicans and moderate or administration Republicans was not related, however, to the series of major laws passed by the wartime Congresses. The Morrill Tariff Act of 1861 marked a turn toward higher protective duties, and subsequent legislation of 1862 and 1864 pushed duties to unprecedented levels, inaugurating an era of extravagant protectionism that would last into the twentieth century. The long fight for free land culminated in the Homestead Act of 1862, granting 160 acres to any family that wished to settle on the public domain. The Morrill Land Grant Act of 1862 donated public lands to the states for support of agricultural and mechanical colleges. In the same year Congress finally authorized the long-projected transcontinental railroad, granting thirty million acres and millions in federal bonds to the Union Pacific and Central Pacific railroad companies to build a line from Omaha to the Sacramento River. By an act of 1863 Congress established a national banking system with member banks issuing a stable currency of uniform national bank notes on the basis of their holdings of federal bonds.

In passing these important measures to serve the interests of northern farmers and business enterprise, the Congress was simply legislating the Republican platform now that the Southerners were no longer there to oppose. None of these measures aroused the controversy in the Republican party that the subject of slavery created. Anxious to mollify the loyal slave states of Delaware, Maryland, Kentucky, and Missouri, Lincoln stoutly resisted doing anything to suggest that abolition of slavery was a northern war aim. In the fall of 1861 he removed the Radicals' favorite general John C. Fremont from command in Missouri for declaring that the slaves of rebels were free. Meanwhile he sought unsuccessfully to interest Congress and the loyal slave states in a plan of gradual, compensated emancipation with the federal government footing the bill.

The Radicals were determined to force the issue, and in 1862 pushed through Congress legislation abolishing slavery in the territories and in the District of Columbia. More important was the Second Confiscation Act of 1862, declaring forfeited the property of all persons supporting the rebellion and proclaiming escaped or captured slaves to be "forever free." By this time Lincoln was becoming aware of the value of an emancipation policy in helping to win the war, especially by gaining friends for the Union in Europe. Finally, on January 1, 1863, he issued his Emancipation Proclamation. This famous proclamation freed only those slaves living in rebel areas and justified the action on the ground of "military necessity." Only as the Union armies advanced did the freedom proclaimed by the proclamation become an actuality for the slaves. Not until 1865 did the Thirteenth Amendment, forbidding slavery throughout the country, become a part of the Constitution.

The Emancipation Proclamation did not allay the Radicals' suspicion of Lincoln, but they failed to block his renomination for President in 1864. In this wartime election the Lincoln Republicans ran as the Union party, appealing to War Democrats by nominating for vice president Andrew Johnson, the Tennessee Senator who had remained loyal to the Union. The regular Democratic nomination went to General McClellan, many of whose supporters were calling for peace negotiations. The long string of Union defeats in the East had so strengthened antiwar sentiment that Lincoln might have been defeated but for some timely military successes in the West on the eve of the election.

TOWARD APPOMATTOX

It is now clear that the fall of Vicksburg and Lee's failure at Gettysburg in July, 1863, had destroyed the last chances of a Confederate victory. And by this time, after trying a long succession of commanders, Lincoln had finally found a general who would justify his confidence. Ulysses Grant, who had capped his doggedly successful western campaigns with the victory at Vicksburg, was called to the East and in the spring of 1864 made general-in-chief of all the Union armies. Before leaving the West he had consolidated Union control of Tennessee with a victory at Chattanooga. Now his grand strategy was a two-pronged final offensive against the South with General William T. Sherman leading one great Union army south from Chattanooga into Georgia and himself leading another south from Washington toward Richmond.

The twin offensives were launched simultaneously in May, 1864, the two Union armies of around one hundred thousand men each pressing back Confederate armies of around sixty thousand. In the West Sherman steadily pushed the Confederates south and by September had won the important rail center of Atlanta. Here he made his audacious decision to abandon his line of supply and wage a war of destruction between Atlanta and the sea. Devastating the countryside as he went, he was in Savannah by December, and the Confederacy had been further segmented. Turning north, Sherman reached Columbia, South Carolina, in February, 1865, and by March was in east central North Carolina.

By demoralizing the Confederate areas south of Virginia, Sherman greatly facilitated Grant's advance on Richmond. In the Spotsylvania Wilderness and at Spotsylvania Courthouse in May, 1864, Lee inflicted heavy casualties on the invading Yankees as he had so often done in the past. But this Yankee general did not withdraw to lick his wounds as had all his predecessors. By flanking movements he kept pressing south toward Richmond. At Cold Harbor Lee again inflicted frightful losses on the Union army, but still Grant pushed inexorably south, passing just east of Richmond and crossing the James River. Lee managed to shield Richmond as Grant moved around it to the south and southwest toward Petersburg. By June the two armies were entrenched facing each other in a long line bending from Richmond southward around the southern side of Petersburg.

Grant simply would not let go, and as the siege went on through the summer and fall and winter his superiority in manpower began to tell. Remorselessly he kept extending his line to the west, and Lee's line became steadily thinner and more vulnerable as he had to keep stretching it farther. By April Lee could extend his line no more and had to pull out of his entrenchments, abandoning Richmond and Petersburg. But by this time Grant had cut all the roads leading south over which Lee might effect a junction with the only remaining Confederate army of any strength. On April 9, 1865, at Appomattox Courthouse Lee bowed to the inevitable and surrendered. One month later the fleeing Jefferson Davis was captured in disguise in Georgia and imprisoned at Fortress Monroe. The Confederacy was dead.

LINCOLN AND THE SOUTH

The treatment of the vanquished South had long since become a new bone of contention between Lincoln and the Radicals. Lincoln wished to bring the rebellious states back into full membership in the Union as rapidly and painlessly as possible. By the time Union forces occupied Arkansas in December, 1863, the President was ready with his "ten per cent plan" of reconstruction. Under this plan he proposed to extend amnesty and restore confiscated property to all Confederates who would take a simple loyalty oath, excluding only high civil and military officers of the Confederacy or its states. As soon as 10 per cent of a state's 1860 electorate had taken the oath, the state could write a new constitution and rejoin the Union.

The Radicals, however, feared with considerable reason that if the southern states were reconstructed on this basis, the old ruling class would return to power and the Negro freedmen would be little better off than they had been under slavery. Anxious for a thorough-going reconstruction of southern society, they insisted that Negroes be given the ballot and that the old rebel leadership be effectively excluded from political life. As a counter to Lincoln's plan they secured the passage in 1864 of the Wade-Davis bill. This measure required a majority, rather than 10 per cent, of the 1860 voters to take a loyalty oath before reconstruction could begin and further insisted on disfranchisement of ex-Confederate leaders.

Lincoln allowed the Wade-Davis bill to die by pocket veto, but the Radicals had one tactical advantage. A state would not be fully restored to the Union until its representatives were seated in Congress, and the Radical-controlled Congress had full power over the admission of members. This power the Radicals used to deny admission to the first southern representatives who appeared under Lincoln's 10 per cent plan. In March, 1865, as the war drew to a close, they gave a further indication of their objectives by creating the Freedmen's Bureau to assist the ex-slaves in adjusting to freedom and to protect their rights in their new state.

The sharpening struggle between Lincoln and the Radicals was suddenly cut short on Good Friday, April 14, 1865, five days after Lee's surrender at Appomattox, when a demented actor and southern sympathizer, John Wilkes Booth, shot a fatal bullet into the President's head as he sat in a box at Ford's Theater.

A grieving nation suddenly discovered its great tragic hero. To Lincoln's strength and humility and eloquence and magnanimity was now added the quality of martyrdom. He had presided over the bloodiest war in the American experience, preserving the Union as the land of liberty and last best hope of man. Hesitantly and grudgingly but nevertheless in the end unmistakably, he had also made the war a struggle to include *all* men within the sphere of American liberty. Yet the Emancipation Proclamation and the Thirteenth Amendment were only a beginning. It was Lincoln's Radical critics who saw most clearly that the task of completing emancipation still lay ahead, and even his great talents could hardly have been equal to this Herculean task. Perhaps it was a timely martyrdom that translated Abraham Lincoln—a man groping toward an ideal only dimly perceptible in his society and age—into the Great Emancipator. For a century and more to come, Lincoln, the symbol, would remind his countrymen that the egalitarian dream was still unfulfilled.

FOR FURTHER READING:

James G. Randall and David Donald have written a comprehensive account of *The Civil War and Reconstruction* (rev. ed., 1961), while the monumental history of the Civil War era by Allan Nevins reached 1863 with the publication of *The War for the Union* (2 vols., 1959–1960). Divergent interpretations of the North's reaction to secession are presented in David Potter, *Lincoln and His Party in the Secession Crisis* (1950); and Kenneth M. Stampp, *And the War Came: The North and the Secession Crisis* (1950).

The northern conduct of the war is best followed through the biographies of Lincoln, the finest single-volume one being Benjamin P. Thomas, *Abraham Lincoln* (1952). For greater detail, see Albert J. Beveridge, *Abraham Lincoln, 1809–1858* (2 vols., 1928); and the chronologically succeeding volumes by James G. Randall (completed by Richard N. Current) on *Lincoln the President* (4 vols., 1945–1955). Current has also written a fine interpretive essay on *The Lincoln Nobody Knows* (1958). Special aspects of the North during the war are treated in T. Harry Williams, *Lincoln and the Radicals* (1941)*; T. Harry Williams, *Lincoln and His Generals* (1952); and John Hope Franklin, *The Emancipation Proclamation* (1963). Clement Eaton has written a good *History of the Southern Confederacy* (1954)*; Rembert W. Patrick describes *Jefferson Davis and His Cabinet* (1944); *King Cotton Diplomacy* (1931) has been well treated by Frank L. Owsley; and Rudolph Von Abele has written a good biography of the Confederate Vice President, *Alexander H. Stephens* (1946). The military history of the war from the point of view of the northern armies may be followed in the vivid volumes by Bruce Catton: *Mr. Lincoln's Army* (1951)*, *Glory Road* (1952)*, and *A Stillness at Appomattox* (1954)*. A more detailed and professional evaluation of the northern military effort through 1863, with greater attention to the western campaigns, is Kenneth P. Williams, *Lincoln Finds a General: A Military Study of the Civil War* (5 vols., 1949–1959). The fighting as viewed from the southern side is best followed in the distinguished studies by Douglas Southall Freeman: *R. E. Lee, A Biography* (4 vols., 1934–1935), and *Lee's Lieutenants* (3 vols., 1942–1944). Also outstanding are two works by Frank E. Vandiver, *Rebel Brass* (1956) and *Mighty Stonewall* (1957). Bell I. Wiley has described the common soldiers in *The Life of Johnny Reb* (1943)* and *The Life of Billy Yank* (1952). Of the multitude of personal accounts by contemporaries, two very different ones may be singled out as having special interest: the *Personal Memoirs* (2 vols., 1885–1886) of General Grant, and *A Diary from Dixie* (1905)* by a Richmond lady, Mary Boykin Chesnut.

---

*Available in paperback edition.

VALUE ADDED BY SELECTED INDUSTRIES, IN 1879 PRICES, FROM 1839 TO 1899 (IN BILLIONS OF DOLLARS)

YEAR	TOTAL	AGRICUL- TURE	MINING	MANUFAC- TURING	CONSTRUC- TION
1899	11.75	3.92	0.55	6.26	1.02
1894	10.26	3.27	.39	5.48	1.12
1889	8.66	3.24	.35	4.16	.92
1884	7.30	3.00	.23	3.22	.86
1879	5.30	2.60	.15	1.96	.59
1874	4.30	1.98	.11	1.69	.52
1869	3.27	1.72	.07	1.08	.40
1859	2.69	1.49	.03	.86	.30
1854	2.32	1.32	.03	.68	.30
1849	1.66	.99	.02	.49	.16
1844	1.37	.94	.01	.29	.13
1839	1.09	.79	.01	.19	.11

(Adapted from *Historical Statistics of the United States* [1960], p. 139.)

CHAPTER 16

THE TRIUMPH OF AMERICAN INDUSTRY

1865–1893

Like a vast and bloody wound, the Civil War seems to divide nineteenth-century American history into two parts. Yet America's industrial expansion, the most important tendency of the postwar years, was under way before the war and continued during it. This immense process would have taken place if slavery or secession had never been heard of and still would have transformed world history. American industrial growth was not unique: England had gone through a similar transformation earlier, Germany underwent one about the same time as the United States, and it was under way before the end of the century in Japan and other countries. But American industrialization was larger in scale than that of any other country and perhaps transformed the national culture more profoundly.

"THE SECOND AMERICAN REVOLUTION"

As we have seen, America had long been exploiting her unique advantages for economic growth. Since 1815, the market revolution had been under way. Like no other country, America had within her own borders nearly all necessary raw materials, a rapidly expanding market, and a swelling labor force. By the fifties she had also an expanding and increasingly mechanized agriculture to feed her city workers, rich sources of capital, demonstrated inventive genius and managerial skill. East of the Mississippi the country was already provided with an adequate transportation network. The American railroad system was the biggest in the world and the country's most important single industry. Yet American trains still ran on British rails. Many historians have credited America's industrial spurt to the Civil War itself. Yet as we have seen, according to one index, the value added by manufacturing, the century's largest percentage gains took place in prewar decades. Obviously, the war created certain immediate demands: woollen cloth for uniforms, shoes, blankets, and guns. Yet it can be argued that these necessities took productive resources away from more important endeavors. Indeed, one of America's great economic advantages in the nineteenth century was that *except* in the 1860's economic growth did not have to be shaped for military ends.

Another theory, advanced by Charles A. Beard and other historians, is that the Civil War was in reality a Second American Revolution in which industrialists, after several generations of frustrated effort, were able to capture control of the government and force it to do their will. This theory deserves a close look.

Until the Civil War, the theory says, the southern-western agrarian majority prevailed, first in Jefferson's and then again in Jackson's time. Thus industry was unable to achieve either a sufficiently protective tariff, an adequate banking system, or (because of sectional bickering) a transcontinental railroad. Now the industrialists seized control of the government in a three-stage operation. First, the Republican party attracted a part of the pivotal Midwest to the support of high tariffs by conceding free homesteads and other farmer-backed measures. Then, while the South was out of the Union and the agrarian majority correspondingly reduced, the spokesmen of industry jammed through Congress the legislation they had long wanted. Finally, through Radical Reconstruction the South was to be kept out of the national councils while the industrialists' program was perfected and entrenched.

Through this daring seizure of power, American industrialists had achieved: (1) a high protective tariff (beginning 1861); (2) a national banking system (1863) and the destruction of the state banks by punitive taxation (1865); (3) the right to import foreign laborers under contracts, signed abroad, which pledged their first year's wages for their transportation (1864; repealed, 1868; practice outlawed, 1884); and (4) a transcontinental railroad system lavishly supported by government land grants and loans (first legislation, 1861). Somewhat more complicated were the benefits gained from the system of wartime finance. Only a quarter of the costs of war were paid by taxation. The rest was handled by the sale of government bonds and the issuance of fiat money (greenbacks). The bonds, which paid 6 and 7 per cent interest, could sometimes be bought in greenbacks which sank, at their lowest, to less than half their face value. Yet the same bonds were redeemed in gold. Thus smart investors could add 100 per cent profit to the interest they had already received. Labor suffered severely from wartime inflation since wages lagged behind prices. Farmers suffered in the chronic deflation of the rest of the century. Only bankers and speculators profited throughout, and the result of government policy was, as Hamilton had said it should be, the accumulation of capital for investment in industry.

Careful research has shown that this thesis of a Second American Revolution, carried out consciously in the interest of businessmen and industrialists, is not valid. To begin with, industrialists and businessmen were by no means united either on the issues of the Civil War and Reconstruction or on the economic program just mentioned. The system of war finance had grown in response to war emergency against the opposition of many powerful businessmen. Interest on government bonds was severely cut into by inflation. After the war, few businessmen were in favor of high tariff and financial deflation at the same time. Many of the politicians who demanded military rule for the South, like Thaddeus Stevens, were inflationists, though they were also often protectionists. The western banking community, on the other hand, supported hard money but opposed the high tariff and was generally in favor of a lenient policy toward the South. In short, the myth of an inside group, dictating economic policy in its own interests and using the slogans of war and Reconstruction to further its interests, must be discarded. In the minds of most people, including businessmen, the war and Reconstruction were political and not economic struggles.

Yet it remains true that industry, whether or not anybody planned it that way, received important and unprecedented governmental support during the war and postwar periods. The tariff, though not really negligible before the war, reached unprecedented heights in wartime and continued to rise, with few interruptions, for the rest of the century. The railroads, in many ways the key to industrial expansion, were indeed given very heavy support by the federal government and by some states. Much of this aid came in the form of the government's most plentiful asset, land.

The banking and currency system were, in the long run, unsatisfactory. Yet they served their wartime purpose for both government and industry. The greenback inflation helped pull the country out of depression and sparked the wartime boom. The national banking system provided a sound and uniform currency and also a steady market for government bonds, which were the basis for the new bank notes. Thus the government was provided with sufficient wartime revenue and could place with confidence its huge orders for munitions and supplies.

After the war the needs of an expanding economy were less well met. The supply of money was often insufficient and bore no relation to the changing needs of business. The banking system was inflexible, and there was still no central authority with power to damp down booms and prevent panics. Businessmen, divided among themselves and often prisoners, like other Americans, of rigid and obsolete economic theories, by no means agreed on what they wanted in the complex world of money and banking. If they had, they probably would have got it.

The triumph of industry was not, then, a planned and masterful capture of the government, and the war itself may have had little to do with the rate of expansion. Yet by the eighties, if not earlier, industrial enterprise was playing a new role in America and contemporaries knew it. The change was partly cumulative and partly psychological. Before the war, industry had been a powerful competitor for public favor and attention. Now, its scale and achievements brought it clearly to the center of the stage. The great drama of exploiting, through private enterprise, the natural resources of a continent, dominated the public imagination. For some time Congress, the Supreme Court, the press, and the pulpit gave business enterprise their unstinting support. State banks, or serious sectional bickering about something as important as transcontinental railroads, seemed memories of the distant past. So, for a time, did Jeffersonian prejudices against the growth of cities and factories.

CONDITIONS OF GROWTH

In many areas outside of politics, postwar conditions were even more favorable to industrial expansion than the conditions which had brought about the boom of the fifties. To begin with, the agricultural revolution, which must precede and accompany any industrial revolution, continued to expand. It was becoming possible for fewer people to grow more food. Wheat furnishes a major example. On the prairies of Illinois and Indiana, in the new and booming spring wheat belt of Minnesota and North Dakota, in the great valley of California, and, in good years, even on the dry plains of Montana, new varieties of wheat produced bigger and bigger crops. Farmers learned to use machinery on an ever-increasing scale. The harvester was followed by the twine binder and the steam thresher. Finally, on the biggest and richest farms, great combines pulled by steam engines harvested and threshed at once. Gigantic elevators stored the wheat at railheads and river ports. Some of it went from there to the new roller mills of flour-producing centers; Minneapolis alone shipped over seven million barrels a year. Both wheat and flour were shipped abroad. American wheat became the mainstay of the British industrial population. European countries, worried about dependence on the United States, sent commissions to study American methods. Meanwhile the many expert speculators in American wheat kept an anxious eye on India, Russia, and Argentina.

Much the same story of geographical expansion, mechanization wherever possible, and entrance into an ever-widening market could be told, with important differences, of other American crops. Like Virginia tobacco in colonial times, American wheat, cotton, and cattle were part of a world economy. After 1870, with farm prices in general falling, trouble was in sight for American farmers, and farm problems were again to become a major headache for politicians. But to those interested in increasing industrial production, more and cheaper food seemed nothing but good news.

The mineral resources necessary for industry turned out to be even more plentiful than anybody had suspected. Deposits of coal and iron, the main essentials for heavy industry, were found within transportable range of each other in many places from the Appalachians to the Great Lakes. The center of copper production moved from Michigan to Montana and Arizona. Like the minerals, the timber of Wisconsin and the far Northwest seemed inexhaustible. The problem was not to save resources, but to multiply methods of using them ever faster.

Somewhat backward as yet in basic science, Americans contributed more than their share to the technological advance needed by industrial society. Some crucial improvements in basic industry, like the Bessemer and open-hearth processes for steel production, were of combined European and American origin. Perhaps because of the needs of a continent-sized democracy, Americans excelled in the field of communication, where they produced the telephone, the typewriter, and the linotype. The problems of new cities brought further adaptations of worldwide scientific advance. By the nineties, electric street railways were taking Americans to work, and electric lights were beginning to brighten their streets and houses.

Population to man the factories and swell the markets continued to pour in from Europe and Asia. Between 1870 and 1900 the population of the United States grew from 38,500,000 to 76,000,000. More than 12,000,000 of this increase came from immigration. Many wondered whether this flood could be absorbed, but the needs of industry for workers, plus the old American commitment to free immigration, beat back the doubters.

Like people, money for investment flowed westward across the Atlantic. Most of the capital needed came, however, from American industry itself. It has been estimated that between 1869 and 1898 about 13 per cent of the national income went into further industrial expansion. This high figure is partly explained by profitable and competitive innovation. In part, it reflects the energy and ability of the period's industrial capitalists, many of them more interested in expanding their vast and complex enterprises than in lavish living.

Nearly all conditions seemed to favor large-scale enterprise. Demand at first seemed inexhaustible. New urban populations with rising income needed consumer goods, and expanding agriculture and industry itself needed machines. Better transportation made it possible to concentrate on mechanization, which often meant bigness. In some industries, like steel, equipment became so expensive that only very big units could meet the fixed costs of production. Prices tended downward during the last half of the century, putting a premium on economic efficiency (sometimes, not always associated with large-scale production). Sharp depressions squeezed out weak competitors, underlining the disadvantages of cutthroat competition and suggesting the desirability of bringing rivals together.

Bigness could take many forms. A great firm might seek to monopolize a single product or a complex empire might tie together many related enterprises. (Carnegie's agglomeration, for instance, included iron and coal mines, shipping lines, steel plants, and rail factories.) Though many of the biggest firms were owned by single individuals or partnerships, the corporate form of organization was used more and more after 1875. It could draw most easily on wide sources of capital, and it could best evade regulation. When public hostility to bigness began to be a problem, gentlemen's agreements could take the place of outright mergers or able lawyers could work out new forms like trusts and holding companies.

Finally, a cause and a result of bigness was the country's rich supply of managerial skill. No other profession, in the period, offered so much wealth and prestige, none was as attractive to ability and ambition as the management of industry, whether or not divorced from its ownership.

Except for their daring, one can find little in common among the great industrialists of the period. Some, like Carnegie, exemplified the traditional poor-boy-to-millionaire pattern though most came from families well above the average in income and education. Some were ruthless pirates, indulging in every kind of misrepresentation and bribery, not hesitating to bring about disastrous panics in order to drive down the prices of stocks they wished to buy. Others were scrupulous Boston gentlemen who tolerated no associate whose moral character and probity were not impeccable. Some spent their money on Fifth Avenue palaces and baronial country estates or on Renaissance pictures. Many poured it out in unprecedented gifts for museums, libraries, and, above all, universities. A few hoarded it for future generations, but, most important, enough plowed it back into expanding production. In doing this, they were constantly assured, by press and pulpit, they were benefiting the whole civilization.

THE ACHIEVEMENT

There was much reason for the widespread public admiration of the industrial accomplishment. Before the end of the century, industrial growth had scattered factories from Michigan to Georgia; drawn workers for them from the farms and villages of the world; linked them to mines, forests, and ports; and made the United States the greatest producer of wealth the world had ever seen.

The most spectacular accomplishment was railroad construction. The already dense network of the northeastern quarter of the country was consolidated and improved and the wrecked southern roads rebuilt. Daring engineers pushed five different railroads clear to the Pacific Coast, throwing steel bridges across the Mississippi, building tunnels and grades through the Rockies and the Sierra, crossing deserts where wood for ties and food for workers had to be brought from the East. Sometimes a whole population to use the railroad had to be brought from the East, too; railroad corporations played during this generation the role of the Virginia Company or the Ohio Company. Everywhere in the West the course of the railroads determined the future of the region. Towns that were bypassed faded away, while at main junctions and terminals whole new cities appeared. It is not surprising that the railroads dominated the politics of the period as they did its economy.

Steel, in midcentury still a luxury product associated with fine cutlery, became the mainstay of the railroad age. Not only was it used for rails, locomotives, bridges, and cars, but also for mining machinery, oil drilling equipment, and steam turbines, and for ships of the new navy and the girders for the first Chicago skyscrapers. By 1900 the United States produced as much steel as its next two competitors, England and Germany, combined; a year later the industry gave rise to the first billion-dollar merger. In a parallel development, oil, a worthless by-product of the salt industry at the beginning of the period, became the nation's chief illuminant and lubricant as well as the source of the Standard Oil Trust, the Rockefeller fortune, and thereby the University of Chicago.

Change affected most consumers' goods as well as heavy industry. Shoe manufacture, a traditional home of the craftsman and home-worker, became dependent on highly complex machines rented from the monopolistic United Shoe Machinery Company. Chicago slaughter-houses and packing plants put the village butcher out of business. Now long lines of cattle cars moved toward Chicago, refrigerator cars in the opposite direction, and meat millionaires built palaces on the lakefront.

Despite the large share of the new wealth that was plowed back into the industrial process, a great deal of it went to make life easier, more efficient, and more pleasant for millions of people. By the nineties the rapid rise of sports, the sharp increase in high school education, the flood of cheap magazines and popular novels, even the bicycle craze and the popular song that commemorated it forever, testified to the presence of a large, relatively leisured middle class. As for the industrial workers, their wage rates stayed about the same during the period while the cost of living dropped. Between 1865 and 1900 real wages rose by something like a half, and the average working day inched downward from eleven hours to ten. If one were to disregard the disastrous impact of seasonal and cyclical unemployment, one could easily conclude that the factory worker made important gains.

By the end of the century, the decisive stage in the process of industrialization and urbanization was completed. Forty per cent of the people were counted as urban in the 1900 census; that is, they lived in places of 2,500 or more. As the figure suggests, even this vast change can be exaggerated. As late as 1900 most Americans lived either in rural areas or in towns that would seem small and quiet in-deed to their descendants today. More of them earned their living on farms than in factories, more of them were owners of businesses—sometimes of very small businesses—than were managerial employees of corporations. Yet nobody, from the most isolated farm in Vermont to the sleepiest village in Mississippi, was wholly unaffected by the power of industry.

Before the nineties, comparatively few tried to balance the costs of industrialization against its benefits. Most Americans in these years assumed, as Jefferson had not, that factories and cities were not only good in themselves but peculiarly American. In terms of human happiness, the balance sheet can never be accurately drawn up. One can be sure, however, that such a change in a nation's way of life has to be paid for heavily, in one way or another, wherever it occurs, whether in Russia or England or America. Though in some ways industrialization was easier in this rich, expanding, ocean-guarded republic than anywhere else, it had its costs. Soon some people were to conclude that the moral, social, and psychic price of industrialization was on the same scale as its tangible benefits.

Only in the mid-nineties, when the third of the period's racking depressions concentrated attention on all the evils of the new way of life, did many Americans stop to regret the landmarks swept away, the traditional patterns destroyed, the difficult questions raised and not answered. Even then nearly everybody knew that the gigantic process could never be stopped. In terms used by economists, the economy of the United States was now mature. In other terms, there was a lot of maturing still to come.

FOR FURTHER READING:

T. C. Cochran and William Miller, *The Age of Enterprise* (1942)*, is a stimulating and highly readable interpretation of the economic history of the United States in the nineteenth and twentieth centuries. W. W. Rostow, *The Stages of Economic Growth* (1960)*, places American industrialization in a world perspective. Some idea of the detailed reinterpretation of American economic history now under way can be gained from the *Journal of Economic History* (March, 1959), which is devoted to that subject. The economic interpretation of the Civil War was brilliantly argued in Charles A. and Mary R. Beard, *The Rise of American Civilization* (1927), and continued into the next period in H. K. Beale, *The Critical Year* (1930). Both are sharply challenged by Robert P. Sharkey, *Money, Class, and Party* (1959). The great range of attitudes toward the period's big businessmen can be suggested by contrasting Matthew Josephson, *The Robber Barons* (1934)* with William Miller, ed., *Men in Business* (1952) or T. C. Cochran, *Railroad Leaders, 1845–90* (1933). The whole subject of the chapter is re-examined in E. C. Kirkland, *Industry Comes of Age* (1961).

A. Hunter Dupree, *Science and the Emergence of Modern America, 1865–1916* (Berkeley Readings in American History, 1963)*, is a documentary study of a subject related to this and later chapters.

---

*Available in paperback edition.

EVENTS OF RECONSTRUCTION

NATIONAL	DATE	GENERAL TENDENCY	STATE
Lincoln Plan announced.	1863	PRESIDENTIAL RECONSTRUCTION	Governments set up in Louisiana, Arkansas.
Wade-Davis Plan pocket-vetoed by Lincoln.	1864		
Lee surrenders. Lincoln shot. Johnson Plan announced.	1865		Governments partly functioning in Virginia, Tennessee.
Freedmen's Bureau bill and Civil Rights bill vetoed. Fourteenth Amendment submitted to states. Congressional elections: Radical gains.	1866		All remaining states reorganized under Johnson Plan. Tennessee readmitted.
Reconstruction Acts. Tenure of Office Act.	1867	HEIGHT OF RADICAL RECONSTRUCTION	Military Rule in effect.
Impeachment of Johnson. Fourteenth Amendment in effect. Grant elected.	1868		North Carolina, South Carolina, Florida, Alabama, Louisiana, Arkansas, readmitted under Radical governments.
	1869		Conservative government restored in Tennessee.

EVENTS OF RECONSTRUCTION (*Continued*)

NATIONAL	DATE	GENERAL TENDENCY	STATE
Fifteenth Amendment in effect. First Enforcement Act. Congressional elections: Republican majorities reduced.	1870	CONFLICT	Virginia readmitted under moderate government. Moderate government restored in North Carolina. Mississippi, Texas, Georgia, readmitted under radical government.
Second and third Enforcement Acts.	1871		Conservative government restored in Georgia.
Grant re-elected.	1872		
	1873		
Congressional elections: Democrats gain control of House.	1874	RESTORATION OF WHITE RULE	Conservative government restored in Arkansas, Alabama, Texas.
Civil Rights Act (Declared invalid 1883).	1875		
Hayes-Tilden disputed election.	1876		Conservative government restored in Mississippi.
	1877		Federal troops removed from Louisiana, South Carolina. Conservative government restored in Florida, South Carolina, Louisiana.

CHAPTER 17

THE SOUTH AFTER THE WAR

1865–1890

In the generation after the Civil War economic expansion absorbed most of the nation's energies. The people's attention, however, centered at first on a more traditional kind of problem, the Reconstruction of the Union and the new order in the defeated South.

THE PROBLEM

The problem of Reconstruction was manifold. Most obvious, and easiest, was the physical rebuilding of shelled cities and ruined railroads. Harder to reconstruct was the defeated section's economic life. The South's industry was at a standstill; much of her farming land was lying idle. Her labor system was destroyed, investment capital was lacking, the savings of many people were wiped out by the collapse of Confederate currency and bonds. Beneath every other problem lay that of a new relation for the South's two races. All that was clear about the country's 4,500,000 Negroes was that none of them were any longer slaves. There were 286,000 in blue uniforms; a few were settled on confiscated plantations in the Sea Islands of the Carolinas, many were simply wandering, drifting from Union army camps to southern cities with great hopes and no means of support. Nearly everybody assumed that they were to continue to work on the land. A few radicals had suggested that they would become landowners and the Sea Islands experiment had raised some hopes. White Southerners assumed that they would work as laborers for white landowners.

In this politically-minded country, most people approached such problems in political terms. By 1865 three southern states had already been reconstructed under the easy terms offered by President Lincoln, which demanded only that 10 per cent of the citizens take an oath of future loyalty and recognize that slavery was ended. Once this was done, elections could be held for both state governments and federal Congressmen. The difficulty was that Congress refused to admit these delegates.

To settle this kind of difficulty, Americans turned to the Constitution. In this unheard-of situation, however, it offered little help. What was the status of a sovereign state which had seceded and been forced to return to the Union? Was it still a state, since secession had been illegal, or was it merely a conquered province? Who could decide: Congress or the president? The president was commander-in-chief of the armed forces and had the power to pardon. But Congress had the right to admit new states, to make rules for territories, and to judge the qualifications of its own members. Long before Lincoln's death, the two branches of government had been at loggerheads over these issues.

More important in the long run than even the constitutional question was the state of mind of three main groups: the ex-slaves, the defeated southern whites, and the citizens of the victorious North. Though able Negro leaders shortly appeared, most of the ex-slaves were not only illiterate but completely inexperienced, both in politics and in such economic institutions as wages and rent. Many pathetic stories are told about the strange hopes and fears of these displaced people. Yet the basic desires of the freedmen were clear and by no means foolish. What they wanted was real freedom, and the signs of freedom were the right to move around, access to education, and ownership of land.

Right after the war, according to northern travellers in the South, shock rather than bitterness was the most common state of mind among southern whites. With their institutions destroyed, what was to become of them? Most pressing of all, without slavery, how was the cotton going to be picked and planted? At first, many looked northward for their answers.

The third and largest group, the victorious northern whites, were by no means a united body. Nearly half, to begin with, were Democrats. Only a few Democrats had been willing to accept the breakup of the Union, but many had sharply criticized the conduct of the war and had opposed emancipation. The sole purpose of the fighting, the party's leaders had insisted, should have been the restoration of "the Union as it was." In the 1864 elections the Democrats had lost some ground, yet they still mustered a formidable 45 per cent of the votes.

Not even the Republicans were sure how much of a change

they wanted. The group called "Radicals" agreed that Lincoln had been too weak and lenient, but they agreed on little else. Republicans were divided on such matters as the tariff and finance, and few had thought through the future status of the Negro.

Two paradoxes made constructive action inordinately difficult. First, slavery had been abolished and the ex-slaves armed by a nation which believed overwhelmingly in the inferiority of the Negro race. This prejudice, mistaken as we now know it to be, was centuries old and almost universal. Even among the abolitionists, only a few had accepted the Negro as an intellectual and political equal. Only part of New England permitted Negroes to vote. Starting with Connecticut, Wisconsin, and Minnesota in 1865, one northern state after another continued to turn down Negro suffrage in the years after the war.

Second, in Reconstruction the North had to undertake a program of drastic, even revolutionary measures. Yet nearly all nineteenth-century Americans had been taught that government action should be sharply limited. This had been said by Jefferson, Jackson, and Lincoln. Schools and colleges taught as gospel truth the maxims of *laissez faire* political economy.

The choice faced by the North, in its simplest terms, was the choice offered to every victor: occupation or conciliation. All the feelings of nineteenth-century Americans were against continued military occupation. Somehow, most agreed, the South must be forced to see its errors and govern itself—according to northern ideas.

Yet to whom in the South could government be confided? To the ex-rebels who were, many Northerners believed, still rebels at heart? To the ex-slaves whom most Northerners regarded as members of an inferior race? Even if they were given the vote, the freedmen, inexperienced in politics and a minority in all but two states, could hardly govern alone. They would have to have the support either of a substantial number of southern whites or of sufficient occupying forces. With or without Negro suffrage the same choice would exist: conciliation or occupation.

PRESIDENTIAL RECONSTRUCTION

The first alternative, conciliation, was tried under the authority of presidents Lincoln and Johnson and is often referred to as Presidential Reconstruction. It is hard to tell how Lincoln's "ten per cent plan" might have worked if it had been continued. As we have seen, this was already sharply challenged by Congress, and Lincoln himself had said it was only one of many possible devices. The Wade-Davis bill, Congress' somewhat more drastic substitute, had been left unsigned by Lincoln.

Like Lincoln, Andrew Johnson embodied the log-cabin presidential tradition. He had been a tailor by trade and had learned to read only as an adult. A resident of eastern Tennessee, where slaves were few, and a former Jacksonian Democrat, he had been an outspoken opponent of secession and a lifelong enemy of the southern planter class. Yet he had no real commitment either to Negro rights or to the Republican party. Like Lincoln, Johnson was honest and able, but he proved to lack completely Lincoln's gifts for patience and political realism.

Like his predecessor, Johnson started by offering amnesty to those who would sign an oath of allegiance. Exceptions to the offer, more numerous than in Lincoln's plan, included important Confederate officials and Confederates who owned more than $20,000 worth of property. This seemed to exclude the leaders of the Old South. Those who had taken the oath were to vote for a constitutional convention in each state. This must repeal the state's ordinance of secession, abolish slavery, and repudiate the Confederate and state debts. Then the state might elect a new government and send representatives to Washington. By the end of 1865 all the states had actually passed through either the Lincoln or the Johnson version of this process, and in conservative or southern eyes Reconstruction was over.

Government was functioning in the South, and the people, Negro and white, were getting back to work. Yet much in the new order was deeply disturbing to northern opinion. Some of the reconstituted states elected prominent Confederates to state and federal office. Most enacted special "Black Codes" to regulate the conduct of freedmen. To former slaveholders, such rules seemed natural and necessary; to many northerners they looked like the next thing to slavery. In some states Negroes were not allowed to assemble; in others the labor of petty offenders could be sold at auction; in some Negro children could be apprenticed to white men without the consent of indigent parents. Most of the codes provided for strict enforcement of compulsory labor contracts. In South Carolina, the code spelled out the intent of such contracts: Negroes were to engage only in agricultural labor or domestic service.

In 1865–1866 northern opinion was further affronted by outbreaks of racial violence in the South. Responsibility for race riots was of course disputed, but the victims nearly always turned out to be Negroes or pro-Negro whites. To Radical Republicans, it seemed that life was not safe in the South for those who really supported a change in southern society, and this change they were determined to bring about. To some it was a moral duty; to others a political necessity.

In the spring of 1866 Congress extended the life of the Freedmen's Bureau, a wartime organization designed to supervise and aid the ex-slaves, and passed a Civil Rights Act prohibiting many kinds of discriminatory legislation. It also refused to admit the representatives of the new southern state governments. Clearly, the President could not hope to carry forward his policy without regard for such formidable opposition. Yet Johnson, like other presidents in other battles with Congress, seemed to grow steadily more stubborn. He blamed the race riots on Radicals, minimized southern denial of Negro rights, and pardoned thousands of southern leaders. In the spring of 1866 he vetoed both the Freedmen's Bureau bill and the Civil Rights Act.

By this time, Johnson had gained the support of Democrats and solidified the Republican party against him. In the fall he toured the country, violently denouncing his opponents as traitors. In the November election the voters gave their answer. The Republicans won two thirds of both Houses and the Radical leadership moved into key positions of power. A new phase of Reconstruction was clearly at hand.

CONGRESSIONAL RECONSTRUCTION

In Congressional, or Radical, Reconstruction, the other alternative, military occupation, was finally given a trial. The purpose, however, was still reform; the South was to be occupied only until her society could be altered and a new electorate formed. This meant something like social revolution, and it was clear that in this revolution the Negroes must play a major part.

The Freedmen's Bureau and Civil Rights bills, both repassed over the President's veto, established the principle that the former slaves were to be protected by the federal government during a transitional state. (They were not, however, to be given land; in this property-loving age only a few suggested such an extreme measure and local experiments in this direction were abandoned.)

Federal protection for the Negroes already implied a change in the relation of the federal government and the states, and such a change was spelled out in the Fourteenth Amendment submitted to Congress in June, 1866. The first section of this amendment provided that no state should infringe any citizen's "privileges or immunities," nor "deprive any person of life, liberty or property, without due process of law," nor deny to any person "the equal protection of the laws." Thus individuals were guaranteed by the *Union* against oppression by the *states*. (The Bill of Rights already protected individual liberties from the federal government.)

The second section of the amendment edged toward Negro suffrage. It provided that if a state denied the vote to any of its male inhabitants, its representation should be reduced accordingly. The third and fourth sections barred leading Confederates from Congress or federal office and forbade states to repudiate the federal or recognize the rebel debt.

Obviously this all-important amendment could not be ratified by three fourths of the states without some southern support. President Johnson urged southern states not to ratify, and Congress, as it might have anyway, moved on to still more drastic action.

The First Reconstruction Act, passed in March, 1867, divided the South into five military districts, wiping out the existing state governments. Under military supervision, each state was to elect a constitutional convention. Delegates to these conventions would be chosen by vote of the whole male population, including the freedmen and excluding leading Confederates. Each constitution was to be ratified by a majority of the state's new electorate and approved by Congress. When the new state had ratified the Fourteenth Amendment its representatives might be admitted to Congress. This Act was clarified and tightened by further legislation, and in 1870 Radical Reconstruction was completed by the ratification of the Fifteenth Amendment, once and for all forbidding suffrage discrimination on the basis of "race, color, or previous condition of servitude."

All these actions were taken against the firm opposition of the President and in the face of the nearly certain disapproval of the Supreme Court. To safeguard Radical Reconstruction, Congress made the most drastic attempt in American history to establish the dominance of a single branch of government.

To disarm the Court, Congress simply withdrew certain kinds of cases from Supreme Court jurisdiction, and the Court prudently refrained from challenging this action. Johnson, however, could be rendered powerless only by impeachment and conviction for "treason, bribery, or other high crimes or misdemeanors." Failing after much effort to find serious evidence of "crimes," Congress saw its best chance for impeachment in the Tenure of Office Act passed in 1867. This Act, of dubious constitutionality, forbade the removal of cabinet officers without congressional sanction. Johnson challenged it by trying to remove Secretary of War Edwin Stanton, an appointee of Lincoln. In the spring of 1868 the House of Representatives impeached the President in a long, confused, and shaky set of charges. Anger ran so high that his accusers failed by only one vote to secure the two thirds of the Senate necessary for conviction.

RADICAL RECONSTRUCTION IN ACTION

How did the Radical program actually work in the South? To this crucial question, historians have developed two opposite answers. A generation ago most accounts said that Radical Reconstruction had been a dreadful mistake. Southern state governments, dominated by ignorant Negroes, self-seeking carpetbaggers, and despicable southern "scalawags" ("collaborationists" would be the modern term), had imposed a reign of terror, extravagance, and corruption. Finally, the South, supported by a revival of decent moderate opinion in the North, had risen in revolt and thrown off the yoke.

More recently this version has been challenged by an opposite one. According to this second, neo-Radical view, Radical Reconstruction was a long-overdue attempt to bring justice and progress to the South. It was sustained in the South not only by federal forces but by determined Negro support. Its defeat was brought about by brutal terrorism and northern betrayal.

The truth about this abortive social revolution is various and complex. It is clear that some of the Radical governments were indeed both extravagant and blatantly corrupt. Yet extravagance and corruption were common in this period in northern states and cities. Moreover, the Radical governments scored some real accomplishments, bringing to the South broader suffrage (for whites as well as Negroes), poor relief, and the beginnings of free, popular education.

Perhaps the key question to ask about Radical Reconstruction is whether it ever had a real chance of success: that is, of effecting a permanent change in southern institutions and customs. The answer is complex. Successful Reconstruction would have demanded either prolonged northern occupation or some degree of cooperation between southern whites and Negroes. For the first the northern people proved to have no enduring appetite. The second seemed more promising initially. Many southern whites did make an effort to accept the new situation (though many did not). Contrary to legend, some "scalawags" were well intentioned, just as some carpetbaggers were honest and some Negro leaders well informed and moderate. Yet any permanent alliance among these elements faced great difficulties. The cooperating southern whites were willing to accept Negro voting under white leadership; the Negroes demanded real political equality. Predictably, if not inevitably, the necessary coalition failed. Violence against the Negroes and their political allies broke out on a larger and larger scale. At first determined to suppress the Ku Klux Klan and other terrorist organizations, Congress grew weary of the attempt. In one state after another, with differing degrees of forcible action, southern whites achieved victory at the polls. In 1877, when President Hayes withdrew the last federal troops, the cycle was complete; the South was under the rule of native whites. At first the new "lily-white" governments, mostly led by members of the prewar planter class, allowed Negroes some token participation in politics. Then, in the nineties, governments representing the poor whites of the section came to power. In a wave of resentment against what they believed to be an alliance of aristocrats and Negroes, these governments drove the southern Negroes almost entirely out of politics. This was done partly by pressure and partly by ingenious suffrage requirements—grandfather clauses, literacy tests, and the like —enforced against Negroes and not against whites.

SOCIAL RECONSTRUCTION

Since the Negroes never received the "forty acres and a mule" for which they had longed in 1865, they had to work for white landowners. Money to pay them was lacking, and the only possible solution was some form of tenantry. The result was the sharecrop and the crop-lien systems. Throughout the South sharecroppers, both white and Negro, received their seed, tools, and staple necessities from landlords to whom they turned over a third or a half of their produce. Most, and often all, of the rest went to pay long-standing debts accumulated by the tenants at country stores with high-monopoly prices and exorbitant rates of interest. The system was not slavery, and it got the crops planted and harvested. Yet the Negro farmer, forever in debt and unable to move, without education or political privileges, subject to white courts and occasionally to white terrorism, could hardly be called free.

In the eighties the South, under white rule again, put on a spectacular drive for industry. Heavy inducements were offered to capital, and much was accomplished in steel, lumbering, tobacco, and, especially, textiles. Yet by the turn of the century southern efforts had barely held even: the South's percentage of the nation's industry was about that of 1860. Even this, in a rapidly expanding economy, was a considerable achievement, but the price was heavy. In southern mill towns disease and child labor were endemic. Most of the profits of industry were flowing out of the section. Until World War II, the South remained both poor and overwhelmingly agrarian.

Perhaps the saddest chapter in all American history is the general acceptance, in the North, of the failure of so much effort. Thirty years after the war most people took for granted a southern system which included not only disfranchisement and rigid social segregation of the Negro but also recurrent violence. In 1892 and 1893, for example, more than 150 Negroes were lynched each year, often with sadistic tortures.

How could the people who had defied the Fugitive Slave Act, fought the war, and voted for Radical Reconstruction accept this situation? For one thing, it was easy to emphasize the seamy side—and it was a large one—of Radical Reconstruction, the greed and corruption with which the process had often been executed. Moreover, most people were convinced that racial differences made political equality impossible. Government, according to nineteenth-century science and social science, could do very little to change customs or alter society. There was, moreover, a bright side to the story. A great Civil War had been settled without executions or confiscations, and the two sides were beginning to be reconciled. It was easy to forget that the Negro was paying most of the bill for this reconciliation.

Responsive in its way to the drift of public opinion, the Supreme Court made its peace with the new situation. In the Civil Rights cases (1883) it decided that the Fourteenth Amendment did not prevent *individuals*, as opposed to states, from practicing discrimination. In Plessy *vs.* Ferguson (1896) the Court held that "separate but equal" accommodations for Negroes in trains (and by implication in restaurants, hotels, and the like) did not violate their rights. Few inquired very carefully whether accommodations were indeed equal.

The upshot, then, of the greatest struggle in American history seemed to be a tragic failure. Yet the story had not ended. The Negro had gained a few rights and a great many hopes. And neither in the North nor the South was the national conscience really at ease.

FOR FURTHER READING:

The older anti-Radical point of view is expressed in J. G. Randall, *Civil War and Reconstruction* (1937), an important summary brought up to date and somewhat revised by David Donald (1961). The most extreme, and one of the most influential, statements of the pro-Radical point of view is W. E. B. DuBois, *Black Reconstruction* (1935)*. A far more moderate defense of the Radicals can be found in John Hope Franklin, *Reconstruction: After the Civil War* (1961)*. The period after Radical Reconstruction is magnificently put together by C. Vann Woodward, *Origins of the New South, 1877-1913* (1951). A recent and challenging reinterpretation of Andrew Johnson is Eric McKitrick, *Andrew Johnson and Reconstruction* (1960). One cannot get far in understanding Reconstruction without reading some of the studies of separate states. Two very different but excellent examples are F. B. Simkins and R. H. Woody, *South Carolina During Reconstruction* (1932), and V. L. Wharton, *The Negro in Mississippi, 1865-1890* (1947).

Grady McWhiney, *Reconstruction and the Freedmen* (Berkeley Readings in American History, 1963)* is a documentary study of this problem.

*Available in paperback edition.

WESTERN HISTORY, 1860–1895

MINING RUSHES	INDIAN WARS	MISCELLANEOUS EVENTS	STATES (IN CAPITALS) AND TERRITORIES
		1858 Butterfield Overland Express (transcontinental stage route)	
1859 Nevada (gold and silver) Colorado (gold)			1859 OREGON
1860–1866 Idaho (gold)			
1860		Pony Express	
		1861 Pacific Telegraph	1861 KANSAS, Colorado, Nevada, Dakota
1862 Arizona (gold)	1862 Massacre of whites, Minnesota	1862 Homestead Act	1863 Arizona, Idaho
1862–1864 Montana (gold)	1864 Arapaho-Cheyenne War		1864 NEVADA, Montana
	Massacre of Indians, Sand Creek, Colorado		
1865	1865–1867 War with Western Sioux	1866 Long Drive to Sedalia, Missouri	
1867 Wyoming (gold)	1867 Indian Peace Commission		1867 NEBRASKA
	1868 War on Southern Plains	1869 Union Pacific Railroad completed	1868 Wyoming
1870	1871 War in Texas Panhandle		
1873 Deeper portion of Comstock Lode, Nevada (richest strike ever)	1874 Red River War	1873 Timber Culture Act	
	1875–1876 War in Black Hills	1874 Barbed wire patented	

WESTERN HISTORY, 1860–1895 (*Continued*)

MINING RUSHES	INDIAN WARS	MISCELLANEOUS EVENTS	STATES (IN CAPITALS) AND TERRITORIES
1875			
1876 Black Hills, Dakota (gold)			1876 COLORADO
1877 Leadville, Colorado (silver, lead)	1877 Nez Percés' uprising, Idaho	1877 Desert Land Act	
1879 Tombstone, Arizona (silver)		1878 Timber and Stone Act	
1880			
1882 Butte, Montana (copper)		1882–1883 Santa Fe, Southern Pacific, and Northern Pacific routes completed	
1885			
	Capture of Geronimo and end of Apache War	1885–1886 Disastrous winters, end of range cattle industry	
	1887 Dawes Act	1887 Drought and western farm crisis	
1890			
	1889–1890 Ghost Dance, battle of Wounded Knee	1889 First Oklahoma rush	1889 NORTH DAKOTA, SOUTH DAKOTA, MONTANA, WASHINGTON
			1890 WYOMING, IDAHO
		1893 Great Northern Railroad completed	

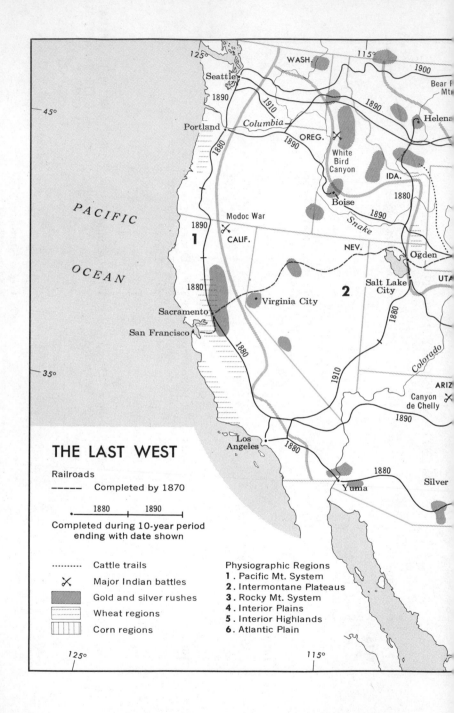

THE LAST WEST

Railroads

- - - - - Completed by 1870

```
        1880        1890
  •━━━━━━━┿━━━━━━━┥
```

Completed during 10-year period
ending with date shown

.... Cattle trails

✕ Major Indian battles

▨ Gold and silver rushes

▤ Wheat regions

▥ Corn regions

Physiographic Regions
1 . Pacific Mt. System
2 . Intermontane Plateaus
3 . Rocky Mt. System
4 . Interior Plains
5 . Interior Highlands
6 . Atlantic Plain

WASH.
Seattle
1890
Portland
Columbia
OREG.
White Bird Canyon
1890
CALIF.
Modoc War
1

PACIFIC

OCEAN

1880
Sacramento
San Francisco
Virginia City
1880

Boise
IDA.
1880
1890
Snake
NEV.
2
Salt Lake City
Ogden
UTA
1880
Colorado
1910

1900
Bear R
Mtn
Helena
1890

ARIZ
Canyon de Chelly
1890

Los Angeles
1880
Yuma
1880
Silver

125°
115°

45°

35°

125°   115°

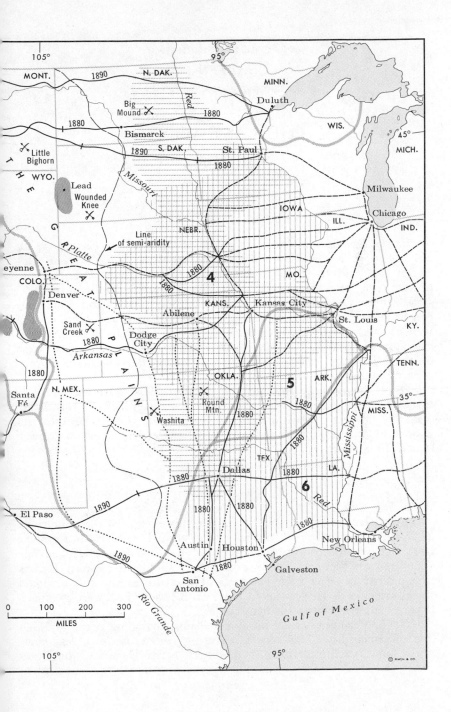

MONT.

105°

95°

N. DAK.

1890

MINN.

Duluth

Red

1880

Big
Mound ✕

1880

Bismarck

WIS.

45°

MICH.

1890

S. DAK.

St. Paul

✕ Little
Bighorn

1880

WYO.

Missouri

Lead
Wounded
Knee

IOWA

Milwaukee

Chicago

ILL.

IND.

Line
of semi-aridity

NEBR.

R Platte

eyenne

COLO.

MO.

Denver

1880

4

1880

Abilene

KANS.

Kansas City

Sand
Creek ✕

Dodge
City

St. Louis

KY.

1880

Arkansas

OKLA.

ARK.

TENN.

1880

N. MEX.

Round
Mtn. ✕

5

35°

1880

Santa
Fé

1880

Washita

MISS.

Mississippi

Rio Grande

1880

TEX.

1880

Dallas

LA.

1880

1880

6

Red

El Paso

1880

1880

1890

1880

New Orleans

Austin

Houston

1880

1890

San
Antonio

Galveston

0   100   200   300

MILES

Gulf of Mexico

105°

95°

© RM*N & CO.

CHAPTER 18

THE LAST WEST

1860–1890

While the United States was struggling with the tragic heritage of an old region, it was also confronting the problems of a new one. Between 1860 and 1890, with no time out for the Civil War, half the present area of the country was occupied and exploited. In 1860 settlers were fast filling up the eastern parts of Kansas and Nebraska. San Francisco and Sacramento were bustling towns and farming was well established in the Willamette Valley of Oregon. Between these two distant borders, the Pacific settlements and the states just west of the Mississippi, lay a vast region of plains and mountains barely penetrated by European civilization.

Two things make this last and greatest West different from all earlier frontier regions. First, far more than ever before, this West was the frontier of an urban and industrial country. Second, its geography made it much less hospitable to settlers than any earlier American frontier.

PLAINS AND MOUNTAINS

From Jamestown to the Mississippi, however hard the conditions of frontier life, there had normally been enough rainfall for farming. Long accustomed to forest, pioneers of the last generation had encountered all the way from northeastern Illinois to eastern Kansas rich prairies covered with tall grass. They had learned to overcome their suspicion of treeless land. This was a lesson they were going to have to unlearn a little further west.

Beyond the prairies lay the Great Plains, beginning at the invisible line of semiaridity. This runs a wavering course, more or less close to the ninety-eighth meridian from eastern North Dakota to the Texas

Panhandle. Some of the area west of this line, particularly in its north-eastern parts, can profitably be farmed by those who know its ways. As one moves westward toward the Rockies, however, the Plains grow steadily higher, drier, and less fertile. In 1860 nothing grew there but the short native grass, and aside from the soldiers who guarded the wagon trails at a few forts, it remained in the possession of its ancient inhabitants. These included the jack rabbit, antelope, coyote, and buffalo, all biologically adapted to live in arid country, and the Plains Indian, culturally adapted to live on the buffalo.

Beyond the Plains lay the Rockies, rich in minerals and long penetrated by fur trappers, and beyond them the intermountain plateaus, mostly made up of sage-brush desert, jagged mountain ranges, and, in the Southwest, true desert dotted with cactus and mesquite. Some of the land of this forbidding province could be irrigated as had been demonstrated by Spaniards on the Mexican borderlands and Mormons near the Great Salt Lake. Beyond these plateaus lay the Pacific mountain chains, first the Sierra and the Cascades, then the Coast Ranges, with rich valleys between.

The whole area had been given the bad name of the Great American Desert. Only the strongest motives could draw settlers into it. The motives that did were the same as those which had first drawn Europeans across the Atlantic: religious freedom (in the case of the Mormons), adventure, independence from one's neighbors, and, most commonly of all, desire for land and gold.

THE MINERS

Between 1859 and 1864 gold rushes occurred at scattered points in what later became the states of Nevada, Colorado, Idaho, Montana, and Arizona. One more major rush, to the Black Hills of South Dakota, took place in 1876. In each case, the boom went through the same stages. First, when a strike was reported, thousands of prospective miners, some greenhorns, some veterans of other mining booms, rushed to the spot. Within a short time merchants, gamblers, prostitutes, and plain bandits appeared to divert some of the wealth from the lucky minority. A certain amount of murder might be tolerated, but claim jumping had to be prevented, and these remote communities soon worked out their own codes of mining law. Sometimes respectable citizens organized vigilante groups to bring about a semblance of rough justice. Before long the diggings were worked out, at least as far as they could be with the picks or washing pans or sluice boxes of the first comers. Sometimes they would close permanently, leaving only ghost towns. Sometimes a second metal would be found, and a second rush take place as in the cases of Colorado silver or Montana copper. Sometimes, as in Nevada in 1873, deeper digging would produce another bonanza. Often after the raw surface metal was gone, organized exploitation with expensive machinery and deeper drilling would produce richer results. Meantime the original prospectors, nearly always broke, would travel to some other likely wilderness, if not in the United States in Canada or Alaska or farther.

This haphazard but intense exploration of mineral resources doubled the world's gold supply with important results for American political history. Silver production, also sharply increased, created in a few western states a special economic interest that held its political power for more than half a century. In many cases, towns created to serve the needs of miners found other means of livelihood and survived when the mines closed. New populations, now present at scattered points in the West, raised new problems, particularly those of transportation and protection against Indians.

TRANSPORTATION

The Oregon migrants and California gold seekers had gone either around the Horn, across the Isthmus of Panama, or over the plains. Beginning in 1861, stage lines and wagon trains reached across the country. At the end of the fifties, the enterprising firm of Russell, Majors and Waddell developed the spectacular pony express which actually got letters from Independence, Missouri, to San Francisco in ten days of fast relay riding. In 1861 this was displaced by a coast-to-coast telegraph line.

Meantime, the secession of the South had settled the old arguments about the route for a railway and in 1862 work was started under heavy government subsidy. The Central Pacific climbed painfully through the Sierra from Sacramento while the the Union Pacific drove along the wagon train route from Omaha via Cheyenne to South Pass. In 1869 while the nation celebrated, top-hatted dignitaries met at Promontory Point, Utah, to watch the driving of the golden spike linking the two roads. For the next decade and a half, much of it a time of depression, the Union Pacific–Central Pacific remained the only through route from coast to coast. Then in the prosperous early eighties three more lines were completed: the Southern Pacific and the Santa Fe systems through the Southwest and the Northern Pacific from St. Paul to Portland. In 1893 a fourth road, the Great Northern, connected St. Paul and Seattle by a route still further north. This last road, unlike its competitors, got along without governmental subsidy, chiefly by promoting the development of its region.

THE INDIAN TRAGEDY

Penetration of the plains and mountains by miners, migrants, and stage coaches had long since made Indian troubles inevitable. The long and bloody struggle for the last West is one of the least pleasant stories in American history. Probably no peaceful solution was possible of this conflict between an aggressive, expanding nineteenth-century civilization and a nomadic, stone-age culture dependent on vast hunting spaces. Yet, as in the case of Reconstruction, mistakes made a hard problem worse. Part of the fault lay with divided councils, civilian administrators squabbling with soldiers, soldiers disagreeing among themselves, settlers arguing with eastern humanitarians. Part of the long tragedy arose from inevitable anger over traditional Indian methods of war. Yet no Indian atrocity is more grisly than such white actions as the Sand Creek massacre of 1864 when several hundred men, women, and children of a tribe trying to surrender were exterminated and their bodies mutilated by a detachment of United States troops.

Many Indians, from the Utes of the Great Basin and the Nez Percés of Idaho to the Modocs of northern California, fought the white man at one time or another. But the most serious enemies of frontier advance were the Sioux of the northern Plains and the Apache of the Southwest. The Sioux, like the other Plains Indians, were superb fighters, fast and indefatigable horsemen, expert shots with bow and arrow and later with rifles and were divided into small, efficient war bands led by such able commanders as Red Cloud and Crazy Horse. The Apache, who had been fighting Mexicans for years, were equally dangerous and still more elusive in their own country of desert and rocky canyon.

The long struggle with the Plains Indians began with a Sioux massacre of whites in Minnesota in 1862. Fierce fighting with Sioux and many other tribes continued through the Civil War years and sporadically in the seventies. The last serious Sioux war broke out in 1876 when the Dakota gold rush penetrated the Black Hills, recently guaranteed to the Indians. As late as 1890 a strange religious frenzy on the Northern Sioux reservation led to an uprising and a last futile slaughter. Long before this the Plains Indian cause had become hopeless with the slaughter of the buffalo. The animals, once among the most numerous in the world, were almost exterminated in the decade after 1870 by meat hunters, sportsmen, and finally by professionals catering to the eastern demand for hides. Meantime the Apache wars in the Southwest dragged on until Geronimo, the last important chief, was captured in 1885.

Ever since the Monroe administration, the government's official policy had been to move the Indians beyond the reach of the white frontier. Once not only Oklahoma but the whole plains had been talked about as permanent Indian country. Inevitably, reservations had become smaller and more crowded with the advance of the settlers, and forced resettlement had been supplemented with doles of beef, staples, and clothing.

As always in American history foolish and cruel policies eventually drew protest. As the Indian menace ebbed, eastern friends of the Indian argued with increasing effectiveness that a policy amounting to conquest and pauperization was not tolerable. The Indian, reformers argued, should be civilized and assimilated rather than maintained in primitive tribal condition. This accorded well with nineteenth-century social theory and also, at times, with the wish of western settlers to break up reservations. After a number of minor reforms the Dawes Act of 1887 reversed Indian policy. Tribal authority and ownership of land was gradually to be extinguished, and reservation land was to be parcelled out to individual Indians, each head of family receiving 160 acres. Such allotments were to be held in trust pending complete ownership after twenty-five years. Indians living in nontribal fashion were to become citizens. Land not so parcelled out could be sold by the government to individual settlers with the proceeds going toward Indian education.

This well-intentioned statute proved disastrous to the Indians. Most of the reservation land went to white settlers. Tribal authority was destroyed, and individual Indians were often victimized by white neighbors. Some received allotments too soon; others were deprived of incentive by the waiting period. In 1934 government policy was reversed again by the Indian Reorganization Act, designed to protect what remained of tribal life.

THE OPEN RANGE

Before the Indians and buffaloes had quite vanished, the plains began to be occupied by the advance guard of the expanding American economy in the form of cattle. The range cattle industry, so much the staple of legend that it is hard to see the reality, was actually a boom-and-bust episode typical of the period's economic history.

Longhorn cattle were developed in Texas, and there, too, the Anglo-American cowboy got his distinctive dress, his high-backed saddle, and some of his vocabulary. Feed was free on the unoccupied grassland and the only thing lacking was a market. This was provided when railroads reached Kansas in the sixties. Huge herds of steers could now be driven fifteen hundred miles across the plains from Texas to Sedalia, Missouri, or Abilene and Dodge City, Kansas. Thence they could be shipped to packing centers. The long drive north from Texas was a dangerous and difficult business beset by Indians, angry home-steaders, diseases, drought, and the tendency of the animals themselves to panic and stampede. It is not surprising that when the herds were safely penned in the railhead towns the cowboys sometimes behaved like sailors in from a long voyage.

Texas longhorns were wiry beasts, and soon it proved more prof-itable to drive them still farther and fatten them up on the open grass-lands of western Kansas and Nebraska, the Dakotas, Wyoming, and even Montana. Sometimes the strain was improved by bulls shipped in from further east. For a while free grass, cheap cattle, and rising de-mand brought about boom conditions. Romance attracted such eastern dudes as Theodore Roosevelt, who had his fling as a rancher in South Dakota, and 30 per cent dividends attracted English syndicates. Soon, inevitably, even the vast plains became overcrowded. As in the mining camps, competition was regulated by semilegal codes. Cattlemen's associations divided up the government-owned unfenced range, regu-lated the annual roundup when new calves were separated and branded, and dealt summarily with rustlers.

By the early eighties, two new enemies of the cattle industry appeared. The first of these was the prairie farmer advancing hopefully onto the dry plains and fencing the land. The second was sheep. The sheep industry had spread from the New Mexico plateaus via the Colorado parks and Utah tablelands to the western plains. According to cattlemen, sheep cropped the range too close, destroyed turf with their hooves, and drove away by their lowly presence the superior and first-coming cattle. Mexican herders had to fight pitched battles with cowboys, and many thousand sheep were driven over cliffs. In the end, however, the undemanding and persistent sheep won this struggle for survival.

The end of the open-range cattle industry came with the disas-trous winters of 1885–1886 and 1886–1887 when the grass was hidden under deep snow and millions of cattle froze and starved. From this point on the successful cattleman abandoned the old wide-open ways, fenced his range, scientifically improved his herd, and put his indignant cowboys to growing feed for the winter.

THE FARMERS

In the thirty years after the Civil War more land was settled than in the whole of American history before that time. This great movement of population belonged only in part to the history of the Great Plains. Much of the new population completed the job of settling the fertile prairies. Yet when the farmers solidly occupied eastern Kansas, Nebraska, and the Dakotas up to the line of semiaridity, they inevitably spilled over it. Some tried their luck as far west as Wyoming and Montana. In many ways, the experience of these western settlers was like that of prairie farmers in the past generation. In other ways, both the new kind of country and the changing national economy made this last chapter of frontier farming different.

This was the first migration of farmers to take place since that great farmer victory, the passage of the Homestead Act of 1862. Under this law any head of family who lived on and cultivated his claim for five years could get title to 160 acres free. This amount of land seemed generous to legislators familiar with conditions farther east, but on the Great Plains, where farming cost more and was more risky, it was not enough to make a profitable venture. Later legislation made some attempt at adaptation to western realities. The Timber Culture Act of 1873 allowed a homesteader another 160 acres if he planted at least a quarter of it in trees. The Desert Land Act of 1877, lobbied through by cattlemen, allowed a prospective irrigator of dry lands to buy 649 acres. He was to pay twenty-five cents an acre down and would get title in three years on payment of the balance, provided he could prove he had irrigated a portion of the land. The Stone and Timber Act permitted the purchase of western lands not suitable for farming but valuable—sometimes very valuable—for timber or stone at the absurdly low price of $2.50 an acre.

All these laws, like many earlier American land laws, played into the hands of speculators, and many of them invited fraud. Cattle, lumber, and land companies used their employees as false homesteaders and hired new immigrants for the same purpose. The country was simply too big for the government to check up on everything that was happening. In the end, all but a small part of the land settled by farmers in this period was aquired not from the federal government directly but from intermediaries. Some of it came from land companies and some from western states which had received land under the Morrill Act for the purpose of promoting education.

The biggest of all the land sellers, however, were the railroads. The first transcontinentals and some other roads had received enormous grants along their rights of way. Their main interest was not in revenue from direct sale of this land but in building population in the areas they served. Thus they offered favorable terms, free inspection trips, agricultural information, and credit. They also advertised, and it is not surprising that the Great Plains sounded, in their promotional literature, a good deal like the Land of Canaan. Railroad agents together with state immigration bureaus and steamship line employees flooded Europe with leaflets about the low prices, phenomenal yields, and easy profits of western farming. In 1882, the peak year for this kind of migration, 105,000 Scandinavians and 250,000 Germans crossed the ocean, most of the former and many of the latter heading for western farms.

As farmers, whether from Illinois or Norway, moved farther west they confronted a host of new problems. Where there were no trees, they had to spend their first winters in dugouts or houses made of thick plains' sod. To keep warm they had to burn buffalo or cattle dung, corncobs, or hay. Fencing presented a worse problem until the invention of barbed wire in 1874 and its rapid spread. To make wells, they had to dig down hundreds of feet in the drier areas. To save what surface moisture there was, they had to learn to plow very deep and then harrow over the top to make a dust mulch. Finally, machines were needed to harvest large areas fast in this region of dangerously changeable weather.

For fencing, for well machinery and windmills to pump the water once found, for steel or chilled-iron plows to break tough sod, for harvesters, threshers, and binders, as well as for land itself, the farmer needed credit. Fortunately or unfortunately, in the good times of the early eighties, plenty of credit was available at high rates of interest.

In the Red River Valley of Dakota as in the San Joaquin Valley of California, wheat ranches of scores of thousands of acres gave an early foretaste of industrialized agriculture. Elsewhere in the new areas, a more modest prosperity prevailed. Farmers built better houses; farming towns paved their streets and improved their schools. The price of land skyrocketed.

To many, it seemed that the Great American Desert had at last been conquered. Advances had been made in techniques of "dry farming," and in the use of new varieties of wheat which could resist drought and cold. As always, the American farmer hoped that good times would continue indefinitely. Experts appeared who said that the climate of the plains was changing: tree planting, irrigation, even the building of railroads and telegraphs were somehow bringing more rain.

Actually, the Great Plains were nearing the end of one of their regular cycles of relatively greater rainfall. In 1887 the first of a series of dry summers withered the crops in the fields. With this grim warning of trouble, credit stopped flowing westward and the boom collapsed. Many of those who had moved beyond the line of semiaridity hastened back in despair. Half the population of western Kansas disappeared in four years, and whole towns were deserted as Colorado mining towns had been when the vein ran out. This disaster, peculiar to the new region in its origins, ushered in a general agricultural depression which in turn gave place to an over-all financial collapse. And unlike other farm crises, this one could not be solved by opening new land at low prices. There was nowhere to go.

THE HERITAGE OF THE FRONTIER

In 1893 the historian Frederick Jackson Turner said that a period of American history had ended in 1890 with the disappearance of the frontier. So far, the frontier had molded American character. It had also, Turner and his followers believed, served as a safety valve for urban discontents. Without it, America would be very different.

Much of this "frontier theory" has been disputed. For instance, it has been pointed out that more government land was disposed of in the decade after 1890 than in the decade before. "Free land," moreover, had always been something of a delusion. Much had gone to speculators rather than directly to small farmers. It had always been particularly difficult for a city worker, without training, equipment, or credit, to "go west." In fact, since the Civil War at least, most people seeking to escape poverty had moved in the opposite direction, from the farm to the city.

Yet it was true, as Turner said, that the 1890 census for the first time found no continuous border beyond which the country was unsettled. It was true also that a great many people in the nineties *felt* that a period was ending with the filling up of the West and that American problems in the future would be different and perhaps more difficult. While few historians agree with Turner that American individualism, equalitarianism, and nationalism come entirely from the West, few would deny that the American temperament owes something to both the reality and the legend of the frontier.

One obvious legacy of the West, and of this last West in particular, was a habit of violence. From vigilantes, frontier sheriffs, and cattlemen's associations the West drew a tradition of rough justice. From mining camps and cowtowns and end-of-track railroad settlements it drew another of just plain roughhouse. And in the twentieth century, violence sometimes hung on in still less attractive forms like the bloody labor wars of Colorado or the persistently high homicide rates of some western states. Perhaps violence was inseparable from some of the more attractive traits of the frontier legend—the devotion to individual freedom and equality we like to think of as western.

In politics the West has shown certain consistent traits. Sometimes the western liking for innovation has made easterners think it radical. Four far-western states pioneered in women's suffrage. The Initiative and Referendum came from the West and so did that last extreme of equalitarianism, the popular recall of judicial decisions. Yet such vigorous ultraconservatives as senators McCarran of Nevada and Goldwater of Arizona are also characteristically western. Sometimes western radicalism and western conservatism are inextricably blended in the same people. What Westerners have in common, perhaps, is a fierce devotion to individual independence, a contempt for tradition, a willingness to try something new, a delight above all in defying whatever mysterious forces are currently meant by the term "the East."

For a long time the heritage of the Far West has been falsified by sentimentalists, perverted by special pleaders, and debased by promoters. Yet those who know the bizarre and unique climate and landscape of desert and mountain, who travel through the region and talk to its old and young inhabitants know that the West is still in some ways difficult to define, different from the rest of the country. How should it not be so? Almost within living memory, large areas of this industrial country were empty, lawless, full of promise and bitter disappointment, and above all inconceivably distant from the civilization of London and Paris, New York, Boston, and Washington.

FOR FURTHER READING:

R. A. Billington, *Westward Expansion* (1949), is a usable general history of the West. L. R. Hafen and C. C. Rister, *Western America* (1941), is a more detailed account of the trans-Mississippi region. Walter P. Webb, *The Great Plains* (1931)*, is a fascinating and controversial interpretation of the region by a devoted native. The best single book on the mining frontier is Mark Twain, *Roughing It* (1872)*. A satisfactory summary of United States Indian policy in the period is L. B. Priest, *Uncle Sam's Stepchildren* (1942). There are many books on the cattle kingdom, including E. S. Osgood, *The Day of the Cattleman* (1929)*; E. E. Dale, *The Range Cattle Industry* (1930); and Louis Pelzer, *The Cattleman's Frontier* (1936). The problems of the plains farmer are authoritatively discussed by F. A. Shannon, *The Farmer's Last Frontier* (1945); and effectively portrayed in the works of Hamlin Garland, especially *Main Travelled Roads*

(1891)*. The social history of the northern plains is discussed by Everett Dick, *The Sod-House Frontier* (1937), and the special problems of the Scandinavian immigrant depicted in Ole Rolvaag, *Giants in the Earth* (1927). R. M. Robbins, *Our Landed Heritage* (1942)*, is a survey of public land policy. Henry Nash Smith, *Virgin Land: The American West as Symbol and Myth* (1950)*, is an important and highly sophisticated interpretation of the effect of the West on American thought and emotion.

*Available in paperback edition.

CHAPTER 19

THE POLITICAL PARADE

1868–1892

The politics of the generation after the Civil War are generally con-
sidered one of the least important and most sordid topics in American
history. During this period, we have often been assured, the American
people were concentrating on industrial development. Politics became
a meaningless side show in which second-rate statesmen made pomp-
ous speeches while special interests maneuvered for advantage behind
the scenes. This picture has much truth in it, but it is not complete.
Much was at stake, though the campaign slogans did not always reflect
the real issues.

THE STAKES OF THE GAME

Politics were, for instance, deeply affected by the period's three
depressions: the major one from 1873 to 1879, the minor one of the
mid-eighties, and the collapse initiated by the panic of 1893. These
depressions and related events such as the fall of farm prices in 1869
and 1887 greatly influenced people's political behavior. They did not,
however, produce effective governmental action. Only in the depression of the mid-nineties did demands for relief and remedy absorb
political argument briefly, and even then the call for action was
temporarily rejected. Throughout the period, depressions affected
people mainly by making them vote for the party out of power. They
also influenced their attitude toward the two big economic arguments
of the period, those over the tariff and the currency.

According to the period's dominant economic theory, it was not
part of the government's duty to interfere with the business cycle.
Distress would always be remedied in the long run by the action of the
invisible, all-powerful laws of political economy. The government's

[241]

role in the economic sphere was simple: (1) it should raise enough money for its own modest wants by equitable means; (2) it should provide a sound currency; and (3) perhaps (there was disagreement on this point) it should seek to advance the national products in the international market. The trouble was that the Civil War had thrown these traditional economic functions way out of kilter. In its great need the government had raised huge sums by any means available. It had placed internal taxes on everything in sight from coal and iron to billiard tables. It had, for the first time, taxed incomes. Partly to make up for these taxes, it had increased the moderate prewar protective tariff. It had issued $450 million worth of fiat money, the greenbacks, and floated immense loans. Now, most people agreed, the problem was to get rid of these burdens and go back to the simple old ways. This proved harder than it sounded.

It was easy enough to remove the income tax and other internal taxes, and this was largely accomplished by 1872. This being done, it seemed obvious that the tariff came next. Many people thought that the high wartime rates constituted unfair favors to special interests and placed a heavy burden on consumers. At first, most politicians took it for granted that the rates must go down. Somehow, though, tariff reduction bills that passed one house tended to be amended piecemeal in the other and then again in conference committee until they were no longer reduction bills.

Part of the difficulty lay in the nature of Congress in which each member represented his constituents and, consequently, very often a geographical and economic special interest. Each commodity was likely to have its own powerful spokesman. It soon developed that the easiest way to compromise between two conflicting interests, such as raw wool and woollen textiles or raw sugar and refined sugar, was to do some kind of favor for each. Thus, despite many attempts, wartime rates were never substantially and permanently lowered. By 1890 the Republican party and a minority of the Democrats were openly committed to raising protection still higher, though the opposition continued to be both sizeable and fervent. Certainly this issue was a real one: the rates on steel rails or woollens mattered a great deal to some people and the price of sugar, for instance, to others.

A problem which the high tariff brought with it—a strange one for modern readers—was the treasury surplus. Governmental functions were so comparatively simple that increased revenues could not easily be spent. Consequently too much of the limited supply of money accumulated in the treasury. One way to handle this problem was suggested by Grover Cleveland in 1888: lower the protective tariff.

Others, however, proved more politically appealing. One could, for instance, lower the nonprotective tariff rates on articles like coffee, tea, or sugar which were not made in this country. This was done in 1872 and again in 1890. It had the advantage of reducing the income of the government only and not of private interests. Or there were always veterans' pensions, river and harbor improvements, and subsidies to silver miners, railroad builders, and other powerful groups.

The other main economic argument arising from Civil War finance centered upon inflation. Right after the war, as we have seen, businessmen were deeply divided on this matter and so were the still prosperous farmers. Gradually, however, as farm prices sank in the seventies and then again in the late eighties and nineties, farm opinion turned toward inflation. At the same time, bankers, eastern editors, and some businessmen became more and more convinced that tampering with the value of money invited disaster. Many economists today would agree that the country's money supply during the whole period was insufficient and inflexible. Certainly many contemporaries believed this as a result of their own bitter experiences.

Three main methods of inflation attracted widespread support. The first was the suggestion, sometimes called the Ohio Idea and incorporated in the Democratic platform in 1868, that the government bonds be paid in the fluctuating greenback currency instead of in gold. Congress turned down this suggestion decidedly in 1869, resolving to pay the bondholders in "coin or its equivalent." It proved possible, however, to refund the bonds at lower rates of interest.

The next method centered upon the greenbacks, toward which there were three different attitudes. One group said more of the "money of the people" should be issued to relieve financial tightness. Another said that the existing greenbacks should be retired as fast as possible. A third, the one which won the argument, said that existing greenbacks should remain in circulation but no more should be issued. In 1875 Congress resolved that $300 million in greenbacks should be left in circulation, but that on January 1, 1879, greenbacks should be made redeemable in gold. Despite a rise, during the depression of the late seventies, of angry demands for more greenbacks, this policy was carried out on time. In the good times of the early eighties, agitation against this accomplished fact gradually declined.

The third proposal to get a big following was the demand for "free" coinage of silver. Traditionally, gold and silver had been the basis of American money, and since 1834 the official ratio between the value of the two metals had been sixteen to one. Since this undervalued silver in terms of world prices, people hoarded the silver dollars and they gradually disappeared. In accordance with Gresham's

1873 - coinage ends -

Law, the "cheap money drove out the dear." In 1873 the coinage of silver was quietly ended. In the decade after this, however, the huge silver strikes of the Far West greatly increased the supply of silver. Now, if the silver dollar had been coined at the old ratio, it would have been the cheaper, and therefore the dominant, coin. This would have expanded the currency and also helped the silver-mining interests, strategically located in underpopulated western states and therefore disproportionately strong in the Senate.

The gold standard, the money of imperial Britain and of international bankers, was blamed for all the farmer's troubles. Pressure to go back to free coinage of silver at sixteen to one became almost irresistible, and twice Congress was forced to make a half-hearted concession to the silver forces. In 1878 the Bland-Allison Act directed the Treasury to purchase $2 to $4 million worth of silver bullion a month and coin it into dollars. In 1890 the Sherman Silver Purchase Act required the purchase of the whole output of the silver mines and the issuance thereon of treasury notes. However, by action of the Secretary of the Treasury, these notes, like the silver dollars coined under the previous legislation, remained convertible into gold on demand so the gold standard was still intact. Despite their lack of major victories, the inflationists remained strong in the West and in Congress.

Aside from the tariff and money, the main recurrent issue was political reform. From the late seventies on, it became painfully clear that the government did not, as standard theory said it should, stay out of economic competition. Its favors in terms of tariffs and tax remissions and subsidies were bought by influence and even money. Some members of the well-established eastern middle class became deeply aroused on moral grounds. Perhaps they were alarmed also by the power of the new rich, who did not share their own traditions of public service. In any case these essentially conservative reformers, Republican by normal allegiance but independent by conviction, became a surprisingly powerful influence. With parties as evenly balanced as they were, professional politicians might hate the unreliable "mugwumps," but they could not ignore them.

The chief proposal of this kind of reformers was the development of a federal civil service. This would end bribery and corruption, take the power of appointment away from unscrupulous politicians, and perhaps create a class of devoted, impartial public servants like those said to exist in England and Germany.

"Snivel service," as the indignant professional politicians called the movement, never achieved its ideal of completely just, impartial administration. It did, however, make it harder to get away with the kind of outright fraud and theft that had become common in the Grant administration. Some of the most powerful politicians of the day were kept out of the presidency because their records were not pure enough to satisfy the reform element. And after many frustrations the civil service movement did finally secure, in 1887, the passage of the Pendleton Act. Under this some federal offices were filled by competitive examination. Since that time presidents have frequently added to the number of offices under civil service, especially when the opposing party has been about to come to power. The increase of federal employees has, however, prevented reform from destroying traditional political methods.

Tariff, money, and reform were the most important of the obvious political issues, and, underlying these, business depressions played a big part in politics. On the surface, however, campaigns were fought over whatever false issue lent itself best to emotional slogans, torchlight parades, and bitter hatreds more or less forgotten between elections. The first of these false issues, sadly enough, was Reconstruction—a real and tragic problem subordinated to the political battle. While people lost interest in the fate of the southern Negro, Republican politicians "waved the bloody shirt," blaming their opponents for all the horrors of war. Conversely, southerners and Democrats dwelt on the horrors of Negro rule.

After attacks on rebels, Negroes, and carpetbaggers began to pall, there were always Catholics, immigrants, and foreigners in general. One big section of the population could be counted on to respond to fear of the Pope, and another always cheered an attack on Great Britain. Finally, the war records, drinking habits, appearance, and marital life of leading candidates could be attacked.

THE RULES AND THE PLAYERS

Part of the explanation of the character of post-Civil War politics lies in two great political facts: the overwhelming power of Congress and the even division between the two great parties. In Reconstruction, Congress had broken the power of the executive. Real power was centered in the Senate. Powerful and arrogant, some leading Senators had built nearly unbeatable personal machines in their home states. Both state and federal officeholders, appointed at their behest, could be assessed for campaign contributions. When this was theoretically outlawed by the Pendleton Act, local business interests could still be heavily tapped. Thus the right kind of governors and Congressmen would be elected, and a subservient legislature would send

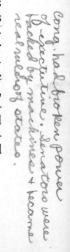

Cong. had broken power of executive. Senators were backed by machines + became real rulers of states.

the real ruler of the state back again and again to the Senate. With the presidency weakened, there was no powerful advocate for general national needs, and politics had to be carried on by log-rolling, that is, by the trading of one particular favor for another.

The Civil War and Reconstruction demoralized the Democratic party, but by no means destroyed it. Though the Republicans held the presidency during most of the period, the Democrats actually won a popular plurality more often and controlled the lower House more than half the time. National elections often depended on a few thousand well-distributed votes.

Since no single interest group commanded a majority, each party had to appeal to many elements. The Republicans could count on the Union veterans and the Negroes, when and where they could vote. Those businessmen who favored the high protective tariff voted Republican and so, usually, did believers in the gold standard (though many western Republicans were inflationists). In good times, midwestern farmers could be counted on for Republican votes. To a large group of respectable middle-class Protestants, it was unthinkable to vote Democratic. The clergyman who said in 1884 that the Democrats were the party of "Rum, Romanism, and Rebellion" went too far and may have lost the election for his candidate, but he voiced a stereotype many took for granted.

After Reconstruction, the Democrats could start with the Solid South. Most immigrants in the coastal cities, neglected by Anglo-Saxon Republicans and helped by efficient Democratic bosses, were also safely Democratic. Western farmers and much of labor tended to vote Democratic when times were bad. Thus the Democrats were always potentially a party of moderate protest, of agitation for low tariffs, and of cheap money. Yet in the East and Midwest as well as the South, some of the party leaders were ultrarespectable lawyers and businessmen. This kind of conservative Democrat, often interested in foreign trade, might favor a low tariff but oppose any other kind of change as vigorously as any Republican.

Thus each party was divided. The Republican factions were three. The "Stalwarts" were all-out believers in party regularity and the bloody shirt. At the opposite extreme were the many Republican reformers. Between these two were the "Half-Breeds," much like the Stalwarts but less blatant. The Democrats included Bourbon reactionaries and near radicals. In presidential years, therefore, each party tended to select a colorless compromise candidate and write a meaningless platform. Precisely because it was necessary to play down divisive issues, it was necessary to play up personalities, scandals, and party regularity. In crucial states in tight years even bribery and violence were not rare.

[246]

Did the system work well? The country and its industry expanded and at least the presidents were reasonably able and thoroughly decent men. Divisive issues were kept out of presidential politics; in campaign years everybody got excited, and after the election most were able to forget about government. One may perhaps conclude that the system worked fairly well as long as the country faced no crises, foreign or domestic. When crisis raised its head, political habits had to change.

THE GRANT ERA

When Grant was elected in 1868, many people expected a dignified, masterly administration in the Washington tradition. Naturally, the chief national hero was flattered by politicians and big businessmen. Equally naturally Grant, who before the war had had little interest in politics and no experience of success, enjoyed the flattery. Originally inclined toward a lenient Reconstruction policy, he was skillfully maneuvered by the Radicals into their camp. His appointments dismayed his admirers. Though they included real statesmen like Hamilton Fish, the New York aristocrat who became Secretary of State, they also included routine politicians, incompetents, seedy relatives of the Grants, military men out of jobs, and plain crooks. Grant's own honesty made his political naiveté all the more tragic.

In financial matters Grant was moderately conservative, vetoing a measure to increase the greenbacks but battling the Supreme Court to defend the validity of those in circulation. Secretary Fish handled foreign affairs with surprising effectiveness. In 1871, the difficult issues arising out of England's wartime friendliness to the Confederacy were sensibly settled by arbitration. To placate reformers, a Civil Service commission was set up, but it was not allowed to interfere with serious politics.

By 1872 the reformers were tired of Radical Reconstruction, irritated by the failure of tariff reduction, and disgusted by the administration's moral laxity. Determined to block Grant's re-election, they held a separate Liberal Republican convention and nominated for the presidency the veteran reformer and crusading editor Horace Greeley. Hoping to make a "new departure" and end the constant attacks on their patriotism, the Democrats nominated Greeley also. As a former Whig, Republican and abolitionist, Greeley was a strange Democratic candidate. Vulnerable to ridicule for his many and sometimes contradictory causes, somehow a relic of the prewar past, Greeley was disastrously beaten.

With Grant re-elected and reformers discredited, the way seemed clear for Stalwart domination. However, the Democrats captured the

House of Representatives in the depression year 1874 and used their victory to investigate the administration. A sinister pattern seemed to repeat itself in one department after another: the purchase of political favors for money. Corruption of this sort touched great causes like the building of the Union Pacific; it honeycombed the Indian Service, the Freedmen's Bureau, and the collection of internal revenue; it touched ambassadors, cabinet members, and even the President's private secretary. Before the end the hero of Appomattox realized that something was the matter and apologized on the ground of his own political inexperience.

THE DISPUTED ELECTION

By 1876 Republican regimes remained in power in only three southern states. With the South back on their side and many northerners hostile to the administration, it seemed likely that the Democrats would return to power. To prevent this unthinkable disaster, the Republicans nominated the honest and able, though rather uninspiring, Rutherford B. Hayes of Ohio. The Democrats also bid for the reformers by nominating Samuel J. Tilden, who as governor of New York had destroyed the grafting Boss Tweed ring in New York City.

Tilden, with a sizeable popular plurality, captured New York and several other northern states in addition to the South. It seemed clear that he had won. The Republicans, however, claimed the votes of the three southern states still under carpetbagger rule: Florida, South Carolina, and Louisiana. In each of these states the Democrats had indeed intimidated Negroes and both parties had been guilty of other dubious practices. After a long and bitter dispute, the conflicting returns from these states were referred to an electoral commission which, acting on strictly party lines, gave the election to Hayes by one vote.

Actually, certain Republicans had approached certain Democrats in advance to make sure the result would be accepted. The Compromise of 1877, as this has been called, somewhat resembles the prewar compromises. Like them, it was made by conservatives for the purpose of preventing trouble. Southern Democratic leaders were assured that, if they accepted Hayes's election, he would remove the troops from the remaining southern states and that the South would receive its share of railroad subsidies and similar federal favors. Actually, conservative southern Democrats, many of them former Whigs, had no love for the potentially radical northern Democrats. The Republican conservatives, on the other hand, hoped to build up their party in the southern states. This hope did not mature, and by the next election the bloody shirt was again waving in the breeze. One result of the

[248]

compromise stood: the North was through intervening on behalf of the southern Negro. Once more white Southerners controlled the South.

THE PRESIDENTIAL SEESAW

Hayes made a serious effort to reform the federal bureaucracy, an effort which involved him in a bitter fight with the Stalwarts of his party but did not go far enough to please the reformers. A financial conservative, he stood firm against inflation. A believer in the principle of a single presidential term, Hayes had made too many enemies to be renominated even if he had changed his mind. After a stalemate between the Stalwart backers of a third term for Grant and the partisans of James G. Blaine, the oratorically gifted but somewhat tarnished "Plumed Knight" of the Half-Breeds, the nomination went to the moderately reform-minded James A. Garfield of Ohio. To placate the defeated Stalwarts, the Republicans gave the second place on the ticket to Chester A. Arthur of the New York Customs House, a perfect representative of machine politics. Garfield won a close election against General Winfield Scott Hancock and, like his predecessor, began struggling with the Stalwarts over patronage. On September 29, 1881, this promising president was shot by a crazy Stalwart officeseeker.

To the surprise and dismay of some of his friends, Vice President Arthur made a good president. Turning against his old cronies, he fought against corruption in the post office and machine politics in his own bailiwick. He backed the Pendleton Act, the first real civil service law, and even attempted to put through a thorough revision of the tariff. In this he failed and the so-called Mongrel Tariff of 1882 was amended out of all reform meaning.

In 1884 the Half-Breeds finally pushed through the nomination of their hero, Blaine. The Democrats nominated Grover Cleveland, the stout and solid governor of New York, who had a deserved reputation for honesty and courage. In a campaign that reached a peak of colorful scandal-mongering on both sides, Cleveland won. To the deep disgust of devoted Republicans, a number of "mugwump" reformers switched parties to support him.

For the first time since 1856, a Democrat was in power. Nothing very dreadful happened; Cleveland, honest and able, was no innovator. The main problem facing him was the rising treasury surplus. Instead of allowing it to be dissipated by continually bigger pensions for veterans, which he courageously opposed, Cleveland insisted on tariff reduction. In 1887, using the most forthright language employed by any president since the war, he attacked the high tariff as the creator of oppressive monopolies and managed to push a tariff reform bill through the House of Representatives though not the Senate.

The protective tariff, therefore, was the one national issue that played a big part in the campaign of 1888. The Republicans nominated the cold and correct Benjamin Harrison of Indiana, grandson of Old Tippecanoe. Since it was clear what was at stake, they were able to go farther than usual in "frying the fat," that is, wringing campaign contributions out of protected industries. Despite these and less savory tactics, Cleveland won a popular plurality, but Harrison secured a majority of the electoral votes.

For some reason, the Harrison administration took this doubtful mandate as a green light for an extreme program along Stalwart lines. With liberal pension acts and rich pork-barrel appropriations for rivers and harbors, post offices, and the like, the new Congress launched a successful assault on the surplus in the old-fashioned manner. The administration leaders gave their cordial support to the complex and ultraprotectionist McKinley Tariff of 1890. To put this across among dubious western Republicans, it was necessary to back also the Sherman Silver-Purchase Act and, still more significantly, the Sherman Anti-Trust Act. This measure, which is discussed on page 257, had little immediate and concrete importance, but its necessity indicated a rising discontent. The admission of six western states and an unsuccessful attempt to give Congress power to control southern elections completed the strategy of the administration high command.

In 1890 the Republicans were repudiated overwhelmingly in Congress and in 1892 Cleveland was vindicated by re-election. Despite the reappearance, however, of his corpulent and familiar figure, there were signs that the conventional pattern of politics was changing. In the heavily Democratic Congress there were several members of a new third party calling itself the People's party and demanding a whole list of radical reforms. Shortly after Cleveland's inauguration a severe financial panic alarmed businessmen. This was only the beginning; the second Cleveland administration was to face a host of new problems at home and abroad. Or, more accurately, old problems that could no longer be ignored.

FOR FURTHER READING:

The only political history of the entire period is Matthew Josephson, *The Politicos* (1938). This is entertaining but dated both in research and point of view. Herbert Agar, *The Price of Union* (1950), is a stimulating interpretation of American politics with much to say about this period. One can approach the economic issues of the period's politics through F. W. Taussig, *The Tariff History of the United States* (1931); D. R. Dewey, *Financial History of the United States* (1936); and W. J. Schultz and M. S. Caine, *Financial Development of the United States* (1938). For the Grant administration, two biographies are very helpful: William B. Hesseltine, *Ulysses S. Grant, Politician* (1935), and Allan Nevins, *Hamilton Fish: The Inner History of the Grant Administration* (1936). The disputed election is convincingly interpreted by C. Vann Woodward, *Reunion and Reaction* (1951)*. For politics from Hayes to Cleveland the best approach is through biographies of the major figures. These are innumerable and range from excellent to mediocre. One of the best is Allan Nevins, *Grover Cleveland* (1932).

---

*Available in paperback edition.

THE INS VERSUS THE OUTS: AMERICAN POLITICS 1868–1896

PRESIDENT	PRESIDENTIAL VOTE (IN THOUSANDS)			REPRESENTATIVES ELECTED			MAJOR TARIFF LEGISLATION	FINANCIAL AND OTHER IMPORTANT LEGISLATION	BUSINESS CONDITIONS
	R	D	other	R	D	other			
							1867 Reduction narrowly beaten.		To 1869 Moderate prosperity for agriculture. Moderate depression for industry.
1868 Grant *R*	3,013	2,707		149	63				1868
								1869 Resolution to pay bonds in coin.	1869 Collapse of farm prices.
1870				134	104	5	Slight reductions.	Bonds re-funded at lower rates.	1870
									1869–1873 Moderate prosperity for industry.
1872 Grant *R*	3,597	2,843		194	92	14	Ten per cent off protected articles. Coffee, tea, free.	Most re-maining in-ternal taxes repealed. 1873 End of silver coinage. Greenback	1872
									1873 Panic.
1874				109	169	14			1874

PRESIDENT	PRESIDENTIAL VOTE (IN THOUSANDS)	REPRESENTATIVES ELECTED	MAJOR TARIFF LEGISLATION	FINANCIAL AND OTHER IMPORTANT LEGISLATION	BUSINESS CONDITIONS
1876 Hayes *R*	4,037 4,284	140 *153*	1875 Ten per cent cut restored.	1875 Resumption Act (greenbacks to be convertible 1879).	DEPRESSION 1876
1878		130 *149* 14		Bland-Allison Act.	1878
1880 Garfield *R*	4,453 4,414	*147* 135 11		1879 Resumption (greenbacks convertible).	1879 Recovery. .... PROSPERITY 1880
1882		118 *199* 10			1882
1884 Cleveland *D*	4,850 4,880	140 *183* 2	1883 "Mongrel Tariff."	1883 Pendleton Act.	Panic and 1884 depression.
					1885 Partial recovery.
1886		152 *169* 4			1886
			1887 Cleveland Tariff Message.	1887 Interstate Commerce Act.	1887 Collapse of farm prices. UNEVEN PROSPERITY

THE INS VERSUS THE OUTS: AMERICAN POLITICS 1868–1896 (*Continued*)

PRESIDENT	PRESIDENTIAL VOTE (IN THOUSANDS)	REPRESENTATIVES ELECTED	MAJOR TARIFF LEGISLATION	FINANCIAL AND OTHER IMPORTANT LEGISLATION	BUSINESS CONDITIONS
1888 Harrison *R*	5,447 5,538	166 159	Mills bill (reduction) passes House.		1888
1890		88 235 9	McKinley Tariff (increase).	1889 Omnibus bill (4 western states). Sherman Anti-Trust Act and Sherman Silver Purchase Act.	Minor panic 1890
1892 Cleveland *D*	5,183 5,555	127 218 11			1892
1894		244 105 7	Wilson-Gorman Tariff (slight reduction).	1893 Repeal of Sherman Silver Purchase Act.	1893 Major panic. 1894
1896 McKinley *R*	7,102 6,493	204 113 40			DEPRESSION 1896

CHAPTER 20

THE RIPENING OF PROTEST

1870–1896

In the nineties, more than in any period before the 1930's, sharp criticism of American industrial and capitalist society broke through the bland surface of American political life. For a few years conservative Americans were deeply alarmed and talked about the menace of revolution. It is hard for present-day Americans to understand the intensity of these fears. Most of the radical demands were for redress and not revolution; many were far from new.

One reason political feelings were so intense was that the two sides in most of the arguments did not speak each other's language. The spokesmen of discontent felt that they had been ignored and frustrated too long. Insistent on being heard, they often sounded more radical than they were. The conservatives, on the other hand, had long taken it for granted that serious discontent in America was impossible. When it appeared they were deeply shocked.

DEFENDERS OF *LAISSEZ FAIRE*

The starting point, for educated Americans of the nineteenth century, was the belief that human affairs were ruled by immutable law. The central law of political economy was that the general good would be best served by the pursuit of individual self-interest. If, under competition, there were difficulties or suffering in society, these were necessary spurs to effort. Rewards went to those who worked hard and deserved them, while poverty was almost always a punishment for vice and laziness. It would be both foolish and immoral for the state or for any private organization to intervene in economic affairs.

These laws of political economy were, said the textbooks, the laws of God. They were also, for those who accepted the new lessons of Darwinian evolution, the laws of biology. The struggle for existence was the means by which the human race had reached its present high development. Interference would simply help the weak and unfit, injure the strong, and thereby weaken the race. Often spokesmen of *laissez faire* combined the two sources of authority: free competition was the means by which evolution took place under Divine superintendence.

This doctrine of *laissez faire* was taught by political economists, preached every Sunday by clergymen, and invoked by lawyers and judges. During the eighties and nineties, the Supreme Court gradually worked out an interpretation of the Fourteenth Amendment which made it a bastion of *laissez faire*. The amendment prohibited states from depriving "any person of life, liberty, or property, without due process of law." "Liberty," the Court said, included freedom of contract and "person" could mean a corporation. "Without due process of law" covered any sort of unreasonable or unnatural regulation (for example of hours of labor or railway rates). What was reasonable depended, of course, on the general knowledge of all educated men, that is on the doctrine of *laissez faire*.

THE REVIVAL OF REFORM

Individualists by tradition, Americans were also reformers. If bad conditions existed, most people believed they could and should be changed. At first, the end of slavery and secession seemed to mean that all was well; gradually, with shocked surprise, many came to realize that this was not the case.

Some of the evils of the period, like recurrent corruption in government and fraud in business, raised no new moral problems; these things were evil and should be punished. Yet, under the new conditions, the line between legitimate competition and dishonesty was not easy to draw. Bribery was wrong, but tips to helpful public officials about likely investments and agreements to give special prices to favored insiders were borderline cases. Closely related to such problems was the old question of monopoly. Since Jackson's day or earlier, most Americans had disliked great accumulations of power. Many businessmen as well as farmers began in the post-Civil War period to feel that great corporations were shutting the door to opportunity and endangering *laissez faire* itself. Understandably the railroads, with their life-and-death power over shippers, drew the earliest fire. By the mid-eighties, when the Supreme Court began to strike down state regulatory laws, demand for national railroad legislation became overwhelming. In 1887 the Interstate Commerce Act forbade certain unfair practices, required that rates be both openly published and "reasonable," and set up a commission to investigate abuses and appeal to the courts for redress.

In 1890, mounting demand for general antimonopoly legislation was met by the Sherman Anti-Trust Act. This law, couched in vague terms, forbade various kinds of action in restraint of interstate or foreign trade. Anglo-Saxon common law had long prohibited harmful restraint of trade, but many lawyers and businessmen believed that what was natural could not be harmful and that most of what occurred was natural. Thus it was most uncertain what was or could be forbidden by the Sherman Act, and for the rest of the century this statute, like the Interstate Commerce Act, remained ineffective. Yet each involved that interesting paradox which was to become increasingly common: government intervention to preserve *laissez faire*.

Perhaps the biggest step in the revival of reform was the discovery of the city. Even for those who believed that poverty was the fault of the poor, it was impossible to ignore the epidemics that periodically spread from the slums or the fires that began in jerry-built tenements and spread to business blocks. Looking a little further, some middle-class Americans were amazed to find whole families living in single, airless, lightless rooms with unspeakable sanitation.

Insofar as they did know about slum conditions, many were at first inclined to blame them on the slum dwellers, that is, the new immigrants. In one of the great migrations of all history, about fourteen million immigrants came to the United States in the last four decades of the century. Through the seventies, most immigrants continued to come from northwestern Europe, particularly the British Isles, Germany, and Scandinavia. In the eighties, however, southern and eastern Europeans started to appear in great numbers, and by the nineties these new sources furnished the majority. Slavs from the Austro-Hungarian Empire, Italians from the poverty-stricken south, and Jews fleeing savage Russian persecution came, like all earlier American immigrants back to the Pilgrims, looking for liberty and opportunity. This was certainly in the best tradition of *laissez faire*, and, moreover, immigration was beneficial to expanding industry.

Many insisted that immigration, like other national problems, be left alone. Yet more and more voices were raised in favor of regulation. Some of the demand for a change in immigration policy was an expression of the ugliest forms of racial prejudice, but much came from other sources. Organized labor feared competition from destitute and hard-to-organize newcomers. Some conservatives worried about the menace to established tradition. To middle-class reformers, the new immigrants presented a perplexing picture. Often destitute, knowing no English, and disoriented by a sudden move from a familiar village to a raw metropolis, the newcomers tended naturally to stick together and to maintain their languages and customs. Equally naturally, they were easily organized for political purposes by bosses who could speak their language and attend to some of their immediate needs. Thus sections of New York and Chicago became, to middle-class Americans, as alien as Naples or Prague. Many people tended to approach the new immigrants with a curious mixture of emotions: compassion, missionary desire to uplift, fear, and resentment.

Whether demand for immigration restriction came from reformist or conservative sources or (as often) from both at once, the inevitable result was government action in a new area. In 1882 Congress excluded Chinese laborers, a group especially disliked by organized labor. In the same year convicts, paupers, and criminals were banned —the list was later to include anarchists and other "undesirables." In 1885 the importation of contract labor was forbidden.

Fear of aliens, resentment of big business, and concern for the urban poor all increased sharply in periods of depression. When thousands of unemployed roamed the streets it became harder to believe that poverty was always a punishment for vice or even that prices and production adjusted themselves automatically to social needs.

In each depression period social violence dramatized the existence of discontent. In the railroad strikes of 1877, mobs took over and looted Pittsburgh and Baltimore until President Hayes sent troops. In 1886 a bomb thrown in the Chicago Haymarket provoked police reprisals and set off a public "anarchist scare." In 1892 the Homestead steel strike turned into a pitched battle between strikers and Pinkerton detectives. Horrified at such episodes, many shocked citizens demanded swift action to restore order and punish violence. This they got, but some went on to ask difficult questions. How could such things happen in America where everyone had an equal opportunity? What had gone wrong with the laws of free competition and inevitable progress?

Among the first flatly to challenge *laissez faire* were certain Protestant ministers. Reacting to personal experiences of city conditions or social violence, some Christians found themselves unable to square the ethics of *laissez faire* with the Gospel injunctions to love one's neighbor. By the early nineties many urban, middle-class congregations heard, to their surprise, that they should apply the law of love to labor relations and the relief of poverty. Some ministers went further than these general injunctions, urging that society be radically reconstructed according to what they considered Christian principles.

Up to this time charitable relief had been either a matter of individual handouts or crowded and inadequate poorhouses. By the mid-century, firm believers in *laissez faire* were organizing to secure charitable efficiency and to make sure that the unworthy poor got nothing and that nobody got enough to spoil his character. By 1890, however, a new group had appeared—the settlement workers. These men and women, of whom Jane Addams was the most famous, actually lived and worked in slum neighborhoods. Being "neighbors to the poor" tended to change their attitudes toward the causes and relief of poverty. At the same time, shocking descriptions of immigrant slums began to be spread by talented reporters like Jacob Riis, author of *How the Other Half Lives*.

By the early nineties, then, many middle-class Americans were finding it hard to accept altogether the theories of *laissez faire*. On the left of this group were believers in drastic social change, like Edward Bellamy, the author of the Utopian socialist novel *Looking Backward* (1888). Somewhat less radical was Henry George, perhaps the most influential American social theorist of the period. George traced all social evils to one single source, the private appropriation of the increase in land values. If this "unearned increment" were taken away from the landlord and used by society, it could be spent for social improvement. At the same time labor and capital would be freed from an unjust burden and true individualism revived.

To the right of George were a host of academic theorists who denied that *laissez faire* and unchecked individual competition had to be the sole law of social evolution. Still to the right of such theorists, and much more numerous, were people who had no answers to current problems and who still believed deeply in individualism, but who found it harder and harder to believe that all was well.

ORGANIZED LABOR

Industrial workers did not need to be told that society was imperfect. It is true that real wages advanced during the period, largely because of falling prices. Yet $1 to $1.50 a day (a common wage for unskilled labor) was hardly lavish, and it left absolutely no margin for illness, accident, or unemployment.

Yet would-be organizers faced great difficulties. Most managers of industry were frankly hostile to all labor unions, and large sections of the press and public shared this hostility. Frequent depressions made labor activity dangerous—there were thousands of unemployed to replace those who were fired and black-listed. Above all immigration meant the yearly arrival of thousands of new recruits to industry who were poor and inexperienced in the American labor market, often willing to work for what they could get.

The first major postwar organizations attacked these problems in the idealistic spirit inherited from prewar reform movements. Up to about 1873 the most important organization was the National Labor Union which was interested in greenback inflation and many other nonlabor causes. Not really sure whether they accepted the wage system or not, some of its leaders tried to start producers' cooperatives and made vague commitments to socialism. Others placed all their hopes on the eight-hour day. Its energies scattered, the NLU ceased to exist in the depression of the seventies.

In the prosperous early eighties, national attention was caught by the Knights of Labor, an organization which had existed since 1869 but now suddenly grown to three quarters of a million. Like its predecessor, the organization was interested in a host of causes including cooperatives and inflation. Though they officially disliked strikes and preferred arbitration, the loosely organized Knights found themselves involved in a series of major railroad strikes in 1884–1886. At first they scored surprising victories, but they ended by losing disastrously. Unfairly, they were associated by the alarmed public with the Haymarket bombing. In the depression of the nineties, the organization perished. It had already failed to meet the competition of a new rival, the American Federation of Labor.

Samuel Gompers, founder of the new organization, was a cigar-maker who had absorbed the craft tradition of his trade. Observing the Knights, he blamed their defeat on loose organization and political involvement. The A. F. of L., which he founded under another name in 1881 and gave permanent structure in 1886, was organized strictly on craft lines and, deliberately or not, appealed mostly to skilled workers. Gompers emphasized what he called "pure and simple unionism," which meant the pursuit of higher wages, shorter hours, and union protection, including if possible the closed shop. The proper methods by which to reach these goals were the strike and the boycott. From the government, the A. F. of L. primarily wanted protection of these methods, not ameliorative legislation. The organization did not oppose capitalism, refusing to come out for any over-all social theory.

By adapting to existing conditions rather than fighting them, the A. F. of L. survived in the hostile world of the nineteenth century. It weathered the depression of the nineties, and by 1900 had won a million members and a limited measure of public recognition. It proved unable, however, to organize the large groups of immigrant workers in heavy industry. Many members of the labor movement, including a strong minority within the A. F. of L. itself, wanted to change the organization's nature—to add political activity to trade union methods, to abandon craft for industrial unions, and, above all, to "organize the unorganized." In the disturbed mid-nineties, this opposition got so strong that Gompers lost the leadership of the A. F. of L. for a year and only narrowly prevented the adoption of a socialist program.

THE FARMERS AND POPULISM

The basic problem of the farmers was the general decline of farm prices from 1870 to 1895. It took more and more cotton, corn, or wheat to pay the farmer's costs, including interest on his debts. Part of the reason for declining prices was that vast areas of the world—Russia, Argentina, and Australia—were coming into competition with America. The farmer, however, tended to blame conditions closer to home. In the first place, he said, the money supply was inadequate and inflexible. It had been wrong to retire the greenbacks, to decrease the number of bank notes in circulation, and, above all, to take silver out of the currency. Second, farmers blamed exploitation by middlemen. Railroad and elevator rates were high and arbitrary, interest rates were going up, and the farmer was being milked by the farm implement trust. Protective tariffs (some farmers said) merely raised the farmer's expenses without helping him.

In two regions, as we have seen, these chronic ills were augmented by local conditions. The overexpanded wheat farmers of the plains were hit by devastating droughts and in 1887 an especially sharp price fall toppled their inflated credit structure. The South, in addition to suffering most of the ills of the West, had to bear in addition the sharecrop and crop-lien system fastened on the section during the postwar shortage of capital. The southern farmer, moreover, suffered from the biracial system, though he did not usually see it that way. Only occasionally, and in only a few southern states, did white agrarian radicals make common cause with Negro farmers against railroads and landlords. More often the discontented white man blamed his troubles partly on his Negro neighbor and accused his conservative enemy of being pro-Negro.

Farmers in the North and South often believed, as their ancestors had for centuries, that the small farmer was by nature a specially valuable and virtuous citizen, that at some time in the past things had been much better for him, and that his troubles were the result of deliberate Wall Street plots. Though conservative in many ways, farmers had an old tradition of calling on the government for help when they felt oppressed. In the late nineteenth century their demands took two main forms: inflation to bring their prices up and regulation to bring their costs down. In the sixties the midwestern Grangers had helped secure state laws regulating railroads and elevators, some of which were invalidated in the eighties by the Supreme Court. Farmers took part in many kinds of inflationary movements, including the greenback and silver struggles and various proposals to issue national currency on the basis of land or crops and lend it at low rates.

When acute farm crisis hit at the end of the eighties, the greatest existing farmer organizations were the two Farmers' Alliances of the North and South. In 1890 two senators and eight representatives were elected on straight Alliance tickets, in addition to a considerable number of closely sympathetic congressmen. Encouraged, representatives of the northern and southern Alliances drew together during the next two years to form the People's party.

In their first national convention in Omaha in 1892 the Populists, as they were called, drew up a platform which summarized, in angry and dramatic language, most of the discontent of the period. It called for inflation by legal tender notes, silver, and other methods. Railroad land grants were to be recovered, and aliens were to be forbidden land ownership. Railroads, and also telephone and telegraph industries, were to be nationalized. In an effort to attract labor support, the platform called for the eight-hour day, immigration restriction, and the abolition of Pinkerton industrial detectives. Miscellaneous radical sentiment was cultivated by denunciation of land monopoly, demand for the income tax, and a general statement that the powers of government should be extended as much as was necessary to secure the end of injustice and poverty. Finally, expressing the deep confidence in increased democracy of most American radicalism, the platform praised the Initiative and Referendum and called for direct election of senators. Running on this platform, General James B. Weaver, the first Populist candidate for the presidency, received a million votes.

Stirred by this promising first effort, some hopeful radicals believed that the Populist movement was going to sweep to power, uniting all the diverse kinds of discontent, upsetting the two-party system as the Republicans had in 1856–1860, and driving out the monopolists and gold bugs.

CLEVELAND'S LAST STAND

Nothing could have been farther from the intentions of the man actually elected to the presidency in 1892. Grover Cleveland incarnated more completely than any politician of the period the doctrine of *laissez faire*. When the Panic of 1893 swept banks and railroads into bankruptcy, when depression set in and unemployment mounted, he had no doubt of his duty. He must fight against the high tariff as always, but still harder against inflation. At all costs demagogues and tamperers must be defeated so as to allow natural forces a chance to bring recovery.

The immediate problem facing the administration was the danger of a lack of gold in the treasury to meet its obligations. Gold had been drained away by the policies of the previous administration. The prohibitive rates of the McKinley Tariff had cut income. Outgo had been increased by political appropriations for rivers, harbors, pensions, and, above all, payments for silver under the Sherman Silver Purchase Act. Cleveland put the administration's whole weight behind a drive to repeal this compromise measure. He won his objective, but thereby permanently alienated the western wing of his party. As a result he lacked the power to force tariff reduction through Congress. The Wilson-Gorman bill, thoroughly amended as usual in the Senate, brought little reduction in existing rates.

With the Silver Purchase Act repealed, the government was no longer obligated to buy the output of the silver mines, but it still had to exchange gold for the outstanding greenbacks and silver certificates. To meet the continuing gold drain, the administration resorted to selling government bonds for gold. Two issues were sold, with difficulty, on the open market. For the third, in February, 1895, the administration sought help in the same quarter that great corporations appealed to in time of stress. This was the international banking syndicate of Morgan, Belmont, and Rothschild. This group was accustomed to performing some of the functions carried out in other countries by central banks. It dealt with governments as equals and demanded high prices for its services. Drawing much of the necessary gold from abroad, the banking syndicate bought the entire bond issue on very profitable terms. The treasury reserve was saved for another year, when another public issue became necessary.

Naturally, this episode raised the pitch of popular emotion, which was already mounting fast. In the congressional elections of 1894, the Republican opposition swept Congress and the Populists increased their popular vote by 40 per cent. In the same year the most serious strike of the period broke out in the model company town of Pullman, Illinois. While Pullman dividends remained high, wages were cut as much as 30 to 40 per cent and employees' rents not reduced. When the desperate Pullman employees appealed for help they received it from the American Railway Union, a new industrial union led by Eugene V. Debs. Around Chicago, A.R.U. men started cutting Pullman cars out of trains and the public began to fear a tie-up in its essential means of transportation.

Welcoming a showdown, the railroad General Managers' Association appealed to the administration. Cleveland's Attorney General, Richard Olney, himself a former railroad lawyer, secured an injunction (invoking among other laws the Sherman Anti-Trust Act) which forbade practically all strike activity. Under this injunction Debs went to jail. Meantime Cleveland sent federal troops to Chicago to maintain order, though the liberal governor of Illinois John P. Altgeld said this was unnecessary. When the troops arrived, riots did indeed break out.

Conservative fears were further roused by the unemployed "armies" which converged on Washington under the leadership of "general" Jacob Coxey and others. Actually these groups were not very large, and their intention was to demand such measures of relief as government loans to finance public work. This proposal seemed to the conservative press the height of extremism and absurdity. In Washington, Coxey was arrested for walking on the grass and the armies peaceably melted away.

As if to complete the anger and frustration of the discontented, the Supreme Court in 1895 sustained the Debs injunction, threw out the very moderate income tax which had been attached to the Wilson-Gorman Tariff, and (in the Knight case) almost completely nullified, for the present, the Sherman Anti-Trust Act.

Still confident in his principles of *laissez faire*, Cleveland spent much of his last two years in office fighting activist foreign policy. Shortly before the end of his term, he vetoed a bill requiring a literacy test for immigrants. Denounced as a traitor by western and southern Democrats, he was a hero to many eastern Republicans. Nevertheless, the Republican party looked forward to the election of 1896, expecting the President's unpopularity to give it an easy return to power.

THE BATTLE OF 1896

William McKinley, nominated by the Republicans on a gold-standard, high-tariff platform, seemed the typical Republican statesman. A former governor of Ohio and a war veteran with impeccable moral principles, he was known mainly for the high tariff that bore his name. His candidacy was managed by his friend Mark Hanna, an Ohio manufacturer with great political gifts. Meeting in Chicago, the Democrats were swept off their feet by the famous "Cross-of-Gold" speech of William Jennings Bryan of Nebraska. Bryan was nominated and a platform adopted calling for free coinage of silver and a number of other reform measures.

For the first time since 1860, the parties were clearly divided on a single issue, and on that issue all the emotions of the period were focused. To one side Bryan was a knight in armor rescuing the people. By the other he was painted as an anarchist, an atheist, and a bringer of revolution. Actually Bryan, in 1896 and throughout his career, reflected accurately the feelings of millions of Westerners, thoroughly traditional in religion and morality and by no means radical in politics. In 1896, in some areas, such solid and conventional citizens felt that they had been cheated out of their rights.

Yet when the votes were counted, the Republicans had won. Bryan had carried only the Solid South, the Great Plains, and the mountain West, losing the border states and the northern Mississippi Valley. There have been many explanations for this result, including a rise in farm prices just before the election and Republican pressure on factory workers. It seems to indicate, however, that the forces of discontent in 1896 were either not large enough or not united enough to win against a determined and skillful opponent. To some conservatives, McKinley's victory seemed a narrow victory for sound principles, the end of a strange aberration, and a green light for prosperity. This impression was deepened when prosperity actually did return soon after the election. Discoveries in South Africa and Alaska increased the supply of gold. European crop failures and rising industrial production helped to raise the farmer's prices. For the next couple of decades, many farmers were comparatively well off. Those that were not usually sought redress through organization and bargaining rather than crusades.

In the South, similarly, normality of a sort returned. In North Carolina at the height of the Populist excitement some Negroes had achieved political office. Now the frustrated agrarian radicals nearly all returned to militant segregationism, a position many of them had never left. For another two generations Southerners stood united in defense of white supremacy.

In other respects, however, the forces of change were not as roundly defeated as it seemed. A small minority of determined radicals emerged from the Pullman strike and other defeats of the nineties to provide articulate criticism of American society in the next generation. The Socialist party, formed in 1900, became for the next generation something close to a coalition of American radicals under the leadership of Eugene V. Debs.

Few of the middle-class reformers who had been aroused by late-nineteenth-century problems returned immediately to a belief in

[265]

laissez faire. Though they did not agree on any over-all social analysis or program, they continued to press for particular governmental actions to redress grievances. Thus the nineties laid down the lines on which conservatives, liberals, and radicals would argue for the next half-century. In domestic controversy, and, also, as we shall see, in foreign policy, the second Cleveland administration marked both an end and a beginning.

FOR FURTHER READING:

The most complete survey of the period's social thought is Sidney Fine, *Laissez Faire and the General Welfare State* (1956). Daniel Aaron, *Men of Good Hope* (1951)*, is a series of essays on reformers. H. F. May, *Protestant Churches and Industrial America* (1949), discusses the development of Protestant social criticism. The starting place for city problems is A. M. Schlesinger, *The Rise of the City* (1933). Oscar Handlin, *The Uprooted* (1951)*, conveys the immigrant's point of view, and John Higham, *Strangers in the Land* (1955), analyzes native hostility to immigrants. On Populism John D. Hicks, *The Populist Revolt* (1931)*, is a thorough narrative, Richard Hofstadter, *The Age of Reform* (1955)*, advances some interesting reinterpretations. C. McA. Destler *American Radicalism, 1865–1901* (1946), treats the effort to unite radicals. Among the many fine autobiographies see especially those of Jane Addams, Samuel Gompers, and William Allen White. The following are a sampling of innumerable biographies: C. A. Barker, *Henry George* (1955); on southern Populism, C. Vann Woodward, *Tom Watson* (1938); on Eugene V. Debs, Ray Ginger, *The Bending Cross* (1949)*.

------

*Available in paperback edition.

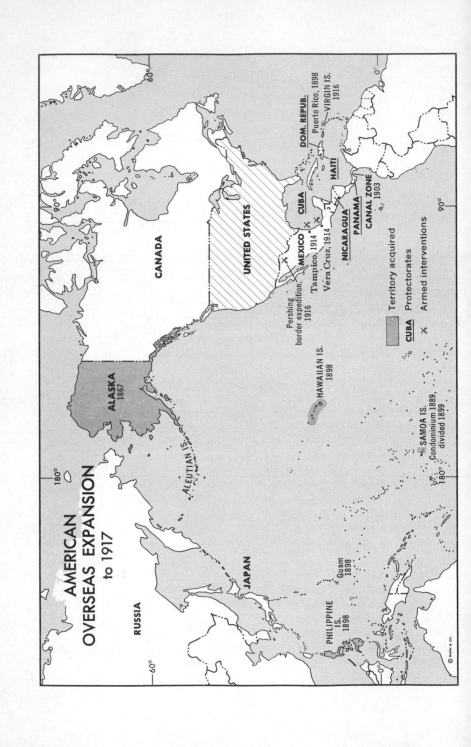

AMERICAN OVERSEAS EXPANSION to 1917

RUSSIA

JAPAN

PHILIPPINE IS. 1898

Guam 1898

ALEUTIAN IS.

ALASKA 1867

180°

60°

SAMOA IS. Condominium 1889, divided 1899

HAWAIIAN IS. 1898

CANADA

UNITED STATES

180°

60°

Pershing border expedition, 1916

MEXICO
Tampico, 1914
Vera Cruz, 1914

NICARAGUA

PANAMA

CANAL ZONE 1903

CUBA

HAITI

DOM. REPUB.

Puerto Rico, 1898

VIRGIN IS. 1916

60°

90°

90°

0°

0°

CUBA   Territory acquired

        Protectorates

×   Armed interventions

© RAND & CO.

CHAPTER 21

OVERSEAS ADVENTURE

1898–1900

From the Peace of Ghent in 1814 until almost the end of the nineteenth century, the United States remained aloof from world affairs. She was enabled to do so by a fortunate combination of circumstances: the European balance of power, British control of the high seas, and her own growing *potential* for armed resistance. Very few nineteenth-century Americans realized the transitory nature of this combination. Most believed that American freedom from foreign danger was permanent and "natural." The United States, Americans believed, was the greatest nation on earth. Following the advice of the founding fathers, she chose to demonstrate this greatness only by peaceful growth.

Through most of the century, public interest in foreign affairs, where it existed at all, centered on four areas. The first had for long been supreme: continental expansion. The second, Far Eastern trade, was the partly unrealized dream of a commercial minority. Yet this interest had led to the establishment of relations with Japan, China, and Korea and helped to justify the acquisition of a few tiny Pacific islands and the development of a protectorate in Hawaii. The other two traditions of American policy were deeply rooted in popular emotions: sympathy for independent, republican governments, especially in this hemisphere, and periodic defiance of the British Empire. Among issues over which America had clashed with the former mother country were New World boundaries of British possessions, American use of the Newfoundland fishing grounds, British interests in Central America, and American sympathy for Canadian rebellion. In each crisis the more irresponsible politicians and newspapers of each country would clamor for war, and then the matter would be settled peaceably. Usually the settlement had been brought about by British concessions made partly in the interest of commerce.

THE END OF ISOLATION

In 1898, with the Spanish-American War, historians have usually seen a break with the past and the full emergence of the United States into world politics. This was not a change in power; since its industrialization the United States had possessed the basis of world power. Nor was it a shift in popular interest. After a flurry of enthusiasm over imperialism most Americans, in the early twentieth century, resumed their habitual concentration on home affairs. However, 1898 did mark something of a tacit change in American commitments. From this point on, the United States, like the other great powers of the day, possessed overseas colonies and took an active interest in world crises from North Africa to the Far East.

Many explanations have been given for this change. The most obvious suggestion is that the American economy had reached maturity and, like other advanced industrial economies, needed raw materials and foreign markets. Most historians believe, however, that this was not true in 1898. American industrialists were principally interested in the gigantic home market. Some of them, especially in the depression of the nineties, were beginning to talk about the desirability of expanded foreign trade. But even these deplored colonial ventures or warlike gestures and heartily advocated the peaceful, nonpolitical spread of commerce.

The traditional idea of "manifest destiny" inherited from the forties and earlier had never died. In the eighties an influential minority had called for a revival of aggressive expansionism on a number of new grounds. Perhaps the commonest was racial superiority. In the nineties this was argued in relation to southern Negroes and new immigrants; it could easily be extended to subject races overseas. Sometimes racialism was linked to a bastard variety of Darwinism. Strong races, it was alleged, needed warlike competition to maintain their virility. Expansion was urged as a religious duty by many, among them the Reverend Josiah Strong, whose best-selling *Our Country* (1886) called for the far-flung physical expansion of American Protestantism, the religion of the future, and of the moral, democratic society that went with it. Another special variety of expansionism was the navalism preached by Captain Alfred Thayer Mahan. Mahan argued that throughout history national greatness had depended on overseas commerce with naval might to protect it. This demanded not only the building of warships but also the aquisition of overseas harbors and coaling stations.

Some of these doctrines were advocated with great force by a group of able, highly-placed young men, mostly of upper-class eastern background, typified by Senator Henry Cabot Lodge of Massachusetts and Theodore Roosevelt. Roosevelt, a rising Republican politician, had already played spectacular roles as Civil Service Commissioner under Harrison and then as Police Commissioner of New York City. In 1897 McKinley appointed him Assistant Secretary of the Navy. At this time Roosevelt, a historian of American naval and Indian fighting, wholeheartedly believed that war—almost any war—was desirable. It would unite the country, take its mind off sordid issues, and develop the manly virtues in its young men.

A third, less obvious cause of the change in American policy was the actual situation in great power politics. The European empires had already divided up Africa and were eyeing the last two remaining areas for expansion: the Near East, occupied by the weak Turkish Empire, and the Far East, occupied by the still weaker empire of China. Each of these was too important to fall to any single power so the leading nations uneasily supported the independence of both, watching each other and staking out spheres of economic influence.

Since the German victory over France in 1871, the European continent had been dominated by Germany and its allies while Britain ruled the seas. Now, however, this pattern was breaking up. Germany, under its ambitious young ruler Wilhelm II, was challenging Britain by a program of naval expansion. Britain, worried by this new menace and sensitive about many threats to her exposed, worldwide empire, was emerging from her stately isolation and looking around for allies. A new great power, Japan, was taking a hand in Far Eastern affairs and challenging traditional Russian interests in Korea and Manchuria. Everywhere the situation was fluid and dangerous. If a country with the potential might of the United States were to show an interest in world politics, she would inevitably be seen as a menace by some powers and as a potential ally by others, whatever her own intentions.

What happened in 1898 reflected all these forces. The United States first became involved in a minor war for a quite traditional objective: political liberty in the Western Hemisphere. When the theater of war shifted to the Far East, the old dream of Oriental commerce was reawakened along with the newer arguments for imperial expansion. Finally, against her will and without quite realizing it, the United States by her Far Eastern acquisitions became involved in great power politics.

FORERUNNERS OF EXPANSION, 1867–1890

Though most of the people in this period had not been much interested in overseas adventure, some active statesmen as well as some propagandists had promoted it. Most of this early expansionist activity involved the Caribbean or the Pacific.

William H. Seward, Johnson's Secretary of State and a vigorous expansionist since prewar days, had bought Alaska from the Russian Empire in 1867. He had also managed to secure for the United States the tiny Pacific island of Midway but had failed in his attempt to aquire Caribbean bases. In the next administration Grant had passionately sought to annex the Dominican Republic. This dream had been frustrated by his conservative Secretary of State, Hamilton Fish, who had also narrowly prevented the country from intervening in the bloody ten years' revolt in Cuba (1868–1878).

Probably the peak of popular isolationism was reached in the complacent eighties. Yet it was also in this decade that the United States acquired a formidable, modern "steel navy," supported in Congress as a means of coastal defense. One statesman who struggled to reverse the isolationist trend was the Republican James G. Blaine, who served as Secretary of State under Garfield (1881) and Harrison (1889–1892). In both administrations he wrangled with Britain, first over rights to build an Isthmian canal and then over protection of the fur seal herd in the Bering Sea. Like Seward, he tried unsuccessfully to aquire Caribbean bases.

More originally, Blaine broached the idea of Pan-Americanism which meant unity of the Western Hemisphere republics under American leadership. In 1885 he called the first Pan-American Conference, which actually met in 1889. This conference was ineffective and the whole Pan-American venture was damaged by Blaine's highhanded efforts to settle South American disputes. It was still more seriously impaired when the United States, in 1891, seemed to threaten war with Chile over a waterfront riot in which two American sailors were killed.

The most important of this period's ventures took place in the Pacific. American interest in the distant and primitive Samoan archipelago was mainly naval. A clash with Germany led, in 1889, to the establishment of a peculiar Anglo-German-American condominium in Samoa.

American involvement in the Hawaiian islands was far more serious. Since the beginning of the century the islands had been visited by American traders, whalers, and missionaries (in that order). Their descendants had become prosperous sugar planters who held actual power in a picturesque native monarchy. From 1842 on, the United States repeatedly made it clear that she would resent European attempts on Hawaiian sovereignty. A treaty of 1875 allowed Hawaiian sugar free entry into the rich American market, yet American contract labor laws did not affect the islands and it was possible to make use of cheap Oriental workers. This idyllic situation, known affectionately in the islands as the Old Monarchy Days, was clearly too good to last.

In 1890 the McKinley Tariff put sugar on the free list, exposing Hawaiian producers to Caribbean competition, and gave a bounty to domestic sugar producers. In January, 1893, a strong-minded Hawaiian queen made a sudden effort to put the American oligarchy out of power and restore autocracy. This gave rise to a revolution. A republic was established which promptly requested annexation to the United States.

The next month, however, Grover Cleveland became president. Nobody was more devoted to the hands-off tradition, both in domestic and foreign affairs. When a presidential commission reported that the Hawaiian revolution had been improperly aided by Americans, Cleveland courageously withdrew the annexation treaty from the Senate. Amid loud cries of outrage from thwarted expansionists, the Hawaiian Republic was forced to wait just outside the gate, much as the Texas Republic had been a half-century earlier.

If the traditionalist Cleveland administration rejected imperialism for the United States, it reacted with unusual sharpness to a suspicion of British imperial expansion in the Western Hemisphere. For some time the British had been trying to redraw a disputed boundary line between British Guiana and Venezuela. In 1895, when Britain rejected American pressure to submit to arbitration, Secretary of State Richard Olney sent her a surprising note. The British were informed that any permanent union between a European and an American state was unnatural, that the United States was "practically sovereign in this hemisphere," and that on certain subjects defined by America her "fiat" was law. Extremists and Anglophobes began calling for war, and for once the Cleveland administration found itself almost popular.

Preoccupied with the South African crisis and concerned about her lack of friends, Britain swallowed her pride and consented to arbitrate the issue. In the long run, she got about what she had wanted. The episode hardly indicated that the United States was sovereign in the whole hemisphere. It did suggest, however, that in the existing state of world politics, American power in the Caribbean might soon come to equal American sensitivity about that area.

In the long run, the most important problem of the Cleveland administration lay still closer, in Cuba. One of the few remnants of Spain's great American empire, Cuba was chronically rebellious yet no Spanish government could afford to let it go. After her Ten Years' War ended in 1878, Cuba entered an interlude of comparative prosperity based in large part on sugar production for the American market. Cuban prosperity was assisted by the McKinley Tariff of 1890 which put sugar on the free list and impaired by the Wilson-Gorman Tariff's restoration of sugar duties in 1894. In 1895, a time of depression in Cuba as in the United States, another insurrection broke out. Far too insecure to handle wisely this difficult situation, the Spanish government talked of eventual concession and embarked on immediate repression. In Cuba, guerrilla methods were met by increasingly drastic reprisals.

Then as now, it was hard for the United States to ignore what went on so close to her shores. The Cuban rebels issued propaganda, raised money, and fitted out illegal expeditions from the United States. The United States had asserted special interest in Cuba since the days of Jefferson. Moreover, the American people throughout the nineteenth century had considered themselves the special patrons of antimonarchical revolutions. Spanish atrocities and Cuban suffering, exaggerated but not altogether false, became a mainstay of the new, ultrasensational newspapers of Joseph Pulitzer and William Randolph Hearst. Patriotic organizations, some labor groups, some reformers, and many congressmen began to demand American action to end Spanish oppression in Cuba. Grimly, as it hung on to the gold standard, the Cleveland administration clung to the dying tradition of nonintervention.

McKINLEY AND CUBA

William McKinley, inaugurated in 1897, represented the more expansionist party. Yet he was sincerely devoted to peace on religious grounds, and his administration was responsive to the wishes of the business community. Many conservative businessmen, feeling that sound government had been narrowly rescued from Bryanism, were heartily opposed to any further crusades, for instance for Cuban liberty. The administration, after giving its first attention to securing the passage of the ultraprotectionist Dingley Tariff, turned toward an effort to calm the Cuban waters. For the moment, the outlook seemed promising. A new ministry in Spain was making gestures toward conciliation and autonomy. Both McKinley and the American minister at Madrid were optimistic when two accidents ended the possibility of peace.

First, Cubans intercepted and gave to the American press a letter from the Spanish minister in Washington, de Lome, incautiously (and inaccurately) describing McKinley as a cheap popularity seeker.

Second, and far more important, the American consul at Havana, disturbed at anti-American riots by pro-Spanish loyalists, persuaded the government to send the battleship *Maine* on a "courtesy visit." On February 16, 1898, McKinley received the appalling news that the *Maine* had blown up and sunk in Havana harbor with a loss of over 260 American lives.

While the press and Congress screamed for vengeance and denounced the President for cowardly subservience to big business, McKinley still tried to preserve peace. The Spanish, who had everything to lose by war, expressed sympathy and regret and denied all knowledge of the disaster. On American demand, Spain abandoned its concentration camps for Cuban civilians, a method particularly distasteful to American opinion, and said it was willing to conclude an armistice with the rebels. At first, however, the Spanish government could not bring itself to request such a truce, nor would it agree to American mediation if negotiations failed. Desperate, Spain tried to secure intervention by the European powers, some of whose rulers sympathized with her and disliked the republican upstart. American power, European disunion, and British opposition put serious international action out of the question. The powers appealed to McKinley for moderation, and both the Pope and the powers put pressure on Spain for further concessions. Finally Spain agreed to request an armistice though not to accept American mediation.

It was too late. Alarmed at a sudden swelling of public passion, reluctant to divide the country, and afraid that Congress might declare war against his will, McKinley on April 11 requested authority to use American troops to create stable government in Cuba. The final Spanish concession, which he had learned of the day before, was reported in an unnoticed sentence of his message. In a mood of patriotic exultation, Congress declared Cuba independent and demanded Spanish withdrawal. Then, to show the purity of American intentions, it added the "Teller resolution" binding the United States not to annex Cuba.

VICTORY

Most Americans, watching Cuba with passionate indignation, did not know much about Spain's larger colony in the Far East, the Philippine Islands, where another colonial rebellion was under way. Theodore Roosevelt, as Assistant Secretary of the Navy, had directed Commodore George Dewey to assemble the United States Asiatic Squadron at Hong Kong and prepare, in the event of war, to attack the Spanish fleet in Manila Bay. Apparently Roosevelt's purpose had been military rather than expansionist: American rule of the Philippines was a possibility beyond even his imagination.

On May 1 Dewey attacked the Spanish fleet in Manila Harbor, destroying it without the loss of an American life. This astounding victory brought the Philippine question into being; it also left Dewey's squadron in a difficult position. Both friendly Britain and less friendly Germany also had naval forces in Manila Bay. Ashore, insurgent Filipinos confronted Spanish garrisons. The American fleet had brought the exiled leader Aguinaldo to the Philippines, but no American policy toward the rebellion had been defined. Finally a small American land force arrived. On the day after the war actually ended, the city of Manila surrendered to American troops, leaving insurgents and Spaniards disputing the rest of the archipelago.

Meantime in its original theater, the war went far less well at first. American coastal cities panicked at mythical rumors of Spanish raids, and mobilization proceeded with lamentable inefficiency. Still worse confusion marred the encampment of American forces in Florida and their embarkation for Cuba. Fortunately for the United States, Spanish equipment, tactics, and morale were in still worse shape.

After many misadventures, the remaining Spanish fleet was finally cornered in Santiago Bay and an American force, including Roosevelt's famous volunteer regiment the Rough Riders, was landed nearby without opposition. A number of small but bloody engagements in the approaches to Santiago gave Americans, including Roosevelt, a chance to prove their courage under fire. On July 3 the decrepit Spanish fleet sailed bravely out of the harbor to meet certain destruction by naval gunfire and on July 17 the city of Santiago surrendered, leaving the United States in control of Eastern Cuba. In early August General Nelson A. Miles completed a nearly bloodless conquest of Spain's other American island, Puerto Rico, and the fighting ended.

Actually, the United States was not in an easy position. American forces occupied only one end of Cuba and one city in the Philippines. Dressed in blue winter uniforms and fed on hardtack and repulsive canned meat (called by the press "embalmed beef"), American forces in Cuba were ridden with dysentery and malaria and threatened with yellow fever. Lieutenant Colonel Roosevelt, among others, was loudly demanding their recall. Even at home in the Florida camps, because of disgraceful neglect of sanitation, disease was spreading. (Eventually many times more lives were lost by disease than by enemy action.) Fortunately, Spain, without a navy, had no hope of continuing hostilities, and on August 12 an armistice was signed.

PEACE AND EMPIRE

As armistice terms, the United States insisted that Spain withdraw from Cuba and cede to the United States Puerto Rico, an island in the Ladrones (Guam), and the city and harbor of Manila. The fate of the rest of the Philippines (more than seven thousand large and small islands with about eight million people) was left for the peace conference to determine. At first reluctant to annex so much distant territory, McKinley feared another upsurge of public opinion like that which had swept the country into war. Finally he convinced himself that it was the duty of the United States to "uplift and civilize" the Philippines. Very reluctantly, Spain agreed to cede them in return for a payment of $20 million.

In the Senate, the treaty faced serious opposition from the anti-imperialists. This diverse coalition included most northern Democrats and the familiar minority of eastern, reform-minded Republicans. It brought together such contrasting individuals as Bryan, Cleveland, Andrew Carnegie, Samuel Gompers, and Mark Twain. Libertarians argued passionately that empire over subject peoples would violate the Declaration of Independence and the Monroe Doctrine. Others pointed out that the Constitution provided no way of governing territories never destined to become states. Racists insisted that Filipinos were unassimilable, and strategists argued, more persuasively, that a Far Eastern possession would endanger American security.

On the other side, it was argued that the flag, once planted overseas, should not be pulled down, that annexation represented the obvious will of God, and that it was America's duty to Christianize the Philippines (which were actually one of the principal outposts of Christianity in the Far East). The strong interest of Japan and Germany in the spoils of the Spanish empire furnished another argument (Germany eventually picked up the Caroline islands and all the Ladrones or Marianas but Guam). The business community, intrigued by the resources of the islands and also by the idea of a base for the China trade, abandoned its opposition to expansion. Reluctantly the conservative Senate leadership agreed to go along with the President. Yet the two sides remained fairly even, and the treaty would not have passed had not Bryan, as head of the Democratic party, decided to support the treaty and fight the issue of annexation in the coming election.

In their 1900 convention the Democrats declared that anti-imperialism was the "paramount issue," and the Republicans accepted the challenge. Theodore Roosevelt, one of the war's principal heroes, campaigned as McKinley's running mate. Actually, however, it cannot be proved that McKinley's solid victory constituted an endorsement of annexation. Many voted once more for the gold standard, the high tariff, and prosperity.

Perhaps the strongest real reason for retaining the Philippines was the lack of a clear alternative. It was obviously out of the question to suppress the revolt and return them to Spain, and nobody wanted to hand them to Germany or Japan. Disunited and in places uncivilized, the islands seemed hardly able to sustain independence without at least the protection of the United States. Yet many continued to feel that annexation was a mistake, both moral and strategic. If this was correct, perhaps the biggest mistake had been the initial occupation of Manila.

The imperialist tide, such as it was, carried with it not only the Philippines, Puerto Rico, and Guam, but also Hawaii and Samoa. Hawaii, whose independent government had assisted American shipping during the war, seemed a useful Pacific halfway house and was annexed by joint resolution. In 1900 the Samoan condominium was ended and the islands divided between Germany and the United States.

Meanwhile in Cuba, which the United States had sworn *not* to annex, American forces performed a heroic job of cleaning up yellow fever. They also quarrelled with their Cuban allies. In 1902 they were withdrawn, but not before the Platt Amendment making Cuba a virtual American protectorate was incorporated in American legislation, the Cuban constitution, and a Cuban-American treaty. This provided that Cuba might not impair its own independence or increase its public debt beyond its capacity. To safeguard either Cuban independence or a government which could maintain "life, property, and individual liberty" the United States was given the right to intervene, which it did in 1906 and several times thereafter. Finally, Cuba was required to sell or lease a naval station to the United States. Not until the Franklin Roosevelt administration was the Platt Amendment finally abrogated, leaving Cuba politically independent but linked to the American economy.

America's imperial experience started unpleasantly when the Filipino insurgents, bitterly disappointed at not receiving independence, turned their guerrilla warfare against the United States. In the ensuing war, which lasted until 1902, Americans suffered more casualties than in the war with Spain. Like most troops fighting guerrilla enemies, American forces sometimes resorted to devastation, concentration camps, and even torture—the same methods for which America had denounced Spain. In a series of complex decisions the Supreme Court

[278]

underlined one of the anti-imperialist arguments by deciding that the Constitution did not necessarily apply in full vigor in "unincorporated territories" and that it was possible to levy tariffs on their products.

Despite these ironies, in the long run the American colonial record was a relatively good one. Everywhere strenuous work in education and sanitation was undertaken, and, despite the Court decision, substantial free trade established. Movement toward popular government began with the establishment of a legislature in Puerto Rico in 1900. In 1901 civil government replaced military in the Philippines, which received an elective assembly in 1907. Thus the worst predictions of the anti-imperialists were not carried out: the United States did not turn, like Rome, from a Republic to an Empire. Neither did the hopes of the imperialists blossom: the resources of the Philippines remained substantially undeveloped, and poverty, in the Philippines and Puerto Rico, was ameliorated but by no means ended. In the twentieth century, most of the American people apparently gave little thought to their new acquisitions. In 1934, partly for ideological reasons and partly because of pressure from competing economic interests, Congress voted to give the Philippines their independence in ten years, and after World War II this pledge was carried out.

WORLD POWER

Thus the American venture into empire seems to have been a temporary enthusiasm. Yet its effects on foreign policy were profound and permanent. American hegemony in the Caribbean, already an accomplished fact, was underlined, and Britain, long the chief rival claimant, was glad to acknowledge it. In the second Hay-Pauncefote Treaty of 1901, England gave in to American demands for exclusive control of the proposed Isthmian canal, abrogating her own treaty rights to equality in this venture. Shortly afterward, Britain cheerfully cut her heavy overseas commitments by reducing her West Indian forces.

Caribbean hegemony was almost inevitable in this era of frank great-power policing of the world. America's ventures in the Far East were far more controversial. To the old, vague, more or less sentimental interest in commercial equality and the independence of Asian states was added a large and vulnerable Far Eastern colony, menaced particularly by the rising power of Japan. Despite her growing naval strength, the United States lacked power to defend these distant commitments.

Since 1895 Japan and the European powers had been forcing China to surrender leased territories and establishing large additional spheres of economic influence. In 1899 Secretary of State John Hay, a friend of Roosevelt and a partisan of the new "large policy," stated traditional American policy in a fresh manner. Partly at the prompting of American commercial interests, he addressed identical notes to the six leading powers asking them to affirm equal treatment for foreign commerce within their spheres of interest in China. Though the answers were ambiguous, Hay announced that the world had accepted this Open Door policy.

In 1900, when the antiforeign Boxer Rebellion endangered the lives of foreigners in Peking, the United States joined an international rescue expedition. At this time Hay broadened the Open Door policy by sending a second note affirming American support of Chinese territorial integrity and calling for commercial equality in all parts of the Chinese Empire, not just the spheres of European influence.

The Open Door policy pleased American opinion and seemed to put the United States in an attractive light. Yet the integrity of the huge, crumbling Chinese Empire and the safety of the Philippines were big commitments, well beyond the actual, developed military power of the United States.

Inevitably, though tacitly, the course of events had drawn the nation closer to its old rival, Great Britain. During the Spanish War, when most European countries had resented America's chastisement of a proud European nation, Britain had supported the United States and Rudyard Kipling, then the most popular Anglo-Saxon author, had urged America to "take up the white man's burden" of empire. Like the United States, Britain wanted the *status quo* maintained in the Far East as well as the Caribbean and welcomed help in achieving this objective. In many American circles, especially in the eastern upper class, the turn of the century saw a revival of sentiment for British friendship on cultural and even racial grounds. The pro-British tendency was by no means shared, however, by the whole American public, large sections of which disliked British policies in Ireland, India, and South Africa and still thought of England as the stronghold of monarchy and aristocracy. Yet as the great powers chose up sides for the world conflict of the twentieth century, there was probably never much doubt that a showdown would find America on the side of the Atlantic, rather than the Central European, powers.

After the turn of the century most Americans were proud of the nation's new empire, fleet, and prestige and were glad that Washington was more often consulted in times of international crisis. They by no means realized, however, that active world politics demanded serious—in the long run even tragic—commitments. And for the first decade and a half of the twentieth century American interest shifted back, for the most part, to its traditional concentration on economic growth and domestic political controversy.

FOR FURTHER READING:

An informative, reliable history of recent American foreign policy is Richard W. Leopold, *The Growth of American Foreign Policy* (1962). The ideology of expansion is described by J. W. Pratt, *Expansionists of 1898* (1936). The best account of the emergence of the United States into power politics is Ernest R. May, *Imperial Democracy* (1961). A lively and sometimes penetrating history of the McKinley administration is Margaret Leech, *In the Days of McKinley* (1959). Walter Millis, *The Martial Spirit* (1931), is an account of the Spanish War, and Frank Freidel, *The Splendid Little War* (1958)*, is a highly entertaining pictorial history. The biographies of Theodore Roosevelt listed in later chapters will also prove useful for this topic.

---

*Available in paperback edition.

CHAPTER 22

ROOSEVELT AND
THE PROGRESSIVE ERA
1901–1908

On September 6, 1901, President William McKinley, a moderately conservative statesman, was shot by an anarchist. When he died a week later the young and dynamic Theodore Roosevelt became president. This tragic incident is often taken to be the beginning of a new period of progressive reform which lasted until World War I. Actually, of course, the Progressive Era was not brought on by the assassin's bullet. Its sources lay deep in the economic, social, and moral history of the country.

THE MATURE ECONOMY

By 1900 the American economy was relatively mature. It was no longer necessary to concentrate all resources and efforts on the expansion of productive capacity. Production continued to increase fairly rapidly in the new century, but not at the fantastic rate of the previous period.

Progressivism owed some of its nature, if not its existence, to the fact that the period 1901–1914 was one of relatively stable prosperity. There was no prolonged depression like those of the seventies or nineties, but only two brief financial panics (1903 and 1907). The farmer, that perennial stepchild of the American economy, entered one of his few periods of relative contentment. Of course many farmers were continually having a hard struggle, and some farm evils like tenancy were still increasing. But average farm income, for a change, was moving upward. This was partly because city population, at home and abroad, was increasing faster than farm acreage. By 1910, 55 per cent of Americans lived in towns.

For some of this urban population, crowded into slums and immigrant ghettoes, things were less than cheerful. Real wages for industrial labor rose more slowly than in earlier decades. Never were social contrasts more extreme, from the still uninhibited multimillionaire, with his Fifth Avenue palace and his fifty room Newport cottage, to the tubercular child in the cotton mill or the garment worker in his tenement sweatshop. America as before led the world in industrial accidents. Thus it is only with careful qualification that one can call the Progressive Era a time of contentment. It is more nearly correct to call it a period of hope, especially for the politically articulate middle class.

Big business grew even faster after the turn of the century. Not all consequences of bigness were bad; one for instance was more money for such advances as electrification and research laboratories. Public relations and advertising received much attention and so did the "Scientific Management" movement of Frederick W. Taylor. Taylor, originally an engineer, urged that each movement of each worker be made as efficient as possible through close study, minute division of function, and rigorous supervision. Working toward similar objectives with less theory, Henry Ford began production of his Model T in 1909. By 1914 he was producing a quarter of a million cars a year.

Another consequence of bigness, and one that seemed to work against innovation, was the tendency toward banker control. Only a dozen great investment houses, led by that of J. P. Morgan, could float the securities necessary for one of the period's giant mergers. These private bankers, controlling insurance and trust companies as well as industries and railroads, could draw on a large part of the national savings. When necessary, they could supplement their resources with those of their foreign connections. Thus they could perform many of the functions of supervision and stabilization traditionally carried out by official central banks; in a sense Morgan was the successor of Nicholas Biddle. Conscientiously, Morgan and his allies tried to end cutthroat competition, prevent risky investment, and rescue sick industries before their financial collapse. In return they exacted not only high fees but control. Through seats on the governing boards of railroads, steel companies, and many other corporations they could enforce their own ideas of sound operation on a large part of American business.

These functions were probably necessary, but they were not without their costs. Sometimes the regnant bankers were unimaginative and unenterprising (they were very reluctant, for instance, to back automobile manufacturers). They did not worry much about working conditions in the industries they controlled. And, as the period's two panics testify, they did not always achieve the stability they aimed at.

Even if the bankers of the age of Morgan had been perfect, however, they would not have been popular. The main single complaint of progressives was directed against what they regarded as immoral and irresponsible power, and this was personified by the mighty, invisible "Money Trust."

THE PROGRESSIVE MIND

Antimonopoly feelings were as old as the Republic, and most of the rest of the progressive ideology was a continuation of the previous period's social criticism. Settlement workers were still discovering urban poverty; ministers were still reinterpreting Christianity in terms of social reform; social scientists were still challenging the basis of nineteenth-century individualist morality. But the discontent of the early twentieth century had a new tone, and this tone was set by a cheerful, though not a complacent, middle class. Careful study has shown that the leaders of early twentieth-century progressivism tended to be fairly prosperous professional or businessmen in their early forties, usually Anglo-Saxon and Protestant, often motivated by personal ambition as well as moral indignation.

Side by side with progressivism, real radicalism was also flourishing. In the century's first decade the Socialist party elected many local officials and one congressman. In 1912 its presidential candidate, Eugene Debs, got 6 per cent of the popular vote. Such Socialist intellectuals as Upton Sinclair and Jack London confidently predicted a socialist America in the near future. On the far left, the syndicalist Industrial Workers of the World, uncompromising advocates of class conflict, organized western miners and lumbermen. In 1912 the I.W.W. began to spread to eastern textile towns.

Except when frightened by such episodes as the Colorado mine wars or the *Los Angeles Times* bombing of 1911, middle-class progressives refused to be deeply alarmed by the rise of radicalism. Only a few of the most hopeful and fearful Americans believed that revolution was close. Theodore Roosevelt, who had stormed about the menace of anarchism in 1896, could find a good word in 1908 for some socialists. The Socialist party itself was sharply divided between advocates of gradual and immediate change.

Neither fear nor personal suffering played much part in the motives of progressive leaders. Doubtless, concern about the high cost of living helped to turn the thoughts of some toward the trusts and the tariff. Many sympathized with the plight of the urban poor. Yet even such obvious evils as child labor and slums looked different in a period without major depressions. Problems like this were not proofs of society's failure, but calls to action. And for most progressives, the most pressing questions were not humanitarian but moral and political.

First, progressives wanted to end corruption, to throw out the crooks and return power to "good citizens" like themselves. Second, they wanted to control "big business," not in the interest of socialism but in that of free enterprise. Some of them wanted to break up large combinations. Others concluded that "the trusts" should be allowed to exist under close supervision.

Because life in America was good, progressives wanted to preserve its promise for the future. They rejected the determinism that had been common in the late nineteenth century. Science, government, and public morality were all changing, and changing for the better. There were no such things as immutable laws, except (for most progressives) concerning moral fundamentals. Following William James, who died in 1910, the pragmatic school of philosophy argued that particular judgments should be made on the basis of concrete consequences rather than according to general metaphysical principles. In educational theory, John Dewey and his followers insisted that children should be taught to solve the problems which arose in their own environment instead of being instructed in the wisdom of the past. The law and even the Constitution were reinterpreted as guides to action rather than unchanging codes. At the height of the Progressive Era, people talked not only of the New Freedom of Woodrow Wilson or the New Nationalism of Theodore Roosevelt, but also of the new literature, the new psychology, even the "new woman."

Optimism gave the reformers of this period much of their confidence and courage. It also blinded many of them to some of the most difficult contemporary problems. Only a few of them gave much thought, for instance, to the disgrace of Negro intimidation and inequality. And only a few really saw the approach of the greatest menace to all their hopes: international war.

THE PROGRESSIVE ACCOMPLISHMENT

Reform started with the exposure of crying evil. The vogue for sensational accounts of corruption and monopoly began with books like Henry Demarest Lloyd's attack on Standard Oil (*Wealth against Commonwealth*, 1894). The new fashion was taken up by sensational newspapers like those of Hearst and by a new crop of popular, cheap, ably-edited magazines led by *McClure's*. For a while one could hardly pick up a periodical without running into a heavily documented exposure of the city traction ring or the patent medicine trust. Muckrakers, as Roosevelt called the new journalists, attacked big business, the unions, the churches, the press itself, state and city government, and finally the United States Senate.

A great many people read about skulduggery in high places for fun, but some were moved to action. Some of the important crusades of progressives started outside politics in such fields as charity organization, education reform, or juvenile courts (concern for the young was characteristic). Sooner or later, however, most concrete accomplishments had to be registered in political action.

The first progressive political offensive was directed against the most obvious target: America's swollen cities, where grafting utilities and protected vice were all too obvious. City reform got under way in the nineties, and in the first decade of the century many cities moved from boss rule to reform. Some moved back soon enough, but often the cycle left a heritage of public waterworks, public or highly regulated street railways, tenement laws, and playgrounds. Sometimes new charters tried to take city affairs out of politics by means of a commission or city manager system.

Still more was accomplished in the states, perhaps the most important laboratories of reform. In 1900 Robert M. La Follette, one of the most militant and uncompromising progressive leaders, became governor of Wisconsin. Working closely with experts from the state university, he made Wisconsin a "laboratory of democracy." Reformers won control of one state after another in the Middle West and then in the Far West and East. (In the South, progressive reform was often tragically allied with anti-Negro demagogy.) Typical state reforms included a great many devices intended to keep the bosses and railroads out of power and "the people" in control. These included the direct primary, the secret ballot, and even preferential popular choice of United States senators, still officially chosen by legislatures. Woman suffrage was adopted by thirteen states, mostly in the West, by 1914. Beginning in Oregon, a number of western states put lawmaking directly in the hands of the people through the Initiative and Referendum.

States were pioneers in such economic measures as close regulation of railroads, utilities, and trusts; progressive taxation; and conservation of natural resources. Labor legislation passed by states included workmen's compensation laws for accident cases, child labor laws, and laws establishing maximum hours and minimum wages for women. (Laws regulating men's labor conditions were sometimes overturned by the courts and always strongly opposed as interference with individual liberty.) By 1917 two thirds of the states, pushed by fervent reformers, had prohibited alcoholic liquors.

Obviously, many of these measures needed to be completed by federal action, and ambitious progressive leaders were eager to move from state capitols to Washington. In 1906 La Follette himself joined what muckrakers called the "millionaire's club," the United States Senate. With other progressive senators, he played a major part in pushing presidents toward reform.

THE PROGRESSIVE HERO

Theodore Roosevelt's inauguration did not cause the Progressive Era, but it was a major event. For the first time since Jackson, a president became the most popular American. For the first time since Lincoln a president stretched the powers of his office. Like Jefferson and Franklin Roosevelt, Theodore Roosevelt was harder to understand than he seemed. On the surface he was noisy, impulsive, and even violent, given to dramatic phrases like "the square deal" and "the strenuous life." He liked to lay down the law about literature, science, or personal morality. Yet most of his impulsiveness came either early or late in his career or was confined to minor issues. His major decisions as president were usually shrewd compromises.

An informal, confident aristocrat, Roosevelt could indulge in pillow fights with his children or drag sweating diplomats on rocky scrambles. This delighted the public and by no means compromised the dignity of the presidential office. A consistent nationalist, Roosevelt took it for granted that the president of the United States was the equal not only of foreign emperors but of domestic millionaires. A born politician, he never quite lost touch either with radicals like Lincoln Steffens or extreme conservatives like Senator Nelson Aldrich. To each he managed to appear as a defender against the other. Like all good politicians, Roosevelt as president was a master of timing. When he became president, he reassured shocked conservatives by announcing his continuance of McKinley's policies and cabinet. At the same time he put out a trial balloon by denouncing the trusts and moved further in that direction when public response was favorable. In 1904, he easily defeated a conservative Democrat, Judge Alton B. Parker, for re-election. President in his own right and conscious of the progressive tide throughout the country, he moved further toward reform objectives. Then in 1907, when the financial panic seemed to demand caution, he followed the suggestions of J. P. Morgan. Finally, in 1908–1909, about to leave office, he called for a whole host of drastic reform measures. This accomplished nothing immediately, but left a program which his successors could not ignore.

[287]

The actual domestic accomplishments of Roosevelt were important, but less important than his demonstration of the possibilities of the presidency. Despite his reputation as a trust buster, Roosevelt was never hostile to big business as such. He disliked practices he considered dishonest and deeply resented defiance of the federal government. His first request in his December, 1901, message to Congress was for the creation of a Department of Commerce and Labor, including a Bureau of Corporations which would collect information about abuses committed by interstate industries. This moderate measure passed against heavy opposition. In 1902 Wall Street was startled to learn that the administration was going to sue the Northern Securities Company, a typical Morgan-sponsored railroad merger, under the neglected and emasculated Anti-Trust Law. Though the administration won this suit and later others, Roosevelt never placed much confidence in sudden punitive assaults against particular mergers. Wanting to prevent unethical practice rather than sheer bigness, he would have preferred (but did not get) legislation providing for the registration and more orderly regulation of all interstate business.

In 1902 the administration had to deal with a bitter anthracite coal strike. Though bituminous supplies were ample, the press played up the prospects of a desperate fuel shortage. Instead of simply sending the troops to the coal fields to "restore order" after the manner of Cleveland, Roosevelt called both parties to the White House. Unwilling to concede equality to their opponents, the operators adamantly refused to discuss concessions. This angered Roosevelt, who began looking into the possibilities of using the army to mine coal, a threat which went well beyond any known presidential powers. After much pressure, the operators agreed to the appointment of a mixed arbitration commission, and in March, 1903, this group made its award. It gave the miners a 10 per cent raise but denied them several of their other objectives, including union recognition. Trouble in the coal fields was long to continue, but a precedent had been established for a new kind of presidential action.

In his second administration Roosevelt had to deal with the demands of the growing group of midwestern Progressive Republicans in Congress. Of all these, the most overdue was railroad regulation. The Elkins Act of 1903, supported by the railroads themselves, had forbidden special rebates to large customers, but the Interstate Commerce Commission was still hamstrung in any effort to regulate rates. After a long process of presidential pressure and compromise, Congress passed the Hepburn Act in 1906. This measure gave the Commission power to set aside existing schedules and determine reasonable rates pending court review. The Commission could also prescribe uniform bookkeeping practices to enable it to keep track of operations, and its jurisdiction was strengthened in other ways. It did not, however, receive the power to make an evaluation of railroad property as a basis for rate-making, an omission which bitterly disappointed Senator La Follette. Similarly, the Federal Pure Food and Drug Act and Meat Inspection Act of the same year gave progressives only part of what they wanted. Some of the worst practices of packers and patent medicine producers were ended, but fraudulent advertising was not prohibited.

Roosevelt, a believer in outdoor life and a vigorous champion of the national interest, prided himself most of all on his efforts for conservation of natural resources. For three centuries Americans had devoted themselves to exploiting their lumber, minerals, and other wealth as rapidly as possible. Now many were becoming conscious of the possibilities of exhaustion as well as the inefficiency and immorality of indiscriminate private appropriation. Under an act passed in 1891 but so far used only a moderate amount, Roosevelt withdrew enormous areas from public entry and set them aside as National Forests. Water power and mineral sites were also withdrawn, and Roosevelt gave his backing to federal construction of irrigation works under the Newlands Act (1902).

Here as elsewhere, however, the President's chief service was probably the exercise of his talent for publicity. A White House conference of notables and a well-staffed national commission reported on the complex problems of land, water, forest, timber, and mineral conservation. A devoted core of conservationists was built up, led by Roosevelt's friend Gifford Pinchot, head of the Federal Forestry Service. Yet opposition by western interests accustomed to private use of public resources continued formidable, and conservationists secured only a start toward their goals.

The considerable list of reforms *not* undertaken by the Roosevelt administration was headed by tariff reform. This was increasingly demanded by midwestern progressives, whose constituents had always been divided in their opinions on the tariff, and were now hurt by foreign reprisals against American agricultural products. The President, however, could never really interest himself passionately in the tariff. Besides, any move in the matter was sure to split the Republican party. So this, with much other unfinished business, was left to Roosevelt's unlucky successor.

IN DANGEROUS WATERS

In foreign policy, Roosevelt seemed to be in his element. An old expansionist, he was both better informed about foreign policy than any recent president and more interested in it. More than most progressives, he seemed to understand the relation between power and objectives. Yet here, more often than in his domestic policy, he betrayed a tendency to rashness. In contradiction to his much quoted adage, Roosevelt did not always speak softly and his stick was sometimes not big enough.

Roosevelt, like many European contemporaries, believed that the world had to be benevolently but firmly supervised by the enlightened great powers. Though he was occasionally irritated by the British, he took it for granted that the Anglo-Saxon powers, as equals and friends, should lead the procession. Then came the other Western European nations, and then a newcomer Roosevelt greatly respected for its martial virtues, Japan.

Part of the job of the enlightened nations was to keep the peace. Earlier, Roosevelt had believed in war for its own sake. Now, however, he thought that it should be prevented between civilized nations. Force was still justified to enforce "progress" on backward peoples, and each great nation must retain the right to protect its vital interests. With these important qualifications, Roosevelt could support some of the goals of the contemporary peace movement. He furthered the work of The Hague conferences on world peace, the establishment of a world court, and the negotiation of treaties for the arbitration of most disputes.

The most obvious accomplishment of the administration was its continued and rapid movement toward American domination of the Central American and Caribbean areas. The Hay-Pauncefote negotiations, under way before Roosevelt took office, cleared away British objections to an American-controlled Isthmian canal. Congress had decided that the best route lay through Nicaragua where the United States had obtained treaty rights to build a canal. However, powerful and somewhat shabby private interests, concerned in part with protecting the investment of the nearly defunct French Panama Canal Company, persuaded the Senate to shift to the Panama route. When the Republic of Colombia, which owned Panama, refused to accept American terms, Roosevelt regarded it as an inadmissable blocking of progress by a backward nation.

A revolution in the Isthmus, carried out with American cognizance and naval protection, made Panama an independent republic. With the new country, the United States immediately negotiated a very favorable treaty providing for American "use, occupation, and control" of a Canal Zone. The French company got its money, Panama got $10 million, work started on the canal, and Roosevelt saw the whole affair as one of his great successes. His critics have said, however, that the episode left deep resentment in Latin America, that the canal could have been built in Nicaragua, and that it could have been built in Panama without a revolution if Roosevelt had shown a little more patience in his negotiations with Colombia.

In 1902 Venezuela, once more the center of an international incident, refused to pay its international debts. According to the great-power code of action of the period, British and German naval units blockaded and even bombarded Venezuelan ports until the Venezuelan dictator agreed to arbitrate his government's obligations. Secretly but forcefully Roosevelt warned the powers to end their naval action. When Germany was slow in complying, Roosevelt backed his warning with a display of naval force.

In Roosevelt's view, if the United States objected to intervention by others in the Caribbean, it was her duty when necessary to police that area herself. In 1904, when the Dominican Republic found itself in similar financial straits, Roosevelt moved in. Against the Senate's opposition, he negotiated an executive agreement under which the United States collected Dominican customs, paid the country's creditors, and put its government on an allowance. This was done so successfully and even tactfully that neither Europe nor Latin America objected. However, Roosevelt accompanied his action with a series of characteristic and sweeping statements constituting a new corollary to the Monroe Doctrine and claiming the right of intervention to prevent "chronic wrongdoing" in the Western Hemisphere.

Under Roosevelt's immediate successors, this "Roosevelt Corollary" was interpreted with less restraint. The relatively conservative Taft administration tried to push American capital into Caribbean countries with the idea of subsequent protection by force. The liberal Wilson administration repudiated this kind of "Dollar Diplomacy," but itself intervened far more forcibly to secure good government. By World War I, the Caribbean was clearly an American lake. The United States owned Puerto Rico and the Virgin Islands (bought from Denmark in 1917), controlled the Canal Zone, had a formal protectorate over Cuba under the Platt Amendment, and had liberal precedent for armed intervention elsewhere in the area. Later during the Hoover and Franklin Roosevelt administrations, the United States gradually modified its policies in an effort to overcome Latin American resentment, abandoning all claims to the right of unilateral intervention.

The other area of increased American activity was the Far East. China, unmilitary and unprogressive, did not meet Roosevelt's standards for being a civilized nation. Thus he had no objection in principle to foreign enterprise there. Like Hay, however, he objected to exclusive control by foreign powers of commercial opportunity in any part of Chinese territory. His suspicion was deeply aroused by Russian domination of Manchuria. When Russia and Japan went to war in 1905 over rival interests in Korea and Manchuria, Roosevelt gave strong diplomatic support to Japan.

The Russo-Japanese War, like the Spanish-American War, was a smashing defeat of a European by a non-European power with considerable effects on the world balance. With the. Russian fleets destroyed and Russia facing revolution, Japan yet lacked resources for continuing the war until Russia surrendered completely. Thus both powers accepted Roosevelt's mediation and gathered to make peace at Portsmouth, New Hampshire. Delighted at his novel role, Roosevelt handled the negotiations with considerable skill. Yet the Peace of Portsmouth, which gave Japan important territorial gains but denied her a money indemnity, proved unpopular in the victorious country.

Thus Roosevelt's hopes for a stable balance in the Far East were defeated, and his major Far Eastern problem during the rest of his term in office was the rising power of Japan. His policies were a characteristic compound of realism, tact, and bravado. Since he could not prevent it, he accepted Japanese domination in Korea and took no action when Japan began to divide actual control of Manchuria with her defeated enemy, Russia. When California and particularly San Francisco started discriminating harshly against Japanese immigrants, Roosevelt put federal pressure on them to desist. At the same time, he negotiated the "Gentlemen's Agreement" (1907) whereby Japan barred emigration of laborers to America. In 1906 he sent the United States fleet, by now the world's third largest, on a trip around the world. Its stop in Tokyo Bay, a daring and imaginative gesture, was a complete social success. More or less in return for all this hard work, Roosevelt was able to secure the Root-Takahira Agreement of 1908. In this both countries agreed to respect equal opportunity for foreign commerce in China, Chinese territorial integrity, and each other's Far Eastern possessions. For the present, this certainly seemed to guarantee the Philippines. How far it protected Japanese mainland gains was not clear.

In 1906, when France and Germany were at loggerheads over Morocco, Roosevelt helped persuade his friend the German kaiser to accept a settlement which left France dominant.

Never had the United States been taken so seriously in world politics. Yet despite Roosevelt's imagination and skill, it is not clear that in the long run his work greatly advanced either American interests or world peace. United States hegemony in Central America, a fact in any case, had been underlined with unnecessary roughness. In the Far East, Japan had replaced Russia as the principal potential threat, and neither the Open Door nor the integrity of China looked much more secure. American commitments in this area still exceeded American power. Throughout the world, the United States had swung a little further toward alignment with the developing Anglo-French-Russian-Japanese entente. The American people, for the most part, were delighted with the country's increased prestige. It is doubtful, however, whether they had been deeply educated in the dangerous realities of foreign policy.

Such carping, however, was little heard at the end of Roosevelt's term of office in 1908–1909. In an unguarded moment at the time of his election in 1904, he had promised not to seek another term. Undoubtedly regretting this, he easily forced the Republican party to accept as his successor his friend and Secretary of War, William Howard Taft. Campaigning against the two-time loser Bryan on a platform of the Roosevelt policies, Taft won easily. Saying goodbye to his "tennis cabinet" and his ambassadorial cronies but not to the nation's affections, Roosevelt departed on an African big-game hunt to be followed by a triumphal tour of European capitals.

FOR FURTHER READING:

The most recent survey of the period, and an excellent one, is George Mowry, *The Era of Theodore Roosevelt* (1958). Mark Sullivan's chatty, journalistic survey of *Our Times* (6 vols., 1926–1935), begins to be useful for this period. Representative recent additions to the enormous bibliography on progressivism are Richard Hofstadter, *The Age of Reform* (1955)*, and Eric Goldman, *Rendezvous with Destiny* (1952)*. The most helpful single book on American socialism is David Shannon, *The Socialist Party of America* (1955); but there is an enormous amount of interesting material in Donald D. Egbert and Stow Persons, eds., *Socialism and American Life* (2 vols., 1952). The best single book on Roosevelt himself is probably still H. F. Pringle, *Theodore Roosevelt* (1931)*. It can be supplemented by Roosevelt's *Autobiography* (1921) and by J. M. Blum's penetrating sketch, *The Republican Roosevelt* (1954)*. Other specimens of the very rich biographical literature are Lincoln Steffens' fascinating and untrustworthy *Autobiography* (2 vols., 1931); William Allen White's solid and revealing *Autobiography* (1946); and F. L. Allen's slight but interesting *The Great Pierpont Morgan* (1949). The intellectual history of the period is outlined in H. S. Commager, *The American Mind* (1952)*, and some important aspects of it interpreted in M. G. White, *Social Thought in America, The Revolt Against*

Formalism (1949)*. Roosevelt's foreign policy has recently been dissected by H. K. Beale, *Theodore Roosevelt and the Rise of America to World Power* (1956)*.

One major facet of progressivism is illustrated and examined in Richard M. Abrams, *The Issue of Federal Regulation in the Progressive Era* (Berkeley Readings in American History, 1963)*.

---

*Available in paperback edition.

THE PROGRESSIVE ERA

	PRESIDENT	DOMESTIC EVENTS	FOREIGN POLICY: EUROPE, ASIA	FOREIGN POLICY: LATIN AMERICA
1898			Spanish-American War.	
1900	McKinley *R* (September 6, 1901, assassinated)	Gold Standard Act.	1899 Open Door Policy. Boxer Rebellion.	1901 Platt Amendment.
1902		Newlands Reclamation Act.		Venezuela Incident.
1904	Roosevelt *R*	1903 Elkins Act. Coal strike settled. Northern Securities case.	1905 Russo-Japanese War and Peace of Portsmouth.	1903 Panama Affair. "Roosevelt Corollary"
1906		Hepburn Act. Pure Food and Drug Act. 1907 Panic	Algeciras Conference on Morocco. 1907 "Gentlemen's Agreement" on Japanese immigration.	

THE PROGRESSIVE ERA (*Continued*)

PRESIDENT	DOMESTIC EVENTS	FOREIGN POLICY: EUROPE, ASIA	FOREIGN POLICY: LATIN AMERICA
1908 Taft *R*	Conservation conference. 1909 Payne-Aldrich Tariff. Mann-Elkins Act.	Root-Takahira Agreement.	
1910	1911 "Rule of Reason" decisions.	1911 Chinese Railway Consortium.	Mexican Revolution.
1912 Wilson *D*	1913 Underwood Tariff. Federal Reserve Act. Federal Trade Commission Act. Clayton Act.		1913 "Watchful Waiting" in Mexico. Tampico and Vera Cruz incidents.
1914		(August) War in Europe. 1915 (May) *Lusitania* sunk.	
1916 Wilson *D*	Federal Farm Loan Act. Adamson Act.	(May) United States threat and German concession on submarine warfare.	Mexican border warfare.

CHAPTER 23

THE PEAK OF PROGRESSIVISM

1909–1917

In 1908 William Howard Taft, proclaiming his devotion to Roose-velt's progressive policies, was an easy winner over the perennial William Jennings Bryan. Pointing to Taft's experience in government —as a judge, as first civil governor of the Philippines, as Secretary of War and presidential troubleshooter—Roosevelt and others predicted an outstanding administration. Actually Taft had experience in every relevant area but that which proved most important: democratic politics.

TAFT AND THE PROGRESSIVES

Later, seeking reasons for the administration's relative failure, critics were to caricature Taft as a fat and lazy reactionary. Actually, Taft was handicapped not so much by his three hundred pounds as by his conception of the presidency. His devotion to the Roosevelt policies was genuine, and for causes he believed in he could work hard. But he was convinced that the president should stay within his constitutional role and not stretch it as had every successful president since Jackson. And in showdowns, he could not help preferring decent and polite conservatives to most progressives with their radical rhetoric and their disregard of constitutional niceties.

Perhaps no Republican president coming to power in 1909 could have been successful. Since the Panic of 1907 times had been a little less prosperous and the growing progressive movement demanded more drastic action about the major unsolved problems: trust control, taxes, tariffs. Roosevelt, sometimes by sidestepping these issues, had managed to avoid an outright split between Republican reformers and Republican conservatives. Yet even his political magic could not have prevented a clash much longer. Standpat conservatives still controlled the party machinery while ambitious, aggressive Republican progressives, mostly from the Midwest, were increasing their strength in both Houses of Congress with every election.

Blaming the rising cost of living on the sky-high Dingley Tariff, many western progressives demanded a tariff cut. Once more a moderate tariff reduction bill sailed through the House only to be modified sharply upward in the Senate. Taft, who was squarely on record for tariff reduction and had succeeded in toning down the bill's worst excesses, believed that the resultant compromise was the best that could be secured. Stung by progressive charges of betrayal, he went so far as to say, in September, 1909, that the new Payne-Aldrich Tariff was the best the Republican party had ever passed. At the same time he failed to support the progressives in their successful attack against the near-dictatorial power of Speaker Joseph G. Cannon. (Taft disliked Cannon but wanted his support for the tariff bill.) Again, because Taft and his Secretary of the Interior Richard A. Ballinger were slower-going and more legal minded in their attitude toward conservation of natural resources, many progressives feared that they were betraying the national domain to private interests. By the spring of 1910, Taft was seen in some progressive circles as a reactionary and a traitor to the Roosevelt heritage.

Like Taft's domestic policy, his foreign policy amounted to a shift of emphasis which seemed to his critics a betrayal of principle. Roosevelt had believed in American political—and, when necessary, military—intervention abroad to protect political stability and the balance of power. Within the limits of these objectives, he favored American capital export. Taft and his Secretary of State, Philander Knox, believed frankly in using American foreign investment as an instrument of policy. Positive efforts to further private foreign ventures would lead both to peace and to the welfare of the recipient countries.

The administration's ventures in what its critics called "Dollar Diplomacy" did not seem to work out that way. In the Caribbean, Taft's program involved him in unpopular military ventures, while in the Far East it led to a startling departure from realism. Roosevelt, after trying various tacks in Far Eastern policy, had finally come to recognize some of the limitations of American power in the area, especially with reference to the rising might of Japan. Taft and Knox insisted on trying to force American participation in Chinese railway development and made a further effort to internationalize Japan's economic ventures in Manchuria. This policy angered Japan and other foreign powers, failed to sustain Chinese integrity, won only grudging and temporary support from American capital, and was reversed by Taft's successor.

Even the most benign aspects of Taft's foreign policy turned out badly in political terms. His long and vigorous negotiations for tariff reciprocity with Canada were regarded by many midwesterners as an effort to sell out western agriculture for the benefit of eastern industry. When he finally pushed a Canadian reciprocity treaty through the Senate, the Canadians, alarmed by loose American talk of eventual annexation, rejected it. Earnestly devoted to peace, the President negotiated treaties with Great Britain and France promising to arbitrate all differences, even those involving vital interests and national honor. Ardent nationalists were alarmed and the treaties were amended into meaninglessness in the Senate.

Despite the President's political ineptitude, it can be argued that his administration brought more solid progressive accomplishments than Roosevelt's. The Taft years saw the introduction of two progressive amendments to the Constitution, the Sixteenth (income tax) and the Seventeenth (direct election of senators). With the latter Taft had little to do, but he played an important part in starting on its way the income tax amendment, potentially the period's most revolutionary change in government.

Progressive legislation passed during Taft's presidency, much of it with his support, included the Mann-Elkins Act strengthening the Interstate Commerce Commission, the Postal Savings and Parcel Post acts, the establishment of a federal Bureau of Mines and a Children's Bureau, and the separation of the Labor from the Commerce Department. Still more impressive is the fact that Taft's administration brought more than twice as many antitrust suits as that of his spectacularly trust-busting predecessor. Actually Roosevelt had lost confidence early in the possibility of halting consolidation and believed instead in federal regulation to prevent unfair competition and deliberate moves toward actual monopoly. This was approximately the doctrine that the Supreme Court, in the Standard Oil and American Tobacco Company decisions of 1912, enunciated in distinguishing between unreasonable and reasonable restraint of trade. Precisely because Taft was more conservative than Roosevelt, he believed more strongly in enforcing the Sherman Act on the assumption that it meant what it said.

In the fall of 1911, for instance, Taft infuriated Roosevelt by moving against United Steel Steel. J. P. Morgan, who controlled the giant steel corporation, had cooperated with Roosevelt in trying to control the Panic of 1907. Roosevelt had promised that the steel company would not be sued for acquiring Tennessee Coal and Iron in that crisis. Now the Taft administration, apparently repudiating his promise, named the purchase as part of the grounds for the suit.

REPUBLICANS AND PROGRESSIVES, 1910–1912

From early in 1910 Taft, stung by progressive criticism, threw the administration's powers, including patronage, against the progressive wing of his own party in the primary elections. In turn, progressives denounced "Dollar Diplomacy," tariff betrayal, and conservation setbacks. The result of the congressional elections was a bad beating for the Republican party as a whole and particularly severe losses for the Taft-backed eastern conservatives. From this point on Democrats controlled the House of Representatives and a Democratic-insurgent Republican coalition the Senate. Needless to say, the rest of Taft's term was a torment to him, and it became increasingly clear that he could not count on renomination, let alone re-election.

In January, 1911, the insurgents formed the Progressive Republican League, apparently backing Senator La Follette for the nomination. La Follette, showing signs of nervous collapse at an important public function, gave progressive Republicans an excuse to switch their allegiance to their real leader. For all but a few, this was the most popular living American, Theodore Roosevelt.

When he had first emerged from the African jungle in the spring of 1910, Roosevelt had heard from Pinchot and others about the administration's misdeeds. Yet when he arrived back in America after a triumphal tour of Europe, he refrained from directly criticizing his successor and former close friend. At the same time he expressed far more radical sentiments than he had ever uttered before. In a famous speech at Ossawattomie, Kansas, in August, 1910, Roosevelt announced that all property should henceforth be held subject to the right of the community to regulate it to whatever degree the public interest might require. This sort of language deeply alarmed the increasingly conservative President.

After the congressional debacle and the steel suit, Roosevelt began openly attacking Taft, and the President, hurt beyond bearing, referred to "political emotionalists or neurotics" with unmistakable reference. Nobody was surprised when in February, 1912, Roosevelt, at the urging of seven progressive Republican governors, announced that his hat was in the presidential ring.

Waging a vigorous primary campaign for the Republican nomination, Roosevelt roundly defeated Taft in those states which had adopted the new direct primary system. Taft, however, controlled the southern Republicans and the party machinery. Using much the same tactics that Roosevelt had used to nominate Taft in 1908, the Taft forces controlled the Republican convention, decided disputes in the President's favor, and secured Taft's renomination.

Amid scenes of weeping, singing, and fighting, Roosevelt's furious followers withdrew to form their own organization and nominate their hero. But the Progressive party of 1912 was more than a vehicle for frustrated Roosevelt worship. It was also an attempt to remodel traditional American liberalism to fit new conditions. Some have seen it as a forerunner of the New Deal, others, more surprisingly, as a harbinger of the partnership between government and business which developed in the Republican 1920's under very different auspices.

The progressives who marched behind the symbol of the Bull Moose in 1912 and waved red bandanna handkerchiefs in honor of the Rough Riders were drawn from several different sources. They included social reformers like Jane Addams, a few of the more daring western progressive politicians, and some spokesmen of the New Business who were urging on businessmen an increase of social responsibility and self-regulation.

Some of the most fervent admirers of the new party were young intellectuals who had been influenced by Herbert Croly's *The Promise of American Life*. This book, published in 1909 and warmly praised by Roosevelt himself, called for a frank abandonment of Jeffersonian individualism and traditional *laissez faire*. The new American progressivism, it urged, should harness and not destroy the creative powers of giant industry. Government, making use of a new, highly-trained elite, should aim at something like a renaissance, at once political and intellectual.

The Progressive platform showed the influence of all these elements. It called for a long list of social legislation, including prohibition of child labor, minimum wages for women, and social insurance. It repeatedly advocated "scientific" and "efficient" government, particularly with reference to conservation and the regulation of business. While it favored international peace, its foreign policy sections were distinctly nationalistic. Showing the influence of western progressives, it backed initiative, referendum, and recall; direct election of senators; preferential primaries for the presidency; woman suffrage; and even (to the horror of Taft and his friends) popular recall of some judicial decisions.

Surprisingly radical on many matters, the Progressive party was distinctly moderate on two. A strong antitrust plank was sidetracked in favor of an appeal for "constructive regulation." Not only was the platform silent on Negro rights, but Roosevelt aquiesced in the exclusion of Negroes from Progressive organizations in the South.

Inevitably, the campaign centered upon the combative ex-President. As his political experience ought to have told him, Roosevelt's exciting venture turned out badly for his supporters and himself. It deepened the Republican split and for the time handed over the party to the old guard. Destroying Roosevelt's own very important role in American politics, it set back the necessary job of adapting traditional liberalism to twentieth-century realities. From Roosevelt's own point of view (or Taft's), it had one further bad result: it brought the Democrats to power.

WILSON AND THE PRESIDENCY

Woodrow Wilson, the Democratic candidate in 1912, was born and brought up in the South. The son of a Presbyterian preacher, he became a political scientist and historian. In 1902 he was chosen president of Princeton. In this position he was at first a distinguished success, but he became entangled in some fierce and complicated battles over university policy. To Wilson, at least, these were fights for moral principle, and he became discouraged when he was fought to a stalemate in 1910. In that year the Democratic politicians of New Jersey invited him to run for the governorship.

Up to this time Wilson's expressed opinions on public issues had been moderately conservative, and he had been tagged by some rich and influential Democrats as a possible savior of the party from "Bryanism." To the surprise and dismay of the New Jersey bosses, Wilson took the campaign and state party away from them, revealing himself as an ardent and idealistic progressive. As governor he equipped New Jersey, the "mother of trusts," with a full set of up-to-date regulatory legislation. An obvious presidential hopeful by now, Wilson carefully conciliated Bryan and other progressives while retaining the support of some conservative elements in the party. In a fierce convention battle, he took the party's nomination at a time when the Republican split made election probable.

Wilson's campaign speeches were as progressive as Roosevelt's but different both in style and content. Where Roosevelt was emotional and combative, Wilson was controlled. Where Roosevelt called for frank recognition of big business and governmental regulation, Wilson insisted on the restoration of opportunity and free enterprise. This too, of course, would mean immediately an increase in government intervention, but only for the purpose of assisting the underdog, the "man on the make." In a series of glowing orations, Wilson insisted that his program would usher in a New Freedom instead of Roosevelt's New Nationalism.

With the support of an undivided party Wilson was an easy winner, but a winner backed by only 42 per cent of the popular vote. Moreover, his party, long out of power, was a curious combination of city immigrants, western followers of Bryan, eastern banking and business interests, and the more than ever Solid South. Some Republicans honestly doubted whether such a group, led by an impractical professor, could govern.

These doubters misjudged both party and President. Able leadership could, up to a point, overcome Democratic divisions as Roosevelt had once overcome Republican divisions, and Wilson was not only an experienced politician but a daring student of American political institutions. The president, he thought, could become an equivalent of the British prime minister, using both party organization and personal popular support to force his own program through the legislative branch.

From their initial doubts, many progressives turned in Wilson's first months in office to amazed enthusiasm. Yet in his career thus far Wilson had shown weaknesses as well as strong points. He demanded and needed complete support from his friends and in showdowns was likely to find his opponents wicked and perverse. Wanting to believe his own program and point of view completely right, he could become bitter and reckless when menaced with defeat. In times of adversity, his intensity and devotion could become handicaps. In his first administration, however, they were superb assets.

In office, Wilson moved immediately against the most formidable redoubts, the tariff and banking. With the help of Republican progressives, he forced through *both* Houses of Congress the Underwood Tariff, reducing the rates to about the level of pre-Civil War days and extending the free list. The tariff bill included a moderate income tax, at last clearly constitutional.

The country's banking and currency system, dating from 1863 and earlier, was unsatisfactory to different groups for opposite reasons. Many lamented the absence of a central bank able to control interest and rediscount rates, to mobilize reserves in a crisis, and thus to mitigate America's all too frequent financial panics. On the other hand, according to a widespread progressive belief currently reinforced by congressional investigation, the "Money Trust," dominated by certain private bankers and especially by J. P. Morgan, had far too much power over American credit and therefore over American economic development. Moreover, for fifty years a large section of

American opinion had believed that the ups and downs of the American economy were partly caused by the inadequacy and inflexibility of the national currency.

Steering with great adroitness between advocates and enemies of a central bank, between believers in public and private control, Wilson with the help of Bryan and others secured the passage of the Federal Reserve Act of 1913. This measure divided the country into Federal Reserve Districts. In each there was to be a Federal Reserve Association which national banks must join and other banks might. A district Federal Reserve Bank was to be owned by the member banks and governed by a mixed public-private board. Each Federal Reserve Bank would receive the cash reserves of its member banks, grant loans to them, and rediscount their business and some agricultural paper. On the rediscounted business obligations, the Federal Reserve Banks would issue a new kind of currency, Federal Reserve Notes, which in addition would be partly covered by a gold reserve of 40 per cent. These notes, part of the national currency, were expected to fluctuate with the needs of business since they were based mostly on business transactions. Federal Reserve Banks would pool resources in time of threatened panic. The whole system was to be supervised by a presidentially appointed Federal Reserve Board which could raise or lower rediscount rates and thus exert some control over the availablity of credit. While the new system by no means solved all America's long-standing banking and currency problems, it was the most satisfactory compromise between efficiency and decentralization which had been developed thus far. After some initial hostility, it was accepted by banking and business.

The third major accomplishment of Wilson's first years, the new trust legislation, was a more doubtful success. It was a compromise between the programs of the New Freedom and the New Nationalism, with a surprisingly large element of the latter. The Federal Trade Commission Act established a presidentially-appointed five man board with power to investigate corporate practice and issue cease-and-desist orders against unfair methods of competition. While its findings of fact were conclusive, its orders could be appealed to the courts.

The Clayton Anti-Trust Act prohibited specific practices such as discriminatory prices, tying agreements, interlocking directorates, or purchase by one firm of stock in another. Such actions were, however, to be illegal only when they tended toward substantially lessening competition, which meant when the courts said they did.

According to the Clayton Act's labor clauses (hailed by Samuel Gompers of the A.F. of L. as "Labor's Magna Carta"), labor was not to be considered a commodity, labor and farm organizations were not to come under the antitrust law's definition of restraint of trade, and the power of courts to issue labor injunctions was (rather cautiously) restricted. Like the Act's other clauses, these were somewhat imprecise and their meaning was whittled down in the courts. Yet the Wilson trust legislation looked formidable, and some business leaders began to consult the government before making moves toward consolidation.

With these major bills passed, the President made it clear that he believed he had accomplished his principal reform objectives. In 1914 and 1915 he seemed to go out of his way to conciliate business and conservative opinion. Many progressives in both parties were disheartened, especially when progressive candidates lost heavily in the congressional elections of 1914.

In 1916, however, perhaps partly because a new election was pending and the Democrats had to attract some Roosevelt voters, the administration turned much more toward progressive reform. Louis J. Brandeis, the prominent antitrust lawyer and progressive intellectual, was appointed to the Supreme Court amid a storm of conservative criticism. Wilson gave his backing, earlier refused, to a Federal Farm Loan Act providing long-term rural credits and to an act prohibiting interstate shipment of goods made by child labor (later held unconstitutional). The dollar-matching principle (federal appropriations to match state expenditures) was extended from agricultural experiment stations to an automobile highway program and (after the election) to vocational education. Finally, forgetting his *laissez faire* principles under the pressure of foreign crisis and the threat of a serious railroad strike, Wilson supported the Adamson Act establishing by law an eight-hour day on the railroads. Thus the Wilson administration, enacting a program not altogether unlike that sponsored by Roosevelt in 1912, represented the culmination of the whole movement of reform which had begun in the nineties.

WILSONIAN FOREIGN POLICY

Despite the scepticism and amusement of much world opinion, Wilson really meant his idealistic pronouncements about foreign policy. He was determined to support and increase American power and prestige, but only for the benefit of all mankind and only according to the most scrupulous methods. Some have seen in this intention a standard for foreign policy never equalled; others have found in it a misunderstanding of the nature and limits of power. To some extent, Wilson's purposes were supported by the new Secretary of State,

William Jennings Bryan, perhaps the only genuine pacifist ever to serve as foreign minister of a great power.

Much of Wilson's early foreign policy involved a startling abnegation of immediate national interest and was carried out amid loud outcries of nationalist indignation. Economic intervention in China was abandoned, the Philippines and Puerto Rico were given more self-government, and the United States, acknowledging treaty obligations denied by the previous administration, stopped discriminating against foreign shipping in the Panama Canal tolls.

In apparent contradiction to this policy of abstention, interventions in the Caribbean were more frequent and bloody than ever before and the United States became involved in what looked like aggression in Mexico. The contradiction was deeply ironic: the Caribbean interventions were aimed at political reform of the area and the Mexican involvement was the result of an altruistic effort to support Mexican democracy.

In 1910 one of the major revolutions of the twentieth century overthrew Porfirio Diaz, the bloody but efficient dictator of Mexico. American investors, who had $2 billion at stake and had gotten along very well with Diaz, were alarmed. When Diaz's liberal successor was murdered, the Taft administration seemed ready to support the new conservative president, Victoriano Huerta. Wilson, however, committed the United States to oppose Huerta without regard to material interests on the ground that he had come to power by violence.

Instead of making Huerta's opponents grateful, Wilson's attempt at intervention in favor of Mexican democracy came close to uniting all Mexican factions against the United States. Always concerned to back American prestige, Wilson supported an admiral who demanded abject apology over a minor incident involving American seamen at Tampico in 1915. In the same year the United States Navy, in order to prevent delivery of German munitions for Huerta, bombarded and occupied the port of Vera Cruz. Wilson was rescued from his increasingly untenable position when the major Latin American powers agreed to mediate. An international conference at Niagara Falls resulted in the coming to power of Venustiano Carranza, Huerta's main opponent, who was by this time no friend of the Wilson administration.

Even then Wilson's Mexican troubles were not finished. Francisco Villa, a picturesque bandit who might be described as a cross between Robin Hood and Jesse James, shot up American border towns, killing American citizens. In 1916 Wilson sent General John J. Pershing into Mexico in pursuit of Villa. Though Villa was a rebel against the

Carranza government, the American action was bitterly resented throughout Mexico and war between the two countries seemed close. When large-scale war became imminent in 1917, the United States had to withdraw the expeditionary force. To Mexicans, America had become the enemy of the very revolution Wilson wanted to assist and guide.

THE MEANING OF PROGRESSIVISM

The progressive movement had not solved the problems of foreign policy. It had not produced, or tried to produce, any new social system. It had made only the barest beginning toward the redistribution of wealth or the control of private accumulations of power. While ultraconservatives lamented the end of free enterprise, the million or so Americans who wanted to move toward socialism were impatient with progressive caution. The problem of Negro equality remained almost untouched. Despite some accomplishments in education and sanitation, the South, white and black, lagged far behind the rest of the country in health and wealth.

Even some of the things progressives had accomplished proved impermanent. Measures like the income tax and the Federal Reserve System were to be given a different meaning in wartime. Many progressive enactments were to be emasculated or abandoned in the postwar decade.

Yet some solid accomplishments remained. The railroads had been tamed and all big business put on some sort of good behavior. Immensely valuable national resources had been saved for the future. New paths for possible later government action were made possible by the income tax and other measures. Clear outside politics earnest reformers, mostly little remembered, had left countless monuments in the shape of playgrounds, schools, clinics, and parks. In architecture, poetry, social science, and psychology, innovation had characterized the Progressive Era. In some fields, indeed, intellectual experiment begun in the Progressive Era was eventually to lead in disturbing directions, pointing far beyond the optimistic reform spirit of the prewar years.

More important than any concrete accomplishment of the progressive movement was its general reassertion of the will to adapt. Like other countries, America had been confronted by the huge problems of industrial civilization. In the face of this challenge, the country had not failed to find resources of courage and vitality. More than anyone yet realized, these resources were to prove indispensable in the coming decades.

FOR FURTHER READING:

H. F. Pringle, *William Howard Taft* (2 vols., 1939), is a sympathetic and interesting biography. Russell B. Nye describes the rise and character of *Midwestern Progressive Politics* (1951). The best account of the Bull Moose movement is G. E. Mowry, *Theodore Roosevelt and the Progressive Movement* (1946)*. Of the immense literature on Wilson, the most valuable long biography is that being written in several volumes by Arthur Link, and an excellent short interpretation that by John A. Garraty (1956). Link summarizes Wilson's first administration admirably in his *Woodrow Wilson and the Progressive Era, 1910–1917* (1954)*. There are good biographies of nearly all major figures. H. F. May, *The End of American Innocence* (1959) discusses the period's intellectual history.

---

*Available in paperback edition.

CHAPTER 24

THE FIRST OVERSEAS WAR

The war which began in August, 1914, was an event of immense importance for the world and for the United States. It brought to an end a century of relative peace, apparent democratic progress, and European domination of the world. It helped to bring about the first Communist revolution. For the United States it ushered in a period of economic world power and political isolation. It brought far greater steps toward governmental direction of the economy than most progressives had dreamed of. Finally, all this drastic innovation produced intense emotional confusion: Americans moved in a rapid zigzag from neutrality to crusading excitement to disillusion and revulsion.

THE WAR AND AMERICA

In 1914 most Americans found it hard to understand why all Europe went to war over the murder of the heir to the throne of Austria-Hungary by a Serb. Actually, the European great powers, all heavily armed, had long been engaged in a struggle for empire and prestige. They were organized in two huge, approximately equal alliances, each fearful of the other. One consisted of the two Central European empires of Germany and Austria-Hungary (with the doubtful adherence of Italy), the other of Britain, France, and Russia. When Austria-Hungary, afraid of the disintegration of her multinational empire, demanded severe punishment of Serbia, Germany backed her ally's demands. Russia felt it necessary to assist Serbia, and France was linked to Russia. When Germany invaded France through Belgium (whose neutrality had been internationally guaranteed), England came somewhat reluctantly into the war. Later the Central Powers were joined by Turkey and Bulgaria; the Western Allies by Italy, Japan, Greece, Rumania, and other countries.

When war broke out, most Americans believed their country could and should stay out of it. Many quoted, or misquoted, the founding fathers on the subject of foreign entanglements. To many progressives, war was associated with reaction, and to the socialist minority it was a product of dying capitalism.

Yet few managed to follow completely President Wilson's advice to remain neutral in thought. Most of the eastern, Anglo-Saxon elite of the nation, including a great many editors and publicists, deeply valued British law and literature and identified their own values with Western European civilization. Still larger groups felt a vague traditional sympathy with France and a genuine moral outrage over the invasion of Belgium. Some influential individuals argued, on less emotional grounds, that American safety depended on British control of the Atlantic Ocean. The drift of American foreign policy for two decades had been toward cooperation with Britain. Thus much Allied war propaganda fell on already friendly ears.

Not all Americans, however, favored the Allies. Many, including most Irish-Americans and many Midwesterners, continued to associate Britain with empire, aristocracy, and oligarchy. To the well-organized and articulate German-American minority, the Fatherland was an innocent victim of Allied encirclement.

Even more clearly than in Jefferson's day, real neutrality was made difficult by America's economic importance and geographic position. In 1914 the country was entering a depression, and war orders promised recovery. From the beginning, America took the traditional and legally correct position that all belligerents were free to buy supplies. British naval power meant that in practice only the Allies could tap American resources, which they desperately needed. Originally inclined to insist on cash sales in the interests of neutrality, Wilson and Secretary Bryan early withdrew their opposition to credit. By 1915 American industry was booming, and American prosperity was bound up in Allied success. Either German victory, an embargo on munitions, a prohibition of loans, or a sudden peace would have meant financial crisis.

Undoubtedly this economic involvement influenced some American opinion. Yet business, and particularly big business, was by no means dominant in the formation of American foreign policy. Some progressives were against whatever business leaders supported. And the President, who bore the responsibility for foreign-policy decisions, had demonstrated in the Mexican crisis a deep hostility to "selfish interests." While Wilson loved British culture and disliked German militarism, he was determined to maintain peace. He was also determined, as always, to defend America's national honor and her power. Both were essential to the overriding goal: the promotion of worldwide democratic progress. Except for the pacifist Bryan, the President's most influential advisers, including his close friend Edward M. House, tended strongly in a pro-Allied direction.

Thus the forces affecting American policy were fairly evenly balanced. Most Americans wanted to stay out, and most hoped for Allied victory. Neither economic interest nor Allied sympathy was strong enough to counter the traditional dislike of becoming involved in Europe's troubles. Perplexed by conflicting emotions, many Americans responded most clearly to surging nationalism. Only a direct challenge to American rights and feelings could tip the balance toward war. This challenge arose out of a familiar problem: neutral rights at sea.

Once again, as in the time of Napoleon, a great land power and a great sea power were fighting an all-out war. Each would prefer to remain on good terms with America, the world's most powerful neutral. Yet neither, in the long run, could afford to give up any weapon necessary to victory. The British, as expected, used their navy to blockade Germany and deny her essential supplies. The Germans, to cut off British supplies, turned to a new weapon, the submarine.

Enormously effective, the submarine was also vulnerable. Traditionally, a blockading warship was supposed to warn an enemy merchant vessel and remove passengers and crew before sinking her. If, however, a submarine surfaced to warn its victim it could fairly easily be sunk by an armed merchant ship. In at least one famous case, a German submarine which had surfaced for this purpose was sunk by a British decoy ship, disguised as an American merchant vessel. Thus the Germans, throughout the war, faced a difficult choice. They could not use their only effective sea weapon in the only effective manner without killing civilians. Yet killing civilians, in 1914, was still regarded by world opinion as illegal and brutal. Submarine warfare, which might bring German victory, could at the same time add to Germany's enemies and thereby bring defeat.

In dealing with blockade and counterblockade, the Wilson administration had three possible choices, and none of these was without its advocates. The first was strict neutrality, favored by Bryan, by many congressional Democrats, and by much midwestern opinion. Of the many methods proposed to implement such a policy, the most plausible was to prohibit American citizens from travelling on armed ships and thus to prevent the most dangerous kind of incidents. Under this plan, protests against both German and British blockade excesses would be filed for postwar negotiation. This policy, or any policy of abandoning or diminishing American neutral rights, was rejected by Wilson on grounds of national honor.

The opposite extreme would have been to intervene, early and frankly, on the Allied side. This would not only have ended the dilemma about neutral rights, it would have shortened the war and given America a more decisive voice in the peace. It was advocated by Theodore Roosevelt, which hardly recommended it to Wilson. Such a choice was completely contrary to tradition and would have divided the country disastrously.

The third choice, and one which attracted Wilson from time to time, was to exert American influence on both sides in favor of a negotiated peace. A beginning in this direction was the effort to induce Germany to give up submarine warfare in return for the relaxation of the British blockade, especially on food. This was rejected by Britain in 1915 and would probably have been rejected by Germany whenever defeat drew closer. Twice during the war, Colonel House visited the belligerent capitals to press for a statement of war aims leading toward negotiation. Neither side was willing to give up the prospect of victory. As always happens in a prolonged war, hatred and fear were aroused to such an extent that compromise was bound to look like surrender.

To force peace, it would have been necessary to threaten both sides with loss of the war. Only a threat to cut off munitions could have compelled Britain to abandon her own war aims. To make such a threat and carry it out might have resulted in German victory. It was clear that the Wilson administration, in a showdown, was unlikely to take such action against the side most Americans preferred. To force Germany to make peace, on the other hand, it would have been necessary to threaten actual intervention on the Allied side. Only a heavily armed America, with a united or docile public opinion, could have made such a policy work. Really effective mediation was made impossible by the whole nature of the American political system. Thus the policy actually adopted was, and perhaps had to be, a constantly shifting compromise among the three alternatives: neutrality, intervention, and mediation.

NEUTRALITY TO WAR IN FOUR ACTS

The first stage of American policy, from the outbreak of war to February, 1915, was characterized by benevolent neutrality toward England. After the shocking invasion of Belgium, the Germans gave little direct offense, while the British blockade became increasingly rigid. Contraband of war was gradually extended to cover most commodities, neutral ships were stopped at sea and taken to port for search, and trade with other neutrals who might transship to Germany was severely rationed. Yet American protests were moderate in tone, British concessions considerable, and, above all, no American was killed. The United States accepted without much ill-feeling even the British proclamation of a mined war zone in the North Sea, where few American ships went.

The second stage, running from February, 1915, until May, 1916, was dominated by German submarine warfare. In February, Germany proclaimed a submarine war zone around the British Isles, cutting the main Atlantic sea lanes. From this point on the administration refused to accept the legality of submarine warfare and announced that Germany would be held to "strict accountability" for American losses.

On May 7, 1915, the liner *Lusitania*, unarmed but carrying some war cargo, was sunk off the Irish coast. Of the 1198 passengers drowned, 128 were Americans. In a series of very strong notes, Wilson demanded that Germany accept responsibility for these losses and abandon her methods of submarine war. After repeated warnings, partial or temporary German concessions, and further sinkings, Wilson, in March, 1916, made it clear that a continuation of unrestricted submarine warfare would mean a break in German-American relations. This clearly implied war, and Germany, somewhat grudgingly, promised that henceforth her raiders would warn before sinking.

In following this policy, Wilson had to fight off critics on both sides. Some of the press wanted war right away, especially when the deaths of American women and children coincided with plausible though inaccurate reports of atrocities in Belgium. Secretary Bryan, on the other hand, resigned from the Cabinet rather than sign a note to Germany he considered dangerously harsh. In early 1916 the administration had to use all its power in Congress to defeat a measure forbidding American travel on armed ships. When Germany accepted American demands, Wilson scored a major victory. The nation was, however, practically committed to go to war whenever Germany changed her mind. To give some meaning to his implied threats of force, Wilson gave his backing, in late 1915, to a preparedness program including increased army and navy appropriations and heavy new taxes.

The third stage, from May, 1916, to February, 1917, brought somewhat less tense relations with Germany, increased irritation against England, and the peak of Wilson's efforts for a negotiated peace. In this period Britain, hard pressed in war and confident of American tolerance, stepped up her enforcement of the blockade. American mail was searched, and American firms believed to have dealt with Germany were black-listed and barred from British trade. Wilson found these actions almost intolerable, and Congress made gestures of retaliation.

In November, Wilson narrowly won re-election against Charles Evans Hughes, a moderate Republican progressive running with the support of a reunited (and largely conservative) party. In the campaign Wilson was attacked by both isolationists and interventionists. His own partisans, however, pointed to his success in keeping America out of war, as well as to his recently increased domestic progressivism.

Once re-elected, Wilson embarked on his most ambitious effort at mediation. This time, instead of approaching the Allies through the sympathetic Colonel House, he publicly asked both Britain and Germany to state war aims. This request, closely following a somewhat specious German offer to negotiate, greatly angered the British. Once more, neither side showed any real wish to compromise, and Wilson became increasingly disillusioned with the Allied cause. On January 22, in an eloquent speech he declared that the world's only hope lay in a "Peace without Victory" for either side.

The fourth and final phase started a week later when Germany, where military pressures had finally defeated civilian resistance, announced the resumption of unrestricted submarine warfare against neutral and belligerent vessels alike. Wilson had no alternative but to break relations, yet he still refused to ask for war. On March 1, the administration released to the press an intercepted German note proposing, in the event of war with the United States, an alliance with Mexico to recover lost territories and an effort to persuade Japan to switch sides. Meantime Wilson, despite a filibuster by Robert M. La Follette and other antiwar progressives, started arming American ships. Only at the beginning of April, after a series of new sinkings, did Wilson finally ask for and get from Congress a declaration of war against Germany.

AMERICA AT WAR: PATRIOTISM AND DISCONTENT

Though many Americans had expected limited, almost painless participation in the war, the state of the Allied war effort in 1917 made this impossible. Germany was sinking British ships faster than they could be built, the French army was exhausted and mutinous, and Russia was knocked out by revolution.

The first Russian Revolution in March, 1917, had caused America to welcome Russia joyfully into the ranks of democratic and constitutional states. In November, however, the Bolsheviks with their slogan of "Land, bread, and peace" had overthrown the moderate Kerensky government and embarked Russia on the Soviet road. In March they signed a treaty with Germany, surrendering large territories and freeing German troops for a one-front war. Germany thus began a series of immense offensives which threatened to defeat the Allies before American help could become effective.

Faced with this desperate necessity, the United States built a conscript army of more than 3,500,000 and by November, 1918, had shipped 2,000,000 men overseas without losses. American naval forces greatly reduced the submarine menace. American ground forces in France played a distinguished and probably decisive part in the bloody operations of 1918 in which the German offensives were finally met and the German armies rolled back.

To do all this, it was necessary to regiment to a new degree the vast economic power of an essentially civilian country. Money for huge loans to the Allies as well as for America's war effort was raised by a fairly democratic system of war finance. About one third of the total needed was raised by taxes as against about one fifth in the Civil War. For this purpose, incomes and corporate profits were taxed at unheard of rates. For 1918, incomes of over $1 million were assessed a total tax of 77 per cent. (In 1913, a top rate of 7 per cent had seemed high.) Federal war bonds were sold to sixty-five million customers in four great drives. Even so, the war was financed partly by inflation and mostly through expansion of bank credit by action of the new Federal Reserve System.

After fumbling with various regulatory devices in the first war winter, Congress in the spring of 1918 gave the President almost dictatorial powers over the war economy. Under him five hundred war agencies policed the productive effort. The War Industries Board allocated raw materials, determined priorities, and standardized products. The War Labor Board opposed strikes and lockouts, but promoted union recognition, the eight-hour day, and uniform wages. The Food Administration under Herbert Hoover guaranteed the purchase and set the prices for major farm commodities, thereby greatly increasing food production. The Fuel Board and the Shipping Administration similarly increased production in their spheres. The railroads were taken over and efficiently run by the Railway Administration.

By 1918 the United States had a fairly efficient regulated economy. Some advanced progressives talked cheerfully of war socialism and prophesied that these gains for collectivism would not be lost.

Most citizens, however, were probably restive under this new system and were held in line only by wartime patriotism. Businessmen resented the siphoning off of some of the enormous war profits through taxes, resented labor's gains, and in general disliked being told what to do. Farmers, faring well, resented the fixing of prices which had never been set in periods of depression. Yet despite its widespread unpopularity, governmental direction of the war economy marked a momentous step in a generally continuing direction. There was no return to *laissez faire*, if indeed *laissez faire* had ever existed. After the war, the government was to act as a partner to business, and later under the New Deal wartime precedents were to be invoked for other kinds of intervention.

Equally great steps, with equally momentous consequences, were taken in the field of manipulating public opinion. Despite evidence of public enthusiasm, the government was apparently disquieted about national unity. The Committee on Public Information blanketed the country with pamphlets and speeches about the goals of the war. Cracking down on opposition, the Post Office barred antiwar publications from the mails. A Sedition Act passed in 1918 forbade abusive language about the American form of government, flag, or uniform or acts bringing into contempt the form of government or the Constitution. About 1,500 persons, including most of the leadership of the Socialist party, were imprisoned for sedition. States and private organizations went much further than the federal government on the road to war hysteria. The German language was driven from the schools, German music was eliminated from concerts, and religious pacifists were physically abused. In some places, the slightest criticism of the administration or the Allies was considered punishable disloyalty. To all this emotion, a reaction was inevitable. For the future, both the possibilities and the dangers of mobilizing emotion had been demonstrated.

Far outrunning measures of compulsion, popular support of the war was extraordinarily general. Yet beneath this unity lay discontent. This was indicated in the congressional elections of 1918 when Wilson, calling for the election of a Democratic Congress as an endorsement of his war leadership, received instead a Republican majority in both Houses.

THE FAILURE OF A WILSONIAN PEACE

On her entry into the war America, democratic and free from either war guilt or aggressive ambitions, was recognized as the most effective Allied spokesman, and Wilson became the worldwide prophet of a democratic peace. On January 8, 1918, he outlined to Congress his famous Fourteen Points.

The first five of these were general liberal formulae: open treaty-making, freedom of the seas, removal of trade barriers, and impartial adjustment of colonial claims in the interest of the natives. Most of the rest of the Points were concerned with the readjustment of boundaries in the interest of the Wilsonian principle of national self-determination even for small nations. The final Point, the most important to Wilson, provided for an association of nations to maintain the peace. A number of the Fourteen Points were contrary to provisions in the secret treaties already negotiated among the Allies. Wilson knew of these treaties but ignored them, doubtless believing that he could force the Allies to abandon them.

On October 6, Germany, her military situation hopeless, asked Wilson for an armistice based on his announced program. Despite Allied objections, the Fourteen Points were accepted as the basis for peace, with some reservations. On November 11, military authorities finished negotiating an armistice which disarmed Germany and made further resistance impossible.

In January, 1919, at Paris, the victorious Allies started negotiating among themselves the peace terms to be imposed on Germany. Accompanied by an undistinguished peace delegation and a large corps of experts, Wilson left for Paris. Frantic ovations throughout Europe apparently convinced him that it was his mission, alone, to force a just peace on the world. Actually, his power was limited by that of two powerful groups of opponents, the Allies and the Senate Republicans. Like Germany, Wilson had to fight a two-front war. Insisting from the outset that the Covenant of the League of Nations be part of the Treaty, Wilson made a quick trip to Washington and found more than a third of the Senate lined up against the Covenant in its negotiated form. Returning to Paris, he had to face the Allied leaders with weakened bargaining powers. These statesmen, bound by the secret treaties, were also understandably determined to secure their nations against further attack and to make Germany pay for the long struggle. Despite a courageous fight, Wilson had to make many concessions. To Italy he had to concede sizeable German-speaking border areas. Japan secured not only Germany's island colonies (which were to play a crucial part in World War II), but also, against Chinese opposition, German interests in the Shantung Peninsula. To France, who desired the actual dismemberment of Germany, Wilson had to concede very severe terms regarding the defeated nation. Germany was stripped of colonies and merchant marine, disarmed, and forced to surrender border areas. Perhaps more important, she was required to admit her guilt for the war as a basis for reparations, whose sum would be fixed later by the Allies.

To Wilson, all concessions were justified by the many gains for self-determination in the Treaty (and in the later treaties with Germany's allies) and above all by the establishment of the League. This would, he hoped, supervise the administration of former German colonies by their new masters under the mandate system. It would secure the reduction of armaments, preserve the independence and integrity of all nations, mediate disputes, and even use force against those resorting to war. For this great hope, Wilson came home to fight.

At first, the Treaty's chances looked good. Wilson's prestige was still great, and the idea of a League of Nations had long attracted American support. Yet the Treaty aroused many kinds of opposition. Among its enemies were the disappointed minorities of German, Italian, and Irish descent, isolationists who feared that the League would involve America in European affairs, liberals who objected to the compromises of democratic principle, and, vaguer but crucially important, many Americans already reacting against wartime enthusiasm and sacrifice.

The Senate, where the struggle centered, was divided into three groups: (1) Loyal Wilsonian Democrats, in favor of the Treaty and the League; (2) A group of only about a dozen Senators including La Follette, Borah, and Johnson of California, who were "Irreconcilable," all-out foes of both; and (3) "Reservationists" who were inclined to accept the Treaty with certain changes defining and restricting the authority of the League.

In the long struggle, opposition to the Treaty was marshalled by Henry Cabot Lodge, an enemy of Wilson and a master tactician. In order to attract the crucial Reservationists, Lodge proposed not the rejection of the Treaty but its passage with a number of changes. These were carefully calculated to sound plausible, but to be unacceptable to Wilson. Lodge knew his opponent. Wilson forbade Democrats to accept the reservations, thus making impossible a two-thirds majority. Without reservations, the Treaty was opposed by Irreconcilables and Reservationists, with reservations by Irreconcilables and loyal Democrats.

Refusing to accept defeat, Wilson embarked on a nationwide speaking tour. The people, he said, must not allow the Senate to "break the heart of the world" by rejecting the Treaty. Prematurely aged and emotionally exhausted, Wilson broke down in the midst of his tour and had to be taken back to Washington. There he suffered a severe stroke and was partly incapacitated for the rest of his presidency. Sick, isolated, but grimly determined, he continued to forbid his followers to compromise. Though the Allies were by now willing to accept the reservations, Wilson's loyal followers rejected them, and the Treaty failed to get ratification.

Once more Wilson appealed to the final authority, announcing in the spring of 1920 that the coming presidential election would constitute a "solemn referendum" on the Treaty. In the campaign the Democratic candidate, Governor James M. Cox of Ohio, did support the Treaty and the League. The Republican candidate, Senator Warren G. Harding of the same state, opposed it only ambiguously, and some of his supporters favored it equally vaguely.

Harding won by the most sweeping majority since Monroe. It is impossible to prove that the election constituted a real referendum on foreign policy. It was certainly affected by many domestic issues, including the breakdown of the President and, to a considerable extent, of his administration. In another sense, however, the election of 1920 was a major decision: the campaign and much press comment as well as the results indicated that the American people wanted a president as little like Woodrow Wilson as possible, and this is what they got.

The United States, a country with a long isolationist tradition, had been moving for a generation toward world leadership. Now her efforts had decided a world war, and her leader had dominated a world settlement. In 1920 the people, exhausted by this break with the past and disillusioned by its results, determined to do their best to return to familiar, cherished ways.

FOR FURTHER READING:

Of the innumerable accounts of America's approach to war, Ernest R. May, *The World War and American Isolation, 1914–1917* (1959) is recent, excellent, and sympathetic to Wilson. C. C. Tansill, *America Goes to War* (1938), is the best of the older, more or less isolationist accounts. A great deal of information is contained in Frederick L. Paxson's authoritative but ill-organized three volumes on *American Democracy and the World War, 1913–1923* (1936–1948). The social history of the home front can be found in P. W. Slosson, *The Great Crusade and After, 1914–1928* (1937) and the wartime state of civil liberties is described in Zachariah Chafee, Jr., *Free Speech in the United States* (1941). The rejection of the Treaty is explained in T. A. Bailey, *Wilson and the Peacemakers* (1947).

Ernest R. May, *The Coming of War, 1917* (Berkeley Readings in American History, 1963)*, is a documentary study of American intervention.

---

*Available in paperback edition.

THE WAR AND THE TWENTIES

PRESIDENT	POLITICAL EVENTS	ECONOMIC CONDITIONS	FOREIGN POLICY	MISCELLANEOUS
1916 Wilson *D*		1914 Depression. 1915–1916 Recovery: war orders. 1917–1918 War prosperity.	1917 (April) War declared. (January) Fourteen Points. (November) Armistice.	1915 Movie, "Birth of a Nation."
1918	Republicans win Senate.			
1920 Harding *R*	1919 (September) Wilson's collapse. Prohibition and woman's suffrage in effect.	1919 Inflationary boom strikes. Deflation and depression.	1919 (June) Versailles Treaty signed. (March) Treaty finally defeated in Senate.	1919 Red Scare. First regular radio station. Sinclair Lewis, *Main Street.*
1922	1921 Immigration quotas established. Fordney-McCumber Tariff. Progressive gains in Congress.	1921 Depression. Recovery.	1921–1922 Washington Conference.	
	1923 (August) Death of Harding 1923–1924 Exposure of "Harding Scandals."	PROSPERITY		

THE WAR AND THE TWENTIES (*Continued*)

PRESIDENT	POLITICAL EVENTS	ECONOMIC CONDITIONS	FOREIGN POLICY	MISCELLANEOUS
1924 Coolidge *R*	La Follette Third Party Movement.		Dawes Plan for Germany.	1925 Scopes Trial; Dreiser, *American Tragedy;* Fitzgerald, *Great Gatsby.*
1926	1927 President vetoes McNary-Haugen farm bill.	1927 Decline in construction and auto industries.	1927 United States–Mexican differences compromised. United States renounces right of intervention in Latin America under "Roosevelt Corollary."	1927 Lindbergh flight.
1928 Hoover *R*		1929 (September–October) Wall Street crash.	1929 Young Plan for Germany.	1929 Hemingway, *Farewell to Arms;* Faulkner, *The Sound and the Fury.*

```
₭₭₭₭₭₭₭₭₭₭₭₭₭₭₭₭₭₭₭₭₭₭
                        ₮
    CHAPTER 25          ₮
                        ₮
>>>>>>>>>>>>>>>>>>>>>>>>
```

THE TWENTIES:
PROSPERITY AND SOCIAL CHANGE

The postwar decade is thought of today in at least three ways. It was the Jazz Age, the roaring twenties, the romantic heyday of flappers and flivvers. It was also the period of Republican prosperity, conservatism, and isolation. Further, it was the period of Hemingway, Fitzgerald, and T. S. Eliot, a time of literary experiment and creation.

These paradoxes are not invented by historians; even at the time America looked different to different kinds of people. Businessmen and farmers, Freudians and fundamentalists were all reacting at different rates and in different ways to a series of changes so rapid as to be deeply disturbing. Some of these changes, like industrialization and urbanization, had been going on a long time and were now accelerated. Others, like the importation of challenging new ideas (among them psychoanalysis and relativity) had begun before the war. Still others were direct results of the war, which was itself a traumatic break with national tradition.

Some Americans accepted change willingly; others fought every departure from the good old ways. Still others accepted innovation in some areas, like technology and transportation, and fought it in others, like manners and morals. Even for the most conservative, however, tradition seemed hard to define or find, let alone restore.

Fortunately, change was cushioned by good fortune. For many Americans the twenties were a time of peace and prosperity—the last for a long time.

THE FAILURE OF WILSONISM, 1918–1920

The first postwar years were by no means placid. The fight over the Treaty was only one aspect of a frustrating struggle to liquidate the war. In 1919, many advanced progressives and labor leaders were talking about planned and masterful reconstruction and even predicting the nationalization of basic industries. Actually, nothing was farther from popular demand or administration intent. From the Armistice on, government contracts were cancelled, employees dismissed, and regulatory powers abandoned. Soldiers were rapidly discharged with only minimum provisions for re-employment.

Congress abandoned regulation and reform less rapidly than the administration. Immediately after the war two progressive causes reached nationwide victory. The Eighteenth (prohibition) Amendment, pushed hard by the Methodist Church and the Anti-Saloon League, was put over the top by a combination of moral zeal, desire to conserve resources, and dislike of German-American brewers. In October, 1919, the Volstead Act, passed over Wilson's veto, ended forever (most of its friends and enemies thought) the manufacture, sale, transportation, or possession of intoxicating beverages. In the same year the Nineteenth Amendment made woman suffrage a nationwide reality.

In dismantling controls the postwar Congress had a mixed record. The railroads, returned to private hands by the administration, were placed under stringent regulation by the Esch-Cummins Act of 1920. This law's purpose, however, was partly to promote rather than prevent consolidation into fewer systems. From now on the railroad industry, threatened with truck and bus competition and in places overbuilt, was to be treated more as an invalid and less as a tyrannical giant. The government-built merchant marine was returned to private interests, and here too subsidy was more needed than control. In one vital area, that of water power, Congress, in 1920, established a new regulatory agency, the Federal Power Commission, with power to license development and operation.

For the most part, however, the wartime-directed economy was dismantled without planning and without disaster. In the spring of 1919, after a very brief postwar slump, business began to pick up. At the time the upturn was credited to unsatisfied consumer demand, but today economists point to government spending, temporarily continued in the form of loans to the Allies and European relief operations. Rapidly, recovery turned into speculative boom, as wholesale prices rose by about 30 per cent.

Instead of Imperial Germany, the main public enemy in 1919 seemed to be the high cost of living. Salaried people were badly pinched, and labor was restive about the possibility of maintaining wartime gains in organization and real wages. Four million workers, more than ever before, took part in strikes. In most of these, including a coal strike and a bitterly fought steel strike, the unions were beaten. Government and articulate public opinion sided strongly with employers.

Many citizens blamed strikes, the high cost of living, and foreign crises on one simple cause: radical conspiracy. The Third International, calling from Moscow for world revolution, was echoed by the two, new, tiny American Communist parties. A few bombings, believed to be of anarchist origin, roused public emotions. Many conservative citizens feared, and a few ardent radicals hoped that revolution was at hand.

In the fall of 1919 Attorney General A. Mitchell Palmer, until now regarded as a Wilsonian progressive, organized his famous series of raids on alleged foreign radical organizations. In the worst of these, thousands of people were arrested with little regard for legal procedure and sometimes treated with considerable brutality. Practically no evidence of dangerous revolutionary activity was uncovered, but many zealous individuals, organizations, and governmental units turned their hostility from Germans to radicals. The New York Legislature expelled five duly-elected Socialist assemblymen, and a drastic sedition bill, carrying the death penalty in certain cases, was introduced (but never passed) in Congress. In one of the last episodes of the Red Scare, two philosophical anarchists named Nicola Sacco and Bartolomeo Vanzetti were arrested for a robbery and murder which few liberals believed they had committed. Despite impassioned agitation for their release, the two men were finally executed in 1927.

Well before this, in fact before the end of 1920, the Red Scare had begun to ebb. For several years, however, fear of the alien, the dissenter, and the nonconformist showed itself in other ways: in race riots and lynchings, in anti-Semitic whisperings, in crusades against alarming ideas, and above all in suspicion of foreigners. All these tendencies played a part in the growth of the Ku Klux Klan, a new organization founded in 1915 in imitation of its Reconstruction namesake. The Klan, a secret organization stronger in the West than the South, was militantly anti-Catholic, antiforeign, and antiliberal. At its height in the early twenties, thousands joined its sheeted parades, perhaps five million enrolled as members, and at least two states came under its political control. Only in the mid-twenties, when most kinds of hysteria gave way to complacency, did the Klan lose strength.

In 1919–1920 many Americans came to associate Wilsonian idealism with frustrated hopes and divisive emotions, with the unsolved problems of Europe, with war propoaganda and foreign entanglements, and with the high cost of living and the Red Menace. Even the most devoted Wilsonians had to admit a shattering contrast between the vigorous leader of 1913 or the inspired prophet of 1917 and the sick, stubborn, old man of 1919, presiding over an administration zealous in hounding radicals but helpless in dealing with social or economic problems. It is not surprising that the country turned with relief toward a leadership as different as possible.

READJUSTMENT AND NEW DIRECTIONS, 1920–1924

Warren G. Harding was a small-town editor, a regular McKinley and Taft Republican, and a handsome, genial man with undemanding moral standards and a third-rate mind. Not unaware of his own shortcomings, he announced a plan to staff his administration with his party's "best minds." A few of these were secured, including Charles Evans Hughes, the new Secretary of State; Herbert Hoover, Secretary of Commerce; and possibly Andrew Mellon, the Pittsburgh aluminum king who became Secretary of the Treasury. In too many cases, though, the administration was staffed with party hacks and presidential cronies in a manner reminiscent of the Grant Era. A major center of power was the famous "little house on K Street" where members of the Ohio Gang played poker and forgot Prohibition. Yet this sleazy regime made decisions of great importance, most of them highly popular in their time.

In the campaign Harding, who had a gift for meaningless oratorical pronouncements, understandably avoided defining his foreign policy. Much of the Republican party was bitterly isolationist, yet an important faction, including ex-President Taft, insisted that the new administration would work out a less offensive substitue for the League of Nations. Whatever the election really meant, Harding drew from it the conclusion that American entry into the League was a dead issue. Even United States membership in the World Court, which Harding and his Republican successors favored, was blocked by ultra-isolationist forces in the press and the Senate.

Despite the strength of isolationist feelings, real isolation was impossible. In the Far East, the original home of the Open Door Policy and the traditional center of Republican foreign interest, a new settlement was urgently necessary. During the war Japan had taken large steps toward the domination of China and military hegemony in East Asia. Yet once more America's traditional commitments in Asia went far beyond her power. In the winter of 1921, an international conference in Washington, sometimes referred to as a Republican Versailles, struggled with the related problems of disarmament and the Far East.

In a series of interlocking treaties the United States attained the following objectives: (1) Japanese expansion was rolled back; (2) the embarrassing Anglo-Japanese Alliance was terminated; (3) the *status quo* in the Far East and the integrity of China were guaranteed by all major powers concerned except Russia; (4) the major naval powers agreed to curtail construction of capital ships, with Japan limited to three fifths of the naval power of each of the Big Two (Britain and the United States). In return for these advantages the United States surrendered the possibility of naval superiority and agreed not to fortify her possessions in the Western Pacific. Much later, in an age of renewed Japanese aggression, these concessions were to be denounced. At the time, however, the United States was in no mood either for an arms race or for contesting Japan's control of the Western Pacific area. The Washington Settlement seemed a great succcess, and Japanese-American relations relaxed.

Even from Europe, it proved impossible to remain aloof. The United States had made huge loans to the Allied nations both during and right after the war. These were viewed by Europeans as American contributions to the common struggle and by most Americans as legitimate business obligations. Not without recrimination, the United States negotiated a series of funding agreements extending payment over twenty-five years with rates of interest scaled down according to ability to pay.

Payment by any scheme turned out to present almost insoluble problems. Sufficient gold was not available, and large imports of European goods were promptly rendered impossible. True to Republican traditions, formed during a period of infant American industry and devoutly upheld long after, Congress, in 1922, enacted the steeply protective Fordney-McCumber Tariff.

To many Europeans, debt payments to the United States seemed inseparably connected with German reparation payments to the former Allies. But in 1923 the Germans, racked by inflation and resentful of the sole-war-guilt principle on which reparations were based, defaulted. France promptly occupied the industrial Ruhr and was challenged by passive resistance from the German population. This situation, clearly threatening prosperity and peace, was a major test for the new foreign policy, and the test was passed. An international commission of experts, headed by an American banker, negotiated the Dawes Plan in 1923, and six years later a like group worked out the similar Young Plan. The basis of these plans was (1) successively scaled-down German payments, (2) stabilization of the German currency, and (3) an international loan to Germany to make these steps possible.

The greatest industrial nation in the world, now also the greatest creditor, could not stay aloof from world affairs. Instead, private investment was substituted for other forms of intervention. American investors, acting more or less in response to State Department suggestions, sustained the German Republic, helped the relatively moderate banker and industrialist regime in Japan, contested Near Eastern oil areas with the British and French, and supported congenial governments in Latin America. Because this was done in the name of profit rather than politics and, above all, because military force was invoked only in minor Caribbean instances, the administration could quote with satisfaction the antientanglement advice of the founding fathers.

Antiforeign emotions were appeased by a drastic change in immigration policy. Well before the war, fear and dislike of "The New Immigration" from southern and eastern Europe had been spread by alarmist propaganda, and pseudoscientists continued to demonstrate the criminal tendencies of Slavs and Latins by their head measurements. Unions had long opposed the admission of cheap labor, and the advance of technology had made a mass of unskilled workers less important to industrialists. The war and the Red Scare had spread suspicion of aliens, and Congress in 1921–1924 took a series of actions designed both to decrease the number of immigrants sharply and to swing the balance back to the north European peoples. In its 1924 version the new legislation established a quota system limiting immigration from each country to 2 per cent of its proportion of resident aliens according to the census of 1890. To the anger of the Japanese, a special provision totally excluded Orientals as "aliens ineligible to citizenship."

This decision, which reduced immigration from a flood to a trickle, broke decisively with a major American tradition and wounded the feelings of important minorities. In the long run, however, its results were far different from those intended by some of its supporters. The end of free immigration, like the disappearance of the frontier, lessened the wide-open, competitive, mobile tendencies of American life. No longer were labor organizers and reform politicians to be frustrated by a continuing stream of newcomers, ignorant of American problems and desperately willing to accept low wages and vote as city bosses told them. Increasingly, the foreign-born and their children were to demand a full place in American politics and with it solutions for the problems of urban society.

The economic policies of the Harding administration were developed in a time of instability. Late in 1920 the postwar boom turned into depression as government supports of basic commodity prices ended and European demand temporarily fell off. In the face of plummeting prices and mounting unemployment, government policy was simple: to do everything possible to encourage business leadership. Secretary Mellon called for strict economy and proposed sharp cuts in taxes on profits and high incomes. (Interestingly, Congress gave him only part of what he asked.) The administration continued the Wilson policy of withdrawal from all forms of government economic enterprise and cooperated still more fully with industry's drive to "discipline" organized labor. Hoover's Department of Commerce strove to further foreign investment and encouraged the formation of trade associations to prevent price cutting and other "unfair" competition. Probusiness appointments to the courts and the new regulatory commissions ended any threat of unsympathetic regulation.

Whether or not because of government policy, recovery began in 1922 and became well-established in 1923. The fact that this depression ended quickly, without government action except to encourage business, was to affect the thinking of many people at the outset of a greater depression a few years later.

One major exception to the encouraging economic tendency was the plight of the farmer. Once more production was far outrunning effective demand, and prices were falling disastrously. During the war, with demand unlimited and prices regulated by the government, farmers had prospered. Right after the war, a land boom had sustained at least the more fortunate. Now, with bumper crops to sell, mechanization putting a premium on efficiency, and European and world competition increasing sharply most farmers were in trouble. Once more large sections of the country confronted the familiar problems of unpayable mortgages and rapidly increasing tenancy.

A series of farm organizations, from the semisocialist Non-Partisan League of North Dakota to the more conservative Farm Bureau Federation, once more voiced demands for relief. In Congress the powerful Farm Bloc secured considerable relief legislation of familiar kinds such as encouragement of cooperatives, facilitation of credit, and regulation of packers and speculators.

Farmers were not the only people to show their discontent with the Harding policies. Prewar progressivism, with its underdog sympathies and anti-big-business emotions, lived on in the hearts of millions of teachers, preachers, social workers, unionists, and others. In the new postwar circumstances, however, both high morale and unity seemed hard for progressives to attain.

In 1922 the most promising of a series of progressive coalitions took shape in the form of the Conference for Progressive Political Action, a federation of farm organizations, discontented labor groups, right-wing Socialists, and assorted Bull Moosers and other progressives. In the congressional elections of 1922 the C.P.P.A. scored some startling successes. Harding Republicans lost many seats both to Democrats and progressive Republicans. To some, it seemed as if Harding's administration might suffer the fate of Taft's. Actually, a comparison to Grant's was closer.

As in the seventies, antiadministration congressional investigations disclosed a shocking series of scandals. Harding cronies in the Veterans' Bureau and a number of other agencies had been dispensing favors for financial inducements. The worst revelation was that government oil lands, held for naval needs, had been transferred in a series of maneuvers to a group of private speculators. Still popular but increasingly conscious of his own inadequacy and of betrayal by his friends, the President fell ill in the course of returning from an Alaskan junket. On August 2, 1923, he died of a stroke in San Francisco. To his party's good fortune, he was replaced by Vice President Calvin Coolidge, a taciturn and parsimonious Yankee who seemed the perfect incarnation of Republican rectitude.

In 1922–1924, however, many people thought that the Harding scandals and the progressive gains foreshadowed a political upheaval. The C.P.P.A. backed the redoubtable Robert M. La Follette as a "Progressive" presidential candidate. The La Follette platform had, to be sure, a rather old-fashioned ring for 1924: antimonopoly, public ownership of railroads, conservation, farm relief, and curbing of the Supreme Court. Yet the Wisconsin Senator, whose antiwar record was now an asset in his own section, looked formidable enough to frighten conservatives. The Republicans, renominating Coolidge on a *status quo* platform, denounced La Follette and his supporters as extreme radicals. Meanwhile the Democrats, deeply divided by their old agrarian-urban split, bogged down in a deadlocked convention and emerged with an unpromising conservative candidate, John W. Davis.

The result of the election was a Coolidge landslide. La Follette, without adequate organization or large funds, had scored 16.5 per cent of the popular vote and ran ahead of Davis in many western states. Yet right after the election his disparate coalition fell apart. Progressivism, for the moment, seemed negative and old-fashioned. The election seemed a green light for business prosperity and its political friends.

THE NEW ERA AND ITS CRITICS

For the rest of the decade, American prosperity was the center of attention both for complacent natives and jealous or admiring foreigners. The principal basis for the good times was an increase in productivity based on advances in technology and management. Between

1923 and 1929, the output per man-hour in manufacturing rose 32 per cent. The basic industrial plant and transportation systems were now largely adequate; this time much of the expansion could go into the kind of production that people notice most easily. Construction, both of suburban houses and urban skyscrapers, electric power and light, and durable consumers' goods scored the most spectacular advances. By 1929 one American in five had an automobile. Radios, household appliances, and prepared foods were almost equally part of the new way of life.

Changing patterns of consumption, stimulated by mass advertising and assisted by time payments, seemed to render obsolete the old "Puritan virtues" of hard work, abstinence, and saving. Leisure and enjoyment became not only permissible but almost obligatory. From perplexing foreign problems and dull domestic politics, public attention turned to the lives of movie stars, the exploits of athletes, or the heroism of aviators like Charles Lindbergh who flew the Atlantic alone in 1927 and immediately became the most popular American.

The new prosperity brought with it a new ideology. Business, according to its spokesmen, had accomplished the dreams of past radicals without coercion or hatred. Poverty and war were both overcome and cutthroat competition had been replaced by cooperation and service. The new businessman was committed to high wages and deeply interested in employee welfare. Thus there was no further use for divisive labor unions or impractical political radicalism.

Actually the results of the new prosperity were less than Utopian. Farm prices rose a little from the postwar depression level, yet farmers as a whole failed to regain their prewar purchasing power. Real wages rose sharply, but not in proportion either to productivity or profits. In 1929, the average factory worker made less than $1,500 a year, and more than 45 per cent of all families got less than $2,000. Even if these figures are doubled to represent post-World War II purchasing power, they do not represent universal well-being. Large groups, like coal or textile workers, southern small farmers, and Negroes, remained in real poverty.

Later, many critics were to point out that the New Era's prosperity was as unsound as it was uneven. Business consolidation, though it did not usually attain the outright monopoly which had alarmed people earlier, often led to dangerous practices. Prices were often inflexible, and insider groups sometimes built crazy pyramids of holding companies. In the late twenties, too much money was going into outright speculation in land or stocks and not enough into genuinely productive investment.

Even at the time, important minorities refused to join in the chorus of complacency. Surviving congressional progressives, led by

Senator George Norris of Nebraska, were able to prevent the administration from turning over to private interests the government-built
nitrate plants on the Tennessee River. (In turn Coolidge and his successor were able to block Norris' own plan for a government-run
Tennessee dam and power system.) Prodded by the Farm Bloc,
Congress passed ambitious farm relief laws. Of these the most discussed was the McNary-Haugen bill, vetoed in 1927. This was a
complex scheme providing for government purchase and sale abroad
of surplus farm commodities.

Perhaps the most important dissenters in the Coolidge era expressed themselves in ways which had nothing to do with politics.
Many people of rural and small town upbringing were uneasy about
the new free and easy ways of living and appalled by the alleged
wildness of the younger generation. Some called for a return to so-
briety, simplicity, and tradition; some swelled the ranks of Protestant
religious fundamentalism. Two generations after the Darwinian controversy, the state of Tennessee passed a law against teaching that man
descended from "lower animals" in the schools. When this law was
challenged by shocked liberals, no less a public figure than William
Jennings Bryan appeared to champion a literal interpretation of
Genesis.

At the opposite extreme from the Fundamentalists but equally
hostile to the dominant business ideology, were the literary intellectuals and their followers. With the war, their exuberant rebellion against
moral and esthetic conventions had turned to a far deeper kind of
alienation. Repelled by postwar intolerance and equally disgusted by
what seemed to them the materialism and conformity of the Coolidge
era, many of the most literate Americans worried out loud about the
fate of American civilization. Some roundly denounced the country
and withdrew to Europe.

The most intelligent of the discontented realized that more was
at stake than any set of national mores. Old questions, put in new
forms, were raising doubts about human nature itself. Americans were
confronting problems common to all men, but particularly distressing
to those who inherited a tradition of individual freedom. To some
popular behaviorist psychologists, man was a bundle of predictable
and controllable responses to physical stimuli. To Freudians he was
ruled by emotional drives far below the level of consciousness. Neither
view seemed to offer much hope to those who cared most for individual freedom. Squarely confronting these and other intellectual
challenges, some Americans produced excellent and profoundly serious
novels or poems. Others laid the foundation for a deeper and richer
criticism of contemporary civilization than had yet been possible.

Self-criticism, however, was the last thing most people wanted.

By no means everybody was either happy or rich in the mid-twenties, but prosperity was still a substantial fact, and those who were the most satisfied were also the most influential. More people than ever before moved to the suburbs, drove to the beach, or dreamed of a summer in Europe. Prosperity could be measured not only in baseball gate receipts but in such substantial terms as houses, schools, and hospitals. What civilization, complacent citizens could legitimately ask, had ever done so much for so many?

Ignoring his critics, President Coolidge could continue to issue his laconic and reassuring statements, take his two-hour afternoon naps, continue the probusiness policies of his predecessor without the corruption, and remain generally popular. The federal government could persist in trimming its costs (especially since states were spending more and more on highways). In 1926 Secretary Mellon was finally able to put over his full program of tax relief for the wealthy.

In foreign affairs, success seemed equally conclusive. In Europe, the mid-twenties were an era of apparent economic stabilization, of Franco-German rapprochement, and of increased prestige for the League of Nations. Despite congressional suspicion, the administration was able to develop a habit of unofficial cooperation with the League for many purposes. In Mexico, where conflict between the forces of social revolution and American business interests dragged on, the Coolidge administration managed to compromise serious differences over subsoil oil rights.

Perhaps the most admirable trait of the New Era was a genuine, nearly universal devotion to the idea of international peace. Barred by Congress from toying with collective security, the Coolidge administration made further but generally unsuccessful efforts to negotiate disarmament in 1927, an effort carried on by Hoover with somewhat more success in 1930. In August, 1928, largely through American efforts, fifteen nations signed the Kellogg-Briand Pact renouncing war as an instrument of national policy. Like Prohibition, this innocuous measure was widely popular among the hopeful. Nearly all nations adhered to it during the remaining interval before World War II.

SMITH AND HOOVER

Neither foreign policy nor domestic economic argument played a major part in the presidential campaign of 1928. On the surface the issues of this contest were personal; at a deeper level it involved the most divisive group loyalties. Herbert Hoover, the Republican nominee, was presented as a self-made engineer, a nonpolitical expert administrator, and a major spokesman of the new business outlook. The Democratic candidate, Alfred E. Smith of New York, though no radical, was known as a friend of the underprivileged, and a champion, during the Red Scare, of civil liberties. The only major issue on which the two sharply differed was Prohibition.

This issue symbolized the real division between supporters of the two men. In many rural and Protestant areas, Prohibition was still regarded as at least a hopeful attack on a great evil, demanding the support of all respectable people. To many city dwellers, on the other hand, it was associated with lawlessness, gangsterism, and puritanical prejudice. Hoover had the conventional presidential background of Protestantism and rural poverty. Smith was a Catholic, a Wet, and a city product with a New York accent. Without concrete issues, the campaign was fought to a large extent in terms of stereotypes and prejudices.

On the surface, the result was another Republican landslide. Hoover carried several states of the Democratic, but Protestant and rural South. Yet later students have noticed that the big cities voted far more heavily Democratic than in previous twentieth-century elections. Despite his religion and his origins, Smith also scored significant Democratic gains in a number of discontented western farm regions. One can glimpse, in the Smith vote, the beginnings of the unbeatable Democratic coalition of the New Deal years.

In 1929, to most people, the new administration seemed to promise increased efficiency and broader humanitarianism within the framework of the Harding-Coolidge policies. Yet Hoover, the ablest of the three postwar presidents, encountered disaster at home and menace abroad. Whether one looked back at the twenties with nostalgia or distaste, they were soon to seem a strange interlude in the tragic and turbulent history of the twentieth century. It was perhaps just as well that the United States had enjoyed an interlude of peace and prosperity, however illusory, between two times of appalling and challenging crisis.

FOR FURTHER READING:

William E. Leuchtenberg, *The Perils of Prosperity* (1958)*, is a readable and intelligent interpretation. John D. Hicks, *The Republican Ascendancy* (1960), is a solid factual survey, political in emphasis. Economic history is excellently summarized in George Soule, *Prosperity Decade* (1947). Foreign policy is illuminated by Selig Adler, *The Isolationist Impulse* (1957)*. F. L. Allen, *Only Yesterday* (1931)* is an informal and very perceptive reminiscence of social change. Preston W. Slosson, *The Great Crusade and After* (1930), is a more academic and comprehensive social history. An influential contemporary sample of American society is R. S. and H. M. Lynd, *Middletown* (1929)*. President Hoover's Research Committee on Social Trends summarizes a great mass of interesting material in *Recent Social Trends* (2 vols., 1933). For literary history the best source is contemporary writing, and the best introduction Alfred Kazin, *On Native Grounds* (1942)*.

Henry F. May, *The Discontent of the Intellectuals: A Problem of the Twenties* (Berkeley Readings in American History, 1963)*, is a documentary study of a familiar but puzzling aspect of the period.

*Available in paperback edition.

THE NEW DEAL

	LABOR	AGRICULTURE	BUSINESS AND INDUSTRIAL RECOVERY	RELIEF	REFORM	MISCELLANEOUS
1932			R.F.C. established.	Relief and Construction Act. Federal Home Loan Bank Act.		Bonus March. Election of Roosevelt.
1933	Section 7A of NIRA.	Agricultural Adjustment Act. Farm Credit Act.	Thomas Amendment to AAA (inflation). Emergency Banking Act. Beer and Wine Revenue Act. Banking Act of 1933 (guaranteed deposits). National Industrial Recovery Act.	Civilian Conservation Corps. Federal Emergency Relief Act. Home Owners Refinancing Act. Farm Credit Act. Public Works Administration. Civil Works Administration.	TVA. Federal Securities Act.	Economy Act. Twenty-first Amendment (Repeal of Prohibition).
1934		Cotton Control Act. Federal Farm Bankruptcy Act.	Gold Reserve Act. Trade Agreement Act (reciprocal trade treaties). Silver Purchase Act.	Civil Works Emergency Relief Act.	Home Owners Loan Act. Securities Exchange Act. National Housing Act.	

THE NEW DEAL (*Continued*)

	LABOR	AGRICULTURE	BUSINESS AND INDUSTRIAL RECOVERY	RELIEF	REFORM	MISCELLANEOUS
1935	National Labor Relations (Wagner) Act.	Resettlement Administration. Relief Electrification Administration.		Works Progress Administration and National Youth Administration.	Banking Act of 1935. Social Security Act. Public Utilities Holding Company Act. Revenue Act (wealth tax).	First Neutrality Act.
1936		Soil Conservation and Domestic Allotment Act.				Neutrality Act extended. Soldier's Bonus. Roosevelt re-elected.
1937		Farm Security Administration.			Court Reorganization Act (not passed). United States Housing Authority.	Neutrality Act revised. Depression (fall).
1938	Fair Labor Standards Act.	Agricultural Adjustment Act of 1938.				Billion dollar naval expansion. Republican gains in Congress.

CHAPTER 26

DEPRESSION AND SOCIAL EXPERIMENT

1929–1938

In the summer of 1929, while stock prices rose beyond all relation to earnings or dividends, most industrial and financial experts predicted nothing but permanent prosperity. Signs of trouble, including declines in both construction and automobiles, the two key industries of the New Era, were generally ignored. In September the market hesitated nervously, and then, in late October, a devastating series of crashes cancelled 40 per cent of the paper values of common stocks.

Despite the continuing optimism of government and business leaders, the crash of 1929 was not a mere correction of inflated values. Like the panics of 1873 and 1893, it turned into severe and prolonged depression. In the years from 1929 to 1933, as stock prices fell ever lower and confidence evaporated, manufacturing production was halved and building nearly stopped. Banks and businesses failed, farm income, already low, was cut in half, and, worst of all, unemployment grew steadily. By 1932 it was variously estimated at from thirteen to seventeen million. American prosperity, and with it the spirit of the New Era, had disappeared.

The impact of the great depression on those who lived through it is hard to exaggerate. At the lowest economic level, the unemployed faced the threat of actual starvation when charities, cities, and states ran out of relief funds. Apple selling and breadlines became common sights, shanty towns sprang up on the edge of cities, men and women were sometimes seen pawing through restaurant garbage. At the opposite end of the scale, some respected financiers were caught misusing investors' funds. Only a few killed themselves or fled to Europe, but both bankers and big businessmen in general rapidly lost public prestige. In the large, previously contented middle class, people unused to disaster lost savings, houses, jobs, and hope. Even those who suffered no personal privation found it hard to dispel fear. Anyone might be the next victim of a disaster nobody understood.

[340]

Why did catastrophe paralyze the richest and most productive country in the world? At the time, many blamed some of the more obvious weak spots in the economy: the loose and ill-coordinated banking structure and the irresponsible financial manipulation that had piled one holding company on another. Later, New Dealers insisted that Republican policies had crippled foreign trade, encouraged inequality and concentration, fostered the boom and then clung doggedly to financial conservatism after the crash. On the other hand, President Hoover was always to believe that the depression was almost beaten when the election of a Democrat destroyed business confidence. In the long run, many historians have concluded that the fault lay in the unsoundness and inadequacy of the previous decade's prosperity. In the twenties prosperity depended as never before on mass consumption. Yet inequality and a too rigid price structure limited consumption. By 1929 effective demand for automobiles and some other products was apparently about filled. Attractive outlets seemed to be lacking for really large-scale investment. In other words, prosperity could not continue as the prosperity of part of one country in a poor world. The New Era picture of liberal and progressive American capitalism, while not without much truth, was not true enough.

HOOVER AND THE DEPRESSION

On coming to office in 1929, President Hoover found himself confronted by two familiar problems of the twenties, farm relief and the tariff. Each of these grew more difficult with the coming of depression.

Like Coolidge, Hoover fought off Farm Bloc proposals which seemed to involve subsidy and price fixing. In their place Hoover secured the passage of a complex measure establishing a Federal Farm Board empowered to promote such time-honored remedies as cooperative marketing. By 1930 the "Stabilization Corporations" also created by this law were buying and storing surplus wheat and cotton. Already the government was up to its neck in undisposable surpluses, and prices were still going down.

As part of his farm program, Hoover proposed another old panacea, tariffs, on agricultural products. This led, in Congress, to further demands for industrial protection and the enactment of the Smoot-Hawley Tariff, signed by Hoover despite the protest of more than a thousand economists. The high rates of this measure ended all prospects of reviving foreign trade.

In his measures specifically designed to fight the depression, President Hoover, the elected representative of New Era know-how, broke sharply with the past. When Secretary Mellon recommended that the government allow prices and wages to fall until recovery set in, according to traditional *laissez faire* formulae, Hoover decided that such a drastic purge might kill the delicate patient. His first action, following New Era doctrine rather than nineteenth-century economic theory, was to call conferences of leading businessmen, which urged employers to maintain wages and production. When this proved ineffective, Hoover used available government machinery to cut taxes, liberalize credit, and prop farm prices.

By 1930, the administration turned to more drastic remedies. In that year, however, the long-brewing revolt against the Republicans was speeded by depression and Hoover lost the support of Congress. Many administration measures failed, but the President managed to secure large public works appropriations and measures to refinance home mortgages and further stimulate credit. His most important new agency, the Reconstruction Finance Corporation, lent large sums to banks, railroads, and businesses and also eventually to states, cities, and agricultural credit corporations. To stem international financial disaster, Hoover called successfully in 1931 for a one-year moratorium on German reparations and Allied debt payments.

Thus, in a major break with the past, the Hoover administration assumed governmental responsibility for fighting an economic crisis. Yet the Hoover measures, sweeping and large scale as some of them seemed by the standards of the twenties, were not on a scale adequate to the dimensions of the crisis. Moreover, the President flatly refused to meet two widespread demands. First, he declined to countenance currency inflation. Second, he fought all measures designed to provide direct federal responsibility for unemployment relief. Either of these actions, he sincerely believed, would have grave effects on American tradition and character.

As the plight of the unemployed became desperate, Hoover was wrongly seen as heartless. By 1932 dejection, apathy, and bad luck seemed to have destroyed the administration's earlier vigor. In that year a "Bonus Army" of unemployed servicemen assembled in Washington to demand immediate cash payoff of twenty-year insurance policies provided for World War veterans by legislation in 1924. Panicking at a minor threat to order, the administration had the Army destroy the veterans' camp with tanks and tear gas. This episode helped to make Hoover, a sensitive man, the worst-hated president since Cleveland. His re-election was obviously unlikely.

The leading Democratic candidate to succeed him, Governor Franklin D. Roosevelt of New York, was little known to most of the public. A Hudson River aristocrat from the Democratic branch of his family, he had yet been influenced by his cousin Theodore as well as by Wilson, whom he had served as Assistant Secretary of the Navy. After his sacrifice campaign for the vice presidency in the Republican year 1920, Roosevelt had been crippled by poliomyelitis. Nonetheless, he had remained active in Democratic politics and in 1928, bucking a Republican trend, had succeeded Smith as governor of New York, where he had tackled depression problems with considerable energy.

The trait the public immediately saw in the new Roosevelt was a gay, jaunty confidence which seemed a welcome opposite to Hoover's dogged gloom. What lay beneath the confidence is a question on which observers never agreed. To Roosevelt's critics, his cheerful nonchalance, his willingness to try anything, his tolerance of contradictions and his impatience of theory meant superficiality and arrogance. To some of his admirers, his flexibility seemed to rest on a bedrock of courage and to be complemented by a genuine humanitarian and religious concern for the underdog.

Nominated by adroit maneuvers in a close convention, Roosevelt in his campaign pledged drastic action to end the depression. What sort of action was not clear; while Roosevelt called for public power development and other progressive reforms, he also pledged a 25 per cent cut in spending and evaded the tariff question. Hoover, meanwhile, asked the people to sustain his own battle with the depression and grimly predicted disaster if his opponent won. The result was hardly in doubt; the Roosevelt landslide approximately equalled the Hoover victory of 1928.

During the interregnum before the new administration could take over in March, Hoover tried hard to persuade the president-elect to commit himself to a balanced budget, maintenance of the gold standard, and other central Republican policies. Roosevelt committed himself to nothing and was blamed by Republicans for a further economic downturn. In February the Governor of Michigan announced a bank holiday to prevent financial collapse, and other states followed suit. By Inauguration Day all banks were shut and some cities had turned to scrip. In the Midwest, farmers had resorted to old methods of semiviolent protest against a hopeless situation; milk trucks had been overturned and mortgage sales forcibly halted. Unemployed vagrants, many of them boys, were roaming the country. As never before, the stage was set for masterful presidential action.

THE FIRST NEW DEAL

In his arresting inaugural, Roosevelt promised that he would, if necessary, ask for powers to fight the depression equal to those given presidents in wartime. America's resources were adequate for the task ahead: the only thing she had to fear was "fear itself." Resounding with confidence and vigor, the speech committed the administration to no single course. For a while nearly all Americans, from bankers to tenant farmers and the unemployed, counted on Roosevelt to help them. The New Deal, taking various forms through the next years, can best be understood as a continuing experimental response to these demands. Back of each measure demanded by the President lay group pressures, party needs, conflicts among presidential advisers, and the balance of congressional blocs. Fully to understand the New Deal, one would have to understand two profound mysteries: American society and Franklin D. Roosevelt.

In the spring of 1933 Congress, with unheard-of speed, passed a series of administration measures. Roosevelt later summarized his objectives as "Relief, Recovery, and Reform," and this First New Deal can be described in terms of these "Three R's."

Relief for the country's most urgent needs started with legislation to open and sustain the sounder banks, leaving the weaker ones shut. Direct federal help for the unemployed began with the Civilian Conservation Corps, which set young men to work on reforestation and other conservation projects. Larger unemployment relief programs included federal grants to states and plans for vast public works. Relief for home and farm owners was the main purpose of further legislation to refinance mortgages.

Recovery of the economy called forth the most spectacular measures of the First New Deal, measures which demonstrated its lack of consistent economic theory. Approaches to recovery included the Economy Act, which reflected the traditional belief that government spending somehow caused economic decline; the Trade Agreements Act, which gave the President power to negotiate low-tariff agreements in order to revive foreign trade; and even the Beer Act, which legalized one promising industry. (By the end of the year, the Twenty-first Amendment swept away Prohibition completely.) The most important recovery programs of the First New Deal, however, relied on two main methods; first, raising prices by restricting output and controlling competition; and second, inflation, now irresistibly demanded by western Democrats.

During the campaign Roosevelt and some of his advisers had declared that the expansion of the American economy, like that of the frontier, was finished. In the future better distribution and planned production would replace violent competition. This theory owed something to Herbert Croly and the Bull Moose movement and something to Herbert Hoover and the trade associations of the twenties. Now the ambitious National Industrial Recovery Act gave industry the legal right to agree on binding codes of common practice. These codes would, it was hoped, end sharp practice, unfair treatment of labor, and unjust, below-cost cuts in prices. How much they would permit prices to *rise* was never clearly settled. To make such agreements possible, the antitrust laws were suspended. To compensate for this favor to industry, workers were promised in the famous Section 7A of the NIRA the right "to organize and bargain collectively through representatives of their own choosing . . . free from the interference, restraint or coercion of employers. . . ."

Reflecting a somewhat similar purpose, the Agricultural Adjustment Act of 1933 sought primarily to raise farm prices by many and complex methods. Its most striking feature was a system of subsidies to be given farmers who agreed to decrease production. Such payments were to be financed by taxes on the industries which processed agricultural products.

Inflation, the other principal recovery device, was provided for in an amendment to the AAA, sponsored by Senator Elmer Thomas of Oklahoma, who remembered Bryan's crusade against gold. The Thomas amendment gave the President power to inflate the currency in many ways. Moving reluctantly at first, Roosevelt took the dollar off gold, sanctioned special measures to support the price of silver, and eventually stabilized the currency at about 60 per cent of its former value.

Reform, that is deliberate effort to render the social system more just or humane, could be seen in the new programs to regulate stock exchanges and investment banking, in the labor clause of the NIRA, and, most clearly of all, in the Tennessee Valley Authority. This daring project, bringing to fruition the long frustrated dreams of Senator Norris and other progressives, was designed to remodel a whole river system by building a series of dams. Among its objectives were cheap power and fertilizer, flood control, soil and forest conservation, the improvement of inland waterways, and new recreation areas. Reform and recovery were both objectives of the National Housing Act of 1934, which provided insurance of loans to promote repair and modernization of homes, farms, and small plants.

NEW DEMANDS AND A SECOND NEW DEAL, 1934–1936

Through these and other laws, the First New Deal seemed to have scored a qualified success. Its first actions brought a sharp rise in production and prices. Then the rate of recovery slowed down, and people realized that the depression had not disappeared. The elections of 1934, increasing the already large Democratic majorities, showed clearly that a majority approved the administration's efforts. Yet more was needed; the First New Deal had brought to light a whole series of new demands.

Farmers had benefited from price rises, but were still distressed. Some of them had been disturbed by the destruction of crops and animals undertaken as an emergency measure in time of surplus. Then in 1934 the worst drought in the nation's history threatened to change surplus to shortage. Thousands of tenants and sharecroppers were driven from the land and left destitute. This seemed to be caused in part by the drought, but also in part by the AAA which encouraged landlords to mechanize and cut acreage. So far, it seemed to many angry small farmers, the New Deal farm program had helped the richest most.

The unemployed demanded faster relief than was provided by the cautious handling, so far, of public works. Organized labor, which had reached a low point in 1933, took new courage from clause 7A with its guarantees of freedom to organize. But as new millions rushed into the ill-prepared unions, hard problems arose. Employers, many of them still hostile to "outside" organizations, thought that Section 7A had authorized them to form more or less docile company unions. Workers insisted that only national organizations could be effective. The National Labor Relations Board, formed by the President to arbitrate multiplying controversies, lacked both authority and consistent policy.

Business and industry, at first eager for New Deal help and willing to promise drastic reform, had become restless with partial recovery. Despite gains made through NIRA codes, many businessmen resented excessive government interference in the details of their operations. Some hoped to exclude the government altogether and make the program into one of simple business self-regulation on the Hoover pattern. On the other hand, progressives were charging that big business already dominated the codes and gouged consumers. Worried liberals, looking both at NIRA and AAA, doubted increasingly whether raising prices and cutting production was the best answer to widespread scarcity.

Thus the administration, which had tried to please everybody, found itself attacked from right and left. Conservatives looked back with nostalgia at the probusiness policies of the Republican years or lamented the end of *laissez faire* and traditional individualism. A little way beneath the surface of some of the most fervent complaints lay a barely unspoken feeling that the balance of power in the country was shifting away from those who ought to be in charge, in the direction of the shiftless, the irresponsible, and the foreign born. Not a few outraged citizens concluded that the whole New Deal was a conspiracy against free enterprise, sound money, and American tradition and even that it was secretly aiming at ushering in socialism or communism.

At the other extreme, it was true that the tiny Communist party of the United States had made some progress. It was aided in 1935 by a sharp change in the international Communist line. Instead of denouncing all non-Communist efforts at reform as insipid and useless, Communists were now to call for a "United Front" and to make every effort to work with "progressives" and "anti-Fascists." During the period from 1935 to 1939, while this line endured, the Communist movement achieved some influence among American intellectuals and among some elements of labor. More important than actual Communist gains, which remained numerically small, was the conviction, or half-conviction, fairly widespread among intellectuals, that capitalism could not recover.

Still more important in practical politics was the rapid spread of economic panaceas. Most of these appealed, as in the past, to disgruntled rural and small town people, and most involved a combination of currency tinkering and old-fashioned anti-big-business rhetoric. Among them were the Townsend Plan for liberal old-age pensions; the inflationary suggestions of Father Coughlin, the radio priest who denounced international bankers in speeches with anti-Semitic overtones; the sweeping production-for-use plan of Upton Sinclair in California; and the glittering, enticing, "Every Man a King" proposal of Huey P. Long, a talented, ruthless spokesman of the dispossessed who made himself governor and near-dictator of Louisiana. All these plans, however illusory, gained their strength from two undeniable truths. First, the richest country in the world had too many poor people. Second, the New Deal had not yet produced a convincing remedy.

In response to all these pressures the President, supported by new advisers, backed a new set of measures. This Second New Deal, often seen as more radical than the first, was not really aimed at systematic alteration of the economic or social system. Indeed, one important group of young men who prepared it were under the influence of Louis D. Brandeis, who had helped to prepare Woodrow Wilson's "New Freedom" program, and imbued his followers with a dislike of bigness and a fervent belief in competition and diversity. The Second New Deal contained no measures aimed at direct regulation of business on the scale of the NIRA and none whose objectives were as sweeping as those of the TVA. Its main object, like that of its predecessor, was to get the economy going and correct in the process some obvious injustices. Some of its measures had the further purpose, a highly traditional one, of breaking up concentrations of power.

The new measures were sometimes proclaimed, however, in combative tones. Often they were carried through with hard-boiled political efficiency. Quite obviously, some of them reflected the demands of newly articulate groups. It is not surprising that some businessmen, remembering the placid twenties, were both resentful and alarmed. To many young people and to believers in social experiment, on the other hand, the Second New Deal brought a time of heady excitement, when almost any goal seemed possible, and almost any method worth a try.

In the sphere of unemployment relief, the administration committed itself to the principle of providing work rather than handouts. A special agency, the National Youth Administration, provided employment for unemployed youths and assisted students to stay in college. The Second New Deal's principal relief agency was the gigantic Works Progress Administration administered by the former social worker Harry Hopkins, a devoted, self-sacrificing, and sometimes ruthless New Dealer. The WPA built roads, schools, parks, and countless other projects. In addition to construction workers it employed actors, painters, musicians, and writers. Astounded conservatives and delighted liberals found the federal government sponsoring symphony concerts, excellent guidebooks, colossal murals of varying quality, and the production of plays, some of them experimental and some left-wing.

Existing farm programs were supplemented by efforts to help the neglected poorest farmers. The Resettlement Administration tried to move families from submarginal land, and the Rural Electrification Administration brought power lines to areas not served by private utilities.

In the Social Security Act, the United States, entering the field much later than other leading industrial countries, laid the foundations for a system of old-age, unemployment, and disability insurance financed largely by employer and employee contributions. The Revenue Act of 1935, though whittled down in Congress, sharply increased taxes on high incomes, corporations, and estates. The Banking Act of 1935 increased the power of the Federal Reserve Board to buy and sell government securities in the open market for stabilization purposes, and the Public Utility Holding Company Act restricted the practice of piling one company on another in the fashion popular in the late twenties.

[348]

Finally, as the new labor problems became more and more pressing, the President, in 1935, gave his backing to a bill long advocated by Senator Robert F. Wagner of New York. The Wagner Act outlawed employer coercion and support of company unions. Henceforth an employer was required to bargain with the union chosen by a majority of his employees in government supervised, secret ballot elections.

Sweeping changes in the size and shape of organized labor were partly a cause and partly an effect of new government policies. Since NIRA days, organizers had turned their attention to the long-unorganized millions in such great industries as steel, automobiles, rubber, and textiles. Inevitably, swelling numbers and this change of direction strained the traditional craft organization of the American Federation of Labor. Led by John L. Lewis, the colorful and domineering head of the United Mine Workers, a group of rebels formed within the A.F. of L. a Committee for Industrial Organization. This group, expelled in November, 1935, became in 1938 the independent Congress for Industrial Organizations.

In a series of hard-fought, sometimes bloody, strikes, the C.I.O. attacked the long-defended bastions of American heavy industry. This time the outcome of labor warfare was a sweeping union victory. Beginning with the surrender of United States Steel and General Motors in 1937, America's most powerful corporations were to make agreements with C.I.O. unions. Already, by that year, organized labor had grown from a depression low of under three million to more than seven million, and it was still growing fast.

Not only the size but the nature of the American labor movement was changed. Most of it, unlike the labor movements of other industrial countries, continued to accept the capitalist system of production. (An important faction of the C.I.O., later to be expelled, was under Communist influence.) But American labor by the mid-thirties was far more deeply committed to political action to further its social objectives than it had been before.

In 1936 the Republicans, sharply denouncing the New Deal, nominated Alfred M. Landon, the moderately liberal governor of Kansas, to oppose Roosevelt. In a victory which surpassed all but Harding's, Roosevelt got more than 60 per cent of the popular vote and carried all states but Maine and Vermont. In this election the Democrats were supported for the first time by an emerging, powerful, but unstable coalition consisting of labor, most farmers, recent immigrants, Negroes, and the South; while the Republicans had the support of most businessmen. Though this pattern was to vary from election to election with changing circumstances, it would affect American politics for a generation.

DEADLOCK AND A THIRD NEW DEAL, 1937–1938

Despite this resounding election victory in 1936, the New Deal in 1937 and 1938 ran into a series of partial defeats. The first was in its conflict with the Supreme Court. In its sessions of 1935 and 1936 the Court had overturned a number of important New Deal statutes, sometimes in five-to-four decisions. These included the National Industrial Recovery Act and the processing tax of the Agricultural Adjustment Act. According to a majority of the Court, Congress during the New Deal had unconstitutionally delegated detailed legislative power to administrative agencies (as in the NIRA) and had gravely misinterpreted the taxing power, the interstate commerce clauses, and other parts of the Constitution.

To the President and many New Dealers, the Court majority seemed to be interpreting the Constitution in a rigid and reactionary manner. Concluding that it would be impossibly slow and difficult to amend the Constitution, Roosevelt in February, 1937, unveiled a drastic proposal for changing the Court's personnel. One justice was to be added for every member who failed to retire after seventy. Some people were shocked by this attack on the Court, and many disliked the President's unsuccessful attempt to present his plan as part of an innocuous program for judicial efficiency. While the argument raged fiercely, the Court itself took a hand in the struggle. A number of important New Deal statutes were suddenly sustained, and one conservative justice voluntarily retired. This made Court reform seem less urgent, and despite the President's refusal to compromise, the bill was defeated in Senate committee.

In the long run, the change in the Court's attitude constituted a major New Deal victory and ushered in a long period of increase in the government's power for social and economic legislation. Yet the prestige of the Court as an institution survived; that of the President was sharply damaged.

It was further injured by the onset of a new depression. In the summer of 1936, production, profits, and wages (though not employment) had been edging toward the levels of 1929. Apparently this was partly because of large government spending for New Deal purposes and for payment of the veterans' bonus (finally provided by Congress over Roosevelt's veto in 1936). The President, worried about deficits and mounting debt, acted to tighten credit and cut the budget, particularly WPA funds. In the fall a sudden collapse seemed to bring back conditions of 1932. Farm prices headed down again, unemployment grew, and some critics concluded that the administration had failed to find a solution for the depression.

Whether this was true or not, the New Deal proved in 1937–1938 that it had not lost its energy. Expenditures were sharply increased for relief, public works, and, under the Wagner-Steagall bill, for public housing. Whereas earlier governmental expenditures had usually been defended only as humanitarian necessities, now spending was advocated partly as a means of inducing recovery. This reflected the increasing influence among economists, in and out of the administration, of the theories of the English economist J. M. Keynes. Keynes argued impressively that in time of depression, deficit spending by government was necessary in order to induce recovery and "prime the pump" of private investment.

Partly to further recovery by breaking up price fixing (a direct reversal of the First New Deal's objective), antitrust prosecutions were vigorously increased. A new Farm Security Administration tried hard to help the tenant farmers and migratory workers who were still America's most poverty-stricken people. A new AAA sought to raise all farm income by many devices, including new measures for crop restriction and government loans on stored surplus crops. Finally, the Fair Labor Standards Act of June, 1938, made possible by the Supreme Court's new attitude, established modest minimum wages and maximum hours for most employees and killed that old and tough enemy of American progressives, child labor. Some of the innovations of this last New Deal, including compensatory spending and wage regulation, proved to be among the most permanent and substantial changes brought about in the whole period.

THE MEANING OF THE NEW DEAL

The 1938 congressional elections ended the New Deal period. Not only did conservative Republicans gain sharply in the West, but conservative Democrats in the South beat off the President's daring attempt to defeat them, and thereby turn the Democratic party into a clear-cut New Deal organization. Though Roosevelt remained popular and existing New Deal measures remained in effect, further concerted or rapid reform action was impossible. For the next quarter-century, the same conservative coalition was normally to control Congress.

Why did the New Deal lose momentum in 1938? Most obviously because foreign crisis began to draw the country's attention away from domestic reform. Yet many have blamed the slowdown partly on the program's own shortcomings, particularly its shifting approach to economic problems, its effort to combine incompatible groups of supporters, and its dependence on Roosevelt's personal leadership. It had, certainly, failed to solve one of the country's most serious problems: in 1938 there were still ten million unemployed. Government spending seemed to be the only really successful way of stimulating recovery, and agriculture still depended on heavy subsidies.

Yet when Americans looked abroad, they could feel more reason for pride. No country had solved the problems of modern industrial society with complete success and several, struggling with those problems, had lost political freedom. Without revolution, without even major constitutional change, the American republic had taken on a big new responsibility. So far, its function had been at most to provide a favorable environment for private economic action and to regulate when necessary. Now, in the face of economic collapse, first Hoover and then Roosevelt had made the government responsible for reaching and maintaining adequate prosperity.

Some of the most important changes brought about by the New Deal were social rather than economic and incidental rather than programmatic. Domination of American society by an elite made up of the native, urban upper-middle class, a domination never secure and never official but long partially effective, had become impossible.

To many who remember these years, however, the most important fact was neither the big accomplishments, the big failures, nor the hidden social changes. It was rather the revival of creativity, daring, and hope, qualities that were to be badly needed in the decades just ahead.

FOR FURTHER READING:

President Hoover's revealing *Memoirs* (3 vols., 1951–1952) describe his own administration well and comment without admiration on the policies of his successor. The 1929 debacle is illuminated by J. K. Galbraith, *The Great Crash* (1954)*. The fullest, liveliest, and one of the most favorable accounts of the New Deal is Arthur M. Schlesinger, Jr.'s *The Age of Roosevelt,* completed through 1936 (3 vols., 1957–1960). Also unfinished and voluminous is Frank Freidel's informative and objective biography of F.D.R. (3 vols., 1952–1956). An intelligent, short interpretation is J. M. Burns, *Roosevelt: The Lion and the Fox* (1956). Among the best first-hand accounts by Roosevelt admirers is Frances Perkins, *The Roosevelt I Knew* (1946); the best hostile memoir is Raymond L. Moley, *After Seven Years* (1939). Dixon Wecter, *The Age of the Great Depression* (1948), is an introduction to the period's fascinating social history. Samuel Lubell, *The Future of American Politics* (1952)* points out underlying political change. Of an enormous literature on American Marxism in the thirties, one of the most readable and understanding accounts is Murray Kempton, *Part of Our Time* (1955).

E. David Cronon, *Labor and the New Deal* (Berkeley Readings in American History, 1963)*, is a documentary study of one important problem of this period.

_____

*Available in paperback edition.

CHAPTER 27

THE REVERSAL OF FOREIGN POLICY

1931–1941

During most of the thirties, American attention was centered on domestic problems. Yet foreign events, occurring in the same period, were to affect the United States even more profoundly than the New Deal. The fragile international order established at Versailles and propped by prosperity broke down. Aggressive military states threatened to dominate Europe and Asia. To meet this challenge, America moved from relative disarmament to colossal military power, and American opinion swung from an extreme of isolationism to unprecedented acceptance of worldwide commitment. This commitment was to prove permanent, and under its stress American tradition and society were to be profoundly altered.

THE BREAKDOWN OF ORDER, 1931–1933

When Hoover took office, he intended to carry on, with only slight revision, the foreign policies of the New Era. More internationalist in outlook than Coolidge, he carried much further the policy begun under Coolidge of substituting conciliation for intervention in Latin America. Cautiously, the Hoover administration moved closer to cooperation with the League of Nations. In any efforts to preserve world peace, however, he was determined to stick to noncoercive political or economic methods. At the London Conference of 1930 the administration worked hard, with some success, to reduce naval armament further according to the pattern set by the Washington Conference of 1921. This was the last victory for disarmament. The effort to limit land armies at Geneva in 1932–1933 resulted in complete failure. By that time, the very idea of arms limitation was rejected by several powerful states.

The Versailles order in Europe had always been unstable. With American power withdrawn, France and England confronted Fascist Italy, Communist Russia, and defeated, unstable Germany. If these discontented powers were united and armed, their strength might outweigh that of the defenders of the *status quo*.

In the late twenties, the Central European order was upheld to some extent by American investment. In 1931, partly because of the withdrawal of American funds, a major Austrian bank failed, and panic threatened to spread to Germany. To prevent further collapse, Hoover suggested a one-year suspension of payments of both German war reparations and Allied debts to the United States. After a damaging delay caused by French suspicions this "Hoover moratorium" was accepted. Frightened by the growing power of the aggressive Hitler movement in Germany, the Western Allies finally, in 1932, agreed to cancel almost all reparations—too late to save the German Republic. The United States refused to cancel war debts in a parallel manner, and most countries paid the first instalments due after the end of the moratorium. These were, in most cases, the last payments made.

In 1931 Britain, the home of *laissez faire* economics, found it necessary to abandon the gold standard for a managed currency, and many other countries promptly followed suit. Hoping to restore currency stability, the United States helped plan a World Economic Conference which would give first priority to exchange stabilization.

The most dramatic collapse of international order occurred in the Far East. Since the Washington Conference, Japan had been ruled by conservative cabinets, and American-Japanese relations had been relatively good. Now, however, the Japanese military were becoming increasingly angry at arms limitation and civilian control. Since Theodore Roosevelt's Treaty of Portsmouth, Japan had possessed railroad and port rights in Manchuria where many Japanese saw an opportunity to acquire raw materials and living space. In 1931, taking advantage of incidents in Manchuria produced by rising Chinese nationalism, the Japanese army embarked on a program of conquest in this vast, nominally Chinese region. This action, carried out apparently against the will of the civilian government in Tokyo, violated not only the League Covenant but also the Republican security structure, consisting of the Washington Nine-Power Treaty and the Kellogg Peace Pact. The Open Door and Chinese integrity, moreover, were part of Republican tradition.

Thus Hoover had to act, but once more American commitments in the Far East outran American power. Furthermore, the deepest beliefs of the Quaker President ruled out either military reprisal or cooperation with the League in economic sanctions. In addition, England, whose collaboration would have been necessary for effective action, had no wish to provoke Japanese threats to her own huge Asian holdings. Resorting to purely moral force, Secretary of State Stimson announced that the United States would not recognize any situation brought about by force in violation of the Open Door or Chinese integrity. After much hesitation, the League took a somewhat similar stand, advising its members not to recognize the Japanese puppet state of Manchukuo. Neither the so-called Stimson Non-Recognition Doctrine nor world disapproval deterred Japan in Manchuria, although she did withdrew from a brief military occupation of Shanghai undertaken in 1932 in retaliation for a Chinese boycott. At the same time, despite Hoover's abhorrence of coercive international action, the United States had become further involved in the defense of the crumbling international order.

THE NEW DEAL AND THE WORLD, 1933–1937

In the first years of the New Deal, American isolationism reached its peak. To the disillusion of the twenties was added the new disillusion of the depression. A host of plays, movies, and novels depicted the horrors of war, and in 1935 a Senate investigation seemed to show that munition makers caused most wars for the sake of sordid profits. Many Americans believed that European propagandists had made a sucker of the United States in 1917 and were trying to do it again. At the same time, our former Allies were defaulting on their obligations and even failing to sustain their own League. (Throughout the decade, European appeasement and American isolationism were to be called on to justify each other.)

Traditional suspicion of Europe was only one of a number of components, all powerful and some mutually contradictory, in the isolationist frame of mind. Many young people were deeply affected by pacifism, and some liberals wanted to concentrate on building a good society at home. On the other hand, conservatives were suspicious of foreign threats to American tradition. Many Midwesterners and most Irish-Americans maintained their historic suspicion of British imperialism.

In the early years of the New Deal, Roosevelt failed to challenge the dominant isolationist creed, though as an old follower of Wilson and his cousin Theodore he could hardly accept it. He was primarily concerned with getting his program of national economic reform through Congress and into action and he badly needed the support of midwestern isolationist progressives. Thus he refrained from opposing such measures as the Johnson Act of 1934 which forbade loans to nations in default.

As Japanese expansion slowed down to assimilate its gains, American-Japanese relations seemed to improve. Though nearly all Americans disliked the brutal Hitler regime which took power in Germany in 1933, few proposed to do anything about it.

In cooperation with some kinds of isolationists or continentalists, Roosevelt backed a modest program of naval building and continued the program of cementing good relations with Latin America. The nonintervention policy was not only restated, but backed in practice by abandonment of the right of intervention in Panama and Cuba. Expropriation by Mexico of the property of United States oil companies was accepted and compensation agreed on. At the Inter-American Conference of 1936, intervention by one state in the affairs of another was condemned, and mutual consultation provided for in case of threats to the peace of the hemisphere. This Good Neighbor policy, though it by no means ended all Latin American suspicion of the United States, was to produce good results in wartime when most of the Latin American countries were to be friendly neutrals and later allies.

In economic matters, the main drive of the early New Deal was nationalistic. In order to save his own program of raising prices through currency inflation, Roosevelt abruptly reversed his early approval of exchange stabilization and in so doing broke up the World Economic Conference in London. On the other hand Cordell Hull, the new Secretary of State, had a deep southern-Democrat belief in lower tariffs, and Roosevelt succeeded in getting congressional backing for the Hull program. From 1934 on, the administration had and used authority to negotiate mutual tariff reductions through reciprocal trade treaties. Hope for a revival of international trade was also involved in Roosevelt's decision in 1933 to recognize Soviet Russia. For several years, this action had been demanded by some business groups who prophesied (wrongly as it turned out) an immense flow of United States–Russian trade.

American isolationist policies were little changed by the new challenges to world order which occurred in the mid-thirties. In 1935 Mussolini's Italy invaded Ethiopia, and in the same year Adolf Hitler felt strong enough to remilitarize Germany in defiance of the Versailles Treaty. In the next year German troops marched into the Rhineland where the same Treaty prohibited their presence. In July, 1936, Francisco Franco opened a Fascist rebellion against the republican government of Spain, and in 1936–1937 the Berlin-Rome-Tokyo axis united the major dissatisfied, essentially aggressive states. All these actions were dealt with ineffectually by the Western European powers. In the Ethiopian affair the League invoked only half-hearted sanctions, England condoned German rearmament in a naval treaty, and Western countries, through a policy of "nonintervention," denied munitions to the Spanish government. Turning increasingly to the left, that government got some aid from Russia while the Spanish rebels were more effectively supported by Germany and Italy.

American policy toward these crises was dominated by a determination to keep out of war rather than to keep war from occurring. The neutrality legislation of 1935–1937 was designed to prevent the particular kinds of mistakes which were believed to have drawn America into World War I. The first neutrality law, passed in 1935, forbade arms shipments to all belligerents, rejecting an administration wish to discriminate between aggressor and victim. In the Ethiopian crisis this was supplemented by a "moral embargo" on oil, the commodity most needed by Mussolini. American refusal to take stronger action gave an excuse for the League also to refuse an outright oil embargo. The second neutrality law (1936) forbade loans to belligerents. In 1937 a congressional resolution, requested by the President, extended the application of the neutrality system from international war to the Civil War in Spain, thus shutting off American arms from the Loyalist government and helping to ensure Franco's success. Finally, the neutrality law of 1937 made the existing prohibitions permanent and, in addition, forbade American travel on belligerent ships. It also gave the President power, for two years, to list commodities other than munitions which belligerents would be required to pay for and transport in their own ships (the cash-and-carry provision). Thus the United States had reversed the policies of Woodrow Wilson and returned to something like those of Jefferson. Neutral rights were waived in order to stay out of war. It seemed clear to the aggressive nations that they had little to fear from American counter action, as long as America herself was not attacked.

DEEPENING CRISIS AND CAUTIOUS CHANGE IN POLICY, 1937–1939

Once more, a shift in American policy was brought on by events in Asia, not Europe. Japan, which had continued to press from Manchuria into North China until 1933, made a truce in that year. In 1937 fighting broke out again near the Peiping-Tientsin railway in relation to which Japan had certain treaty privileges. Since the ensuing war, though full scale, was undeclared, the American neutrality legislation was not automatically applied. Partly in order not to cut off arms to China, and partly to keep some anti-Japanese action in reserve, Roosevelt refrained from invoking the neutrality laws, and America shipped some war materials to each belligerent. However in October, 1937, Roosevelt expressed his feelings about Japanese action with new vigor. Referring to a "spreading epidemic of world lawlessness," he suggested that aggressors be "quarantined."

Alarmed isolationist reaction made it plain to the President that he had moved beyond public opinion. The United States joined in League of Nations' condemnation of Japanese action but opposed sanctions. In December, when Japanese planes sank an American gunboat on the Yangtze, apologies were accepted without much excitement. Once more, world disapproval without action failed to deter Japan, and her forces proceeded to bomb and occupy the principal Chinese cities. By 1938 she had set up a puppet government in China and committed herself fatefully to the establishment of a New Order in East Asia.

Lacking a clear European policy, the United States played only a minor role in the major European events of this period, periodically and fruitlessly appealing for moderation and conciliation. In 1938 Hitler absorbed Austria and began threatening Czechoslovakia. This led to the Munich Agreement among Britain, France, Italy, and Germany, which forced Czechoslovakia to surrender certain strategic frontier districts inhabited by German-speaking people. This settlement was brutally nullified in March, 1939, when Hitler took over the rest of Czechoslovakia. During the same spring Italy invaded Albania, while Hitler seized the Lithuanian town of Memel and unmistakably began threatening Poland. This time, however, Britain and France guaranteed the prospective victim, and it become evident to nearly everybody that major war was imminent.

Roosevelt, who shared this opinion, believed also that Britain and France could win with American material help. He therefore called for a somewhat cautious and moderate program of rearmament mainly on the basis of continental naval and air defense. He also asked Congress to repeal the arms embargo in order to make it possible for belligerents to buy American munitions on a cash and carry basis. Though most press opinion favored this action, it was defeated by isolationists in Congress. This was to be their last major victory.

In the summer of 1939, while Britain and France were making a rather half-hearted effort to make a defensive alliance with Russia, Stalin instead suddenly concluded pacts of trade and nonaggression with Hitler. This apparently left Germany free to attack Poland without becoming involved in a major two-front war, and on September 1, Hitler's troops crossed the Polish frontier. France and England, this time, declared war as they had promised. Poland, destined to be the most tragic victim of World War II, was quickly overrun. As German troops advanced through western Poland, Russian troops occupied the eastern part of the country.

Now that war was a fact, Roosevelt was able (in November, 1939) to prevail on Congress to repeal the arms embargo and place shipments of both munitions and other commodities on a cash and carry basis. Once more, as in 1914, the Western Allies were free to come and get American arms, provided that they could pay cash and provide shipping. This seemed enough to assure Western victory without further American commitment. Most observers predicted that the major belligerents would settle into a long stalemate, confronting each other in the "impregnable" Maginot and Siegfried lines.

CATASTROPHE AND THE END OF NEUTRALITY, 1940–1941

In the spring of 1940 the stalemate war came to a sudden end as the Germans conquered first Denmark and Norway and then the Low Countries. In a lightning assault from Belgium, mobile German units poured into France and in a month had crushed and demoralized the French army, supposed by many to be the world's strongest. It seemed as if there was no possible resistance to the new German combination of parachutists, divebombers, and tanks. On June 22 France surrendered. The Germans occupied half the country, leaving the collaborationist government at Vichy in charge of the rest.

Thinking he had won his war, Hitler hoped that England would make a compromise peace. Instead, though isolated and almost without land armament, the British replaced their ineffective premier with Winston Churchill, who announced his determination not only to resist but ultimately to destroy the Nazi regime. In the ensuing battle of Britain, though British cities were heavily bombed, the Royal Air Force defeated the German effort to clear the way for invasion. It began to seem once more possible that American support might sustain England, and many Americans wanted to do this at all costs. Others, however, insisted that the most important objective still was to keep America out of war.

In the ensuing foreign policy argument, perhaps the most important in American history, both sides were made up of diverse elements. On the anti-interventionist side with the traditional midwestern isolationists, were Anglophobes, including many Irish-Americans; people who thought Britain's cause hopeless; pacifists; young people who had heard with horror about the intolerance and hate generated by World War I and middle-aged people who had shared the postwar disillusionment; progressive reformers reluctant to give up domestic objectives; and some, but not by any means all, of those who disliked Roosevelt because of his domestic policies. This diverse coalition was supported by the small group influenced by the Communist party, which had supported collective security until 1939 and was to support war after 1941, but which was isolationist during the two years of the German-Soviet alliance. Those who favored drastic action in support of Britain included, as in 1914, many influential Americans conscious of deep ties to British culture. These were joined by those who were outraged by atrocity stories, this time true, about Nazi barbarism. Most important, perhaps, was the increasing group which felt that American security would be seriously threatened by Nazi control of the Atlantic.

Most Americans, probably, were neither isolationists nor outright interventionists. Most continued to hope for British victory, and most now wanted America to furnish arms to Britain. Most wanted also to stay out of war. The decisive question was which of these last objectives was the more important. Before the fall of France, opinion polls seemed to show that most Americans wanted first of all to keep out of war. After it, the majority gradually shifted; most concluded that British survival came first. This decision, however, was neither universal nor clear-cut, and the administration did not help to clarify the choice.

Insofar as one can understand Roosevelt's policy after twenty years of debate about it, the President was by no means neutral in his sympathies and clearly wanted to contribute as much material aid as possible to Britain. This policy, he said, would keep America out of war. At first he doubtless believed that this *would* be so, and until very late he hoped that it *might* be the case. Always conscious of the dangers of hostile public reaction, and once more desperately anxious to put over his program, he continued to say that America would stay out of war when he must have known that this was no longer certain. Whether a franker policy would have had better results, either at the time or in the long run, will long be debated.

The steps taken by the administration, and approved by a majority of Congress and public opinion, were drastic enough. In May, Roosevelt called for a billion-dollar defense appropriation and for airplane production of fifty thousand a year. At Charlottesville on June 10, he promised continued material help to "opponents of force."

In September, by executive agreement, he traded fifty over-age destroyers, desperately needed by Britain, for defense bases in British Western Hemisphere possessions. In the same month, Congress adopted the first peacetime conscription law in American history.

In the fall of 1940, foreign policy argument was channelled into an election campaign. Because of the national emergency, the Democrats broke the anti-third-term tradition to renominate Roosevelt. His opponent Wendell Willkie, though a utility company president who had fought TVA, was a representative of the liberal wing of the Republican party. Accepting much of the New Deal, Willkie attacked mismanagement and bureaucracy. Since Willkie accepted the necessity of aiding Britain and since both candidates promised that America would stay out of actual foreign war, there was little difference on foreign policy. In the closest victory of his presidential career, Roosevelt got 55 per cent of the popular vote.

Once more securely in office, Roosevelt asked for and got a still more binding commitment to British victory. In March Congress passed the lend-lease bill, giving the President authority to transfer equipment, rather than money, directly to nations whose defense was vital to that of the United States. In response to urgent appeals from the beleaguered British, munitions were furnished in enormous quantity. In the spring of 1941 British and American staff officers discussed common strategy in the event of American belligerency. In August Roosevelt and Churchill, meeting at sea, committed themselves to the liberal principles of the Atlantic Charter, promising a free and warless world "after the final destruction of the Nazi tyranny."

Committed to Hitler's defeat, America could not allow her shipments of munitions to be destroyed by the increasingly powerful German submarine offensive. In the summer of 1941, the United States entered into undeclared naval warfare with Germany. American ships reported submarine sightings to the British. American troops occupied Greenland and Iceland, and finally America began convoying British and American shipping to Iceland, halfway across the Atlantic. Sinkings occurred, and in September Roosevelt, denouncing German "piracy," ordered American naval vessels to "shoot on sight."

Meanwhile the nature of the war in Europe had profoundly changed. Unable to knock Britain out of the war before American deliveries became effective, Hitler decided to secure his continental flank. In October, 1940, German troops occupied Rumania and in April, 1941, moved into Yugoslavia. This intensified Hitler's difficulties with his quasi-ally, Stalin. In June, 1941, the Germans invaded the Soviet Union, penetrating so deeply that it looked for some months as if they would win another major victory. Promptly both Churchill and Roosevelt announced that any enemy of Hitler was a friend of theirs, and lend-lease aid to Russia began. While Russian participation stimulated anti-interventionism in some quarters, it reduced it in others. For the first time, it seemed, a coalition existed which actually could destroy the Nazis, and the United States was a member of it in all but actual land fighting.

For some time, Roosevelt had concluded that official American participation in war would be desirable, and a majority of the public had decided, according to the polls, that war would be preferable to British defeat. Hitler, however, was by no means eager to provoke further American intervention and add another great power to his already formidable list of opponents. Once more, the crucial development came from the other side of the world.

WAR WITH JAPAN

In the Far East also the Hitler breakthrough of 1940 precipitated great changes. To Japan, it seemed to offer a last chance to consolidate her new East Asian order and thereby to end the costly and indecisive "China incident." By moving southward toward the colonies of occupied France and Holland and hard-pressed Britain, Japan could secure needed supplies of oil, rubber, and tin.

So far Roosevelt, concentrating on the European danger and not eager for involvement on another front, had continued the United States' rather ambiguous policy toward Japan with one important change. In July, 1939, the United States threatened future economic measures by giving a six-months' notice of the abrogation of her 1911 commercial treaty with Japan. In July, 1940, sensing that a Japanese forward movement was at hand, the President prohibited the export of some kinds of oil and scrap metal. Later measures tightened this embargo and increased the pressure on Japan to find alternate sources.

In September, 1940, the Japanese with Hitler's diplomatic assistance forced the Vichy government to concede ports and bases in the northern part of French Indo-China. In September Germany, Italy, and Japan signed the Tripartite Pact, obliging each to help the other in case of attack by any power not now at war. Since a special article excluded Russia, this could mean only the United States.

There were still, however, powerful Japanese who hoped to achieve Japan's goals without war with America. Through much of 1941, the attitudes of both countries were set forth in a series of negotiations. Japan was willing, at most, to refrain from armed aggression in Southeast Asia and even to "interpret" in America's favor the promises of the Tripartite Pact. To pay for peace in the Far East even in the event of war with Germany, the United States would have had to restore Japanese-American trade, help Japan to obtain oil supplies from the Netherlands East Indies, and recognize (or at least cease to obstruct) her new order in China. The United States was unwilling to accept these terms and offered instead to restore trade and help Japan gain some of her economic goals provided she gave up her military objectives both in Southeast Asia and China. Once more, the American commitment to the Open Door and Chinese integrity assumed enormous importance.

In July of 1941 Japanese forces moved into southern Indo-China and clearly headed for Malaya and the Dutch East Indies. Roosevelt promptly responded by freezing all Japanese funds in the United States. In August, still hopeful of keeping the United States neutral, Prince Konoye, the Japanese premier, requested a "Pacific Conference" with Roosevelt. Though Konoye suggested the possibility of further important concessions, Roosevelt refused to meet unless there was some preliminary agreement on basic issues. In October the Konoye government fell, and the new Tojo government prepared for war.

Well before the complex Washington discussions of November, 1941, the positions of each side had been repeatedly made clear, and the two positions had proved incompatible. The American government considered trying to gain time by presenting proposals for a temporary Pacific truce, but decided against this. Knowing that an attack was at hand, the Americans restated for the record their earlier position. On December 7, 1941, Japanese planes attacked and severely crippled the American fleet at Pearl Harbor. The next day Congress declared war, and three days later Germany and Italy declared war on the United States.

Later, Roosevelt was much criticized, first for not pursuing further the effort for peace with Japan and second for not preventing the Pearl Harbor disaster. It was to be argued bitterly that his real objective was to force Japan to attack the United States and thereby to get America into war with Hitler by the "back door."

Probably a real compromise with Japanese ambition, short of surrender of old American commitments and betrayal of America's allies, would have been difficult to achieve. It is arguable, however, that a Roosevelt-Konoye meeting might have gained time and, less plausibly, that it might have strengthened the opponents of Japanese militarism. As for the second charge, it seems that by late November, 1941, the American government had decided that war was inevitable and that further stalling would be no use. Roosevelt knew before December 7 that a Japanese movement was actually under way and indeed warnings were sent to American Pacific bases to that effect. Apparently because an attack was expected further west, the warnings to Pearl Harbor were insufficiently frequent and emphatic and defensive action was neglected. Thus a small cloud remained over the official version of the Pearl Harbor incident. At the time, however, the Japanese "sneak attack" united the American people for war as nothing else could have.

FOR FURTHER READING:

The most formidable of many attacks on the Roosevelt foreign policy is Charles A. Beard, *President Roosevelt and the Coming of the War* (1948). Roosevelt is defended in Basil Rauch, *Roosevelt: From Munich to Pearl Harbor* (1950). W. L. Langer and S. E. Gleason, *The Challenge to Isolation, 1937–1940* (1952), is a well-documented and informative study, generally favorable to United States policy. Herbert Feis, *The Road to Pearl Harbor* (1950)*, is a detailed study of Japanese-American negotiations. See also the references for Chapter 28.

*Available in paperback edition.

THE SECOND WORLD WAR

	DIPLOMATIC	MILITARY		HOME FRONT
		PACIFIC THEATER	EUROPEAN THEATER	
1939 OUTBREAK	March 14 Germany annexes Czechoslovakia. March 31 Anglo-French pledge to Poland. August 23 German-Russian Pact.		September 1 Germany invades Poland. October 14 Russia invades Finland.	November 4 Neutrality Act of 1939 (cash and carry).
1940 DISASTER	September 3 United States–British "Destroyer Deal." September 27 Japan-Germany-Italy Tripartite Pact.	September 22 Japan gets bases in French Indo-China.	April 9 Germany invades Norway, Denmark. May 10 Germany invades Benelux. June 22 German-French armistice. August – September Battle of Britain.	September 16 Selective Service. November 5 Roosevelt defeats Willkie.
1941 INTERVENTION	July 26 United States freezes Japanese funds. August 14 "Atlantic Charter" statement by Roosevelt and Churchill. November United States–Japanese Washington negotiations.	July 24 Japan occupies French Indo-China. December 7 Pearl Harbor.	April Germany invades Greece, Yugoslavia. April–May United States extends protective action in Atlantic. June 22 Germany invades Russia. September 11 "Shoot on sight" order in Atlantic.	March 11 Lend-Lease Act. November 17 Neutrality Acts repealed. December 8 Declaration of War.
1942 LOW POINT	May Molotov in Washington. June Churchill in Washington. August Moscow Conference (Stalin, Churchill, Harriman).	February 15 Singapore surrenders. May 6 Corregidor surrenders. May 7–8 Coral Sea. June 3–6 Midway. August–February Guadalcanal.	January–June German offensive North Africa. Summer German offensive Russia. September–February Stalingrad. November 4 El Alamein. November 8 United States landings in North Africa.	January 30 Office of Price Administration established. February–March Japanese-American "relocation." November Republican gains in Congress. December 2 First self-sustaining nuclear reaction (Chicago).

THE SECOND WORLD WAR (*Continued*)

	DIPLOMATIC	MILITARY		HOME FRONT
		PACIFIC THEATER	EUROPEAN THEATER	
1943 **ALLIED UNITY**	January 14–24 Casablanca Conference (Roosevelt, Churchill). August 11–24 Quebec Conference (Roosevelt, Churchill). November 22–26 Cairo Conference (Roosevelt, Churchill, Chiang). November 28–December 1 Teheran Conference (Roosevelt, Churchill, Stalin).	Throughout year Allied gains in South Pacific (Solomons, New Guinea). November 21 United States invades Gilberts (Tarawa) (start of central Pacific offensive).	January–May Allied victory in North Africa. July–December Russian offensive. July 10 Sicily invaded. September 9 Italy invaded (Salerno).	November 5 Senate resolution for international organization.
1944 **VICTORY IN SIGHT**	July 1–22 U.N. Monetary and Financial Conference (Bretton Woods). August 21–October 7 Dumbarton Oaks Conference (plans U.N.). October 9–18 Second Quebec Conference.	January 31 Marshalls invaded. June 18 Marianas invaded. October 23–25 Philippine Sea. November 24 Beginning of air attack on Tokyo.	June 6 Normandy invaded. July 25 St. Lô breakthrough. September 12 United States enters Germany. December "Battle of the Bulge" (German counter-offensive).	United States reaches twice Axis war production. November 7 Roosevelt defeats Dewey.
1945 **THE ATOMIC AGE**	February 4–11 Yalta Conference. April 23–June 26 San Francisco U.N. Conference. July 17–August 2 Potsdam Conference (July 26, ultimatum to Japan). September 2 Japan surrenders.	February Manila recaptured. February–March Iwo Jima. April–June Okinawa. August 6 Hiroshima. August 9 Nagasaki. August 15 V-J Day.	March 7 Rhine crossed. April 25 United States and Soviet forces meet on Elbe. May 8 V-E Day.	April 12 Roosevelt dies. July 16 First atomic bomb exploded, Alamogordo, New Mexico.

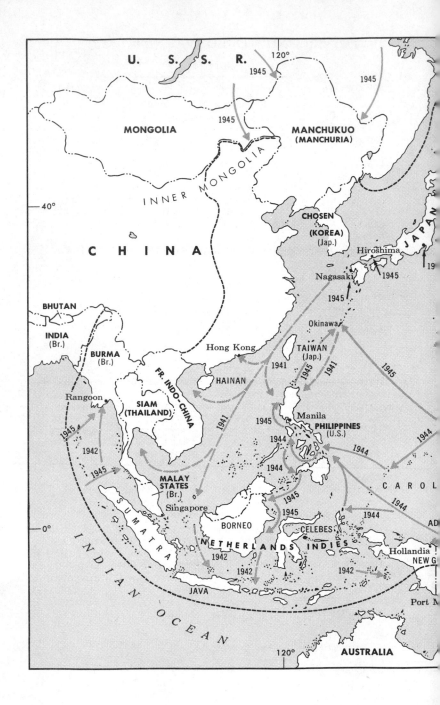

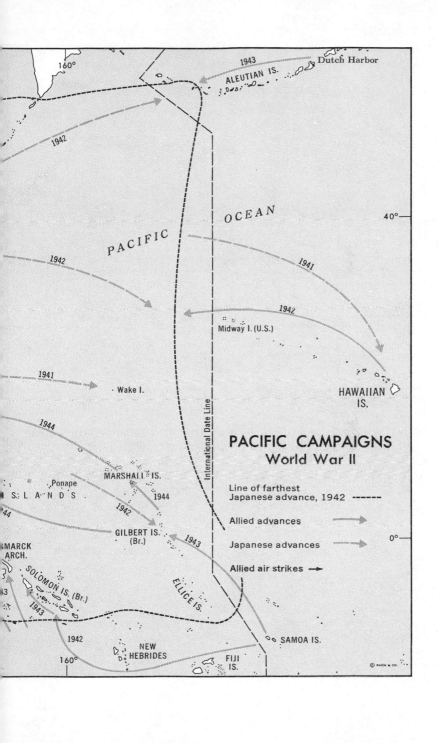

1943   Dutch Harbor
ALEUTIAN IS.

1942

OCEAN   40°

PACIFIC

1942   1941

1942

Midway I. (U.S.)

1941   · Wake I.

HAWAIIAN
IS.

1944

Ponape

MARSHALL IS.

S L A N D S   1944

44   1942

GILBERT IS.
(Br.)   1943

MARCK
ARCH.

SOLOMON IS. (Br.)

3

1943

1942

160°

NEW
HEBRIDES

ELLICE IS.

International Date Line

SAMOA IS.

FIJI
IS.

0°

PACIFIC CAMPAIGNS
World War II

Line of farthest
Japanese advance, 1942   - - - - - -

Allied advances

Japanese advances

Allied air strikes →

© RAND & CO.

RECONQUEST OF EUROPE
World War II

Atlantic Ocean

15°
0°
55°

NORWAY

SWEDEN
(Neutral)

EIRE
(Neutral)

UNITED
KINGDOM

North Sea

DENMARK

55°

London

NETH.

1945

Berlin

Landings, 1944

Calais

GERMANY

Cherbourg

1944

BELG.

1945

Brest

Paris

1944

1944

CZECH.

Nantes

1944

1944

1945

FRANCE

SWITZ.
(Neutral)

AUSTRIA

Toulouse

1944

Genoa

Venice

YUGO.

PORT.

40°

Marseille

Cannes

1945

1944

SPAIN
(Neutral)

Landings
1944

ITALY

1944

Rome

1943

40°

1943

Mediterranean Sea

SICILY

Allied advances

0

150

300

MILES

0°

Landings
1943

15°

© RAND & CO.

CHAPTER 28

WAR FOR THE WORLD

1941–1945

FROM DEFEAT TO VICTORY, 1941–1944

Through the winter and spring of 1941–1942, the United States confronted her most serious challenge since 1861. One headline after another reported successful Japanese invasions: Malaya, Guam, Wake, Hong Kong, Singapore, the Dutch East Indies, Burma, the Western Aleutians. On May 6, 1942, the last organized American forces in the Philippines surrendered at Corregidor. The New Order in Greater East Asia was almost a fact. Any counteroffensive against Japan, it seemed, would have to conquer concentric rings of islands scattered over vast ocean areas.

Hitler, meanwhile, held firmly the productive power of Western Europe. His first invasion of Russia was turned back in the winter of 1941 after reaching the outskirts of Moscow. His second, beginning in June, 1942, reached deep into the Caucasus and entered Stalingrad on the Volga. Britain was threatened with the collapse of her Atlantic supply line. Sinkings mounted after American entry, many of them occurring within sight of American coastal cities. The worst fears of Western leaders were that Russia would collapse and Britain starve long before American power became really effective.

Already Anglo-American staff conferences had decided that the main Allied offensive must be directed against Germany, the more formidable enemy, while a holding action was carried on in the Pacific. But any offensive seemed a long way away, and even a holding action was not immediately apparent.

By summer and fall of 1942 more hopeful news began to appear. Japanese naval power, checked at the Coral Sea in May, was ended as an offensive threat at Midway in June. In August American troops began a grim and bloody offensive in the Solomon Islands. In October the British stopped the German drive toward Suez at El Alamein,

[371]

the next month American forces landed in North Africa and began fighting German troops. In the gigantic battle of Stalingrad, the Russians captured a German army and began the reconquest of the vast territories they had lost.

In 1943 the Allies passed decisively to the offensive. After hard fighting, German forces were cleared from Africa, and in the summer and fall Anglo-American forces invaded Sicily and Italy. Though Mussolini fell from power and Italy surrendered, the Italian dictator escaped and bitter German resistance formed in central Italy. In the Pacific War, the island-hopping strategy indicated the means of American victory. Sea and air power made it possible to isolate and bypass Japanese garrisons; it would not be necessary to reconquer the vast Japanese holdings one by one. Bitter fighting brought control of the Solomons, and in November the battle of Tarawa began the Central Pacific campaign.

By this time the technique of amphibious warfare was so highly developed that it became possible to land on any hostile shore with sufficient preparation, provided one was willing to accept immense casualties. The crucial difficulty was maintaining the beachhead after landing. This was borne out in June of 1944 in the long-awaited landing in Normandy. This attack on the heavily defended French coast, the greatest amphibious operation in history, was seriously endangered by bad weather and stubborn resistance. By the end of July, however, a breakthrough at St. Lô ended the Normandy campaign and opened that of France. American tank units were able to sweep around the defenders as German forces had in 1940. By November most of France and Belgium had been liberated by Anglo-American forces, but in December a fierce counterattack surprised Americans in the Ardennes Forest.

On the eastern front in 1944 the Russians entered Poland, Yugoslavia, Hungary, and even East Prussia. In the Pacific the island-hopping campaign continued through the Marshalls, Marianas, and Carolines. In November bombers from the Marianas began devastating raids on the Japanese home islands. In the Philippines, American re-entry brought on the greatest naval battle in history at Leyte Gulf, where the remaining power of the Japanese navy was broken. By the end of the year, though much fighting remained in Europe and on the Pacific, victory was clearly in sight and so were its problems.

THE HOME FRONT

Perhaps the greatest single factor in this victory was American production of ships, tanks, planes, and the infinitely varied tools of modern war. In 1941, though the buildup had begun, there was still a long way to go. Shipments to Britain had depleted American supplies, and once more it proved difficult to organize American economy and society for war production. The gigantic task was handled with all the best and worst features of New Deal government, with imagination and vast scale, and also with a full complement of reversals, reorganizations, bureaucratic battles, bottlenecks, and waste. Yet by 1943 the huge machine was operating, and by 1944 America was producing double the combined total of the Axis countries.

This goal was won, moreover, without the extreme measures of coercion urged by some experts. There was no single production "czar," and there was no draft of labor. Adjustment of incentive seemed to work far better than totalitarian force. Industrialists received very high rewards in depreciation allowances and government construction of war plants. Yet corporation profits and high individual incomes were again taxed at confiscatory rates. Business, and especially big business, played a major part in planning and accepted a partnership with the government as it had in World War I and had not in the New Deal period. Labor strikes, much denounced in the press, were actually few in proportion to manpower. Labor kept the gains of the New Deal, including a forty-hour week with time and a half for overtime. Earnings rose rapidly, and unions expanded from ten to nearly fifteen million men.

The biggest wartime gains of all went to the previously depressed farmers or, more accurately, to some of them. Their continued strength in Congress pushed the regulated farm prices up to 110 per cent of parity, and government efforts to keep food prices down were at first only partly successful. While 17 per cent of the farm population left for the cities, the income of the remainder went sharply up and so did their production.

While many people in Europe and Asia were starving, American consumers had to cut down their driving, go without new cars, and accept rationing of food and some other products. From 1943 on control of most prices was reasonably successful. Not only was there no real civilian suffering, but many people—especially people previously deprived—lived and ate better than ever before.

Not the long efforts of the New Deal, but the incidental effects of war brought prosperity, and with it, fundamental social change. Apparently the mechanism was government spending on a new scale. In 1936, the biggest New Deal spending year, a federal outlay of $8 billion had caused many citizens to worry about the foundations of the Republic. In 1945, when federal expenditures reached $98 billion, unemployment practically vanished and the country seemed to reach new levels of production and prosperity. High wages and farm prices, together with war taxes, produced a greater measure of economic equality than had ever existed. As war industry redistributed the population, the Pacific Coast gained wealth and power. Many Negroes changed jobs and homes, and racial customs began to shift even in the South.

Superficially, the war seemed to bring political unity. Since America had been attacked, overt opposition to the war was negligible. Startling worldwide commitments seemed to be accepted, and many said that isolationism had died at Pearl Harbor. In contrast to 1917, unity seemed to exist without hysteria. Civil liberties were generally preserved with one large exception: 117,000 Americans of Japanese ancestry, two thirds of them citizens, were moved from their West Coast homes first to barbed-wire temporary camps and then to isolated relocation centers in the interior. Though most were resettled in the East or Midwest before the war was over and some eventually received financial compensation for their losses, the scars of this ruthless and unnecessary action remained.

If there was less overt opposition and less hysteria than in World War I, there was also less idealistic enthusiasm. The Four Freedoms, Henry A. Wallace's glowing picture of a "Century of the Common Man," Wendell Willkie's commitment to "One World" were highly effective in liberal circles. None of these, however, came as close to producing a nationwide response as Wilson's appeal to "make the world safe for democracy." For many Americans, this was less a crusade than (as Roosevelt called it) a "War for Survival."

American opinion, deeply divided in 1941 over both the New Deal and Roosevelt's interventionist foreign policy, was not magically reunited in wartime. But division had to manifest itself in indirect ways—in hostility to the Europe-first policy, resentment of price control, exaggeration of strikes, and (despite much countereffort) criticism of the Allies. Some liberals attacked the government for its tactical compromises with Vichy or alleged tenderness toward the British Empire. A larger group remained deeply suspicious of collaboration with Russia, and a still larger faction was determined to prevent the postwar survival of the New Deal.

In 1942 the Republicans sharply increased their strength in Congress. In 1944 Roosevelt, like Lincoln, won a wartime election, this time against the rather ineffective opposition of Thomas E. Dewey, and in the same year many archisolationists lost their seats in Congress. Thus Franklin Roosevelt, again like Lincoln, retained the decision-making power of a wartime president. But for this he paid a price. It was necessary—or so he decided—to postpone discussion not only of important unsettled domestic controversies, but also of some of the thorniest unresolved international problems. The only goal on which all could agree was military victory.

THE GREAT ALLIANCE

In international relations, as in so many fields, World War II seemed to reverse American precedents. In World War I, America had been a gingerly cobelligerent; now she was a full-fledged ally bound to refuse a separate peace. She took the lead in the efforts to make the wartime international coalition into a new international organization. Both public opinion and, this time, the Senate seemed heartily to back the proposal for a new United Nations.

America's most important wartime relations were, of course, with her major allies, and here success was less complete. President Roosevelt placed his major hopes both for victory and postwar stability on the "Four Policemen": Britain, China, Russia, and the United States. Only with Britain was real cooperation achieved. Similar national traditions plus the mutual admiration of Roosevelt and Churchill helped to make the Anglo-American war effort the most successful combined operation in history, yet even here major differences appeared.

The Americans were used to thinking of war in terms of an all-out drive for victory followed by a return to peace and normality. The British had some experience of victory's delusions and costs. Many of the American leaders were suspicious of British efforts to cling to empire. Above all, Roosevelt and Churchill differed in the later stages of the war over Russian relations.

In 1942 American political and military leaders demanded an immediate cross-channel invasion of Europe, partly to prevent collapse of the eastern front. Churchill accepted the necessity of such an operation in the future, but thought it impossible without further buildup and fought hard for diversionary operations in southern Europe. After 1943 his reasons were partly political: Western penetration of the Balkans and Central Europe would prevent Russian domination of these areas. This argument was settled by compromise. To Stalin's chagrin, the Normandy invasion was put off until 1944, while the North African and Italian campaigns represented a partial concession to Churchill's views. A Balkan front was never opened.

Roosevelt's program for making China a great power was a complete failure. Chiang Kai-shek's Nationalist government shared control of the huge country with a well-intrenched Communist movement, and each side fought the other as well as Japan. Exhausted by long war, the Nationalist government was further weakened by corruption.

A SYNOPSIS OF AMERICAN HISTORY

Neither General Joseph Stilwell nor anybody else could bring about a major Chinese contribution to victory. Yet at Cairo in November, 1943, Roosevelt, Churchill, and Chiang agreed that after the war China would get back Manchuria as well as Formosa and the Pescadores. The first of these pledges was largely nullified by the Yalta Agreement, and the second was to be the source of endless trouble.

By far the most difficult relationship was, of course, with Russia. America began this wartime association with a recent past of deep hostility toward that nation. During the period of the Russo-German Pact, American opinion had been outraged by Russia's moves into eastern Poland and Rumania; by her absorption of the three small Baltic states, Latvia, Lithuania, and Estonia; and, above all, by her Winter War with Finland who had refused to surrender certain border districts considered by Russia necessary to her own defense. With the German-Russian break, however, both Roosevelt and Churchill immediately saw the possible importance of Russian contributions to the war. To help keep Germany occupied in the east, America sent Russia lend-lease aid amounting to $11 billion. Temperamentally optimistic and used to thinking in terms of only one opponent at a time, many Americans managed to convince themselves that Russian society and government had fundamentally changed. Russia and America were to remain friendly after the war, and this friendship was to be the mainstay of world peace. This opinion was held by Roosevelt and by his principal advisers, liberal and conservative, civilian and military.

Through 1943 some success was achieved in shaping common military objectives. Good feeling reached its height in late November, 1943, when Roosevelt, Stalin, and Churchill met at Teheran, Persia. There the coming offensive against Hitler was roughly coordinated. It was agreed that German military power must be permanently eliminated, perhaps by division of the country. In Yugoslavia, Allied aid was to go only to Tito, the Communist leader of one branch of the underground. Both the eastern and western frontiers of Poland were to be shifted radically to the west.

From here on, as Soviet armies penetrated Eastern and Central Europe, postwar control of this area became the principal subject of inter-Allied argument. Churchill, while fully aware that Russia's losses entitled her to some security and even more conscious of her unquestioned power in the area, wanted to bargain sharply with Stalin. He was willing, for instance, to concede Russian preponderance in Rumania and Bulgaria in return for Western predominance in Greece and equality in Yugoslavia and Hungary. But even this was an ambitious program; to achieve these goals it would have been necessary to use Amer-can military power for political purposes. This American military leaders, by tradition and training, were unwilling to do. It would, moreover, have been very difficult to convince the American people that American casualties should be incurred for any other purpose than defeat of present enemies. Eager to mediate between Russia and Britain, overconfident of his own ability to charm and persuade Stalin, and conscious of American public and military opinion, Roosevelt refused to play the game of inter-Allied power politics. He tried, instead, to build a future based on genuine Russian-American collaboration.

This effort shaped the most important of the Allied conferences which took place at Yalta, in the Crimea, in February, 1945. By this time, the approach of victory made it necessary to agree on some concrete plans. Though the political future of Germany was left undecided, it was agreed that she would be divided into four zones of military occupation. Stalin here conceded that one zone, formed out of previously constituted Western zones, would be occupied by France, now back in the war under the leadership of Charles de Gaulle and jealous of equal treatment. Germany, it was further agreed, would pay heavy reparations in the form of goods and labor. At Russian insistence, the United States agreed on a figure of $20 billion, half of it for Russia, as a basis for future discussion.

The Polish boundaries agreed on at Teheran were confirmed. This meant that Russia gained large territories in the east, to some of which she had historic and ethnic claims. In the west, Poland was to be liberally compensated with German territory, though the final German-Polish boundary settlement was postponed until a German peace conference. The Communist Polish government set up by the advancing Russians was to be broadened by the inclusion of new members from the exile government in London and from the underground. Free and secret elections, in which all democratic parties could take part, would be held as soon as possible. Similarly, in the rest of liberated Europe, interim governments would be formed on a basis "broadly representative of all democratic elements," and free elections would be held as early as possible.

Another section of the Yalta Agreement dealt with world organization. The nations united against the Axis were to meet in the United States to form an organization, some of whose structure had already been determined at a conference in Dumbarton Oaks near Washington. Of the two most important organs, the Assembly and the Security Council, the latter was to act by unanimity alone. This "veto" provision, much criticized later, was wanted by the United States as well as by Russia. The new organization would not, it was recognized, be in a position to coerce great powers; its effectiveness would depend on the close collaboration of the major states.

Finally, by a secret section of the agreement, Russia was obligated to enter the war against Japan within two or three months after the defeat of Germany. For this Russia was to receive liberal compensation. The *status quo* was to be recognized in Outer Mongolia, a Soviet puppet state nominally a part of China. Russia was to get back what she had lost to Japan in the Treaty of Portsmouth, including railroad and port concessions in Manchuria and possession of the southern portion of the huge island of Sakhalin. Russia would also receive the Kurile Islands north of Japan. Roosevelt was to "take measures" to secure the concurrence of Chiang Kai-shek in these terms which would, however, be "unquestionably fulfilled."

In later years, the Yalta Agreement was to be subject to bitter criticism which made two sorts of cases against it. The first of these was idealistic and humanitarian. America had conceded forced labor as part of German reparations and, despite many pious references in the text to the "principles of the Atlantic Charter," had disposed of millions of people without their consent. Moreover, important rights in Asia, which the United States had refused to concede to Japanese pressure, were handed over to Russia without consulting China.

The second case was concerned with the postwar balance of power. The complete destruction of German power and the concession of new Polish boundaries brought Russia into the heart of Europe and left her potentially dominant on that continent, while the Far Eastern terms brought her back into the crucial Manchurian region. Thus one potentially hostile great power was substituted for another in each area.

Defenders of the Yalta Agreement on the basis of power politics have answered these criticisms mainly by pointing to the current military situation. The Russians were in occupation of much of Poland and the Balkans. Anglo-American forces were not within reach of these areas and had no way of getting there. American Pacific commanders, expecting a fanatical resistance in the Japanese home islands and wrongly informed about the size of Japanese forces in Manchuria, were demanding that Russia be brought into the Far Eastern war.

The moral indictment of Yalta has been answered in several ways. First, defenders have pointed out that the hope for collaboration with Russia was a hope for world peace, noble and natural however unrealistic. The incredible Nazi atrocities, increasingly exposed by the reconquest of occupied territory, did not dispose America to be tender of German rights or to think about resurrecting German power. These

[378]

disclosures served also to take American attention away from the brutality of some Russian behavior in Poland and elsewhere. Second, it
has been argued that the provisions regarding free elections in Poland
and other reconquered countries would have safeguarded democratic
principles if they had been carried out by Russia after Yalta. Finally,
the objectors have been reminded that the Far Eastern provisions were
accepted by Chiang, when he learned of them, with little protest. The
Soviet Union shortly concluded a treaty with Nationalist China promising to support only the Chiang regime as the central Chinese government.

Taken together, these defensive arguments explain many things.
The errors of Yalta were not caused by treason, as extremists later alleged, but by optimism. Yet even the best that can be said is not
entirely reassuring. Certainly the agreement did not meet the standards
of idealism which America had so often invoked in the past, even
when power to enforce these ideals was lacking (as in Manchuria in
1931). On the other hand, if the Yalta Agreement is to be judged in
terms of hard-boiled realism, it can hardly be called an American
success.

Nonetheless, when Roosevelt returned from his long journey, exhausted but triumphant, most Americans gratefully accepted his heart-
felt statements that a future of democracy and peace had been assured.
That spring the Soviet Union failed to reconstitute the Polish government as promised, and elsewhere in the occupied areas made it clear
that such phrases as "free elections" and "all democratic elements" had
different meanings in the East and West. Roosevelt was angered by
Russian suspicions that Britain and America were negotiating for a
separate peace with the Nazis in Italy. To some extent, Roosevelt began to doubt the future he had planned. Before these doubts could
lead to action, however, he died (of a cerebral hemorrhage on April
12).

Most Americans, and nearly all Europeans, believed that a great
leader was lost. Surely they were right: Roosevelt's confidence and
optimism had been as important in war as they had been earlier in
depression. His mistakes flowed from the same great qualities.

FROM YALTA TO HIROSHIMA

The victory of 1945 was clouded by Allied dissent and darkened
by cruelty and destruction. In the spring of that year, however, this
was not apparent to the American people, and even the President's
death failed to spoil the news of success on every front. In Europe,

the German counteroffensive was stopped at Bastogne, Belgium, before the end of 1944. By March, 1945, American forces had crossed the Rhine. In early April, when American troops reached the Elbe, General Eisenhower decided on military grounds not to push forward toward Berlin, but to make sure first of the Southern Alpine redoubt where it was believed that the Nazis might make a last stand. This decision, communicated to Stalin, was protested by Churchill. It was, however, upheld by Truman, the new President, who was as yet eager to continue Roosevelt's policy of good relations with Russia. A little later, for similar reasons, Eisenhower refused to press toward Prague, and the Russians occupied both Central European capitals. On May 1, while Soviet troops were entering Berlin, Hitler killed himself, and three days later Germany surrendered to England, Russia, and the United States.

As American forces drew closer to the Japanese home islands, they continued to meet fierce resistance. No Pacific battles were harder fought than Iwo Jima, in February, or Okinawa, in May. Off the latter island, as in the Philippines, Japan made use of a strange and effective weapon, the suicide plane. Hundreds of pilots dove deliberately at American ships. This and other fanatical behavior convinced most Americans that they were in for a desperate fight in Japan itself.

Actually, Japan's resistance was almost at an end. American submarines had cut off necessary supplies, and since November American bombers had inflicted terrible destruction. In June the Japanese war cabinet fell, and a new government began unsuccessfully to seek Russian mediation.

President Harry Truman and Winston Churchill, meeting at Potsdam, demanded on July 26, that Japan surrender. If she did, they promised, the Japanese would neither be destroyed nor enslaved; if she did not she would meet "utter destruction." Since Truman had received word of the first explosion of an atomic bomb, he was in a position to carry out this threat. When compliance did not seem to be forthcoming, an atomic bomb was dropped on the city of Hiroshima on August 6. The next day Russia hurriedly entered the war in advance of the agreed time. On August 8 another atomic bomb hit Nagasaki, and on August 14 Japan agreed to the Potsdam terms. A formal surrender was signed aboard the *Missouri* in Tokyo Bay, September 2.

Even in the euphoria of victory celebrations, some Americans could not avoid asking themselves how it happened that their country, with its deeply humanitarian traditions, had been the first to use history's most terrible weapon. The Hiroshima bomb killed eighty thousand people and injured many more, some of whom died horribly in the ensuing weeks and months. Yet in 1915, the United States had been genuinely outraged by the death of 1,198 civilians on the *Lusitania*. Throughout the thirties, and as recently as 1939, American spokesmen had denounced aerial bombing of civilian populations.

The advent of the atomic bomb typified several tendencies, good and bad, that ran through the history of the war. It was, in the first place, a typical result of the American civilian war effort. It depended on a bold decision based on immensely complex science and engineering. It was conceived by scientists from many countries, some of them refugees. Thus it was a product of a liberal society associated with some of the best American traditions.

At the same time, its use in war was the climax of a period of mounting inhumanity for which all major nations bore some responsibility. The worst atrocity of the period was the systematic German annihilation of six million Jews. In places Russian treatment of political and national minorities was almost as bad. Bombing of cities was carried out by Axis nations from Shanghai in 1932 to Rotterdam in 1940. City destruction was carried to new lengths by Britain and America in Germany, in 1943–1944, when three hundred thousand civilians were killed. The American fire bombings of Japan killed about 330,000 people. Thus the annihilation of two cities in 1945 could be taken for granted by callous people, while more sensitive ones defended the action as a means of shortening the war and thus reducing both Japanese and American losses in the long run.

Postwar examination by American experts seemed to indicate that Japanese resistance had been almost over before Hiroshima. (Somewhat similarly, precision bombing of industries and transport turned out to have been far more decisive than city destruction in Germany.) But whatever the military or other judgments on the use of the atomic bomb in 1945, its existence became henceforth a major and incalculably frightening fact.

Thus the United States came to the end of a period of great and revolutionary achievement. From a policy of isolation she had emerged to a stance of worldwide involvement. She had helped to build a great alliance, and through this and her productive and military achievements she had helped destroy perhaps the worst regime in history. All this had been accomplished without dictatorship, without the destruction of either economic or political liberty at home.

The price for these great achievements started with a million American casualties, but that was only a beginning. Millions of people in Europe and Asia were starving in their ruins. Hate and fear were rampant as never in modern history. Another totalitarian state had been brought to immense worldwide power. The peaceful, democratic world promised by Roosevelt, and by Wilson before him, seemed nowhere in sight.

FOR FURTHER READING:

For military and diplomatic history, probably the single most valuable work is Churchill's monumental though not infallible *The Second World War* (6 vols., 1948–1953)*. A very short account of American fighting is Fletcher Pratt, *War for the World* (1950). Walter Millis, *Arms and Men* (1956)*, is a humane and enlightened study of American military policy from the beginning and is especially valuable for this period. The tangle of Washington bureaus is to some extent unravelled in Eliot Janeway, *The Struggle for Survival* (1951). One of the most thorough accounts of inter-Allied negotiations is Herbert Feis, *Churchill, Roosevelt, Stalin* (1957). The same author's *Japan Subdued* (1961), discusses the decision to drop the atomic bomb. Robert Sherwood, *Roosevelt and Hopkins* (2 vols., 1948)*, gives a highly favorable picture of the American effort to achieve good relations with Russia. Chester Wilmot, *The Struggle for Europe* (1952), provides a stimulating and intelligent English criticism of American strategy and diplomacy. Among important memoirs are those of secretaries of state Cordell Hull, Edward R. Stettinius, and James F. Byrnes; of Admiral William D. Leahy; and of Generals Dwight D. Eisenhower and Omar Bradley.

---

*Available in paperback edition.

THE TRUMAN YEARS

	DOMESTIC	THE ATOM	EUROPE	ASIA
1945	April 12 Death of F.D.R. November Coal strike.	Baruch Plan. McMahon Act (AEC). Bikini atomic explosion.	July 17–August 2 Potsdam Conference. August 21 End of lend-lease. November 20–October 1 Nuremburg trial.	August 14 Sino-Soviet Treaty. December Beginning of Marshall mission to China.
1946	June–November End of price controls. November 5 Republicans capture both Houses.		November 4–December 12 Foreign ministers complete treaties with German allies (ratified 1947).	January–April Iran incident.
1947	March 22 Truman loyalty program. June 23 Taft-Hartley Act. July 26 National Security Act.		March 12 Truman Doctrine (aid to Greece and Turkey). June 5 Marshall Plan announced. November–December London Conference (Britain, Russia, United States) breaks up over German question.	January End of Marshall mission to China.
1948	November 2 Truman defeats Dewey.	Eniwetok explosion.	February Communist coup, Czechoslovakia. June Yugoslav-Russian break. June 24 Berlin blockade begins.	May 15 Israel independent, recognized by United States.

THE TRUMAN YEARS (*Continued*)

	DOMESTIC	THE ATOM	EUROPE	ASIA
1949	October 14 Smith Act convictions.	First Russian atomic explosion.	April 4 North Atlantic Treaty. May Russians agree to end Berlin blockade.	January 20 "Point Four" announced. Chinese Nationalist defeats. December 8 Chiang to Formosa.
1950	January 21 Hiss convicted. February 9 McCarthy attacks State Department. September 23 McCarran Act. November 7 Republican election gains. December Hoover attacks Truman foreign policy.	United States starts work on hydrogen bomb.		January Acheson "defense perimeter" speech. June 25 North Korean attack. November 26 Chinese attack in Korea.
1951	1951–1952 Corruption disclosures, foreign policy and communism argument.		April 2 Eisenhower Headquarters in Paris opens.	April 11 MacArthur recalled. July 10 Korean peace talks open. September 8 Japanese Peace Treaty.
1952	April 8 Truman seizes steel mills. June 30 McCarran-Walter (immigration) Act. November 4 Eisenhower defeats Stevenson.	British atomic explosion. United States hydrogen explosion.	August 2 West German peace Contract (occupation ends).	

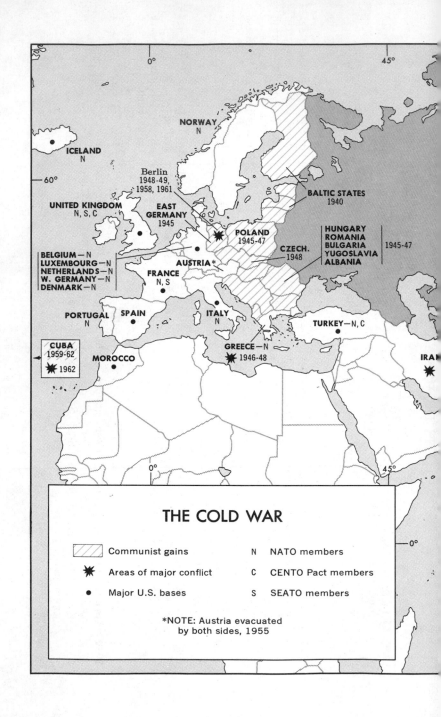

ICELAND
N

60°

UNITED KINGDOM
N, S, C

NORWAY
N

Berlin
1948-49,
1958, 1961

BALTIC STATES
1940

EAST
GERMANY
1945

POLAND
1945-47

CZECH.
1948

HUNGARY
ROMANIA
BULGARIA
YUGOSLAVIA
ALBANIA

1945-47

BELGIUM—N
LUXEMBOURG—N
NETHERLANDS—N
W. GERMANY—N
DENMARK—N

AUSTRIA *

FRANCE
N, S

PORTUGAL
N

SPAIN

ITALY
N

TURKEY—N, C

CUBA
1959-62

1962

MOROCCO

GREECE—N
1946-48

IRAN

45°

0°

45°

0°

THE COLD WAR

Communist gains

Areas of major conflict

Major U.S. bases

N   NATO members

C   CENTO Pact members

S   SEATO members

*NOTE: Austria evacuated
by both sides, 1955

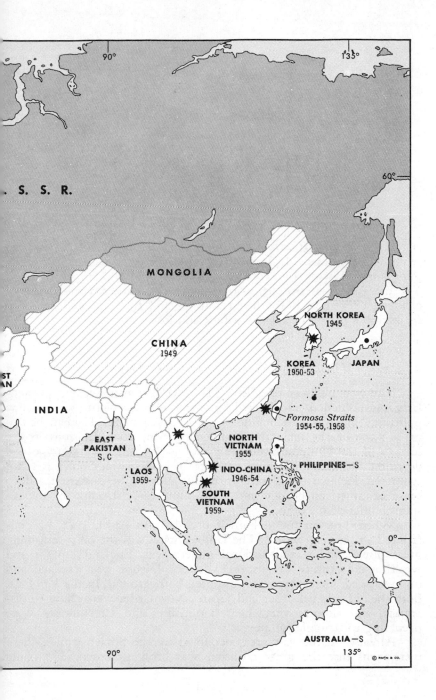

U. S. S. R.

90°

135°

60°

MONGOLIA

NORTH KOREA
1945

KOREA
1950-53

JAPAN

CHINA
1949

INDIA

Formosa Straits
1954-55, 1958

EAST
PAKISTAN
S, C

NORTH
VIETNAM
1955

PHILIPPINES—S

LAOS
1959-

INDO-CHINA
1946-54

SOUTH
VIETNAM
1959-

0°

AUSTRALIA—S
135°

90°

© RMcN & CO.

CHAPTER 29

NEITHER PEACE NOR WAR

1946–1952

After World War II, American history became impossible to separate from world history. The scene grew too large for a historian to grasp, just as events were too complex for contemporaries to understand. Yet the American people, who lived through these years, had not changed overnight. Both their traditions and their leaders had been formed in a period of relative safety and isolation.

THE END OF THE GREAT ALLIANCE

The first postwar president, Harry S. Truman, seemed particularly old-fashioned. He looked to many like a small-town machine politician. He was this, but he was also much more. Truman had to make some of the most tremendous and dangerous decisions in the history of the United States. He made all of them with courage and devotion and many of them with great intelligence. Sometimes hot tempered, inclined to tolerate unreliable cronies, he possessed a deep sense of American history and a profound understanding of the responsibilities of his office.

When Truman found himself president, in April, 1945, he confronted an alarming world. The United States was the only remaining great power under constitutional government. England's might and wealth were nearing exhaustion, Western Europe was wrecked and impoverished, Germany was a disputed battleground. In the Far East, both the old colonial order and Japan's New Order were about to disappear, and almost everywhere nationalists and Communists were preparing to struggle for power.

Already, in the vast areas occupied by the Soviet armies, there were signs that the great coalition was breaking down. The Yalta

Agreement had conceded that Russia would receive large areas that had been part of prewar Poland and that Poland would be compensated at the expense of Germany. Not only had Russia moved up her own borders to the newly conceded line, she had also turned over to the new Polish government large areas in the west—far larger than those envisioned by the Western Allies—expelling nine million Germans. While the promised broadening of the Warsaw government was endlessly discussed, Polish underground leaders were lured out of hiding only to disappear in Soviet prisons. Still hoping for the best, Truman and Churchill both recognized the Warsaw government in July. This meant the destruction of the exile regime in London whose sizeable army had fought hard for the Allies.

With the important exception of Finland, the other countries in the sphere of Soviet power seemed to be heading for the same process. Coalition governments in the next few years were to fall more and more clearly under the control of Communist minorities, which in turn would be purged of all possibly anti-Stalinist elements. Looking back, it seems clear enough that Stalin had always intended to secure his power in Eastern Europe. It may be that he assumed that this area was conceded to be a Russian sphere of influence despite various phrases about free elections. After all, Stalin could point out, he was making no military effort to contest areas occupied by the Western powers, such as Greece or Italy. Disturbingly, however, Russian intransigence in Eastern Europe was accompanied by increased Communist militance throughout the world.

To stem this strange military-political, national-international offensive was a hard assignment and one for which America was ill prepared. Urgent demands from the people and Congress were forcing the rapid discharge of the vast American armies. The principal remaining American weapon, the atomic bomb, could be used only in a new world war. This was a possibility nobody could contemplate.

From 1945 to 1947 the American government made an effort—not without misgivings but with some success—to maintain friendly relations with Russia. At Potsdam, in July, 1945, Truman met Stalin and Churchill (replaced during the conference by Clement Attlee of the British Labor party). The Potsdam Conference sent an ultimatum to Japan and agreed on a complex set of principles for the government of Germany by Russia, the United States, Britain, and France.

The foreign ministers of these four powers, meeting periodically in the next years, managed with much difficulty to draw up treaties with the German allies, and these treaties were confirmed at an international conference in Paris in February, 1947. An International Military Tribunal, sitting at Nuremberg in 1945–1946, condemned twelve major Nazi war criminals to death. (A similar international court, meeting in Tokyo in 1946–1948, resulted in the hanging of seven Japanese war leaders.)

The earliest and worst breakdown of four-power cooperation took place in Germany. The provisions worked out at Potsdam and earlier for four-power government had been based on an assumption of continued East-West cooperation. For a situation of East-West disagreement, they were absurdly impractical. Berlin, the German capital, was to be governed by the four powers jointly. Though it lay a hundred miles inside the agreed Russian zone, no definite access routes from the west were provided.

According to the Potsdam agreement, Germany was to be denazified, demilitarized, stripped of her warmaking power, and left with a standard of living no better than that of the average for Europe (at that time very low). Though no central German government was to be set up for the present, the country was to be administered as an economic unit through the agreement of the four zonal administrations. Though the final amount of reparations was not set, removal of German industrial equipment was to commence. In addition to what it removed from its own zone, Russia, which had suffered frightful destruction at German hands, was to receive 25 per cent of the equipment removed from the Western zones, part of which was to be paid for by shipments of German food and raw materials from the Russian zone. For the present, the United States went ahead with this program, including the dismantling of German industry.

It was soon clear that completely different social systems were emerging in the Eastern and Western zones. As German productive facilities were further weakened, it proved difficult to feed the West German population, swollen by twelve million refugees from the east. Food from the Russian zone was not forthcoming.

In 1946 the United States announced a change in policy, including revision upward of German production, eventual political unification of Germany on a decentralized basis, and re-examination of the German-Polish frontier. To make this palatable to Russia, the United States offered to guarantee German disarmament for twenty-five or even forty years. This offer was promptly refused. In January, 1947, Britain and America agreed to join their zones. Later that spring, a foreign ministers' conference completely failed to agree about reparations, and the deadlock over Germany was complete.

In Austria, four-power occupation worked a little better, partly because an Austrian government had been recognized, though a peace treaty proved impossible to make. In Japan the United States governed substantially alone, despite Russian protests and minor concessions. Under General MacArthur, with extraordinary Japanese cooperation, occupation authorities embarked on an ambitious program of making over Japanese government, society, and even culture along democratic and pacifist lines. Korea was divided arbitrarily at the thirty-eighth parallel of latitude between Russian and American military occupation, pending the establishment of independent government.

A dramatic plan for international control of atomic energy, drawn up by a committee headed by Bernard Baruch, the veteran financier, was rejected by the Soviet Union on grounds that were to become familiar. The Baruch plan called for destruction of American bombs only after international inspection and control had become effective, while the Soviet Union demanded immediate destruction. Meanwhile the Russians, with the aid (perhaps unnecessary) of espionage, were working hard on their own weapon. In August, 1946, Congress created its own system for tight government control of American atomic research and development by an Atomic Energy Commission.

Immediate relief for starving people was carried on by the United Nations Relief and Rehabilitation Administration (UNRRA) with the United States necessarily footing most of the bill. More fundamental moves to restore the world's shattered economies were clearly necessary. Here the prospect of international cooperation was weakened by an unwise American action. Without considering consequences, the United States abruptly cut off lend-lease aid at the end of the European fighting. (Fortunately it was agreed that supplies used in fighting need not be paid for and thus another war debt problem was avoided.) This action deepened Russian suspicions and forced Europe to buy American goods on the open market. In 1945 the United States made a new loan to Britain. By the winter of 1946–1947, with her debts mounting and her dollars gone, Europe faced economic and political disaster and further American action was clearly necessary.

Obviously the vast scheme for postwar Russian-American collaboration was creaking badly. Yet America was reluctant to admit its failure and embark once more, and so soon, on an independent program of worldwide action. Only fear for her own eventual safety would make such a program possible.

In March, 1946, Winston Churchill warned at Fulton, Missouri, that an "Iron Curtain" had cut Europe in two and that Stalin, who did not want war, might gain his objectives without it. Like Roosevelt's "quarantine-the-aggressors" speech, this warning was received with incredulity and hostility. Yet some Americans, and perhaps the administration, began to wonder if there was not once more a danger of hostile domination of Europe and Asia.

In case of aggression, feared or actual, the most obvious recourse was the United Nations. Yet the veto provision of the Charter, and indeed the whole structure of the organization, made it difficult for the United Nations to deal with great-power aggression. In the spring of 1946 Russian forces did indeed withdraw from the northern provinces of Iran after an appeal to the Security Council. In Greece, however, the problem proved more difficult. The conservative government, supported by English troops which had occupied the country with Stalin's consent, was being attacked by guerrilla forces. Apparently these forces were being powerfully assisted by Greece's Communist neighbors. United Nations commissions sent to deal with the problem divided on East-West lines. In February, 1947, the British government informed the Americans that it could no longer carry out its Greek responsibilities. At this point Truman made up his mind that independent American counteraction was necessary.

CONTAINMENT IN EUROPE, 1947–1949

The new American policy, known as "containment," was described by George F. Kennan of the State Department in 1947. Soviet policy, Kennan said, was dominated by a belief in the inevitable triumph of communism. World Communist victory, while it might be pursued with patience, could not be abandoned as an objective without a fundamental change in the Soviet system. Such a change might eventually be induced if the United States (1) demonstrated to the world its own vitality and (2) frustrated Soviet plans by the patient application of counterforce wherever necessary.

Counterforce was first applied under the "Truman Doctrine" announced in March of 1947. Calling for economic and military help for people menaced by armed minorities or outside pressures, Truman persuaded Congress to appropriate funds for Greece and also for Turkey, who was being pressed by Russia to cede border provinces and permit partial Russian control of the strategic Dardanelles. In neither country were all problems quickly solved; in both the immediate threat to independence was met.

In June the United States proposed a more general program for European economic relief. In a speech at Harvard, General George Marshall, now Secretary of State, offered to assist the recovery of all European nations including the Communist ones. Russia forced her satellites to refuse, but the Western European countries willingly presented a united recovery plan. After considerable debate, Congress established the European Cooperation Administration and, in the next three years, appropriated more than $10 billion for its purposes. This "Marshall Plan" was the greatest success of American postwar policy. It laid the basis for the startling European recovery and unprecedented European unity of the fifties.

Naturally, these American actions produced sharp Russian reactions. The Communist parties of Western Europe, through strikes and political agitation, tried hard though unsuccessfully to make the Marshall Plan a failure. Communist control of Eastern Europe tightened, and in February, 1948, Communists in a *coup d'état* took over Czechoslovakia, a country already aligned with Russia in foreign policy but until now governed by a coalition. This event, which deeply alarmed Europeans, was partly balanced by a break between Yugoslavia (hitherto the most important European Communist satellite) and the Soviet Union. From then on Tito's realm was to be Communist but independent in foreign policy. This development might, it seemed, indicate one road toward the disintegration of Stalin's empire.

In the summer of 1948, Russia decided on drastic countermoves in the crucial German area. Reacting sharply to a reform of the currency in the Western zones, Russia announced that the division of Germany ended all reason for Western presence in Berlin. Russian forces cut all surface communication between West Germany and the former capital, threatening with starvation the city's Western garrisons and West Berlin's two million pro-Western inhabitants. This threat, the most dangerous so far, was resolutely met by flying supplies into Berlin in American planes. In May, 1949, the Russians suddenly decided to end the blockade, but the division of Germany was already complete. In September the (West) German Federal Republic was proclaimed at Bonn, and in the following month the (East) German Democratic Republic was created with its capital East Berlin. Thus the most difficult American-Russian problem had taken shape. It was obvious that most Germans wanted their country united and most clearly preferred Western alignment. It was equally obvious that the Russians would never allow a united Germany to join the Western bloc.

Alarmed by the Berlin threat and encouraged by economic revival, the European countries made gestures toward unity and asked for American commitments. In April, 1949, the United States broke with its ancient dislike of binding alliances and signed a treaty of mutual defense with thirteen nations of Western Europe. Later this North Atlantic Treaty was signed by Greece and Turkey.

Obviously, such commitments to defend vast areas demanded military means. In July, 1947, the National Security Act overhauled the defense establishment, creating the office of Secretary of Defense, the National Security Council, the Central Intelligence Agency, and other new organizations. In June, 1948, Selective Service was revived and at the same time two bomber groups, capable of delivering nuclear bombs, were sent to air bases in Britain.

Despite these steps the United States had only begun to build forces sufficient for a sustained worldwide power struggle. Congress was still reluctant to make very large appropriations, and the President was determined to make further cuts. Up to 1950 defense expenditure was limited to $15 billion, and the armed forces to little over a million men. This meant that the nation was still depending heavily on the atomic bomb. In September, 1949, a Russian nuclear explosion announced the end of American atomic monopoly. In the winter of 1949–1950 the administration decided to begin work on the hydrogen bomb which would be far more devastating than any existing weapon.

Thus by 1949 the United States had adopted, in theory and practice, the policy of containment. It was not quite clear whether she was bound to undertake counter action in *any* area of Communist activity or only in those areas where resistance seemed promising. This problem was to cause immense difficulty later. So far, however, the most obvious threat had been to Western Europe, and here there was no doubt of America's commitment. She was bound to support European freedom with her economic might and also, if necessary, with weapons of incredible and unknown powers of destruction. Apparently public opinion supported this commitment more fully than it had approved resistance to the Nazis before 1940.

THE NEW AMERICAN SOCIETY, 1945–1949

In domestic as in foreign affairs, the first Truman years were a time of profound change, of conflict, and of considerable success. Remembering 1921 and 1929, many people predicted a postwar depression. Instead, it soon became apparent that the most serious economic problems were to be shortages and inflation. Price controls, fairly efficient in the last years of the war, were mostly destroyed in the summer and fall of 1946 in a long wrangle between the President, who favored them, and the Congress, which distrusted them. Between December, 1945, and December, 1947, prices rose by about a third.

As in 1919, organized labor wanted to protect its wartime gains and defend wages against inflation. This time its efforts were successful. In several rounds of strikes beginning in 1946, unions achieved compromise settlements with employers, usually providing considerable wage increases for which the consumers paid most of the bill in higher prices. For the first time in American labor history, a period of major strikes passed almost without violence. Yet both the public and the administration were concerned about the growing power of labor to bring the economy to a standstill. In 1946 the government briefly took over the coal mines, and Truman threatened to have the army run the railroads if necessary.

By no means placid, postwar American society was richer and more productive than any in history. America's gross national product, in the prosperous year 1929, had been worth a little over $100 billion and in the depression had fallen below $70 billion. By 1948 it was above $174 billion (using the same dollar value) and only beginning a spectacular upward movement.

At first prosperity was apparently stimulated by pent-up consumer demand. Undoubtedly, federal spending for European relief and other purposes helped sustain it. From the wartime peak of $98 billion, federal spending fell to $33 billion by 1948, as against the $3 billion which had seemed normal in the twenties. In the gloomy thirties, certain economists had said that booms were unlikely to be sustained in the future either by a rising birthrate or new industries. Now they were proved wrong by a spectacular "baby boom" and by important new developments in such fields as electronics and aviation.

Once more, as in the twenties, spokesmen for American capitalism claimed that it had outstripped the dreams of past radicals. This was at least more nearly true than it had been in the earlier period. Continued high taxes and high wages were redistributing wealth to a significant degree. While farm income once more started downward after 1947, wages continued to rise and so did the share which workers had in the country's total net income. While some corporations were huge and powerful, all business including small business had grown. Most people did not believe that the gloomy predictions of 1900 trust-busters were about to be fulfilled. Competition did not seem to be disappearing.

Compared to the early twenties, the new postwar period saw far less hostile reaction to national and racial minorities, partly, no doubt, because there were fewer foreign-born Americans. Definitely, though too slowly, the Negro scored major advances. (Truman's desegregation of the armed forces and presidential support for civil rights assisted this process.) The "G. I. Bill of Rights" sent thousands of veterans to college who would never otherwise have gone. It was arguable that the postwar American society, with its vast new middle class, its burgeoning suburbs, and its high-paid labor, was not only the richest but the most equalitarian society the world had seen. Yet, when one looked into the pockets of poverty that lay beneath the rich surface, one found many people who did not share in the new well-being. Among these were small farmers, teehnologically displaced workers, the old, the mentally deficient, and, despite all advances, most Negroes.

These paradoxical facts shaped the politics of the postwar period. Most Americans, not directly affected by the new kinds of distress, wanted neither to abandon the New Deal nor to extend it. Thus both left and right were frustrated, and the political pendulum swung indecisively, almost regularly, back and forth between a moderately conservative Congress and a surprisingly liberal President.

In September, 1945, Truman called for a long list of reform measures which he called the "Fair Deal." These included higher minimum wages and broader social security, public housing and slum clearance, more regional development along TVA lines, federal assistance to education and health protection, and an attack on racial discrimination in employment. The familiar Southern-Democrat–Republican coalition frustrated most of these aims. Yet the Employment Act of 1946 marked official acceptance of federal responsibility for the maintenance of maximum employment.

In 1946, during the peak of inflation and strikes, the Republicans gained control of both Houses of Congress. Liberals predicted disaster, yet few New Deal laws were repealed. One important new measure, the Taft-Hartley Act, indicated a conservative swing in labor policy, but regulated unions much less strictly than many conservatives wanted (it outlawed the closed but not the union shop). The same Republican Eightieth Congress, denounced by Truman for frustrating his Fair Deal, cooperated remarkably with his spectacular and novel foreign policy.

As the election of 1948 approached, most people still underrated both Harry Truman and his chances. While conservatives disliked the Fair Deal, labor and liberals were tired of Truman's peppery intervention in strikes and longed for a leader of Roosevelt's inspirational gifts. Even the Democratic party itself seemed to be falling apart. The left wing threatened to follow Henry A. Wallace, who roundly denounced Truman's foreign policy for unnecessary hostility to Russia. A strong civil rights bill in the platform brought the secession of most conservative Southerners, who supported the "Dixiecrat" movement of Governor J. Strom Thurmond of South Carolina. The confident Republicans, once more fighting back their right wing, renominated Governor Dewey of New York.

Actually, the situation was less unfavorable to Truman than it seemed. The people were not yet deeply divided about foreign policy, and some had resented the tendency of a Republican Congress to frustrate reform and curb labor. The two secessions actually proved advantageous. Wallace's well-intentioned protest movement was captured by the Communists, which doomed it to insignificance and drew antiradical fire away from the Fair Deal. Thurmond carried only four Deep South states, and his candidacy helped keep northern Negroes in the Democratic camp. Truman's startling victory brought with it a Democratic Congress.

Jubilantly, the President called once more for the enactment of the Fair Deal, to which he added a new farm program, civil rights measures, and repeal of the Taft-Hartley Act. He called also for a new "Point-Four" in foreign policy, providing for American technical assistance to the vast underdeveloped areas of the world. Congress passed some of the milder Fair Deal measures in such familiar fields as minimum wages, social security, and housing. But there were no new TVA's, no dramatic new farm program, and no drastic revision of the Taft-Hartley Act. Point Four operations were commenced with an appropriation of $35 million for all Asia, Africa, and Latin America.

If they looked to history, rather than to their highest hopes, for their standards of comparison, Americans had some reason to be pleased with their government's record in the first four postwar years. At home they had achieved great prosperity and retained sufficient political unity. Abroad they had assumed vast responsibilities and scored some successes. In the middle of the century, this relatively cheerful picture was shattered by unforeseen events.

CHALLENGE IN ASIA, 1949–1951

As in 1941, disaster struck not in Europe where America had reliable allies and a clear policy, but in the Far East where allies were doubtful and commitments unclear. In China, at the end of the war, the government of Chiang Kai-shek faced a well-entrenched, experienced, and armed Communist opposition which controlled about a fourth of the Chinese population. Russia, which occupied Manchuria as a result of her brief war with Japan, recognized the Chiang government as sovereign throughout China, including Manchuria. Stalin's forces gave limited assistance to the Chinese Communists, but turned over the Manchurian cities to Nationalist garrisons often flown in from the south by America. (It is by no means certain that Stalin, at this time, wanted a Communist success in China which would provide him with a powerful rival in the Communist world.)

In the era of high hopes and Roosevelt-Stalin accords, many American observers, not all of them left-wing, found the Chinese Communists efficient and honest and the Nationalists corrupt and hopeless. Some advocated an effort to produce a coalition government. Encouraged by a few gestures in this direction from both Chinese sides, Truman sent General Marshall to try to bring about such a union. By December, 1946, Marshall concluded that the task was hopeless and asked to be recalled.

By this time the Truman administration had apparently concluded, with little articulate domestic opposition, that the cause of Chiang was lost. In 1949 the Nationalist armies disintegrated, the Communists captured city after city, and in December Chiang's government moved to the island of Formosa. Suddenly the American people awoke to the fact that China, whose integrity America had long upheld, was now indeed united, but under hostile control. From the Baltic to the Yellow Sea over the whole vast Eurasian mainland, Communists were in power.

Later many argued that America should have given Chiang more active support. At the time very few demanded the kind of massive commitment that would have been necessary to keep the tottering Nationalists in power. Here as elsewhere, the faults of American policy were to a large extent the result of traditional American optimism. Roosevelt's program for making Nationalist China a great power, Truman's hope for Nationalist-Communist coalition, and later suggestions that Chiang could have been sustained with a little more effort were all equally unrealistic.

Many Americans were genuinely shocked at events for which they were unprepared. Neoisolationists and Asia-firsters blamed the Roosevelt policies for the disaster, and some partisans saw in the loss of China a means of ending Republican defeat.

Accused not only of mistaken judgment but also of deliberate treason, Truman and his Secretary of State, Dean Acheson, stuck to their guns. An American White Paper blamed the Chinese Nationalists for their own defeat, and the President announced that the United States would not get involved in Chinese civil war in behalf of Formosa. And in January, 1950, Secretary Acheson made a speech defining a broad American "defense perimeter" in the Pacific—very broad, but covering neither Formosa nor Korea. This raised in a new form the most difficult problem concerning the containment policy. *Any* announced boundary for American intervention might seem to invite Communist attack in the area left outside. Was the only answer American commitment *everywhere?* Or was it possible, in a democratic

[398]

country, to decide for or against action in each case without advance commitment or public preparation?

Perhaps because Korea, a narrow peninsula bordering on both major Communist countries, was a very poor theater for American action, that was where the next challenge came. Postwar zones of Russian and American military occupation had solidified into opposing political entities, and on June 25, 1950, the (Communist) North Koreans crossed the South Korean border in force. Immediately the matter was taken by the United States to the United Nations Security Council which Russia happened to be boycotting. With no Russian member to cast a veto, the Council demanded North Korean withdrawal and urged its members to assist South Korea.

In obedience to this order, and also to sustain a regime created and fostered by the United States, President Truman sent to Korea first American air and sea forces and then ground troops under General MacArthur. Reversing the earlier policy of aloofness from the Chinese civil war, he stationed the Seventh Fleet between Formosa and the Chinese mainland. This last action was not altogether approved by America's allies, but fifteen other nations sent small contingents to the UN army in Korea. Thus the situation was an ambiguous one: MacArthur was nominally in command of an international army under UN orders. Actually, his army was made up of 90 per cent Americans and South Koreans. Thus this international "police action" was also an American war. It turned into a bloody and frustrating struggle with profound effects on American foreign and domestic policy.

At first the North Koreans swept the raw American troops southward. In September, holding only a small area around the port of Pusan, the UN force started a northward counterdrive. By a brilliant landing behind enemy lines at Inchon, near Seoul, Mac-Arthur achieved a major victory. This raised the question whether the UN troops would stop at the old boundary or push on to unify the nation under the South Korean government (both Korean governments claimed to represent the whole peninsula). When the General Assembly resolved that its aim was to create a "unified, independent, and democratic Korea" MacArthur's troops crossed the thirty-eighth parallel and drove northward toward the Chinese boundary at the Yalu River, which MacArthur was forbidden to cross. Though President Nehru of India and others warned of possible Chinese intervention, General MacArthur assured President Truman that this was most unlikely. At the end of November, however, Chinese troops surprised the UN Army near the Yalu, inflicted a severe defeat, and started a drive southward against stiff resistance.

Chagrined at what he called a new war, MacArthur demanded

new measures to win it. These included permission to bomb the "privileged sanctuary" in China from which Chinese troops and some Russian-made planes were coming, the use of Chinese Nationalist troops from Formosa, and an all-out commitment to victory over the new enemy, with or without the support of America's European allies. When MacArthur carried his protest to the extent of press interviews and letters to members of the Republican opposition, Truman promptly recalled him from command.

This bold action, taken by Truman to protect what he considered the all-important control of the president over foreign policy, precipitated an angry debate. MacArthur received a hero's welcome from Congress, and at first the public seemed to agree with his eloquent argument that there is no substitute for complete victory as a goal in war. General Omar Bradley, Chairman of the Joint Chiefs of Staff, warned, however, that an all-out war with China would be "the wrong war, in the wrong place, at the wrong time." The administration stuck to its policy of limited war, and in Korea the line between the two sides was stabilized at about the old border between North and South. In July representatives of the two sides began a long, frustrating effort to negotiate a compromise peace.

The Korean War was the signal for a major overhaul of American defense and foreign policies. Not primarily for Korean purposes, but to prevent a worldwide Communist victory, the military budget was quadrupled and the armed forces increased to 3,500,000 men. In Europe, where recovery was now well under way, American aid shifted from an economic to a military emphasis. At American suggestions, the North Atlantic Treaty Organization decided to build a Combined Western European force to deter possible Russian attack. Headquarters were established in Paris, and once more Eisenhower was placed in supreme command of an allied army.

Almost inevitably, European rearmament raised the question of contributions from West Germany, the most exposed and now the most prosperous European state. A separate German army was still an intolerable idea to the French and other victims of the Nazis. In 1952, following a French suggestion, the Western European nations formed a European Defense Community in which national components, including a German one, would be placed under a single command.

Japan had proved an important base for the Korean action, and in September the United States signed a peace treaty dropping all restrictions on Japanese economic growth or even rearmament. A separate security treaty gave American forces the right to remain in Japan. At about the same time the United States signed mutual defense treaties with the Philippines, Australia, and New Zealand.

Thus the Korean War, following the Berlin blockade and the Russian atomic explosion, changed the nature and degree of American commitments once more. A remarkable combination of courage and restraint had turned back Communist aggression and prevented the development of a third world war. For this achievement, a heavy price had been paid, and not all of it by Americans. The United States had lost twenty-five thousand men, Korea was devastated, and the Korean civilian population had suffered almost incredible losses. Yet it seemed that victory, or even an end of the fighting, was not in sight. Instead of guarding a limited defense perimeter, the United States seemed to have undertaken to resist Communist advances in even the most remote and difficult theaters. Europe seemed permanently divided, and the German question farther than ever from solution. War had brought its usual accompaniment of conscription, inflation (comparatively moderate), and high taxes. Military expansion seemed to threaten more than ever the traditional civilian character of American society and government. Both America and Russia were known to be developing the hydrogen bomb, potentially a thousand times more powerful than the weapon that had destroyed Hiroshima. It is not surprising that the American people, most of whom remembered years of apparent security, were very deeply disturbed.

CONFUSION, HYSTERIA, AND THE END OF
THE TRUMAN ERA

Popular unrest first took the form of a new debate over foreign policy, similar in some ways to those of 1898–1900, 1914–1917, and 1939–1941, but more violent than any of them. Some extremists argued that the whole diplomacy of Roosevelt and Truman had been part of one gigantic plot, including the New Deal, Pearl Harbor, the buildup of Russia, the sellout of China, and war without victory in Korea. Less violent critics of the administration argued, as former President Hoover did in 1950, that it was a mistake for America to make any commitments on the continents of Europe or Asia. Senator Taft and others called for a reliance on air power rather than ground troops, and many urged that timid or uncooperative allies be disregarded. On the other hand the somewhat demoralized liberals maintained that the real mistake had been support of corrupt and reactionary regimes or reliance on military rather than economic methods of defense against communism.

Though none of these arguments held up very well in its extreme form, discontent was not to be dismissed lightly. Nobody knew just where, if anywhere, the limits of American commitment were, and the long-run positive goals of foreign policy were not clear. American "cold war" resistance had been improvised to meet unforeseen threats. Attempts to provide it with a theory were not altogether convincing, and its opponents offered no clearly feasible alternatives. Thus the argument centered, increasingly and disastrously, on one emotional issue: Communists in government.

Unfortunately, neither the facts nor the arguments affecting this issue were simple. Liberals usually appealed to free speech, and it was true that the United States, since its beginnings, had normally tolerated advocacy of revolution. But free speech, even revolutionary speech, did not clearly cover new forms of secret political activity. No earlier radical group had been under the control of a foreign great power. And it was not quite clear whether, during a cold war, wartime or peacetime precedents should govern.

Between 1941 and 1945, when Communists throughout the world were supporting the anti-Hitler alliance, some Communists had found employment in Washington, usually in low-echelon jobs. A few of these had been exploited by the Soviet Union for espionage. In some intellectual circles and in sections of organized labor, the Communist party had regained a portion of the strength it had held in the thirties. These facts, exposed and greatly exaggerated at the moment Americans were dying in a frustrating war with Communists in Korea, produced an explosive reaction.

Responding to early disclosures of Communist activity, Truman established a government loyalty program in March, 1947. Employees were investigated by the F.B.I., and those found disloyal (later, also those considered "security risks") were discharged. Despite efforts for fairness, the novel and secret character of this program led to some abuses and much uneasiness. Turning from the problem of secret infiltration to a quite different area, Truman's Justice Department started in 1948 to prosecute the leaders of the American Communist party under the Smith Act of 1940, which forbade advocacy of, or conspiracy to advocate, forcible revolution.

Though these actions were disapproved by many liberals, they were not enough to pacify current fears. The demand for more drastic measures arose partly from the House of Representatives' Committee on Un-American Activities whose methods had long drawn liberal criticism. The most spectacular, though not the only or the clearest, case of communism in government arose in this Committee in 1948 when Whittaker Chambers, an ex-Communist, accused Alger Hiss of having been a Communist and, a little later, of having engaged in espionage.

Hiss, a brilliant and widely admired young man, had held a

moderately influential State Department post and had attended the Yalta Conference. Nearly all liberals believed him innocent, and President Truman referred to the Committee's work as a "Red Herring." Yet Chambers' melodramatic and baffling charge proved very hard to refute. In 1950 Hiss was finally convicted in court, not of espionage but of perjury in his denial of Chambers' charges. Still more alarming to the public was the discovery that spies had been operating in wartime atomic installations. Now the threat of annihilation was added to the loss of China as a result of Communist conspiracy.

In 1950 Congress passed, over Truman's veto, the McCarran Internal Security bill which among many drastic provisions required the registration of Communist organizations and provided that subversives could be interned by presidential order in time of war. In 1952 the McCarran-Walter bill severely increased political restrictions on immigration. And in 1950, when fear of communism had reached its peak, the Communist issue was discovered by its great promotional genius, Senator Joseph McCarthy of Wisconsin.

Charging that many Communists (the number varied) were employed in the State Department and moving on to attack as traitors General Marshall and Secretary Acheson, McCarthy succeeded in creating a wide following and an unparalleled amount of public alarm and confusion. In the congressional elections of 1950, the new political technique of extreme, unsupported charges seemed to work remarkably well, as critics of McCarthy went down to defeat and clever politicians adopted his tactics. As in the anti-German hysteria of World War I, states, cities, and private organizations took up the crusade. Soon self-appointed groups were purging libraries, harassing teachers, and listing dangerous television stars. For a time, it seemed as if traditional individual freedom, decency, and common sense were to be sacrificed in the search for a complete, impossible security.

In this disturbing atmosphere the 1952 election campaign began. In April, when a threatened steel strike seemed to threaten paralysis, Truman seized the steel plants, an action held unconstitutional in June. A series of sordid political scandals in the administration, not enormous by Harding or Grant standards but still disturbing, began to be exposed. Opposition extremists spread the picture of an incompetent President, surrounded by traitors and crooks, committed to a hopeless war.

Actually, in the summer of 1952 the nation's right-wing extremists received their severest blow when the Republican convention nominated not a McCarthyite demagogue and not even the widely-respected conservative Senator Taft, but General Eisenhower. The General, long identified with both the Roosevelt and the Truman foreign policies, could hardly lend himself to McCarthy's charges of "Twenty Years of Treason." Eisenhower did, however, support all Republican candidates, including McCarthy, while he confined himself to more moderate discussions of "the mess in Washington" or at most "creeping socialism." In foreign policy, the Republicans promised both peace and victory. John Foster Dulles, their leading foreign policy spokesman, promised that Republicans would roll back communism instead of merely containing it. Near the end of the campaign, Eisenhower promised that if elected he would fly to Korea and bring the war to an end.

The Democrats nominated the eloquent Governor of Illinois, Adlai Stevenson, who aroused immense liberal enthusiasm but proved unable to stem the Republican tide. Surprisingly, the overwhelming Eisenhower victory failed to produce much change in Congress, where Republicans barely gained a two-house majority. Ironically, and fortunately, the first election of a Republican president since Hoover guaranteed that there would be no sharp change in American foreign policy.

FOR FURTHER READING:

Among general histories of the period, Herbert Agar, *The Price of Power* (1957)*, is thoughtful and very brief; Eric F. Goldman, *The Crucial Decade* (1956)*, is colorful and anecdotal. F. L. Allen, *The Big Change* (1952)*, points out some of the differences between this period and the previous postwar era. Foreign policy is briefly summarized by William G. Carleton, *The Revolution in American Foreign Policy, 1945–1954* (1954), and a section of it is examined in detail in Herbert Feis, *Between War and Peace, The Potsdam Conference* (1960). John Lukacs, *A History of the Cold War* (1961)*, is a balanced essay. Of the mountainous literature on the Communist issue, Alistair Cooke's account of the Hiss case, *A Generation on Trial* (1950), best conveys the atmosphere of the period. The list of memoirs starts with those of Truman.

Hugh Ross, *The Cold War: Containment and Its Critics* (Berkeley Readings in American History, 1963)*, is a documentary study of postwar foreign policy.

*Available in paperback edition.

EISENHOWER AND AFTER

	DOMESTIC	SPACE AND THE ATOM	EUROPE	ASIA, LATIN AMERICA, AND AFRICA
1952	November Eisenhower elected.	November 1 Eniwetok hydrogen explosion (United States).		December Eisenhower visits Korea.
1953	1953–1954 McCarthyism. Recession.	August 20 Russian H-bomb.	March 5 Stalin's death. June Riots in East Berlin. September 26 United States bases in Spain.	July 27 Korean armistice.
1954	April–June Army-McCarthy hearings. May 17 Court outlaws school segregation. November Democrats capture Congress.	March 1 Bikini H-bomb (United States).	September 8 SEATO Pact.	May–June Guatemala Crisis. July 21 Indo-China divided.
1955	July 11 Dixon-Yates contract cancelled.		May 15 Austrian Peace Treaty. July 18–23 Geneva meeting (Eisenhower, Bulganin).	
1956	November Eisenhower elected with Democratic Congress.	Stevenson proposes H-bomb ban.	February Khrushchev denounces Stalin crimes. October–November Hungarian insurrection.	October Suez Crisis.
1957	Recession. September 24 Troops to Little Rock.	May 15 British H-bomb. October 4 Sputnik.	March 28 European Common Market.	January 5 "Eisenhower Doctrine" in Middle East.

EISENHOWER AND AFTER (*Continued*)

	DOMESTIC	SPACE AND THE ATOM	EUROPE	ASIA, LATIN AMER- ICA, AND AFRICA
1958	November Democratic gains in Congress.	January 31 United States satellite. March 31 Russia suspends tests (United States follows).		May Lebanon Crisis.
1959	July Steel strike.	September 13 Soviet "Lunik" hits moon.	September Khrushchev visits United States.	February 16 Castro premier of Cuba.
1960	Recession. November Kennedy elected.	February 11 French atomic explosion. July 20 Polaris sub launches missile.	May U2 incident. November West Berlin threatened.	June Tokyo riots. June 30 Congo independent; civil war. August Laos Crisis.
1961		April 12 Gagarin first astronaut. August Russia resumes testing in atmosphere (United States underground tests follow).	August Berlin wall.	January 3 United States breaks relations with Cuba. April 17 "Bay of Pigs" invasion of Cuba.
1962	May 28 Stock market crash. September Troops to U. of Mississippi. November Democrats retain control of Congress.	February 20 John H. Glenn first United States astronaut. April United States resumes testing in atmosphere.		February United States military Command in South Viet Nam. July Laos treaty. October India-China border fighting. October Cuba crisis.

CHAPTER 30

THE AGE OF PERMANENT CRISIS

1953–1963

Some Americans had hoped, and others had feared, that the Eisenhower administration would sharply change American foreign policy and re-shape post-New Deal American society. It did neither. In nearly every sphere, the history of the administration seemed to go through three stages: first, announcement of sweeping change; second, reversion, with overwhelming public approval, to a slightly modified version of earlier policies; finally, frustration and renewed crisis. One explanation of this cycle is not hard to find. In the circumstances confronting American policy-makers of this period, real alternatives were few, and completely satisfactory solutions impossible. Yet the American people did not give up easily their search for security and contentment. In 1953 many wanted a change; in the middle fifties most believed that they had found security; by the end of the decade it was apparent that they had not.

In 1960 a narrow majority voted once more for change. By 1963 it had become clear that real innovation was still hard to effect.

FROM REACTION TO COMPLACENCY

In 1953, fear of domestic subversion reached panic proportions. The federal security program was drastically tightened, while con-gressional committees searched for disloyalty in education, entertain-ment, and private foundations. For a while Senator McCarthy, now chairman of the Committee on Government Operations, seemed the most powerful individual in Washington. Far from admitting that Re-publican victory had ended the danger of Communist infiltration, he intensified his accusations. The State Department, long his principal victim, seemed to have surrendered. Officials who criticized the Senator were suspended, and books which offended him were removed from American information libraries and destroyed (sometimes their authors were called to Washington and harshly grilled). Two junior members of McCarthy's staff junketed through Europe issuing portentous reports on the loyalty of senior American officials after talking briefly with shady foreign informants. Civil servants and even army officers were encouraged to disobey their superiors and disclose confidential information. The morale of federal employees sank dangerously, and some of America's staunchest friends abroad were dismayed.

In 1954, the Senator fell from power as rapidly as he had risen. The President had shown signs of disquiet, and, perhaps more important, the public was beginning to be bored. A prolonged and complicated controversy with the Department of the Army resulted in a series of television hearings in which McCarthy's manners and methods shocked the public. Finally a select committee of the Senate condemned his conduct as contradictory to senatorial traditions. Discredited and comparatively ignored, McCarthy died in May, 1957.

Later in the decade the Supreme Court, now presided over by Earl Warren, a liberal Republican, delivered a number of decisions which restricted the scope of congressional committees and in other ways reaffirmed the importance of traditional individual freedoms. At the polls, the congressional elections of 1954 demonstrated that the "Red issue" had lost its potency, and in 1956 it was hardly used. In the sunshine of the middle Eisenhower years, hysteria could not survive. Yet the age-old problem of liberty and security had received no permanent answer and continued, in many forms, to plague the national conscience. Some of the most important and difficult issues of foreign policy seemed to have been placed beyond the range of effective public discussion. And a minority on the far right, small but not negligible, added Eisenhower and Warren to their list of worldwide conspirators.

In the same period the administration's economic and social policies shifted from right to center. At the outset, many cabinet members were wealthy businessmen, the conservative Senator Taft apparently wielded great power in Congress, and the President's own pronouncements on domestic matters were highly conservative. Senator Taft died in July, 1953. In the winter of 1953–1954 a recession set in causing the Treasury Department to modify its conservative, anti-inflation policies. Without drastic government action, recovery came swiftly, and in the mid-fifties an unparalleled prosperity prevailed. Despite this fact and despite the President's great and continuing popularity, Democrats recovered control of Congress and kept it throughout the Eisenhower administrations. With the Korean War over and

the McCarthy hysteria abated, it became clear that the country's domi
nant mood had not changed greatly since the Truman years. Few
Americans wanted to dismantle the New Deal, and few wanted radica
new departures. Under these circumstances, the Eisenhower instinc
for compromise and conciliation had free rein.

In the prosperous mid-fifties, the political pattern seemed to con
sist of (1) administration friendliness to business, (2) administratio
efforts, seldom strikingly successful, to promote economy and decen
tralization, and (3) compromises between President and Congress i
support of moderate, familiar kinds of reform programs. Efforts t
win business confidence included tax concessions, increased "partner
ship" of government and private enterprise in the development o
public power and even nonmilitary atomic energy, and support fo
state, rather than federal, control of tideland oil resources. On th
other hand, Eisenhower's first, Republican Congress created the De
partment of Health, Education, and Welfare, extended social security
and gave moderate support to public housing. Even after the Demo
crats recovered control, few measures more startling than these wer
passed. Such controversial programs as health insurance or federa
support of education were regularly defeated or heavily amended.

A major effort to change the direction of New Deal and Fai
Deal farm policies was made by Ezra Taft Benson, Eisenhower's con
servative Secretary of Agriculture. Amid loud outcries from farn
spokesmen, price supports were made "flexible" rather than rigid; tha
is, lowered. Yet, since farm income was declining, many New Dealist
measures, including a "Soil Bank" scheme to reduce acreage, received
administration support. Neither farm subsidies nor the farm problen
seemed at all likely to disappear.

A surprisingly vigorous program of antitrust prosecutions and
various efforts to help small business failed to achieve a significan
movement in the direction of *laissez faire*. Government spending, so
long denounced as the road to socialism, was cut back only moderately
after the Korean War. It remained higher than the 1950 post-World
War II low of $45 billion and by 1957 was to reach a new peacetime
high of $82 billion. Government decisions of many kinds continued to
affect every part of the economy. To the President's obvious distress
it became clear that this fact placed vast temptations in the way of
competing interests. In 1955 the Dixon-Yates contract, an effort to
provide for private construction of a huge power plant for Memphis
proved to be improperly negotiated and was cancelled by Eisenhower
The next year disclosures of attempted bribery of a senator forced
the President to veto a bill to exempt natural gas producers from fed
eral rate control.

The most important advance of the period, that made by the Negroes, was not primarily a product of executive action. In 1954 the Supreme Court reversed its 1896 position on segregation. Until now, "separate but [nominally] equal" treatment of Negroes in transportation, recreation, and education had been legal. Now segregation, specifically in education, was pronounced inherently unequal. This decision, tightened and interpreted by later Court pronouncements, produced fierce defiance in the South, and only the border states began effective school desegregation during the decade. Without specifically approving the Court's position, the President supported it in the name of constitutional obligation. In 1957 he sent federal troops to Little Rock, Arkansas, where Governor Orval Faubus, alleging fear of mob action, was using state guards to obstruct court-ordered integration of the high school.

Probably even more important than the Court decision was the new determination of southern Negroes to achieve the equality so long promised and denied. Most Negro efforts were directed at ending segregation in transportation, restaurants, and housing. Usually campaigns were carried on with remarkable discipline, in a spirit of passive resistance, often under the leadership of ministers and sometimes with the help of northern white sympathizers. Progress in integration and equality was probably greater than in any decade since Reconstruction. Yet delays and frustrations were many, and before the end of the decade the program of nonviolent desegregation was challenged by a Negro minority who called for militant, pan-African, black nationalism.

In its social effects, Eisenhower prosperity had something in common with Coolidge prosperity. Like the twenties, the forties and fifties added large numbers of citizens to the complacent, suburban, moderately conservative ranks of the middle class. As in the twenties, however, the culture of prosperity excluded some people and was repudiated by others.

Until nearly the end of the decade, few middle-class citizens noticed that a large minority remained poor. Esthetic blight and moral sluggishness were the main targets of criticism. Perhaps the most obvious failure of America—here the critics were repeating strictures made since the eighties and nineties—was her cities. Traffic choked them, old slums disgraced them, and new jerrybuilt housing spread from their edges into the countryside. In the slums and, more shockingly, in some wealthy suburbs juvenile delinquents expressed their confusion and frustration in acts of meaningless violence.

As in the twenties, intellectuals denounced dulness and conformity. The successor of Babbitt was the Organization Man who was said to live and breathe in the cheerful, noncontroversial manner pre scribed by the head office on the basis of personality research. T‹ repudiate, defy, and outrage this monster seemed to a few seriou people the main need of the hour. "Beatniks," bearded and bizarre proclaimed a new religion of defeat and withdrawal rather than de fiance. The gospel of passivity was sometimes proclaimed, however in a militant enough manner. Often the new Bohemians seemed recog nizable heirs of earlier American nonconformists and eccentrics, driver to new extremes by the new difficulties of resisting an immensel powerful society.

To most Americans, however, Eisenhower prosperity and it genial symbol were apparently highly satisfactory. An unassuming president who left many administrative decisions to his subordinates praised free enterprise, disowned corruption, and cooperated with : cautiously reformist Congress seemed to fit the needs of the hour Surely one of these needs, though hardly the only one, was for re assurance and rest after decades of fierce controversy. Despite a hear attack in 1955, Eisenhower was renominated in 1956 and scored : landslide victory over a visibly less-confident Adlai Stevenson. Insteac of the "Three K's" of 1952 (Communism, Korea, and Corruption) alliterative Republican campaigners invoked Peace, Progress, anc Prosperity.

FROM MASSIVE RETALIATION TO PEACEFUL COEXISTENCE

In 1952, many Republicans had denounced war, governmen spending, and appeasement. Some had promised in contrast peace economy, and a rollback of world communism. The difficulties of this commitment were made greater by a change in the tactics of the opponent. In March, 1953, Joseph Stalin died. Nikita Khrushchev who emerged as Russia's new leader, repeatedly proclaimed a relax ation of the Russian police state and a foreign policy of peaceful competition with capitalism. The main theater of this competition was to be the underdeveloped countries just emerging from colonial rule. In many of these countries the new, comparatively "soft" Communist line, coupled with unquestionable Russian technological achievement. seemed to have considerable appeal. Thus American policies had to be adjusted at once to old commitments and to a new situation.

During most of Eisenhower's presidency, foreign policy was for mulated, and to a considerable extent formed, by Secretary of State John Foster Dulles. Dulles announced that America, instead of merely containing communism, would adopt a policy aimed at liberation of Communist-oppressed territories especially in Eastern Europe. Instead of reacting locally to Communist threats, America from now on would answer with "massive retaliation" at times and places of its own choosing.

This policy led to a change in military emphasis. Expenditures and ground troops were to be cut back. This would eliminate indecisive local wars like that in Korea. Nuclear weapons would be further developed and the air arm expanded. This would give the country, as the newspapers were soon putting it, "more bang for a buck." Corollaries of this "New Look" in military policy were tight alliances and the development of a string of air bases abroad from Spain to Iran. NATO armies in Europe would be equipped with tactical atomic weapons.

The new policies drew heavy criticism abroad and at home. Critics charged that they would make American resistance to aggression impossible except in cases justifying all-out nuclear war. This became harder to contemplate as American tests made clear the colossal destructiveness of the H-bomb, and scientists made conflicting statements about the effect of fallout on cancer, leukemia, and birth deformities. In October, 1954, Eisenhower said that war had become obsolete under modern circumstances. Since the Russians were saying much the same thing, the world breathed a little easier. Yet crises still occurred, and the "massive retaliation" policy for dealing with them seemed to have lost part of its meaning.

The new military-diplomatic policies were severely tested in the Far East. Carrying out a campaign promise, the administration succeeded in negotiating a Korean peace on approximately the same terms Truman had been willing to accept. The massive retaliation policy may have contributed something to Communist willingness to sign, since Dulles announced that if war persisted it could not be confined to the Korean Peninsula. Prisoners of war were allowed, as both Truman and Eisenhower had insisted, to choose whether to go home or not, and a large number of Communist soldiers chose Formosa. The peninsula was left divided, leaving America committed to assist and defend an economically and politically shaky South Korean state.

With peace in Korea, attention shifted southward to Indo-China where since 1945 the French had been fighting a bloody and unsuccessful war against the Viet Minh independence movement, by now under solidly Communist leadership. At first the United States had been skeptical about colonialism here as elsewhere, but since the Korean War America had been supporting the French heavily with money and material. In March, 1954, it suddenly became clear that northern

Indo-China could no longer be held unless the United States com
mitted at least its air power. Both Dulles and Eisenhower proclaime
that the loss of Indo-China would lead to Communist domination o
all South Asia. Yet despatch of American ground troops to fight i
the Indo-Chinese jungles seemed incompatible with the New Loo
policy, and air power alone would be ineffective there. According t
the new military doctrine, this seemed a clear case for massive retalia
tion against the centers of opposing power. Such a terrible alternativ
was, however, hardly considered in practice. Eisenhower, overrulin
both his military and civilian advisers, decided against even local a
assistance to the French. France rapidly moved to end the war, an
in 1955 the United States accepted, though it did not itself negotiate
a solution which divided Indo-China. Three more weak and divide
states, Laos, Cambodia, and South Viet Nam, were added to the lis
of American responsibilities.

One of the administration's early acts was to carry out Repub
lican promises to "unleash Chiang Kai-shek." The Seventh Flee
patrolling the Straits of Formosa mainly to protect Chiang's Nationa
ists against mainland assault, was instructed to present no furthe
opposition to attacks in the other direction. In 1954 the Chinese Com
munists loudly proclaimed their intention of capturing Formosa whicl
quoting the Cairo Declaration of 1943, they insisted was part of Chin
It had long been clear that the United States would not allow Formos
to fall, and she had just assisted in the movement there of forme
Communist soldiers. American policy was less clear toward the tin
islands, within ten miles of the Chinese coast, which the Nationalist
had garrisoned. When mainland batteries began shelling these offshor
islands, the United States announced that America would defend then
if the assault seemed to be part of an attack on Formosa itself. In
treaty with Chiang, the United States pledged herself to defend For
mosa and the Pescadores, but Chiang promised not to invade the main
land without United States consent. Thus his brief "unleashing" wa
ended.

In September, 1954, the United States signed the SEATO treaty
of military alliance, modeled on the Atlantic Pact, with Britain, France
Australia, New Zealand, the Philippines, Pakistan, and Thailand. Thu
a Far Eastern policy not much unlike that of Truman had emerged
The United States had divided two crucial areas with the Communist
and guaranteed the resulting *status quo*. The Formosa Straits now, lik
Korea in 1950, were an area of great danger where the limits of Amer
ican commitment were not clear.

The Eisenhower policies were further tested in a new theater, th
Middle East, whose problems to some extent typified those of the en

THE AGE OF PERMANENT CRISIS, 1953-1963

ire underdeveloped two thirds of the world. More and more, it began
o be said that the outcome of the world struggle for power lay not in
Europe or East Asia but in the vast, backward, impoverished, restless
countries of Africa, Southern and Western Asia, and Latin America.
Yet America's great wealth and special political traditions made it immensely difficult for her to achieve any understanding of these huge
areas. United States interest in the Middle East was especially acute
because of the region's immensely important oil resources, long de-
ended by Britain and coveted by Russia, and also because of America's relation to the new state of Israel. The courage of Israel in fight-
ng for its independence and welcoming all the survivors of Hitler's
pogroms appealed to many Americans. Yet most Moslem nations hated
he Israelis as interlopers and refused to accept the existence of the
new state.

The United States fostered, but did not join, the Baghdad Pact
igned in 1954 by Great Britain, Turkey, Pakistan, Iraq, and Iran.
America agreed also to assist President Nasser, the Egyptian dictator
who aspired to Pan-Arab leadership, to build a huge dam on the upper
Nile. When Nasser seemed to bargain for Russian support as well, the
American offer to build the dam was suddenly withdrawn. Nasser
promptly seized this excuse to nationalize the French-built, British-
and-French-owned Suez Canal which had been for generations the
ifeline of the British Empire and was now a funnel for vitally needed
European supplies of oil. At the end of October, 1956, Egypt was
attacked by Israel, Britain, and France. Siding against her traditional
allies, America condemned this use of force. American pressure, in
strange combination with Russian threats of intervention, forced a
humiliating British-French withdrawal.

Alarmed at declining Western prestige and strong signs of Soviet
nterest in the Middle East, the President, in January, 1957, persuaded
Congress to endorse the "Eisenhower Doctrine." This authorized the
President to provide military assistance to Middle Eastern nations re-
questing aid against Communist aggression. This pledge proved difficult to implement. Within two years crises occurred in Jordan, Syria,
and Iraq. Each, however, involved the threat of a Communist coup
from within, rather than that of external aggression, and American
help was not sought. In July, 1958, the United States did send troops to
Lebanon, whose president had requested them. At the end of the
Eisenhower era, conditions in the Middle East seemed a little less
dangerous despite the baffling dilemmas of American policy. So far,
nationalism in this area seemed to be gaining on communism.

In Europe, where the President was personally popular, the program for collective defense ran into serious difficulties. The NATO

scheme had been formulated when Stalinist threats and Far Eastern aggression had alarmed the European nations. Now, with the Korean peace and the new Russian tone of conciliation, immediate fear of communism subsided. In some circles, not all of them left-wing, fear of possible American rashness and consequent nuclear war took its place. Moreover, Europeans, like many Americans, were more interested in their own burgeoning prosperity than in problems of defense.

In August, 1954, the European Defense Community scheme, a French suggestion heartily endorsed by the United States, was killed by the French parliament. Secretary Dulles threatened angrily an "agonizing reappraisal" of American policy, which seemed to suggest withdrawal of American forces or perhaps a separate relation with Germany. Under British leadership, the European nations in 1955 developed a complex substitute. Germany was invited to provide a limited proportion of NATO troops. The (West) German Federal Republic received full sovereignty, was guaranteed by France, England, and the United States, and promised not to pursue reunification by force. Yet West Germany still claimed the lost territories, West Berlin was still isolated, and no Central European settlement had been accepted by Russia.

Despite such points of conflict, relations between America and Soviet Russia moved from unexampled harshness to unexampled mutual toleration. At the outset of his administration, Eisenhower announced that Russian goodwill could be demonstrated by a Korean peace and an Austrian peace treaty. Not only the first but, to everybody's surprise, the second condition was satisfied. In 1955 Austria was evacuated and became an independent, neutral, Western-oriented nation. Russia made peace with Yugoslavia without a Yugoslav return to the orthodox Communist fold and recognized West Germany. At a major Communist congress in 1956 Khrushchev denounced the crimes of the Stalin period in startling terms. Western scepticism about the new Russian line was lessened when the Chinese began to denounce it as a betrayal of Leninism.

In the summer of 1955, while the new line was still unfolding, Eisenhower consented to meet with the British, French, and Russian heads of government at Geneva. The conference settled no outstanding problems. Its most dramatic moment came with Eisenhower's suggestion of an "open sky" formula under which each side would receive full military information from the other and be free to verify it by aerial inspection. Acceptance of this proposal, either by Russia or by the American Congress, was doubtful. Yet an exchange of military information seemed a promising avenue toward peace and became a recurrent goal of American policy. The new "spirit of Geneva" seemed for a while more important than concrete negotiations, as America and Russia exchanged delegations of ballerinas, farmers, and other ambassadors of goodwill. The Dulles policy of massive retaliation was dead, and even the Truman policy of building collective resistance became harder to implement.

If the new Soviet line raised problems for Western policy, it raised still harder ones for Stalin's heirs, who had no thought of abandoning Stalin's East European gains. From Warsaw to Berlin people longed to test the limits of the new policies. Some remembered that Secretary Dulles had promised American support for liberation. In 1953 strikes and riots in East Germany produced no American action. In 1956, Poland, a country especially important to the United States because of immigration, daringly defied the Russians and established a regime which, while still Communist and part of the Eastern alliance, offered considerably greater liberty of expression. Taking the cue, and tragically taking it too seriously, the Hungarians revolted with greater violence and seemed on the point of leaving the Soviet sphere altogether. After considerable initial hesitation, Russian troops brutally suppressed the revolt. Later, its leaders were executed. Since the United States took no action, it seemed that liberation was as dead a policy as massive retaliation.

Despite these disturbing events, the country apparently entered Eisenhower's second term in a cheerful and optimistic mood. Within two years new threats at home and abroad made optimism far more difficult.

THE END OF COMPLACENCY, 1958–1960

The administration's troubles began with an economic downturn in late 1957. This recession, more serious than its postwar predecessors, focussed attention on three problems. The first of these was unemployment which hovered around 5 per cent, declining only slightly with economic upturns. The second problem was the rate of American economic growth which was far slower than that of either Russia or Western Europe. The third was the American balance of payments. Declining European purchases and continuing American arms and aid programs were causing an outflow of gold and threatening American capacity to maintain her massive responsibilities.

Aside from these immediate problems, analysis began to show more and more clearly that Eisenhower prosperity, impressive as it was, had never spread to all the people. The war and the early cold war periods, with their colossal new government expenditures, high taxes, and demand for labor, had benefited the lower economic groups most. The group considered poor by economists had shrunk from something like two thirds of the people in the depression to about a quarter in 1953. Since then, while the well-to-do group had grown sharply, the proportion of poor had remained about the same, and their share in the national income had decreased. The poor fourth of a rich society were too easy to overlook and neglect. Most were untrained and undereducated, and automation was rapidly lessening demand for unskilled labor. Many were old, and many were Negroes. Neither unions, social security, nor housing legislation seemed to reach the problems of these rejected people. Even an economic upturn might pass them by.

These moral, social, and economic challenges did not become clear overnight. Yet it was obvious enough that distress existed in some areas (like West Virginia coal fields and big-city slums) and that the economy had lost some of its drive. At the same time the administration was wounded when Sherman Adams, Eisenhower's chief administrative aide, was forced to resign after disclosure of his acceptance of improper gifts from favor-seeking cronies. Rumors of corruption, the fact of recession, and worry about foreign policy were registered in the election of 1958. Democrats, and especially liberal Democrats, scored their biggest gains since 1936. The President accepted this blow with good grace and continued to cooperate with the anything but radical Democratic leadership in Congress.

Abroad, challenges and disasters mounted dramatically from 1957. In October of that year, the Russians placed in orbit their "sputnik," the first man-made earth satellite. This was not only a major feat of applied science, but also a demonstration of military power. Russia had already boasted that she possessed an intercontinental ballistic missile capable of delivering a nuclear warhead anywhere. Now this claim seemed probably true. Sputnik set off a wave of American self-criticism which tended to exaggerate the achievements of Soviet education, science, and weapons as much as these had been underrated earlier.

Many tasks were quickly accomplished to remedy the American lag in rocket building and the penetration of space. In January, 1958, a small American satellite was put in orbit, and in November the Air Force fired a huge rocket six thousand miles. Probably the strongest American answer to the Soviet lead was the firing of a rocket from the "Polaris" submarine in July, 1960.

Like the competition between European powers from the sixteenth to the nineteenth centuries, the "space race" had both a peaceful and a warlike aspect. It was a new field for "peaceful competition" in which each country spent vast resources for scientific and exploratory prestige. It was also a sinister and complex struggle for military superiority and particularly for possession of mobile, hard-to-destroy, and infinitely powerful nuclear weapons. Whoever was ahead, it was clear that the terms for American foreign policy had changed. America's historic invulnerability was gone; war would mean immediate and vast destruction in the United States as well as in enemy territory.

In confronting the new threat the administration was handicapped by the fatal disease (1957) and death (1959) of Secretary Dulles. No new policy seemed at hand to replace his consistent though unsuccessful system. And the Soviet Union, full of self-confidence, intensified both the conciliatory and the belligerent phases of its offensive.

American-Russian negotiations about disarmament and an end to nuclear tests continued under immense pressure from alarmed world opinion. In 1958 both countries announced a temporary cessation of testing, but the Soviet Union, which acted first, got most of the credit. In November of that year Khrushchev renewed Russian pressure on Berlin. In the absence of an acceptable settlement, he announced, Russia would in six months sign a peace treaty with East Germany. This would turn over the Berlin approaches to the most intractable and rigid of the satellite states. From time to time in the next years the deadline was extended, but the threat remained. Pressing hard for negotiations on the Berlin issue, Khrushchev secured an invitation to visit the United States in September, 1959. Once more nothing was settled, but an atmosphere of strained cordiality was maintained.

Making a further concession, Eisenhower agreed to meet Khrushchev in Paris in May, 1960, without the preliminary lower-level negotiations which the United States had earlier demanded. Just as the meeting was getting under way, the Russians shot down an American photographic plane 1,300 miles inside Russian territory. At first, American spokesmen denied the charge of espionage but the pilot, who had been captured, confessed. Contrary to international custom in such matters, the administration now acknowledged and justified the practice of secret photographic flights over Russian territory. Dramatically Khrushchev demanded an impossibly abject apology from the President and, in its absence, angrily broke off the Paris meeting and withdrew an invitation for a presidential return visit to Russia.

In Asia affairs went little better. Communist China bombed the offshore islands again in 1958 and bloodily subdued autonomous Tibet in 1959. Immediately after the Paris fiasco, an Eisenhower visit to Japan had to be postponed because of student riots against a Japanese-American security treaty. In two weak states of former French Indo-

China, Laos and South Viet Nam, Communist guerrilla movements seemed to be stronger than non-Communist governments.

In Algeria prolonged insurrection absorbed the energies of France and threatened the United States with a difficult choice between anti-colonialism and a traditional alliance. Further south in Africa, the French, British, and Belgian empires were liquidated with great rapidity, leaving in their wake many large and small nations, mostly lacking experienced leaders or viable economies. In one of the weakest and largest of these, the former Belgian Congo, disintegration threatened to spread East-West conflict to a new theater.

Most distressing of all to Americans were the developments in Latin America. Since the wartime triumphs of the Good Neighbor policy, little had been accomplished in this region by American diplomacy. Despite statements of democratic solidarity, both the Truman and Eisenhower administrations had made cordial gestures toward oppressive military regimes. The most spectacular action of the Eisenhower administration in the region, applauded at home but reviving memories of intervention among Latin Americans, had been to assist a right-wing coup against a pro-Communist government in Guatemala. No program like the Marshall Plan had been developed to complement political with economic action, and the region's desperate economic problems were steadily growing more acute. In 1958 Vice President Richard Nixon, touring Peru and Venezuela, was the target of violent hostile demonstrations.

In January, 1959, in Cuba, the guerrilla forces of Fidel Castro triumphed over the government of Fulgencio Batista. Many Americans sympathized with the Castro movement's program of needed economic reform and blamed American policy for close relations with the previous right-wing regime. But before long, executions and confiscations in the island seemed to indicate that Castro was drawing closer to the Communist bloc. By the end of the Eisenhower administration, American investments in Cuba were confiscated, American trade nearly cut off, and Castro's violently anti-American and by now pro-Soviet movement was threatening to attract support throughout the poorer regions of the hemisphere.

Probably the position of the United States in 1960, difficult as it was, seemed even worse because of the apparent lull of the mid-fifties. Straining for a vanished security, the American people still felt a deep affection for the immensely likable President, while at the same time they repudiated his party in Congress and increasingly criticized his policies.

This situation was dramatized, as so much of American history has been, in a presidential campaign. Richard Nixon, Eisenhower's vice president, received the Republican nomination and campaigned on the administration's record. Senator John F. Kennedy of Massachusetts, forty-four years old, able, rich, and Catholic, promised sweeping change and vigorous forward movement. The outcome of the election, a hairline Kennedy victory, proved difficult to analyze. It seemed to demonstrate that (1) the obvious ability, political skill, and vigor of Senator Kennedy impressed the public; (2) a great many people, though many fewer than in 1928, still voted according to historic ethnic and religious loyalty; and (3) the American people, though shaken from the complacency of 1956, were still not in the mood for large-scale new departures. This last point was underlined by the congressional elections. Democrats retained control, but Republicans and conservatives of both parties registered gains. Thus the Kennedy administration came to power in no position to implement the bold new programs it had promised.

IN SEARCH OF THE NEW FRONTIER

In the spring of 1963, it was still too early to evaluate, and almost too soon to describe, the Kennedy administration. New departures were most clearly evident in fields subject to executive action, among them military policy. On leaving office Eisenhower eloquently warned the nation against allowing the further growth of a powerful "military-industrial complex." The new administration, which regarded Eisenhower's defense program as inadequate, devoted an ever larger proportion of the country's financial, engineering, and scientific resources to weapons development. At the same time administration was streamlined, ultraconservative political activities of a few officers were curbed, and, where possible, economies were suggested. But Congress was now as resistant to military cutbacks as it had once been to military increases. State pride, local economic interest, and national fears all played a part in this kind of opposition to executive action.

The main note of Kennedy military policy, aside from expansion, was diversification. Liquidating whatever remained of the Dulles reliance on massive retaliation, the new regime tried to achieve a balance of "conventional" and nuclear forces and thus to provide alternatives to either holocaust or surrender. Ironically America's European allies, once critical of American concentration on nuclear weapons, now resisted diversification.

Kennedy, insisting on the need for national vigor in a manner sometimes reminiscent of Theodore Roosevelt, sharply increased expenditures for rocket development and space exploration and committed the United States to a "race to the moon." In 1962 three American astronauts were put into orbit around the earth. Though Russia retained a lead in the special field of human space exploration, it soon became clear that earlier Democratic talk about American missile inferiority had been exaggerated and that any "missile gap" which had existed had been closed.

Here on earth, prospects for peaceful relations with Russia, though not with China, seemed at first to improve. Repeatedly the President called for serious negotiation and reasonable concessions as well as firmness. Yet negotiations achieved few clear results. New and alarming threats to Berlin in 1961 led to a temporary buildup of American power, but the complex German issue was again postponed rather than settled. A little later Russia resumed the testing of hydrogen bombs of tremendous size, and the United States shortly followed suit. Sporadically, negotiations for an end of testing seemed close to success. So far, however, American concessions (chiefly on the amount of inspection necessary and chiefly in response to technological development) seemed at once too small for Russia and too big for some powerful congressional critics.

Calling for far more attention to the underdeveloped countries, Kennedy asked a reluctant Congress for large-scale, long-range American aid. He insisted that social and political progress were indispensable for economic development, pressed for social reform abroad, and was willing to tolerate neutrality or socialism as long as the new nations stayed outside the Russian or Chinese spheres. A small, but important success in this vast undertaking was the formation of the surprisingly popular Peace Corps which recruited and trained idealistic young people to make a personal contribution of work in underdeveloped countries.

In larger terms, success varied from continent to continent. In Africa, a combination of anticolonial votes in the United Nations and support for the United Nations' arduous efforts for Congo unity produced a mildly favorable response. In Southern Asia, where Kennedy shifted American support from a conservative Laotian faction to a neutral coalition and at the same time stepped up antiguerrilla warfare in South Viet Nam, only a slight measure of stabilization seemed to be in sight. In Latin America the record was mixed. Kennedy's call for an "Alliance for Progress" was received with some enthusiasm. But much goodwill was lost by inexplicable and serious bungling in Cuba. In April, 1961, the administration gave organizational and logistic, but not all-out military support, to an attempted invasion. The invaders were Cuban refugees recruited and trained secretly under the Eisenhower administration. The resulting defeat at the "Bay of Pigs" led to severe criticism abroad of American aggression, and serious concern at home about American indecision.

Much of Kennedy's foreign policy depended on an attempt to get the economy "moving again" and correct the nagging injustices of American society. Here too success proved elusive. Some measure of recovery was achieved, but the growth rate continued to lag, unemployment figures remained about the same, and poverty continued to dominate the lives of large minorities. Yet, as it had since World War II, Congress resisted proposals for social innovation. Administration appeals for medical care for the aged under social security, federal support of education, and urban renewal were among those defeated. Kennedy's principal congressional success was a bill giving the administration power to alter tariff rates by as much as 50 per cent, mainly in order to bargain with the highly successful West European Common Market. More vigorously than the Eisenhower administration, but less constantly than Negro leaders demanded, the new administration supported the growing Negro struggle for civil rights. In September, 1962, troops were sent to Mississippi to protect a Negro who had registered in the state university.

In the fall of 1962 two other events seemed to sharpen the rather blurred picture. Since the Bay of Pigs failure, congressional critics had been demanding still stronger action in Cuba. The administration took severe measures to reduce the island's foreign trade by economic pressure, but insisted that the Cuban threat was political rather than military. Then suddenly in October the President announced that aerial observation had disclosed the presence in Cuba of Russian intermediate missiles and that these, in his opinion, constituted a serious threat to American security. Apparently Khrushchev had taken this means to correct a balance of military power inclining toward the United States.

Looking tense and grim, the President announced that he had ordered American warships to stop and search vessels coming to Cuba which might contain offensive weapons. In case this proved insufficient, he ordered military concentrations preparatory to possible invasion of the island. Since this would mean killing Russian personnel in Cuba, nuclear war seemed a real possibility.

To Khrushchev, Kennedy offered a pledge not to invade the island if Russian offensive weapons were withdrawn under inspection. To the great relief of the world, Khrushchev's answer was conciliatory and Russian ships heading for Cuba turned around. Visibly alarmed, the Russian leader first suggested reciprocal disarmament of foreign bases and then, when no such concession was forthcoming, accepted Kennedy's terms. Missiles and bombers were removed from Cuba under

American aerial surveillance, although Castro refused to allow ground inspection.

Gratifyingly, the Organization of American States, which had hesitated to support drastic anti-Castro action, unanimously backed Kennedy's bold action, as did America's somewhat startled European allies. Meantime a Chinese seizure of Indian border districts inclined some neutral countries a little in America's direction. For the moment it seemed as if American boldness and address, together with Russian realism and restraint, had produced not only an American victory but a better chance for a peaceful future.

The second Kennedy success, and a far more equivocal one, was in the congressional elections which closely followed the Cuban crisis. Instead of the usual midterm losses for the party which holds the presidency, the Democrats retained about the same narrow majority in Congress. Analysts were quick to point out, however, that this was partly because the narrow Democratic victory in 1960 left little to lose and that the Democratic popular vote had declined slightly.

Certainly in the first months of 1963 it did not seem that the balance of forces had altered very decisively, either in the nation or the world. Undoubtedly the Russians and others respected American determination more than before. Yet either real victory or real conciliation still seemed elusive, and there were some signs in Russia of a turn back from cautious liberalization to Marxist rigidity. Castro was still in Cuba, and the opponents of the administration began once more to demand action to get him out.

More vigorously than in years, and in some instances more plausibly, critics of past policies were demanding selective cuts in foreign aid. In Europe the President's program received a hard blow. Kennedy had hoped to use his hard-won tariff reduction powers to achieve closer economic relations with the continental Common Market countries. Britain seemed about to join this powerful and prosperous grouping. Suddenly President Charles de Gaulle of France vetoed British adherence, explaining his action partly as a wish to avoid Ango-Saxon domination. Efforts to promote Atlantic military unity, now in the form of a multinational missile-equipped submarine force, ran into similar difficulties.

Reports on the economic health of the nation showed a familiar pattern: general prosperity, occasional record corporate profits, lagging growth, 5 to 6 per cent unemployment and pockets of stubborn poverty. So far, the Kennedy administration seemed a reasonably creditable continuation of recent history and not the bold break with the past promised in 1960.

To some commentators on the mixed record of this vigorous, intelligent assault on the country's hard problems, the obstacle seemed political. The old deadlock between executive and legislative power, common throughout American history and practically unvaried since 1938, placed barriers in the way of sweeping departure. Yet in other periods as recent as the thirties and forties, operating under the same system of checks and balances, the nation had broken with the past to meet new challenges.

Beneath the political problem lay the powerful, intangible realities of tradition and history. Colossal in its power, the United States was limited by its history of peace and success. Nostalgia for a past of easy economic expansion and effortless national safety (a past whose simplicity was often exaggerated) made major innovation difficult to undertake. To extreme danger, at Pearl Harbor, in Berlin, or in Cuba, the country responded without question. But positive and consistent goals for American policy were a different matter. Either belligerence or timidity presented immense dangers. Responsibilities and limitations needed equally to be reassessed.

Innovation at home was similarly hard. Changes in American society made in the 1930's and before were generally accepted. Only a noisy few wanted to repeal the income tax amendment, break the power of labor unions, or shove the emerging Negro back into his prewar status. Yet new ventures failed to attract wide support. For one thing, every development of the public sector of the economy, every effort to fight remaining destitution or speed up growth cost money. According to many economists, American nondefense spending was not unduly high either in relation to other advanced countries or to the power of the economy. Yet according to tradition—and this was a surprisingly traditional country—government spending or any new governmental undertaking was acceptable only as a response to a major catastrophe.

Perhaps further crisis would be necessary to produce responses on the scale of the best ventures of the American past. Perhaps gradual adaptation would fit American goals and powers to each other. Looking around at the world of the 1960's, none could doubt the difficulty of the problems. Looking back at the past, none could doubt the greatness of the resources.

FOR FURTHER READING:

Only a few books and articles on the most recent period are written with a sense of history. Among the most incisive estimates of the Eisenhower administration are Richard H. Rovere, *The Eisenhower Years* (1956), and William V. Shannon's brilliant essay in the

November, 1958, *Commentary*. John W. Spanier, *American Foreign Policy Since World War II* (2nd ed., 1962)*, offers a useful summary of the Eisenhower foreign policies. Samuel Lubell, *The Revolt of the Moderates* (1956), interprets the political situation just before Eisenhower's re-election. Certain important extremes of American opinion are illuminated in Norman Graebner, *The New Isolationism* (1956), and one of the strangest careers in American history is objectively assessed in Richard H. Rovere, *Senator Joe McCarthy* (1959)*. Theodore H. White, *The Making of the President 1960* (1961)*, is an extraordinarily full analysis of a campaign. One helpful preliminary estimate of the new administration is contained in the April-June, 1962, issue of the (London) *Political Quarterly*. The new poverty is discussed in Michael Harrington, *The Other America: Poverty in the United States* (1962), and the literature on this subject is brilliantly summarized by Dwight Macdonald in *The New Yorker* (January 19, 1963), pp. 82–132. Francis M. Bator, *The Question of Government Spending* (1960)*, is a helpful analysis of this problem.

An important episode in the security crisis of the early Eisenhower administration is presented in documentary form in Cushing Strout, *Conscience, Science, and Security: The Case of Dr. J. Robert Oppenheimer* (Berkeley Series in American History, 1963)*.

*Available in paperback edition.

INDEX

PRINTED IN U.S.A.